DEVELOPMENT OF EDUCATION IN INDIA

Vol. I : Development of Education in India: A Survey of Educational Documents before and after Independence
A. Biswas and *S.P. Agrawal*

Vol. II : The Second Historical Survey of Educational Development in India: Select Documents 1985-1990
S.P. Agrawal and *J.C. Aggarwal*

Vol. III : Third Historical Survey of Educational Development in India: Select Documents 1990-1992
S.P. Agrawal and *J.C. Aggarwal*

Vol. IV : Development of Education in India: Select Documents 1993-94
S.P. Agrawal and *J.C. Aggarwal*

Vol. V : Development of Education in India: Select Documentation 1995-97
S.P. Agrawal

About the Author

S.P. Agrawal (*b*. 1929) was Director, National Social Science Documentation Centre, ICSSR, Government of India and Member Secretary, Indian Association of Social Science Institutions. He was also the Vice-Chairman of the Asia and Pacific Information Network in Social Science (APINESS). In 1998 he was awarded the degree of Doctor of Philosophy in Education (*Honoris Causa*) by International University Foundation. Presently, he is Member, IFLA Round Table on Research in Reading, International Committee for Social Science, Information and Documentation, Board of Studies of National Archives of India and Hindi Advisory Committee, Ministry of Coal, Government of India. He is also Fellow of the Society of Ethnobotanists. Born and brought up in the cradle of freedom movement, which he joined at the tender age of twelve, he gained an insight into political problems and developed a sense of responsibility which bore fruit as an information scientist. He has written extensively on various aspects of Education, Indian Polity and Library and Information Science.

CONCEPTS IN COMMUNICATION INFORMATICS and LIBRARIANSHIP - 80.

General Editor: **S. P. AGRAWAL**

DEVELOPMENT OF EDUCATION IN INDIA

SELECT DOCUMENTATION 1995-1997

VOLUME - FIVE

S.P. AGRAWAL

former Member Secretary
Indian Association of Social Science Institutions,
and
former Director, National Social Science Documentation Centre (ICSSR)
New Delhi

Assisted by

M.W.K. Sherwani

former Assistant Educational Advisor,
Ministry of Human Resource Development, New Delhi

CONCEPT PUBLISHING COMPANY, NEW DELHI-110059

ISBN 81-7022-661-9

First Published 1999

Published and Printed by
Ashok Kumar Mittal
Concept Publishing Company
A/15-16, Commercial Block, Mohan Garden
New Delhi-110059 (India)

Phones : 5648039, 5649024
Fax : 091-11-5648053

GENERAL EDITOR'S INTRODUCTION

During fifty years of independence despite numerous Committees and Commissions which Government of India had set up from time to time to examine almost all the aspects of our educational system and spell out the ways and means to improve the situation the educational scenario in the country if not depressing is not very much cheering indeed. There are a number of factors for the failure of the system to deliver the goods. Both the bureaucrats and the political leaders are to blame for the present state of our educational situation. The inadequate financial provision, the apathetic attitude of the politicians and civil service and the frequent politically inspired shift in educational policies have been responsible for lack of sense of direction and effectiveness of programme implementation. The politicians masquerading themselves as educationists and specialists and throwing to the winds all the considered views of the educators and the educationists have taken important decisions on important issues which have done more harm than good to the educational health of the nation. They impose their own half-baked ideas and whims which have worsened the situation. For instance, decades back in Uttar Pradesh by the diktat of the politicians English was banished from the schools in utter disregard of the views of the knowledgeable and meaningful persons who were opposed to such a course of action. However, after playing havoc with the careers of lakhs of children they realized their folly and reversed the decision. The other States too have made similar such preposterous decisions on political expediency and they have to make hasty retreat after ruining the careers of the students concerned.

It needs no prophet to tell that before taking any decision on any important issue, it is very necessary for a decision-maker to have full understanding about the strengths and weaknesses of the issue in question and its consequences for those for whom it is meant. We can have such an understanding only when we have full facts about both the negative and positive aspects of the subject, views of the important persons who matter in the particular field and the deliberations of the Committees and the Commissions that have been constituted to make a thorough examination of the issue.

Keeping these things in view we decided to bring out a series of historical surveys about educational developments in the country from pre-independence to post-independence period. The First Historical Survey covering the period before and after independence upto 1985 was published in 1986. The Second Survey spanning the period 1985-1990 was brought out in 1991. Since these Surveys were very well received by the discerning educators, educationists and educational administrators we were encouraged to publish the Third and Fourth Surveys covering the period from 1990 to 1994. It may be pointed out that Third Volume reflects the attempts made in the direction of implementing the National Policy of Education 1986 and modified in 1992.

In this publication the material has been grouped in four parts. Part One presents an overview of educational developments in the country in all its important aspects. The Part Two includes select documents covering diverse facets of education. Particularly it is concerned with the reports of the important commissions and committees presented by them during the period covered. The Third Part is devoted to educational statistics. The last Part consists of Appendices relating to topics not covered earlier.

Acknowledgement

Main documentation sources are: Ministry of Human Resources Development, Department of Education, Government of India, New Delhi; University Grants Commission, New Delhi; National Council of Educational Research and Training, New Delhi; National Institute of Educational Planning and Administration,

New Delhi; Important Indian newspapers and journals of standing. We are grateful to all research institutions/organisations for using their documents in this Volume.

S.P. Agrawal

Contents

PART – THREE

PART – FOUR

APPENDICES: SIGNIFICANT DOCUMENTS NOT INCLUDED IN THIRD AND FOURTH SURVEYS

PART – ONE

DEVELOPMENT OF EDUCATION

1

Development of Education : An Overview

1.1 ELEMENTARY EDUCATION

The education policy of the Government of India in the post-Independence era has been to provide free and compulsory education to all children at least upto the elementary stage. Recognising the need for a literate population and provision of elementary education as a crucial input for nation building, the Government's stand was reiterated in the National Policy on Education (NPE 1986) and the Programme of Action 1992, to work towards provision of education of a satisfactory quality to all children upto 14 years of age before the commencement of the 21st century.

The targets fixed for the VIII Five Year Plan have the following three broad parameters:

I. *Universal Access:* (i) Universal enrolment of all children including girls and persons belonging to SC/ST; (ii) Provision of primary school within one km of walking distance and facility of non-formal education for school dropouts, working children and girls who cannot attend formal schools; and (iii) Improvement of ratio of upper primary to primary schools from the existing 1:4 to 1:2.

II. *Universal Retention*: Reduction of dropout rate between class I to V and I to VIII from the existing 46 per cent and 60 per cent to 20 per cent and 40 per cent respectively.

III. *Universal Achievement*: Achievement of minimum levels of learning by almost all children at the primary level, and introduction of this concept at the upper primary stage.

Progress over the Years

The concerted efforts over the years have improved performance in enrolment and resulted in increase in institutions, teachers as shown in Tables 1.1, 1.2 and 1.3.

Table 1.1: Number of Institutions *(in lakhs)*

	1950-51	1995-96
Primary Schools (Classes I-V)	2.10	5.90
Upper Primary Schools	0.13	1.71
	2.23	7.61

Table 1.2: Number of Teachers *(in lakhs)*

	1950-51	1995-96
Primary Schools (Classes I-V)	5.38	17.40
Upper Primary Schools	0.36	11.65
	5.74	29.05

Table 1.3: Gross Enrolment

	1950-51	1995-96
Primary Stage		
Total Enrolment (in millions)	19.2	109.8
Gross Enrolment Ratio (percentage)	43.1	104.3
Upper Primary Stage		
Total Enrolment (in millions)	3.1	41.0
Gross Enrolment Ratio (percentage)	12.0	67.6

In pursuance of Constitutional directives, State Governments have abolished tuition fees in the Government, local bodies and aided schools upto the upper primary level.

Accessibility of schooling facilities is no longer a major problem. 8.26 lakh habitations covering 94% of the country's population have now schooling facilities within one km distance at primary stage. At upper primary stage also 726 lakh habitations covering 83.98% of rural population have a school within 3 km distance. Enrolment ratio is 104 for classes I-V and 67 for classes VI-VIII.

While the gross enrolment ratio (GER) at primary stage in the country as a whole and in most of its States exceed 100 per cent, there are quite a few States including Bihar, Haryana, Jammu and Kashmir, Meghalaya, Rajasthan and Uttar Pradesh where the ratio is considerably low. At the upper primary stage, these States and in addition, Andhra Pradesh, Orissa and Sikkim have GERs lower than the national average. Most of these States have literacy rates lower than the national average also. There is thus a strong regional dimension of Universalisation of Elementary Education (UEE).

Gender Disparities

While UEE is the ultimate goal, no strategy or programme of action can succeed without addressing itself to gender and regional dimensions specifically. Gender disparities are conspicuous in regard to enrolment and retention. Girls' enrolment has grown at the primary stage from 5.4 millions in 1950-51 to 47.7 millions in 1995-96 and at upper primary stage from 0.5 million to 16.0 million. The rate of growth of enrolment of girls has been higher than that of boys. But disparities still persist as girls still account for only 43.2 per cent of enrolment at primary stage and 39.0 per cent at upper primary stage. The dropout rate of girls is much higher than that of boys at the primary and upper primary levels.

Scheduled Castes and Scheduled Tribes

According to the 1991 census, the population of Scheduled Castes (SCs) was 138.12 million (16.33%) and that of Scheduled Tribes (STs) was 67.8 million (8.01%) of the country's population.

Scheduled Caste and Scheduled Tribe population are heterogeneous target groups in all respects. There are wide variations among different SC and ST groups regionally. Thus, SC girls in Kerala are likely to be better placed than non-SC boys in some of the more backward States and districts.

The enrolment of SCs and STs has increased considerably at the primary stage. The participation of SCs and STs is now more or less in proportion to their share in population at the primary level. Dropouts, though declining over the years, are significantly large. Gender disparities are very conspicuous among SCs and STs also.

Strategy Frame

In order to achieve UEE by 2000 A.D., the following key strategies have been worked out in consultation with States and UTs : (i) Overcome the problem of school dropouts and lay emphasis on retention and achievement rather than on merely enrolment; (ii) Strengthen the alternatives of schooling, particularly the Non-Formal Education system for working children, girls and children from other disadvantaged or marginalised sections of the society; (iii) Shift focus from educationally backward States to educationally backward districts; (iv) Adopt disaggregated approach with a focus on preparation of district specific and population specific plans; (v) Provide universal access of schooling facilities, particularly to girls, disaggregated groups and out-of-school children; (vi) Improve school effectiveness, teacher competence, training and motivation; (vii) Introduce Minimum Level of Learning (MLL) for enhancement of learners' achievement; micro planning will provide the framework of universal access and universal participation while MLLs would be the strategy for universal achievement; (viii) Overall planning and management and stress on participative processes; and (ix) Convergence of different schemes of elementary education and related services such as early childhood care and education and school health and nutrition programmes etc.

Minimum Levels of Learning (MLL)

India is one of the few developing countries which took the initiative in 1991 to lay down MLL to be achieved at primary stage. This new approach integrates various components of curriculum, classroom transaction, evaluation and teacher orientation. The first phase of the programme was implemented through 18 voluntary agencies, research institutions, SCERTs etc. The results of these projects showed significant improvement in learning attainments of school children.

It has now been decided to upscale the MLL programme through institutional mechanisms throughout the country. National resource institutions like the National Council of Educational Research and Training (NCERT), Regional Institutes of Education (RIEs), SCERTs, and DIETs are being networked for this purpose. In 1996-97, more than half of the States were implementing the programme with the assistance of more than 200 DIETs. Curriculum revision, rewriting of textbooks to make them competency based, enhancing their pedagogical value, training of teachers in the classroom processes are the major activities being undertaken.

Andhra Pradesh, Bihar, Goa, Gujarat, Karnataka, Kerala, Manipur, Pondicherry, Rajasthan, Sikkim, Tamil Nadu, Uttar Pradesh and West Bengal have reported introduction of MLL in some of their primary schools. Madhya Pradesh, Chandigarh, Haryana and Lakshadweep are in the process of introducing MLL in their primary schools. The District Primary Education Programme (DPEP) has adopted MLL as a major strategy for improvement of quality for primary education. Non-formal education programme is also adopting MLLs wherever appropriate.

Laying down of MLLs is a part of the larger curriculum reform endeavour to achieve greater relevance and functionality in primary education. The implications of this exercise are: (i) Lightening the curriculum of its textual load and also the burden of memorising unnecessary and irrelevant content of facts; (ii) Relating textual content with a meaningful process of understanding and application; (iii) Ensuring the acquisition of basic competencies and skills to such a level where they are sustainable and would not easily allow relapsing into illiteracy; and (iv) Facilitating mastery in learning not only by brighter children in the class but also by almost all children including first generation learners.

A committee under the Chairmanship of Prof. R.H. Dave is currently working to prescribe learning competencies for various subjects taught at the upper primary stage.

New Initiative taken by Central Government in 1996-97

Proposal to make the Right to Free and Compulsory Elementary Education a Fundamental Right

The Common minimum programme of the United Front Government resolved to take on the enormous challenge of UEE by making the right to free and compulsory elementary education a Fundamental Right and enforcing it through suitable statutory measures. The resolution was discussed in a Conference of State Education Ministers and State Education Secretaries held on August 9-10, 1996. The Conference recognised the momentous significance of the resolve and urged the Government to consider the financial, administrative, legal and academic implications of the proposal. The Conference recommended the constitution of a Committee of State Education Ministers to consider the implications. Accordingly, the Ministry of Human Resource Development (Department of Education) constituted a Committee of State Education Ministers under the Chairmanship of Union Minister of State for HRD (Education). The Committee has since submitted its report.

Exemption from Payment of Excise Duty

With a view to cushioning the impact of the rising costs of text books and exercise books, the Government has exempted writing and printing papers supplied to all State Text Book Corporations from excise duty in the Union Budget for 1996-97. It is expected that this would make school text books and exercise books affordable for students from weaker sections of society.

Scheme to Assist Voluntary Agencies in the Establishment of Residential Primary Schools

The Union Finance Minister had in his budget speech for 1996-97, announced a new scheme of assistance in the establishment of residential primary schools. The basic features of the scheme as outlined in the speech were: (i) The scheme envisaged provision of financial assistance for residential primary schools in rural areas for the poor, irrespective of caste or creed; (ii) the scheme was intended to be implemented through NGOs; and (iii) an initial sum of Rs. 5.00 crore has been set apart in the Union Budget for 1996-97.

The Department of Education constituted a Committee headed by Union Education Secretary to formulate guidelines to operationalise the scheme. The Committee has since submitted its report. It has recommended that the scheme may be implemented on a pilot basis in 1996-97.

Based on the report of the above Committee, guidelines and operational modalities in respect of this scheme have been finalised and approval of the Standing Finance Committee is being obtained. The scheme is likely to be operationalised during the current financial year, i.e., 1996-97.

It is proposed that a detailed feasibility study would be undertaken by NCERT for its implementation on a long term basis beyond 1996-97. NCERT has been requested to formulate the detailed scheme accordingly.

Operation Blackboard

The National Policy on Education, 1986 recognising the unattractive school environment, unsatisfactory condition of buildings and insufficiency of instructional material in primary schools, which function as demotivating factors for enrolment and retention, called for a drive symbolically called "Operation Blackboard" for substantial improvement in the quality of primary schools. The scheme was started in 1987-88 to bring all existing primary schools in the country upto a minimum standard by way of physical facilities by providing them with: (i) At least two reasonably large all-weather rooms along with separate toilet facilities for boys and girls; (ii) At least two teachers as far as possible, one of them a woman; and (iii) Essential teaching and learning material including blackboards, maps, charts, a small library, toys; and games and some equipment for work experience. Central assistance is provided for item numbers (ii) and (iii) which has been fully provided to all the targeted primary schools.

Under the scheme of OB, the construction of school buildings is primarily the responsibility of State Governments. However, in consultation with the Department of Education, the Ministry of Rural Areas and Employment has worked out a formula under the Jawahar Rozgar Yojana (JRY) to ensure availability of funds for construction of primary school buildings under the OB Scheme. According to this formula, 48 per cent of the funds for construction are provided by the Ministry of Rural Areas and Employment as central matching share of JRY, if the States raise 12 per cent JRY State share and 40 per cent Non-JRY share.

Expanded Operation Blackboard

The scope of the scheme has been enlarged to provide 3 class rooms and 3 teachers in primary schools where enrolment exceeds 100. The scheme has also been extended to cover upper primary schools.

The components of the sub-scheme for upper primary schools comprise the provision of: (i) at least one room for each class;

(ii) a Headmaster-cum-office room; (iii) necessary toilet facilities; (iv) a contingency grant of Rs. 1000 per annum; (v) library facilities; (vi) essential equipment; and (vii) at least one teacher for each class/section. Primary schools with enrolments more than 100 and two teachers are now being provided with a third teacher.

According to the guidelines of the extended scheme, the salary of one additional teacher will be provided by the Central Government for the plan period. Rs. 50,000 is provided to each school for essential teaching learning equipments including Rs. 10,000 for library facilities. In order to promote community participation in this venture, preference is given in selection to the villages where community contributes 20% (Rs. 10,000) towards equipment in which case central contribution will be Rs.40,000. However, in tribal (ITDP) areas entire 100 per cent assistance will be provided.

Table1.4: Achievements under OB

Physical	Provision of Teaching Learning Equipment to Pr. Schools (in lakh)	Sanction of additional Teachers for Primary (in lakh)	Construction of class rooms (in lakh)	Financial (Rs. in crores)	
				From 1987 to March 1997	During 1996-97 till Oct. 1997
1	2	3	4	5	6
Target	5.23	1.53	2.63	1515.95	116.58
Achiev-ements	5.23*	1.49	1.74		

* In addition 4,000 teachers have been appointed by State governments.

It is proposed to sanction third teachers to about 7220 primary schools with enrolment exceeding 100 during the remaining part of the financial year 1996-97.

During the current year as well as the next year the thrust is essentially on monitoring of the system and close follow-up with the States on the progress and utilisation of the funds sanctioned under the scheme. It is proposed to set up a system of concurrent monitoring and evaluation of the scheme through external agencies from the current financial year. This is expected to provide feedback on areas which might require further strengthening. Because of constant monitoring the utilisation of funds by States has gone up from 79 per cent during 1994-95 to 82 per cent during 1995-96.

Table 1.5: Achievements under Expanded OB

Expanded OB	8th Plan targets	Achievements
Sanction of third teachers to primary schools with enrolment exceeding 100	42,000 (30%)	34,780
Coverage of upper Primary schools; supply of Teaching learning material	47,000 (30%)	47,589

A new initiative namely Special Orientation Programme for Primary Teachers (SOPT) has been taken up since 1993-94 to give training to primary teachers in use of OB material and MLL strategy with focus on teaching of Language, Mathematics and Environmental Studies. About 18 lakh teachers are likely to be covered by the end of Eighth Five Year Plan under this programme.

Non-Formal Education

Objectives and Description of the Scheme

The National Policy on Education, 1986 taking a realistic view of the enormous task of achieving UEE in its entirety (access, retention, as well as achievement), envisages that free and compulsory education of satisfactory quality be provided to all children upto the age of 14 years before commencement of 21st century. For the first time in 1986, an educational policy had admitted that the schools would not reach all children particularly millions of girls and working children whose participation in the school system is thwarted by socio-economic conditions. The policy, therefore, called for a large and systematic programme of non-formal education as an integral component of the strategy to achieve UEE with enough flexibility to enable the learners to learn at their own pace and at the same time having quality comparable with formal education.

The scheme was conceived in 1979-80, scaled up in 1987 and revised in 1993 with emphasis on organisation, flexibility, relevance of curriculum, diversity in learning activity to suit the needs of learners through decentralised management. The scheme primarily covers the educationally backward States, namely Andhra Pradesh, Arunachal Pradesh, Assam, Bihar, Jammu and Kashmir, Madhya Pradesh, Orissa, Rajasthan, Uttar Pradesh and West Bengal. It also covers urban slums, hilly, desert and tribal areas and areas with concentration of working children in other States as well.

The main features of the scheme include: (i) short course with duration of about two years; (ii) part-time instruction at a place and time convenient to learners in small groups; (iii) flexibility in mode of delivery; and (iv) special emphasis on girls education.

At present, the scheme is being implemented in 21 States/ UTs. Under the Scheme, Central assistance is provided to States/ UTs and Voluntary agencies on the following pattern:

1. Co-educational centres and	60% Administrative support
2. Exclusively girls centres	90%
3. Centres run by Voluntary agencies	100%

Implementation in 1996-97

State Sector – There is an allocation of Rs. 158.20 crore (Rs. 128.20 crore under the State Sector and Rs. 30 crore under Voluntary Sector) for the current financial year for running NFE programme in 21 States/UTs, being the last year of the Eighth Five Year Plan, 2.41 lakhs NFE centres sanctioned under State Sector in 15 States/UTs in 1995-96 are being continued covering about 70 lakh children. Out of 2.41 lakh centres under State Sector, about 1.18 lakh centres are exclusively for girls, covering about 29.50 lakh beneficiaries.

Voluntary Sector – An important achievement in the current financial year has been enlisting the increased participation of NGOs in the programme. At present, 590 Voluntary Agencies are running 38,900 centres in the country. Under Experimental and Innovative programmes, new strategies on a pilot basis for micro-planning survey training, material development, education for the disabled and working children, running of NFE centres, health education programmes are taken up. At present, 41 such projects are in operation. In addition, NGOs are running District Resource Units for providing resource support to the programme.

New Initiatives: The Conference of Education Ministers of the States/UTs held in August 1996 considered NFE scheme as one of the important components for achieving universalisation of elementary education in the country and decided that the NFE scheme should continue as a Centrally Sponsored Scheme in the year to come. It was also decided in the Conference that the Scheme should provide for greater flexibility in implementation and allow greater autonomy to the States to make local contextual modifications.

An outlay of Rs. 704.00 crore (Rs. 625 crore under State Sector and Rs. 79 crore under Voluntary Sector) has been approved for the 8th Plan period with a target of 3.50 lakh NFE centres.

National Council for Teacher Education (NCTE)

NCTE has been established as a national level statutory body by the Government of India vide its notification dated August 17, 1995 with the objectives of achieving planned and coordinated development of teacher education, regulation and proper maintenance of norms and standards of teacher education and for matters connected therewith. The mandate of the NCTE is quite wide and includes regulatory as well as developmental functions. Some of the major functions are laying down norms for various teacher education courses, recognition of teacher education institutions, laying down guidelines in respect of minimum qualifications for appointment of teachers, surveys and studies, research and innovations, prevention of commercialisation of teacher education, etc.

As per the provisions of the Act, four Regional Committees for the Northern, Southern, Eastern and Western regions have been set up with Headquarters at Jaipur, Bangalore, Bhubaneshwar and Bhopal respectively. These Regional Committees have to consider the applications of institutions of teacher education for recognition/permission in accordance with the provisions of the Act. So far, 1524 applications have been received, 108 institutions have been recognised, 226 institutions have been granted provisional recognition and 62 institutions have been refused recognition. The remaining applications are under consideration of the Regional Committees.

During the brief period that the Council has been in existence, it has laid down norms and standards for pre-primary, elementary and secondary level teacher education institutions. Norms for B.Ed. through distance education mode and M. Ed. have also been prepared and are likely to be notified soon. On the basis of the recommendations of an expert committee, the NCTE has taken a decision that the education for the first degree/diploma should be only through face to face institutional course of teacher education of minimum of one year academic duration.

The decision has been communicated to all State Governments, Universities, Boards of Education, etc. However, with a view to providing avenues for professional growth of in-service teachers and to clear the backlog of untrained teachers in some regions of the country, B.Ed. through correspondence/distance education is being continued on a limited scale. For this purpose, NCTE has issued regulations laying down guidelines for the universities/institutions running B. Ed. through correspondence/ distance education mode on the basis of recommendations of an expert committee headed by Prof. Ram Takwale, Vice-Chancellor, IGNOU as approved by UGC.

During the year 1996-97 a number of seminar, workshops, symposia, awareness meetings, etc. were organised, and number of projects and studies taken up including: (i) Formulation of competency based teacher education curriculum for elementary teacher education institutions; (ii) Restructuring of curriculum framework of teacher education; (iii) State level studies on teacher education –current status, issues and future projections; (iv) Development of quality training material for teacher education institutions; (v) Human rights and national values for teacher educators; and (vi) Study of profile of teacher educators.

In addition, a few projects were also taken up with the assistance of international agencies, including a UNESCO sponsored conference on professional status of teachers and preparation of its reports and compendium of papers presented in the conference, preparation of self-learning modules for teacher educators in Language, Mathematics and Environmental Studies with the assistance of Commonwealth of Learning Hindi translation of ILO/UNESCO recommendations concerning the status of teachers and the report of experts on the applications of the recommendations.

Shiksha Karmi Project (SKP)

SKP is being implemented in Rajasthan since 1987 with assistance from the Swedish International Development Agency (SIDA). The project aims at Universalisation and Qualitative improvement of primary education in remote and socio-economically backward villages in Rajasthan with primary attention being given to girls. The project identifies teachers' absenteeism as a major obstacle in achieving the objective of UEE. The project is being implemented by the Government of Rajasthan through Rajasthan Shiksha Karmi Board (RSKB) with the assistance of voluntary agencies. During the first phase from 1987 to 1994, 90 per cent of the project outlay was funded out of the plan budget of the Central Government which was subsequently reimbursed by SIDA. The Government of Rajasthan shared 10 per cent of the project cost.

The second phase of the SKP is being implemented from July 1, 1994 and is for a period of three years up to June 30, 1997. The cost sharing between SIDA and Government of Rajasthan has been revised from 90:10 to 50:50 during Phase-II of the project. An outlay of Rs. 48.00 crores has been envisaged for Phase-II. SIDA has committed an assistance of 60 M SEK (Rs. 24.00 crores) for Phase-II.

Implementation structure and mechanism of the project have been designed to ensure that the State Government and non-governmental organisations work in partnership. NGOs work hand in hand with the Project Director to design, organise and conduct training for SK trainers and oversee training of Shiksha Karmis. NGOs are also responsible for the Project supervision and support of Shiksha Karmis. The Project design is based on the assumption that education services must have community support if they are to meet the needs of deprived sections of the rural areas. At the grass-root level, Panchayat Samiti, Shiksha Karmis Sahayogi, Subject Specialists of non-government organisations, Shiksha Karmis and the village community constantly interact with each other to achieve the aims of the project.

Shiksha Karmi Project (SKP) is innovative, educational, interventionist which aims to overcome major problem of poor enrolment and high drop-out of children, particularly girls. The SKP runs Prehar Pathshalas, Angan Pathshalas, Mahila Prakashan Kendras as innovative activities.

Shiksha Karmi Project (SKP) has emerged as a successful experiment in tackling the problems of teacher absenteeism, social and gender inequality in access and the quality of education. There has been a three-fold increase in enrolment of children in the schools taken over by the project. Nearly a fifth of those of whom the project is targeted are attending Prehar Pathshalas; 62 per cent of these are girls. A significant number of children covered by the SK schools are from Scheduled Caste and Schedule Tribe households.

Evaluation exercises in the field reveal that the grasp over literacy, numeracy and environmental awareness is higher among the children in SK schools than in the panchayat-run schools in neighbouring villages. In alertness of children and in their enthusiasm, the SK schools scored much higher.

A pilot scheme to integrate disabled children in SKP has been launched recently in Ghatol (Tribal) and Balotra (Desert) Blocks. A survey has revealed that 6 per cent of children upto 14 years of age in the two Blocks suffer from physical disabilities. So far 458 disabled children have been enrolled in SK schools in these blocks.

A Monitoring Mission commissioned by SIDA held first Bi-annual Review of the SKP in February-March, 1996. The major findings of the Monitoring Mission reveal that the project has made great strides in involving key persons at all levels in planning, monitoring and management. A vital factor in the successful functioning has been the evolution of procedures based on field experiences and consensual decision-making. There has been greater decentralisation and more community involvement as the project gears up to enter the third phase. The overall scholastic achievement has been rated to be good and several initiatives have been taken to promote gender sensitivity as reflected in increased participation of women in the programme.

Parliamentary Standing Committee on Human Resource Development also visited Rajasthan in the first week of November, 1996 for undertaking a review of the performance of the SKP. A second Indo-Swedish Joint Bi-annual Review of the SKP was held in October 1996. The preliminary proposal prepared by the SKB for sanction of Phase III of the project was discussed in this review. An expenditure of Rs. 1545 million for committee liabilities up to 2002 AD and Rs. 750 million for coverage of an additional 4000 villages upto 2000 AD have been envisaged in these preliminary estimates. It was agreed that SIDA would examine this proposal in the light of the positive achievements of the SKP so far.

The project now covers 1785 villages in 113 blocks of Rajasthan. 4271 Shiksha Karmis provide primary education to approximately 1.50 lakh children in day schools and Prehar Pathshalas (schools of convenient timing). The project has achieved success in universalising enrolment and attendance of children in several project villages. Level of learning have improved and so has retention of enrolled children. SKP has devised an effective model for support, supervision and monitoring of quantitative and qualitative aspects of primary education in partnership with NGOs. The project is known for its open participative style and continuous innovations and experiments to achieve its objectives. The approach, strategies and achievements of the SKP have attracted national and international recognition.

National Programme of Nutritional Support to Primary Education (NP-NSPE)

For the first time in the country a nation-wide programme of NSPE commonly known as Mid-Day-Meal Scheme was launched on August 15, 1995. The programme is intended to give a boost to universalisation of primary education by increasing enrolment retention and attendance, and simultaneously impacting upon nutritional levels of students in primary classes (I to V).

The ultimate aim under the programme is to provide wholesome cooked/processed food having a calorific value equivalent to 100 gm of wheat/rice per student per school day through the implementing agencies, such as, panchayats and nagarpalikas which are expected to develop institutional arrangements for serving of cooked/processed food within a period of two years from the date of commencement of the programme in the local areas. During the interim period, foodgrains (wheat/rice) at the rate of 3 kgs per student per month are being distributed subject to a minimum attendance of 80 per cent.

The Programme has since commenced in all the States/UTs. The existing programmes of providing cooked meals in Gujarat, Kerala, Orissa, Tamil Nadu and U.T. of Pondicherry have been dovetailed with the national programme. Haryana, J&K and Madhya Pradesh started the national programme by providing cooked meal in 1995-96. However, Haryana has reviewed its decision recently and opted for distribution of foodgrains from the academic year 1996-97.

In National Capital Territory of Delhi processed food (Sweet Bread) is being supplied to the primary school children in urban slums. The remaining States/UTs are distributing foodgrains (Wheat/Rice) as a prelude to the provision of cooked/processed food.

The programme has been expanded to cover 5.57 crore primary class children in the 4426 Blocks comprising Employment Assurance Scheme (EAS)/Revamped Public Distribution System (RPDs) and LFL blocks (having female literacy lower than national literacy rate). All primary classes in the remaining blocks and urban areas in the country will be covered during the next year, i.e. 1997-98.

District Primary Education Programme (DPEP)

DPEP is a Centrally Sponsored programme providing special thrust to achieve Universalisation of Elementary Education (UEE). The programme takes a holistic view of primary education development and seeks to operationalise the strategy of UEE through district specific planning with emphasis on decentralised management, participatory processes, empowerment and capacity building at all levels.

The programme is structured to provide additional inputs over and above the provision made by the State governments for expenditure on elementary education. The programme fills in the existing gaps in the development of primary education and revitalises the existing system. DPEP is contextual and has a marked gender focus. The programme components include construction of classrooms and new schools, opening of Non-Formal/ Alternative Schooling Centres, appointment of new teachers, setting up of Block Resource Centres/ Cluster Resource Centres, teacher training, development of Teaching Learning Material, Research based interventions, special interventions for education of girls, SC/ST etc. A new initiative of providing integrated education to children with disability and a distance education component for improving teacher training is also being planned.

Objectives: The programme mainly aims at providing access to primary education for all children, reducing primary dropout rates to less than 10 per cent, increasing learning achievement of primary school students by at least 25 per cent, and reducing the gap among gender and social groups to less than 5 per cent.

District Selection Criteria

The district is the Unit of programme implementation and selected on the basis of twin criteria, viz, (i) Educationally backward districts with female literacy below the national average, and (ii) Districts where Total Literacy Campaigns (TLCs) have been successful, leading to enhanced demand for elementary education.

Funding

District Primary Education Programme is a centrally sponsored scheme, 85 per cent of the project cost is shared by GOI and 15 per cent by State Government. Both the Central share and State share are passed on to State Implementation Societies directly as grant. The Central Government share is resourced by external funding. Several bilateral and multilateral agencies are providing financial assistance for the DPEP. The World Bank has provided a credit amounting to US $260 million (approx. Rs. 806 crore) under phase I of DPEP. The European Community has signed a financial agreement with the Government of India to provide a grant of 1.50 million ECU (approx. Rs. 585 crore) as programme support for DPEP in Madhya Pradesh. An agreement has been signed with IDA for a second credit amounting to US $ 425 million for DPEP-II. The Government of Netherlands is likely to provide a grant of US $ 25.8 million for DPEP in Gujarat. A financial agreement with ODA for a grant of $ 42.5 (Rs. 220 crore) has been signed for Andhra Pradesh DPEP.

Coverage

The programme was formally launched in 1994 in 42 districts of 7 States viz. Assam, Haryana, Karnataka, Kerala, Maharashtra, Madhya Pradesh and Tamil Nadu. The programme has been extended to another 15 districts in 4 additional States namely, Andhra Pradesh, Gujarat, Himachal Pradesh, and Orissa under DPEP-II. The programme is poised to expand to cover a total of about 120 districts in 13 States by the end of 1996-97.

Lok Jumbish Project (LJP)

An innovative project called "Lok Jumbish" (People's Movement for Education for All) with assistance from Swedish International Development Authority (SIDA) has been undertaken in Rajasthan. The basic objective of the project is to achieve education for all by the year 2000 through people's mobilisation and their participation.

Aims and Objectives

(i) Providing access to primary education to all children upto 14 years of age through the school system as far as possible and part-time non-formal education where necessary;

(ii) Ensuring that all enrolled children attend school/NFE Centre regularly and complete primary education;
(iii) Ensuring that the quality of education is improved and all children achieve at least minimum levels of learning;
(iv) Creation of necessary structures, and setting in motion processes which would empower women and make education an instrument of women's equality;
(v) To pursue the goal of equity in education between boys and girls and between socially and educationally disadvantaged sections and the rest of the society and also to initiate measures for provision of basic education to the handicapped children;
(vi) Making necessary modifications in the content and process of education to better relate it to the environment, people's culture and with their living and working conditions; and
(vii) Effectively involve people in the planning and management of Education.

The project is implemented by "Lok Jumbish Parishad", an Autonomous Society registered under the Societies Registration Act.

During the first phase of the project 1992-94, Lok Jumbish covered 25 blocks spread over several districts with an expenditure of Rs. 14.03 crore shared by SIDA, Government of India, Government of Rajasthan in the ratio of 3:2:1.

The second phase of LJP was recently approved to be implemented between 1994-97. In this phase the project would be extended to 50 blocks. An outlay of Rs. 80 crore has been envisaged to be shared by SIDA, GOI and GOR in the ratio of 3:2:1.

Decentralised management structure is the hallmark of the LJP. Lok Jumbish has been able to build partnerships with the local communities and voluntary sectors and developed strategies for community participation. People's participation is ensured at every level like school mapping, micro-planning, training of core teams as well as in village surveys.

In spite of large scale expansion in recent years, several dhanis and chaks have remained unserved by primary schools.

Lok Jumbish is able to set up several new schools, Non-Formal Education Centres through systematic school mapping exercises with the help of local communities. So far school mapping exercises were completed in 1388 villages; 246 new primary schools; 185 Shiksha Karmi Schools and 1016 NFE centres have been opened by LJP.

Lok Jumbish attaches utmost importance to woman's education. It has set up Mahila Shikshan Vihars for providing quality education in a residential type of atmosphere to rural women. Women's participation is ensured in all LJ activities. There are at present 6078 women members in 1611 core teams working in villages. Vihan, an NGO promoted by LJP, has taken up 245 Anganwadi centres for strengthening the programme of pre-primary education and its linkages with primary education.

Lok Jumbish has also initiated several innovative programmes/activities like school health programme to generate awareness among the school children on health issues, special efforts to bring children belonging to minorities to mainstream education, special incentive schemes like supply of free uniforms, free text books to school children which has resulted in better enrolment and retention of children especially girls in the schools; low cost hostels for the benefit of tribal children, etc.

1.2: SECONDARY EDUCATION

Vocationalisation of Secondary Education

In accordance with the priority accorded to vocationalisation of education in the National Policy on Education, a Centrally Sponsored Scheme of Vocationalisation of Secondary Education was introduced in February 1988. The main objectives of the scheme are to enhance individual employability, reduce the mismatch between demand and supply of skilled manpower and provide an alternative for those pursuing higher education without particular interest or purpose. A Centrally Sponsored

Scheme of Pre-Vocational Education at Lower Secondary Stage has also been introduced from the year 1993-94 primarily to impart training in simple marketable skills to the students of classes IX and X, to develop vocational interests and to facilitate students in making a choice of vocational courses at the higher secondary level. The target laid down in the revised policy is to divert 10 per cent of higher secondary students to the vocational stream by 1995 and 25 per cent by 2000 A.D.

In order to provide expert inputs in policy formulation and implementation on a continuing basis, a Joint Council of Vocational Education (JCVE) has been set up at the national level under the Chairmanship of Minister of Human Resource Development, with counterpart organisations at the State level. To ensure that the tasks laid down by JCVE are performed effectively, a Standing Committee of JCVE has been constituted under the Chairmanship of Education Secretary.

Pt. Sunderlal Sharma Central Institute of Vocational Education (PSSCIVE) was set up at Bhopal on July 1, 1993 under the overall umbrella of NCERT. The Institute acts as an apex level research and development organisation in the field of vocational education and provides technical and academic support to the programme. PSSCIVE has developed 82 competency based curricula in 6 major areas which can be adopted by States/UTs with modifications based on the need and relevance of those courses in that particular area. The CIVE has now been entrusted with the task of standardising the curricula/textbooks/instructional material for vocational courses. The CIVE is also *inter alia* engaged in conducting programmes for training of teachers and orientation of key functionaries.

The Scheme at +2 level is implemented through the State Governments/UTs Administration. So far all the States/UTs, except Lakshadweep, have joined the programme. Upto the end of 1995-96, 18,709 vocational sections had been approved in 6,476 schools, creating capacity for diversion of 9.35 lakh students to the vocational stream at the +2 level. This is 11 per cent of the enrolment at +2 level. The actual enrolment is, however, likely to be less as optimum utilisation of facilities created may not be achieved. During 1996-97 main emphasis has been, therefore, on consolidation and qualitative improvement of the programme.

So far assistance for introduction of Pre-vocational courses in 527 schools has been provided to 9 States/UTs, i.e., Assam, Chandigarh, Delhi, Karnataka, Manipur, Madhya Pradesh, Punjab, Rajasthan and Uttar Pradesh.

The courses are selected by the State Government on the basis of assessment of manpower requirement through district vocational surveys. About 150 vocational courses have been introduced at the +2 level in six major areas, viz., Agriculture, Business and Commerce, Engineering and Technology, Health and Para-Medical Services, Home Science Services and others. It has been recommended that 70 per cent of the total instructional time be devoted to vocational theory and practice, and the remaining to the study of general foundation courses and language course. On-the-job training forms an integral part of the curricula.

The Scheme at the +2 level envisages setting up of administrative structure at the Centre, State, District and School levels. The Bureau of Vocational Education is operating at the Central level to oversee the implementation of the programme. In the major States/UTs separate structures at the State level have been created. However, all States/UTs have not created these structures particularly at the district level for various reasons. To facilitate exchange of experiences amongst States so that successful models could be replicated, inter-State field visits were organised.

The Scheme lays considerable emphasis on practical training of students both during the course of study as well as after completion of the course. 60 Vocational subjects fields have so far been covered under the Apprenticeship Act to enable the vocational graduates at the +2 level to avail of the benefit of Apprenticeship Act.

The main weaknesses witnessed in implementation of the programme have been (i) a general preference in society for formal education and a corresponding disparagement of vocational education, low priority accorded by States/UTs, (ii) lack of micro level attention, non-availability of trained teachers and text books, (iii) inadequate linkages with industries and limited avenues for vertical mobility. During the last eight years of implementation of the Vocational Education Programme, several review meetings with State Governments/UTs have been conducted. In April, 1997, a review meeting was conducted with Education Secretaries of all States/UTs to bring to their notice the above weaknesses and discuss strategies for the implementation of Vocational Education Programme during the 9th Plan.

Since the success of Vocational Education Programme would depend upon the placement of vocational students in wage or self-employment, the Department of Personnel and Training has impressed upon the Ministries the need to amend Recruitment Rules to enable vocational pass-outs to be eligible for Government jobs. States/UTs Administration have been suitably advised in this direction. The Department of Education has also set up an inter-Ministerial Committee to review the position department-wise about the posts available in various departments and organisations under them, in respect of which preference can be given to persons with relevant vocational training.

Efforts have been made to introduce need-based courses to ensure ready employment for vocational students. Collaborative arrangements have been worked out with the Ministry of Railways, Ministry of Health, Handicraft Board, etc. A large number of industrial enterprises, in both public and private sectors, were also addressed by the Ministry with a view to involving them in the vocational education programme. Based on the responses received, some collaborative arrangements are being worked out.

The policy also emphasises the need for making available non-formal, flexible and need-based vocational programmes to school drop-outs, neo-literates, etc. The Scheme, therefore, provides for funding of innovative programmes in the field of vocational education undertaken by voluntary organisations. So far 56 voluntary organisations have been assisted under the Scheme.

A computerised Management Information System (MIS) has been developed for vocational education to obtain necessary information on different aspects of programme implementation. The National Informatics Centre (NIC) in collaboration with Department of Education and NCERT has prepared two guidelines – one for filling up the format and the other for feeding the data through Computer Software prepared for the purpose.

With a view to evaluating the performance of the Vocational Education Programme, 4 external agencies/ institutions were awarded the work of conducting a region-wise evaluation. The final report has been submitted by Operations Research Group (ORG). Follow-up meetings in four regions with States/UTs have been planned for dissemination of the findings.

Integrated Education for the Disabled Children (IEDC)

The Kothari Commission (1964-66) had recommended the education of disabled children in regular schools. In 1974 the then Department of Social Welfare launched the Centrally Sponsored Scheme of IEDC. The implementation of this Scheme was transferred to the Department of Education in 1982.

The National Policy on Education, 1986, focuses special attention on the education of disabled children for achieving the goal of Education for All. It advocates the approach of providing integrated education for the mildly handicapped and of special education for the severely handicapped children.

IEDC Scheme purports to provide educational opportunities for the disabled children in common schools, to facilitate their retention in the school system and ultimately their integration in the general school system.

The Scheme is implemented through the Education Department of the State Government/UT Administrations. Voluntary Organisations also assist the State Governments in implementing the Scheme. An Administrative Cell is to be set up by the State Education Department to implement, monitor and evaluate the programmes in the State. The salary component of this Cell is fully met under this Scheme.

Under the scheme, 100 per cent financial assistance is admissible for the education of disabled children studying in common schools by way of supply of aids/equipments, allowances for books, uniforms, transport, readers in respect of blind children, escorts in respect of the severely orthopaedically handicapped and employment of helpers/attendants. The Scheme also provides for meeting the cost of salary of special teachers, setting up of resource rooms, carrying out assessment of disabled children, training of special teachers, removal of architectural barriers in schools and production of instructional material.

The Scheme was revised in 1987 to rationalise several existing provisions and incorporate some new ones considered necessary for proper implementation of the Scheme. The Scheme was again revised in 1992 mainly with a view to increasing the financial ceilings in respect of certain provisions, prescribing qualifications of special teachers and to enlarge the scope of the scheme so as to extend special teacher support to all categories of handicapped children except those orthopaedically handicapped.

In 1987, the NCERT with UNICEF assistance, launched the Project Integrated Education for the Disabled (PIED) for strengthening the implementation of the IEDC Scheme. Here the Composite Area Approach was adopted, where a cluster, usually a block, was taken as the project area. All schools in the area were expected to enrol disabled children. Since 1987, this project has been implemented in one administrative block each in Haryana, Madhya Pradesh, Maharashtra, Mizoram, Nagaland, Orissa, Rajasthan, Tamil Nadu, Delhi Municipal Corporation and Baroda Municipal Corporation.

Promotion of Yoga in Schools

The National Policy on Education (NPE) 1986 lays down special attention on Yoga, as a system to promote integrated development of body and mind. Efforts are in progress to introduce Yoga in all schools and in teacher training courses.

Based on the evaluation of the experimental programme of Introduction of Yoga in Kendriya Vidyalayas in consultation with Yoga experts and keeping in view the NPE 1986, provisions of a Centrally Sponsored Scheme for Promotion of Yoga in Schools was launched in 1989-90.

This Scheme is implemented through the Education Departments in the States/UTs as well as Yoga Institutions of repute. Under the Scheme financial assistance is provided for training of teachers in Yoga and for building of infrastructure necessary for the purpose. In addition, Institutions of all India character are given assistance for maintenance as well as developmental expenditure for promotion of basic research and/or for teacher training programmes in various aspects of Yoga other than the therapeutical aspects. Financial assistance to Yoga Institutions for promotion of therapeutical aspects is being extended by the Ministry of Health and Family Welfare.

Based on the experience in implementation of the Scheme, the Scheme was revised in 1992 to enhance assistance for training courses of Yoga teachers. A provision was also made to meet the travel costs of teachers as the States were finding it difficult to bear this expenditure and were therefore unable to depute teachers for training.

Assistance under the Scheme has so far been provided to a number of organisations/institutions in 12 States/UTs. The Kaivalyadhama Shreeaman Madhava Yoga Mandir Samiti, Lonavla, Pune continues to be assisted under the scheme both for maintenance and developmental expenditure on research and for teacher training programme.

Science Education

To improve the quality of science education and promote scientific temper, as envisaged in the National Policy on Education, 1986, a Centrally Sponsored Scheme, "Improvement of Science Education in Schools", was initiated during 1987-88. Under the Scheme, financial assistance is provided to State Government/Union Territory

Administrations and Voluntary agencies. While Voluntary agencies are provided assistance for conduct of experimental and innovative programmes, States/UTs are assisted for provision of Science Kits to upper primary schools; upgradation and strengthening of science laboratories in secondary and senior secondary schools; supply of books on science related subjects to secondary and senior secondary schools; and training of science and mathematics teachers.

Table 1.6: Achievements during 1987-88 to 1995-96

	7th plan	1990-91 1991-92	1992-93	1993-94	1994-95	1995-96	Total
Amount Spent (Rs. in crore)	80.03	39.57	24.94	22.08	22.70	23.91	213.23
No. of States/ UTs covered	30	26	14	15	9	15	32
No. of Schools covered							
(i) Upper Pr. (Science Kits).	42398	13671	11099	5756	6852	5833	84776
(ii) Sec./ Higher Sec (Library Assistance)	16382	7514	4906	3874	2969	2985	39245
(iii) Sec./ Higher Sec. (laboratory assistance)	15073	7764	5576	3914	3163	3122	38790
No. of Institutions assisted for setting up of District Resource Centres**	115	82	–	–	–	–	197
No. of Voluntary organisations assisted (for innovative programmes cumulative)	13	16	7	12	11	14	32

** This component does not qualify for assistance during the 8th Plan.

All the State Governments/Union Territory Administrations have received assistance under the Scheme during the period 1987-88 to 1995-96. Voluntary agencies have also availed of assistance for conduct of various innovative programmes during 1995-96.

An outlay of Rs. 120.00 crore has been approved for continuance of the Scheme during the 8th Plan.

International Mathematical Olympiad (IMO)

With a view to identifying and nurturing talent in mathematics at school level, IMO is held every year. India has been regularly participating in IMO since 1989. Each participating country is required to send a team consisting of not more than six secondary schools student contestants, a team leader and a deputy leader.

The Indian team in the last 8 Olympiads was jointly sponsored by the Department of Education, Ministry of Human Resource Development and the National Board for Higher Mathematics (NBHM), Department of Atomic Energy. The cost of international travel was paid by the Department of Education, while all other expenses on selection of students, internal travel, incidental expenses etc. were borne by the NBHM.

IMO 96 was held at Mumbai in India in July 1996. Ministry of Human Resource Development sponsored the event and also provided requisite financial support; while the responsibility for organisational matters rested with the National Board for Higher Mathematics.

The Indian contingent to IMO-96 held in July 1996 won one gold, three silver and one bronze medals.

Educational Technology

This is a Centrally Sponsored Scheme combining certain elements of a Central Plan Scheme. The scheme aims at applying technological innovations to improve the quality of education. Under the scheme, the entire cost of Radio-cum-Cassette players in primary schools and 75% cost of colour T.V. in upper Primary Schools is provided by central government. To enable production of suitable programmes for these schools, six autonomous State Institutes of Educational Technology (SIETS) in Andhra Pradesh, Bihar, Gujarat, Maharashtra, Orissa and UP, have also been funded under the scheme.

The scheme also extends financial support to the Central Institute of Educational Technology (CIET) for producing programmes for the school sector for telecast/broadcasting through Doordarshan and Akashvani.

At present all the programmes for the school sector for broadcasting through Akashvani and Telecast through Doordarshan are produced by CIET and SIET system, and are funded under the scheme.

Achievements

So far 3,66,732 Radio-cum-Cassette players and 64,952 colour T.V.s have been sanctioned to States and UTs for installation in Primary/Upper Primary Schools respectively. During 1995-96 CIET and SIETs have together produced 359 Audio,1045 Video (Total-1404) Programmes.

Central Institute of Indian Languages, Mysore has been funded for production of cassettes for learning certain Indian languages at the school levels.

The scheme has been evaluated by the National Institute of Educational Planning and Administration (NIEPA) and Social and Rural Research Institute (SRRI). The evaluation report recommendations have been brought to the notice of Sates/UTs for taking up follow-up action.

National Award for Teachers

The Scheme of National Award for Teachers was started in the year 1958-59 with the object of raising the prestige of teachers and giving public recognition to the meritorious teachers working in

Primary, Middle and Higher Secondary Schools. In 1967-68 the scope of the scheme was enlarged to cover the teachers of Sanskrit Pathshalas, Tolls etc. run on traditional lines. In 1976 the scheme was further enlarged to cover Arabic/Persian teachers of Madarsas run on traditional lines. From the Award Year 1993, the scheme has further been enlarged to cover teachers from Sainik Schools, Navodaya Vidyalayas and schools run by the Atomic Energy Education Society.

Each award carries a certificate of merit, a cash payment of Rs. 10,000 and a silver medal.

The number of awards given have been increased from 296 to 302 from the Award year 1993.

Two hundred and seventy eight teachers were selected for the National Award for 1995. These awards were given away by the President of India on 5th September, 1996 at a function organised at Vigyan Bhawan, New Delhi. For the National Award, 1996 selection process is in progress.

Scheme for Strengthening of Boarding and Hostel Facilities for Girl Students of Secondary and Higher Secondary Schools — Financial Assistance to Voluntary Organisations

One of the main factors responsible for the slow pace of growth of enrolment of adolescent girls in rural, tribal and other remote areas is the traditional societal inhibitions against their movement outside the family precincts. Since High/Higher Secondary schools in such places are sparsely located, girls remain particularly disadvantaged.

In order to actualise the recommendations in POA 1992 for formulating a special enabling plan to ensure increase in enrolment of girls in secondary education and the NPE directive for encouraging NGO participation in education, it was decided to launch the above mentioned scheme during the VIII Plan period with the objective of providing: (i) non-recurring assistance as a one time grant for the provision of essential furniture, utensils and meeting basic recreational need at the rate of Rs. 1500 per boarder; (ii) recurring assistance for food, emoluments of cook and bearer at the rate of Rs. 5000 per annum per boarder to the existing hostels run by the NGO.

During the year 1995-96, 31 voluntary organisations have been supported and an amount of Rs. 60.34 lakhs has been released.

National Council of Educational Research and Training (NCERT)

The National Council of Educational Research and Training (NCERT) is an apex resource organisation set up by the Government of India, with headquarters at New Delhi, to assist and advise the Central and the State Governments on academic matters related to school education. The NCERT provides academic and technical support for improvement of school education through its constituents viz. (i) The National Institute of Education, New Delhi, (ii) The Central Institute of Educational Technology, New Delhi, (iii) Four Regional Institutes of Education located at Ajmer, Bhopal, Bhubaneshwar and Mysore, (iv) Pandit Sunder Lal Sharma Institute of Vocational Education, Bhopal and (v) Field Offices.

During 1995-96, the NCERT had a fresh look at its functioning and reprioritised some of the programmes in response to national concerns in school education. Elementary education received special emphasis. The outreach of academic support and consultancy services was extended to State and district level agencies, particularly in the states implementing the District Primary Education Programme. Special steps are being taken to attend to the development of the school education sector in the North Eastern region.

National Open School (NOS)

NOS was established in November 1989 as an autonomous organisation under the Department of Education. This institution provides education to its students through the distance education mode.

Significant Achievements during 1996-97

The admission to various courses of the NOS have reached an all time high and is expected to cross the figure of 80,000 during 1996-97. The number of study centres continue to increase every year and have reached the figure of 642 and is likely to exceed 700. Many more number of Boards/Universities have recognised the courses of NOS and the number has now reached 111. The percentage of women students in NOS will be about 33 per cent and that of SC/ST 23 per cent. In collaboration with the National Literacy Mission, NOS has taken up the project on Open Basic Education for providing education to the neo-literates at III, V, and VIII Standards. It has also developed learning materials in 14 subjects.

Ninth Plan Proposals

The NOS has decided to create exclusive departments for Vocational Education and Student Support Services. Apart from two languages which NOS offers viz. Hindi and English, it has introduced Urdu, Gujarati, Telugu, Bengali and Kannad. It proposes to introduce more languages in the coming years. NOS has provided guidance for the establishment of State Open Schools (SOS) in Haryana, Madhya Pradesh and Karnataka and similar such schools are likely to be established in West Bengal, Gujarat and Punjab.

Kendriya Vidyalaya Sanghathan (KVS)

Government of India approved the scheme of Kendriya Vidyalayas in 1962 on the recommendations of the Second Central Pay Commission, with the idea of encouraging the growth of Secondary Schools with a common syllabus and medium of instructions for providing uninterrupted education to the children of Central Government employees who are liable to frequent transfers. Initially, 20 regimental schools in different states were taken over as Central Schools. In 1965, an autonomous body, called the KVS was set up to run these Vidyalayas. Over the years, the number of Kendriya Vidyalayas increased to 858 at present.

Kendriya Vidyalayas have been set up with the following salient features : (i) Kendriya Vidyalayas are fulfilling their commitment to provide educational needs of the transferable Central Government employees to a large extent; (ii) Preference in admission is given to children whose parents had the large number of transfers during the preceding seven years; (iii) All Kendriya Vidyalayas are co-educational and composite; (iv) Common Text books, bi-lingual medium of instruction, i.e. English and Hindi and common curriculum are followed; (v) All Kendriya Vidyalayas are affiliated to Central Board of Secondary Education; (vi) Teaching of Sanskrit from Class V to IX is compulsory. However, the student can offer Sanskrit as an additional optional subject at Class X also; (vii) The quality of teaching is kept high by maintaining a proper teacher-pupil ratio; and (viii) No tuition fee is charged from students upto class VIII. The wards of staff of KVS, SC/ST, Children of officers and men of the Armed Forces killed or disabled during hostilities in the wars of 1962, 1965 and 1971 against China and Pakistan and girl students are exempt from paying tuition fee upto class XII.

Navodaya Vidyalaya Samiti

In order to provide high quality modern education to the talented children predominantly from the rural areas, without regard to their socio-economic conditions, Government of India launched the scheme to establish one Navodaya Vidyalaya in each district of the country. Navodaya Vidyalayas are fully residential co-educational institutions providing education upto Senior Secondary stage. Education in Navodaya Vidyalayas including boarding and lodging, textbooks, uniforms,etc, is free.

Opening of NVs

So far 380 NVs have been sanctioned. It is expected to sanction 10 more new NVs by the end of 1996-97 and 30 during 1997-98.

Admission

Admission in Navodaya Vidyalayas is made at the level of Class-VI through a test conducted by NCERT in the concerned district in which all children who have passed Class-V from any of the recognised schools in the district are eligible to appear.

Academic Results

CBSE results for 1996 are given in Table 1.7.

Table 1.7: Results for 1996

Class	No. of Vidyalayas	Appeared	Passed	Pass %
Class X	279	13464	11313	84.0%
Class XII	213	8975	7314	81.5%

Education of SCs/STs and Women

Navodaya Vidyalayas are meant for children from rural areas and admission of children from urban is restricted to a maximum of 25 per cent. The scheme also provides for reservation of SC/ST in proportion to their population in the concerned district subject to a maximum of 50 per cent provided that in any district such reservation will not be less than the national average.

Efforts are made to ensure that atleast 1/3rd of the students selected are girls. The percentage of SC/ST and Girl students in JNVs is 21.6 per cent, 12.9 per cent and 30.9 per cent respectively.

1.3: HIGHER EDUCATION AND RESEARCH

University Grants Commission

Growth of Higher Education System

At the beginning of the year 1996-97, the total students enrolment in universities and colleges was 64.26 lakhs. The enrolment in the University Departments and 10.64 lakhs and that in the affiliated Colleges was 53.62 lakhs.

Four out of ten students in higher education are in the faculty of Arts, enrolled for courses in social sciences and humanities which include History and Culture and Languages. Three out of ten students are enrolled for courses in Sciences, Engineering, Medicine, Agriculture and related disciplines. The faculty of Commerce absorbs two out of 10 students while remaining are in the faculty of Education, Law and 'Others' (Fine Arts etc.). Enrolment at the first degree level was 56.67 lakh (88.2%); at the Postgraduate level 6.04 lakh (9.4%); at research level 0.71 lakhs (1.1%); and at the diploma and certificate level 0.83 lakh (1.3%). The total number of teachers increased to 3.10 lakh during the year. Of these, 0.71 lakh were in the University Departments/ University Colleges and the rest in the affiliated colleges. Of the 71,084 teachers in the Universities, 9,099 were Professors, 18,624 were Readers, 40,518 were lecturers and 2,843 were Tutors/ Demonstrators. In the affiliated colleges, the number of senior teachers was 33,289, the number of Lecturers was 1,95,662 and that of Tutors/Demonstrators was 10,537.

Presently, the total number of Universities in the country was 171 and the total number of Institutions deemed to be Universities was 38.

Higher Education among Women

The enrolment of women students at the beginning of the year 1996-97 was 21.91 lakh. At the Postgraduate level, the enrolment of women was 34.0 per cent of the total enrolment. The enrolment of women students was the highest in Kerala (52.4%), followed by Goa and Punjab (51.1%) each, Pondicherry (45.2%), Delhi (44.6%), Manipur (42.8%),Tamil Nadu and Jammu and Kashmir (39.9% each) and Meghalaya and Nagaland (39.7% each). The enrolment of women was the lowest in Bihar (18.6%).

Programmes and Activities of the Commission

Some of the major thrust areas pursued during the year were: Human Resource Development, Environment Education, Vocationalization of Education at the first degree level, Academic Staff Colleges for Orientation of Teachers, Eligibility test for recruitment of lecturers, Inter-University Centres and Consortiums, Distance Education, COSIST, Adult Education and National Literacy Mission, Spread of Mass Communication and Educational Technology network, Computer Education, Education for Scheduled Castes and Scheduled Tribes and for the minorities and weaker sections among the minority communities, Education for women and the handicapped and Population education.

Human Resource Development

The Commission has been striving to develop human resources and towards this end, it provides assistance for various programmes which enable teachers and researchers to upgrade professional competence and keep abreast of the latest developments in their disciplines. Assistance for various types of scholarships and Fellowships is provided to achieve this objective. Junior Research Fellowship is awarded to those research scholars who have qualified in national level tests conducted by the UGC, CSIR, GATE etc. Teachers of outstanding eminence are awarded national fellowships for a specified period to devote themselves exclusively to research and writing. Similarly, under the Scheme of Research Scientists, 200 positions have been created at any given time. The awardees are placed in two slabs viz., Rs. 2300-3500 and Rs. 4000-6500. The scheme provides opportunities to those who wish to pursue research as a career. Selections under this scheme are made directly by the Commission. A scheme of Career Awards also exists which aims at identifying young talented teachers to devote themselves to research with lesser teaching responsibilities.

Under the scheme of Visiting Professors/Fellows, assistance is provided to universities for appointment of Visiting Professors/Fellows. During the year, the Commission continued the scheme of "Visiting Faculty" in the universities so as to provide teaching/research assignments outside Kashmir to the teachers from Kashmir Universities and its affiliated colleges due to disturbed conditions there.

Research and Studies in Emerging and Inter-Disciplinary Areas

These courses include courses like Super-Conductivity, Atmospheric Science, Environmental Education, Computer Application, etc.

(i) *Super Conductivity Programme*

The UGC programmes on Super conductivity has been in operation since 1987 for assisting universities in developing education and research capabilities in both basic and applied areas of Super Conductivity. Periodic review through group monitoring meetings and annual/bi-annual reports are inbuilt features of the programme. The Commission was supporting 35 universities in both basic and applied areas.

These institutions have come up as Centres of Excellence in their particular areas. The programme has generated a positive impact on the university system for collaborative approaches to R&D and educational activities.

(ii) *Atmospheric Science*

This programme has been in operation since 1987, with the object of promoting meteorological and atmospheric sciences in the universities and providing employment opportunities for persons trained on the computer systems installed at the council of Meteorological and Earth Sciences for medium range forecasting. The Commission was supporting seven universities under this programme.

(iii) *Environment Education*

In view of the growing concern for Environment and in the light of the Supreme Court Directive in this regard, UGC has impressed upon universities to introduce a course on Environment as a compulsory subject at the undergraduate and post-graduate levels. The UGC has constituted expert groups to consider proposals received from universities in this regard. Assistance for the following programmes was approved by the Commission.

1. Workshops/Seminars on environment education at P.G. level in different departments in universities/colleges.
2. Introduction of a special paper on environment education at P.G. level in different departments in 15 universities/colleges.
3. Introduction of M.Sc. course in environment education in 22 universities.
4. Seven research projects on 'Flyash Accumulation and Imperatives of Finding of Avenues for its Mass Scale Utilisation'.
5. Environmental components to be introduced at B.Ed./ M.Ed. level in 19 universities.

Nearly 100 episodes for promoting environment awareness have also been telecast by the UGC through the 'Country-wide Classroom' programmes. The Commission has also prepared a text book and some popular literature for undergraduates with the help of Expert Groups on Environment.

Vocationalisation of Education at the First Degree Level

In conformity with the National Policy on Education 1986 (revised in 1992), a programme of vocationalisation of education at the first degree level was launched by the UGC from 1994-95. Funds to the tune of Rs. 26 crore were provided by the Ministry of Human Resource Development for implementation of the programme.

On the recommendations of the Standing Committee on Vocational Education (SCORE) and its sub-committee/regional committee constituted for the purpose, the UGC identified 209 institutions (19 Universities and 190 Colleges) in the first instance, for starting vocational courses at the first degree level during 1994-95. These institutions introduced one to three vocational courses in 35 subjects identified by the Core Committee. A list of these 35 subjects is given below:

1. Functional Hindi
2. Functional Sanskrit
3. Communicative English
4. Archaeology and Museology
5. Principles and Practices of Insurance
6. Actuarial Science
7. Office Management and Secretarial Practices
8. Tax Procedures and Practices
9. Foreign Trade Practices and Procedure
10. Tourist and Travel Management
11. Advertising, Sales Promotion (Sales Management)
12. Computer Application
13. Industrial Chemistry (Seven streams)
14. Food Sciences and Quality Control
15. Clinical Nutrition Dietics
16. Industrial Microbiology
17. Bio-technology
18. Biological Tech. and Specimen Preparation
19. Seed Technology
20. Sericulture
21. Industrial Fishing and Fishery
22. Instrumentation
23. Optical Instrumentation
24. Geo-explorational and Drilling Technology

25. Mass Communication Videos Production
26. Still Photography Audio Products
27. Electronic Equipment Maintenance
28. Computer Maintenance
29. Electrical Equipment Maintenance
30. Environment and Water Management
31. Rural Technology
32. Automobile Maintenance
33. Refrigeration and Air-conditioning Maintenance
34. Construction Technology Management
35. Manufacturing Process

During the year 1995-96, another 198 institutions (7 Universities and 191 Colleges) were identified for support for starting vocational subjects involving a total financial commitment of Rs. 1740.50 lakh (recurring and non-recurring) for 1995-96 and Rs. 416 lakh p.a. for the next four years. Another 325 institutions (6 Universities and 319 Colleges) have been covered under the programme during 1996-97, thus bringing the total number of institutions upto 1996-97 to 732. During the year, training programmes were also organised for equipping teachers of the respective institutions for teaching the vocational subjects which were being offered at their parent institutions. The Standing Committee on Vocational Education constituted Regional Monitoring Groups from amongst its members and conducted monitoring exercises at Bhopal, Bombay, Bangalore, Calcutta and Delhi to assess the progress made by the institutions in starting vocational courses.

Media and Educational Technology

The UGC has undertaken initiative to utilize the time slot available for higher education to telecast programmes in higher education titled "Country-wide Class Room" through which higher education has spread to remote and backward areas of the country. The Commission is at present supporting seven Educational Media

Research Centres (EMRCs), at the University of Pune, Gujarat, Jamia Millia Islamia, Jodhpur, Madurai Kamraj, and at the Central Institute of English and Foreign Languages and St. Xavier College, Calcutta. In addition, Audio Visual Research Centre (AVRCs), at Roorkee University, Osmania University, Anna University, Devi Ahilya University, H. S. Gour University, Mysore University, Kashmir University, Manipur University, Punjabi University and Calicut University are being supported for training of personnel and production of soft-ware. Nearly 85 per cent of the higher education programmes transmitted on T.V. are produced indigenously.

In order to make distance learning more effective and bring best faculty within the reach of all sections of students, including semi-urban and rural students, a project to produce non-broadcast syllabus-based video lecture tapes for under-graduate students has also been undertaken. Out of 15 subjects selected for the purpose, video lectures in eight subjects have been completed. The Consortium for Educational Communication (CEC) provides the institutional framework to sustain and enhance the on-going media activity of the EMRCs and AVRCs and explore new technological advances in the field. It has also started making monthly programmes and producing educational programmes for transmission through the Enrichment Channel of Doordarshan.

The CEC has also taken steps to produce programmes on contemporary issues like environmental awareness, safe drinking water and prevention of AIDS. During the year, new project titled "Educational International" was started with a view to promote and widely disseminate abroad the Indian educational material on economic terms.

The project is to be implemented by the Consortium for Educational Communication, New Delhi. Other agencies which have agreed to work for the project are the Indira Gandhi Open University. National Council of Educational Research and Training and National Open School. The UGC has also established a Consortium for export of educational material as a project mode of CEC.

Adult, Continuing and Extension Education and Population Education Programmes

Adult, Continuing and Extension Education Programmes have the following goals:

(a) Eradication of Illiteracy
(b) Promotion of Continuing Education
(c) Promotion of Population Education
(d) Promotion of Legal Literacy and Awareness of various Development Programmes
(e) Support for Science Education and Transfer of Technology.
(f) Promotion of Other Welfare and Community Development Programmes.

To achieve these goals, the Commission is providing financial assistance to universities for the implementation of the Total Literacy Campaign (TLC), through their departments of Adult, Continuing and Extension Education. The guidelines for these programmes envisage internal evaluation/monitoring system through State Level Nodal Agencies/Universities. The Commission is also deputing university/college teachers to work with Bharat Gyan Vigyan Samithi on whole time basis for nationwide literacy movement. Population Education Programme, assisted by the UGC, is implemented by the universities as part of the United Nations Population Fund (UNFPA)–UGC project through the Population Education Resource Centres (PERCs) which are 12 in number. These have been set up by the UGC in the departments of the Adult, Continuing and Extension Programmes to provide support services for various activities like material development, curriculum development and training for the functionaries. Thrust has been given to new emerging areas such as AIDS, Drugs abuse, environment and ageing. The PERCs have been organising training programmes, national level programmes and other activities like debates, poster competitions, one-act plays, exhibitions in different parts of the country as well as a series of extension lectures on population-related issues. Efforts have also been initiated to integrate Population Education components for undergraduate and postgraduate curriculum, starting with selected themes on Population dynamics, like having a controlled family size, spacing of children, age at marriage etc. The scope has gradually been expanded to cover larger areas like health, immunization, nutrition, drug addiction, AIDS awareness and environmental issues to focus on the quality of life.

Action plan for the prevention and control of AIDS has been drawn up by the UGC, according to which additional grants are to be provided to universities and colleges for the purchase of books on AIDS, Population Education, Environment and Drug abuse.

Distance Education/Correspondence Courses

Distance Education, which is mix of correspondence education, Distance Education and open learning, accounts for nearly 12 per cent of the total enrolment in higher education and is the emerging reality in the educational sense of the country. Assistance is provided to universities to the tune of Rs. 10 lakh, as seed money for the first five years for introducing distance education programmes/correspondence courses. Further assistance to the tune of Rs. 5 lakh to Rs. 7.5 lakh is provided after 5 years for running undergraduate and postgraduate courses respectively. Improvement in the quality of Distance Education Programmes is being brought about with the help of audio, video, radio and television facilities. Audio-Visual Research Centres (AVRCs) have been set up in each of the four regions to support distance education programmes in the universities. The Centre in the Northern region is producing programmes in Hindi, English and Urdu; the Centre in the Western region is developing programmes in Marathi, Gujarati and Kannada; the Southern regional centre is producing programmes in Tamil, Telugu and Malayalam, while the Eastern region centre is preparing programme in Oriya, Bengali and Assamese.

Facilities for Scheduled Castes/Scheduled Tribes, Handicapped and the Weaker Sections of the Society

In addition to the Junior Research Fellowships reserved for Scheduled Castes and Scheduled Tribes out of the total number of such fellowships instituted for various universities, the Commission is directly awarding every year 50 fellowships for these categories. Also, the Commission has reserved 40 Research Associateships for Scheduled Castes and Scheduled Tribes. In order to provide opportunities to teachers belonging to Scheduled Castes and Scheduled Tribes in affiliated colleges, 50 teacher fellowships have been earmarked for them to improve their qualifications by doing M.Phil/ Ph.D. Special cells in various universities have also been set up to ensure effective implementation of the various schemes for the Scheduled Castes/Scheduled Tribe students. Relaxation has also been prescribed in the criteria for financial assistance to colleges having SC/ST enrolment and to those located in backward regions. There is also a scheme of "Remedial Coaching for Scheduled Castes and Scheduled Tribes" being implemented in universities and colleges which aims at improving the skills and linguistic proficiency of the students in various subjects and raising their level of comprehension in such subjects where qualitative techniques and laboratory work are involved.

Under the scheme, a university/college is eligible to receive grant on 100 per cent basis upto a ceiling of Rs. 1.5 lakh and Rs. 0.75 lakh per annum respectively. During the year 1995-96, proposals of 101 colleges and 6 universities were approved for conducting remedial coaching. The Commission continued to provide assistance to identified centres and cells (in universities and colleges respectively) for conducting coaching classes for the educationally backward among minority communities for preparing them for competitive examinations other than the higher civil services. The Commission has also identified some additional Centres in different universities/colleges in order to cover more areas of minority concentration. At present, there are 21 universities and 60 colleges running the scheme. Also, 10 colleges have been identified as coaching centres exclusively for women candidates.

In order to oversee the implementation of the reservation policy in Central Universities, the Commission has appointed a Monitoring Committee under the Chairmanship of Secretary, UGC. A series of meetings of this Committee have been held with the Registrars of Central Universities, Representatives of Ministry of Human Resource Development and the Ministry of Social Welfare to assess the steps taken for implementation of the reservation policy. The Commission has also been organising regional meetings of the Registrars of State Universities/Deemed Universities for implementation of the reservation policy.

Women's Studies

Under the Commission's programme of promoting women's studies, assistance is provided to universities and colleges for setting up centres and cells for women's studies. The Centres/Cells are required to undertake research, develop curricula, and organise training and extension work in the areas of gender equity, economic self-reliance of women, girls education, population issues, issues of human rights and social exploitation. The centres are not expected to be like other conventional departments of the universities, in that they are not required to run courses that lead to undergraduate or a postgraduate degree. Presently, the UGC assisted 33 centres/cells for women's studies. In addition, assistance for research projects concerning women's studies was also provided. Forty part-time Research Associateships for women have also been created in Science, Humanities, Social Sciences and Engineering/ Technology to enable them to take up post-doctoral research.

Project on Information and Library Network (INFLIBNET)

Project on Information and Library Network is a Computer Communication network for linking library and information centres in universities, deemed to be universities, institutions and colleges through the application of computer and communication technologies to enable them to optimally utilize their resources.

The INFLIBNET has created a centralised data base of academic holdings in which data received from these institutions is entered, which will ultimately lead to a national union catalogue for on-line access. INFLIBNET is also helping university libraries to computerise their records by offering them facility of down-loading from its authenticated master file. Development of an appropriate library management software has also been taken up in collaboration with DESIDOC taking into account requirements of the university libraries. During 1995-96, the INFLIBNET programme was converted into an Inter-University Centre under Article 12(ccc) of the UGC Act and the Centre has been registered as an autonomous society.

The UGC has funded, so far 114 university libraries for library automation under this programme and personnel from over 100 academic libraries, including executives, have been trained in computerised operation and management.

Fake Universities

The problem of fake universities awarding unrecognised degree has been engaging the attention of the University Grants Commission and the Government of India for the past few years.

A Fake University is an institution which is not entitled to call itself a university and award degrees under its name. According to the provision of the University Grants Commission Act, 1956 only those universities which are established under an Act of Parliament or a State Legislature, or are granted deemed to be University status are entitled to call themselves "University" and confer degrees. As many as 20 universities have been identified as fake universities by the UGC. The UGC has set up a separate cell in its office to look into the complaints pertaining to fake universities. This cell would liaise with different agencies of the Government and take such measures as are necessary for arresting the menace of fake universities.

1.4: TECHNICAL EDUCATION

Technical Education is one of the most significant components of human resource development spectrum with great potential for adding value to products and services, for contributing to the national economy, and for improving the quality of life of the people. In recognition of the importance of this sector, the successive Five Year Plans laid great emphasis on the development of technical education.

During the past four decades, there has been a phenomenal expansion of technical education facilities in the country. But, a lot still needs to be done in respect of increasing its coverage and enhancing its accessibility to the needs of the organised as well as the unorganised and rural sector and in improving its relevance to productivity. Moreover, the changing scenario by the turn of the century in socio-economic, industrial and technological areas needs to be considered to enable the system to play its role with greater relevance and objectivity. Based on these considerations, several initiatives were taken to further revamp the technical education system. They include: modernization and removal of obsolescence, promoting institution-industry interaction, providing continuing education for upgrading the skill and knowledge of technical personnel working in industry and service sectors, transfer of technology to the rural sector/setting up of Technology Development Missions to meet the emerging challenges in Science and Technology.

Considerable progress has been made in implementing the various programmes and schemes. A major project has been undertaken with the assistance of the World Bank, to upgrade the technical education system in the country for enabling the polytechnics to improve their capacity, quality and effciency. Vested with statutory authority the All India Council for Technical Education (AICTE) continues to fulfil the tasks assigned to it. The proposals to establish two new Indian Institutes of Management at Indore and Calicut and the Indian Institute of Information Technology and Management at Gwalior have been approved during 1995-96.

Indian Institutes of Technology

The five Indian Institutes of Technology (IITs) at Bombay, Delhi, Kanpur, Kharagpur and Madras were set up in the country as Institutes of National importance and premier centres of education and training in engineering and applied sciences at the undergraduate level and to provide adequate facilities for postgraduate studies and research.

The IITs conduct four-year undergraduate programmes (Bechelors degree) in various fields of engineering and technology. They also offer integrated Master's degree courses of five years duration in physics, chemistry, mathematics, biochemical engineering and bio-technology. In addition. IITs offer M.Tech. degree courses in various specialisations and one-year post-graduate diploma courses in selected areas. The Institutes also offer Ph.D. programmes in different branches of engineering sciences, humanities and social sciences. There are also advanced areas of training and research in each institute, in identified areas of specialization.

Over the years the IITs have succeeded in developing patents and their exploitation by the industry. The IITs have earned a sizeable revenue through sponsored research projects, consultancy works undertaken by their faculty members.

The institutes are the leaders in education, training and research for the development of technical manpower at levels comparable to the best in the world. Selection of the brightest students through JEE for entrance to undergraduate courses and the very high quality of training thereafter speak volumes of the IITs system, which is committed to the pursuit of excellence. The Insti-tutes continued to modernise their laboratories with funds provided by the Government of India for the purpose.

A special preparatory course of 10 months duration continued to improve the intake of SC/ST students in the IITs. Those SC/ST students who fail to qualify the Joint Entrance Examination (JEE) for admission in the IITs but score a certain minimum per centage of marks are offered admission to the preparatory course.

At the end of the preparatory course, the students are subjected to a qualifying test on the basis of which they are offered admission to the B.Tech. Programme without having to appear in the JEE again. This has improved the position of intake of SC/ST students in the IITs. The SC/ST students also continued to get financial support from the Institutes by way of pocket allowance, loans and discretion grant, apart from free messing.

As per the Assam Accord, another IIT has been set up in Assam, the sixth in the chain of IITs. For declaring the IIT, Guwahati – the sixth in the fraternity of IITs, as an Institute of National Importance, the Institute of Technology Act, 1961 was further amended and it came into force with effect from 1st September, 1994.

Academic programmes commenced from the academic year 1995-96 in three disciplines, namely Computer Science and Engineering, Electronics and Communication Engineering and Mechanical Engineering with a total intake of 65 students. During 1996-97, 75 students were admitted.

Indian Institutes of Management

The four Indian Institutes of Management (IIMs) located at Ahmedabad, Bangalore, Calcutta and Lucknow were set up by the Government of India with the objective of providing high quality management education through teaching, training, research and consultancy. These Institutions are the centres of excellence.

The three Institutes in Ahmedabad, Bangalore and Calcutta continued their usual academic programmes, viz., Postgraduate Programme in Management (equivalent to M.B.A.), Fellowship programme (equivalent to Ph.D.), Management Development Programmes, Organisation Based Programme and Research and Consultancy for Industries.

The fourth Indian Institute of Management at Lucknow started functioning from 1985-86 session. This is still in a developing stage. The Institute is conducting Post-Graduate Programme, Management Development Programme and undertaking Research and Consultancy for Industries.

As a follow-up of National Policy on Education, these Institutes have established Research Centres to meet the needs of other non-corporate and under-managed sectors like Agriculture, Rural Development, Public Systems Management, Energy, Health Education, Habitat, etc. These institutes have also set up computer-aided Management Centre with the objective of promoting the development of application of software in the area of industry-oriented management techniques.

Recently, the Government has established two more Indian Institutes of Management (IIMs), one at Indore (Madhya Pradesh) and other at Calicut (Kerala). Academic activities will be started from the session 1997-98.

All India Council for Technical Education (AICTE)

The AICTE set up in 1945 as an advisory body was given a statutory status through an Act of Parliament in 1987. The Act came into effect on March 28, 1988. The main functions of the AICTE includes proper planning and coordinated development of technical education in the country, qualitative improvement at all levels in relation to planned quantitative growth and regulations of the system and maintenance of norms and standards.

In order to streamline the system of approval of new courses and programmes the Council has issued regulations for establishment of new institutions/starting of new courses, etc.

The Council has come to an understanding with the Council of Architecture (functioning under the Architects Act) and the Pharmacy Council of India (under the Pharmacy Act) in the procedure for assessment of courses and institutions in their respective fields.

The Council has laid down norms and standards for diploma, degree and postgraduate courses in various fields. In pursuance of Supreme Court judgements, the council has issued regulations fixing norms and guidelines for charging tuition and other fees and providing guidelines for admissions of students to professional colleges.

The AICTE has also issued Regulations for granting approval to technical institutions, courses and programmes in the fields of technical education. Under these Regulations approvals are given to private unaided technical institutions also.

Asian Institute of Technology, Bangkok

The Asian Institute of Technology (AIT), Bangkok is an autonomous international Graduate Institute providing advanced education in Engineering, Science and allied fields. It enrols about 600 students from more than twenty countries and has international faculty members. The Institute is governed by an international Board of Trustees, whose members come from different countries along with those from India.

The Government of India has agreed to provide assistance to the Asian Institute of Technology for: (i) Deputation of Teachers/ Experts in specialized areas of Engineering and Technology, meeting the entire cost of their deputation; (ii) Annual Grants upto Rs. 3 lakh for purchase of equipment from India; purchase of books and payment for subscription on academic and technical journals published in India; and expenditure on academic related activities in India.

Regional Engineering Colleges (RECs)

Under the scheme of establishment of Regional Engineering Colleges, a Central Plan Scheme, seventeen Colleges have been established, one each in the major states, to meet the country's growing requirement for trained technical manpower for various development projects. Each college is a joint and cooperative enterprise of the Central Government and the State Government concerned. While all the seventeen colleges offer 1st Degree Courses in various branches of Engineering and Technology, fourteen of these have facilities for Post-Graduate and Doctoral programmes.

The Colleges are administered by a Board of Governors (BOGs) with a fair degree of autonomy, both financial and administrative. The Chairman of the Board is the Minister for Technical Education of the respective State in which the College is located.

At the National level, there is an Advisory Council for RECs, with the Union Minister for Human Resource Development as its Chairman for giving advice on the broad policies for the REC system.

Academically, the Colleges are affiliated to the respective Universities in the region where the RECs are located. Within this framework some of the Universities have granted academic autonomy to RECs affiliated to them.

The Government of India meets the entire non-recurring expenditure and 50 per cent of the recurring expenditure on undergraduate courses of these Colleges. The balance of 50 per cent recurring expenditure is borne by the respective State Governments. The entire expenditure on postgraduate courses is met by the Government of India.

The admissions are made on the basis of entrance examinations conducted by the Technical Education Department of the States concerned for admission to all Engineering Colleges in the State. 50 per cent of the seats in each Regional Engineering College is filled by the students qualifying from the State where a particular REC is located. The rest 50 per cent seats are filled by the students coming from other States/UTs based on pre-decided distribution.

Ministry of Human Resource Development has taken a number of initiatives for developing curriculum in tune with present day needs and forging links with the industry and also to help RECs to achieve excellence in education and research and development.

U.K.-India Technical Cooperation Project for RECs

An Indo-UK Technical Cooperation project to strengthen technical education in India through assistance to 8 RECs in four technical themes: DESIGN (RECs at Allahabad and Jaipur), ENERGY (RECs at Bhopal and Tiruchirapalli), INFORMATION TECHNOLOGY (RECs at Surathkal and Warangal) and MATERIALS ENGINEERING (RECs at Nagpur and Rourkela) commenced in April, 1994 after a formal MEMORANDUM OF UNDERSTANDING was signed between the Government of India and the UK on January 12, 1994.

The project is curriculum based and aims to meet changing industrial needs by improving the quality and relevance of REC's graduate in-service training, consultancy and R&D services. This will be achieved by improving teaching skills, developing the curriculum, equipping laboratories in each college, developing management information systems and strengthening links with industry.

There is a Project Steering Committee (PSC) which monitors the overall progress of the project at the national level and has met twice (i) on June 13, 1994, (ii) on May 22, 1995, and (iii) on 12th September 1996 to take stock of the progress achieved so far. Joint Educational Adviser (Tech) dealing with the RECs is the National Project Director (NPD) of the Project and oversees all aspects of implementation of the project on behalf of the GOI, including release of finances from MHRD. The Chairman, AICTE is the Chairman of the Project Steering Committee (PSC).

There are four Theme Sub-Committees one each for each major areas, viz, Design, Energy, Information Technology and Materials. An eminent expert from industry is the Chairman for each of them. These Committees meet once in every four months to review activity in the theme areas, over the previous four months, plan activities and procedures for consultancy, equipment specifications and reception for confirmation by Project Steering Committee (PSC) and recommend adoption of new curricula to the respective REC Board of Studies, who report to the PSC twice per year. Each of theme Sub-Committees also form an appropriate Curriculum Planning Group with industrial participation.

Centres of Excellence Programmes of RECs

During 1993-94 the Government have taken an important initiative of providing a special grant of Rupees one crore each to a REC annually under the Plan for the remaining period of the 8th Five Year Plan in addition to the general Plan grant, to develop 17 RECs into institutions of excellence at par with the IITs.

High Power Review Committee

A High Power Committee to Review the RECs has been constituted on June 17, 1996 under the Chairmanship of Dr. R.A. Mashelkar, Director General and Secretary, C.S.I.R.,New Delhi. The Terms of Reference of the Committee are as under:

(i) To review progress made by RECs and achievements vis-a-vis their Mission Statement as stipulated in their Memoranda of Understanding and suggest the future role of RECs in building a high quality Technological Education base in the country.
(ii) To initiate methods of teaching practices, formulation of new programmes and curriculum; industrial, research and consultancy activities etc. to cater to the goals and objectives.
(iii) To examine the administrative and funding arrangement of RECs and propose changes, keeping in view the challenges offered by the Global Technology Scenario and also suggest an alert organ within the system for keeping RECs at the cutting edge of Technology Education.
(iv) To suggest mechanisms for close participation of RECs with industry, society and other institutions.
(v) To suggest methods of selection of excellent faculty and teacher training programmes for existing teachers.
(vi) To make recommendations on any other matter which the Committee deems fit for the Growth of RECs as leaders in Technical Education.

World Bank Assisted Technician Education Project

Recognising the need for revamping technician education as projected in the National Education Policy the Government has launched a major project which is being implemented in two overlapping phases with the assistance of World Bank to enable the State Governments to upgrade their polytechnics in capacity, quality and efficiency.

The World Bank Assisted Project to support technician education is estimated to cost Rs. 1650.00 crore including World Bank Credit Assistance of Special Drawing Rights of 373.3 million over the period 1990-99. The project under two phases covers 17 States and 2 Union Territories involving 535 polytechnics. It is primarily a State sector project and the entire cost is provided by the participating State Governments from their respective State Plan allocations. The project is being implemented by the State Governments under the overall guidance, support and monitoring by the Department of Education for which a small central component covering strengthening of four Technical Teachers Training Institutes in the country, establishment of National Project Implementation Unit and a National Project Directorate in the Ministry have been provided in the project. The World Bank Assisted Technician Education Project gives thrust for women's education through creation of additional places of 9,200 for women in polytechnics by establishing 39 new women polytechnics besides providing seats for women in Co-ed polytechnics. The project also provides for additional hostel facilities for girl students, and quarters for faculty and staff of the polytechnics.

Mid Term Review of Phases-I and II of the Project were conducted by the World Bank. The World Bank has expressed satisfaction on the performance and noted that the objectives envisaged would be achieved.

1.5: ADULT EDUCATION

National Literacy Mission

Literacy is a major component of Human Resource Development and is basic to any programme of social and economic progress. Development can never become self sustaining unless it is accompanied by corresponding changes in the attitude, value, knowledge, and skills of people as a whole. The only way this change can be accomplished is through education and literacy is the first step towards education. The National Literacy Mission was set up in 1988 with the goal of making 80 million people literate by 1995. The Total Literacy Campaigns is the dominant strategy for achieving the literacy goals of the nation. The Indian experience in literacy has aroused the interest of the international community and has become the role model for many Asian and South Asian countries. At the national level the aim is to consolidate the gains of literacy and to concentrate efforts in the four major Hindi-speaking States in the Hindi heartland where the bulk of the illiterate population resides.

The Mission which was set up with the objective of imparting literacy to 80 million non literates in the age group of 15-35 by the year 1995 has now been set with the goal of covering 100 million non literates by the year 1999. Children in the age group 9-14 are also included where there are no NFE Centres. The Total Literacy Campaigns have been extended to 417 districts in the country of which 178 have entered post literacy phase. An estimated 90 million learners have been enrolled in the programme and 56 million are reported to have been made literate. A number of programmes were taken up under the NLM this year which include: (i) A national workshop to review the UNFPA funded Population Education Project and to decide on future perspectives, issues and strategies for the implementation of the project in the 3rd phase from 1997-2001 was organised on May 27-28, 1996 at Kodaikanal, Tamil Nadu; (ii) A regional workshop on the Scheme of Continuing

Education for neo literate was held from June 26-28, 1996 at Hyderabad; (iii) As part of the International Literacy Day celebrations, a Saksharta Utsav was held in New Delhi on September 7, 1996; (iv) On the occasion of the 30th International Literacy Day on September 8, 1996 in New Delhi, two books, viz. *Women and Literacy* and *Our Hopes and Our Dreams – In Our Words* were presented to the President of India; (v) A Conference of Chairpersons/Directors of State Resource Centres was held in New Delhi on September 24-25, 1996; (vi) A SAARC Conference of Voluntary Agencies working in the field of Literacy and Continuing Education was held from October 14-16, 1996 in New Delhi in which representatives from the countries of Nepal, Bangladesh, Pakistan and Sri Lanka participated.; (vii) The second National Conference of State/UT Directors of Adult/Mass Education was held in New Delhi on October 17-18,1996; (viii) A SAARC Conference of Voluntary Agencies working in the field of literacy and Continuing Education was held from October 14-16, 1996 in New Delhi in which representatives from the countries of Nepal, Bangladesh, Pakistan, Sri Lanka and India participated; (ix) In collaboration with State Resource Centre, Bhubaneshwar, ACCU-UNESCO held its 14th Regional Workshop on the preparation of literacy follow up materials for adults in rural areas in Asia and the Pacific in Bhubaneshwar, Orissa from November 12-23, 1996; (x) An orientation workshop for literacy consultants on Operation Restoration on TLC/PLC projects was held in New Delhi on November 29-30, 1996; (xi) In collaboration with the Government of Maharashtra and SAHAS (Saksharta Hak Samiti), Greater Bombay, National Literacy Mission organised a National Conference on Urban Literacy Campaign in Indian context on December 27-28, 1996 in Mumbai, Maharashtra.

Special Projects for Eradication of Illiteracy – TLC/PLCs

National Literacy Mission Authority set a target of making 100 million citizens functionally literate in the age group of 9-35 by the end of 1999.

The Total Literacy Campaign (TLC) is the principal stra-tegy of the NLM for eradication of illiteracy in the country. The literacy campaigns under the Scheme are area-specific, time-bound, delivered through voluntarism, cost-effective and outcome-oriented, and are implemented by Zilla Saksharta Samitis usually headed by District Collectors.

The campaigns are initiated with appropriate environment-building activity coupled with a door-to-door literacy survey during which potential learners and volunteers are identified. Suitable primers are developed and primer-specific training is provided to the required personnel. The environment-building activity as well as monitoring and internal evaluation are continued through the teaching/learning activity which accounts for a total of 200 hours spread over a period of 6 months. An external evaluation is made at the conclusion of the teaching.

After completion of the TLC, Post Literacy Campaign (PLC) is launched to mop up the left-over illiterates to consolidate the gains of literacy acquired during TLC, and to enable the neo-literates to develop abilities for self-learning.

The literacy campaigns are implemented through direct funding to the ZSS by the Central and State Governments in the ratio of 2:1. However, for districts under Tribal Sub Plan their ratio is 4:1.

Implementation of TLCs in various parts of the country has evoked an enthusiastic response from the weaker sections of the society, especially the Scheduled Castes and Scheduled Tribes. Experience has also shown that more than 60 per cent of the learners attending classes are women. The number of TLC/PLC projects have covered 417 and 178 districts either fully or partially in the States of Andhra Pradesh, Assam, Bihar, Delhi, Goa, Gujarat, Haryana, Himachal Pradesh, Jammu and Kashmir, Karnataka, Maharashtra, Madhya Pradesh, Manipur, Meghalaya, Orissa, Rajasthan, Tamil Nadu, Tripura, Uttar Pradesh, West Bengal and the U.T.s of Chandigarh, Daman and Diu, Dadra and Nagar Haveli and Pondicherry.

The focus of the TLC has now shifted to the Hindi speaking areas where bulk of the illiterate population resides. So far 172 districts under TLC and 32 districts under PLC have been sanctioned in the four major Hindi-speaking States of Bihar, Madhya Pradesh, Rajasthan and Uttar Pradesh. Besides, the special measures taken under NLM in these four States are: (i) Sensitization workshops for collectors and other officials and non-officials involved in literacy campaigns and similar workshops for writers and media personnel for sensitization on literacy issues are organised regularly; (ii) The State Governments have been reviewing the progress of literacy campaign, with a view to improving the implementation of projects; and (iii) The State Resource Centres of all the four States have been strengthened and their financial assistance augmented.

Rural Functional Literacy Project

The centre based Rural Functional Literacy Programme has been phased out with effect from April 1991 except in States/UTs of Jammu and Kashmir, North Eastern States, Sikkim, border districts of Rajasthan under the Border Area Project and Dadra and Nagar Haveli. These areas have relatively low literacy rates as well as extremely difficult terrain, hindering communication and mobility. During 1995-96, no viable proposals were received. Most of the projects sanctioned during 1994-95 have been carried over to 1995-96 for implementation.

Shramik Vidyapeeths (SVPs)

The Shramik Vidyapeeths represent an institutional framework for offering non-formal, adult and continuing educational and polyvalent training programme to industrial workers. Shramik Vidyapeeths are working under auspices of State Governments/ Universities/Voluntary Agencies. During 1996-97, 53 Shramik Vidyapeeths are in operation, 44 in voluntary sector and remaining 9 are under State Governments/Central Government.

Scheme of Continuing Education for Neo-literates

The National Literacy Mission (NLM) lays specific emphasis on Continuing Education for Neo-literates which is the modified form of the Scheme of Post Literacy and Continuing Education, launched in March 1988. The basic objectives of the scheme of Continuing Education are: (i) Provision of facilities for retention of literacy skills and continuing education do enable the learners to continue their learning beyond literacy stage; (ii) Creating scope for application of functional literacy for improvement of living conditions and quality of life; (iii) Dissemination of information on development programmes and widening and improving participation of traditionally deprived sections of the society; (iv) Creation of awareness about national concerns such as national integration, conservation and improvement of the environment, women's equality, observance of small family norms and sharing of common problems of the community; (v) Improvement of economic conditions and general well-being through short duration training courses for providing vocational skills and linkages between continuing education and developmental activities; (vi) Provision of facilities for library and reading rooms for creating an environment conducive for literacy efforts.

Voluntary Agencies

The Scheme of financial assistance to Voluntary Agencies working in the field of Adult Education continued to encourage and provide financial assistance to the non-governmental organisations who are considered to be the partners in achieving the goals of the National Literacy Mission.

The main objective of the Scheme is to provide financial assistance to voluntary agencies for their involvement in the following activities: (i) Implementation of time-bound, area specific, result oriented and voluntary based literacy projects; (ii) To take responsibility in well defined non-ZSS areas for eradication of illiteracy and running of post-literacy and continuing education programmes; and (iii) To take up innovative and experimental projects, environment building activities including organisation of seminars and conferences, etc.

The scheme is continuing with its endeavour to encourage greater participation of voluntary agencies in the adult education programmes.

Directorate of Adult Education

The Directorate of Adult Education (DAE), a subordinate office of the Department of Education, continued to function as the National Resource Centre in the field of Adult Education and Literacy campaigns. The Directorate has different units with identified professional and administrative functions. The main activities of the Directorate included preparation of materials and surveillance under which the Directorate organised (i) 12 monthly meetings of the Improved Pace and Content of Learning (IPCL) Advisory Committee for review of the teaching learning materials developed by the SRCs/RRCs, TLC Districts and other related agencies concerned. Guidelines were laid down for preparation of material for Basic literacy, Post literacy and Continuing Education Programmes; (ii) Training and orientation workshops for writers and artists were organised at Bhubaneshwar, Itanagar, Dimapur, Leh and Imphal for orientation of writers in techniques of designing IPCL materials plus preparation of sample material in Assamese, English, Dogri, Urdu, Kashmiri, Bodhi and other tribal languages; (iii) Three regional workshops were organised at Mysore, Gangtok and Ahmedabad for assessment of Population Education Components integrated in the Basic Literacy, Post Literacy and Continuing Education materials and preparation of supplementary materials on the messages not adquately covered in the serials so far, and (iv) One national workshop was organised at Udaipur in collaboration with the SRC, Jaipur as follow-up programme of the Nepal Workshop of Asian Cultural Centre for UNESCO (ACCU) Japan on Developing Basic Literacy Materials for Women and Girls in Asia and Pacific.

State Resource Centres (SRC)

SRCs had been providing academic and technical resource support to literacy campaigns in the country. With the increase in number of Literacy Campaigns upto 414 districts in the country, responsibilities of SRCs by way of development of materials, training of field functionaries, monitoring and evaluation of campaigns, etc., have increased manifold.

Resource Centres extended resource support to voluntary agencies and other educational institutions. In this regard, several of the SRCs intensified collaborative action with Zilla Saksharta Samitis.

The National Literacy Mission (NLM) took several measures to strengthen the SRCs, upgrade their capability and involve them more vigorously and intimately in the literacy efforts. In view of this, a National Conference of Directors of State Resource Centres was organised by the National Literacy Mission/Central Directorate of Adult Education on September 23-25, 1996. Some Chairpersons and the State Directors of Adult/Mass Education also attended the conference.

The activities of SRCs were monitored regularly and the Annual Report on State Resource Centres for the Year 1995-96 was brought out.

Shramik Vidyapeeths (SVPs)

The scheme of SVP is one of the prominent programmes of non-formal adult and continuing education for the urban community. 53 SVPs were set up by the Year 1995-96 and likely to be expanded during Ninth Plan.

The basic idea behind the multi-dimensional or polyvalent approach to the education of urban working community in SVP is to meet the various inter-related needs of target groups with specifically tailored programmes. This provides knowledge and imparts skills simultaneously and in an integrated manner.

The prime concern of the SVP is to conduct courses of varying duration involving vocational/technical skills for skill development/upgradation to participate in income generating activities. It is to improve socio-economic status of the poorest of the poor beneficiaries. The programmes of SVPs have been very widely recognised as very potential means of promoting continuing education and develop attitude for lifelong learning. The Directorate of Adult Education is extending Technical Resource Support Services for smooth functioning of the SVPs in the countries.

During the Year1995-96 the SVPs conducted 10119 programmes and benefited 376802 persons. The participation of women in programmes was to the extent of 63.21 per cent and that of males was 36.79 per cent only. 87.84 per cent persons were of the age group of 15-35 Years. 83.55 per cent were income group below Rs. 155 per month.

1.6:WOMEN'S EDUCATION

Mahila Samakhya

The Mahila Samakhya programme is a direct outcome of the commitment of affirmative action in support of women's education mandated in the National Policy on Education. A programme for women's education and empowerment, Mahila Samakhya endeavours to create a learning environment where women can collectively affirm their potential, gain the strength to demand information and knowledge, and move forward to change and take charge of their lives.

Education is understood as an ongoing process of learning and empowerment which transcends mere literacy. The programme, which is not constrained by present agenda or predetermined targets, responds and designs interventions to meet the articulated needs of rural poor women. The *sangria* (village level women's collective) is the nodal point around which the programme revolves.

The process of mobilising and organising women is facilitated by a *sahayogini* (a cluster co-ordinator in charge of 10 villages). She is crucial link between the village Sangha and the district implementation unit of the programme. The latter provides resource support and inputs to meet the needs of the women. The district units in turn are supported by a State Office which ensures a facilitative environment and brings in necessary resource inputs for the programme. At the State level, an autonomous registered society an as empowered body has been set up to oversee the programme. At the national level the programme is coordinated by a Project Director. A National Resource Group, an advisory body of eminent women activists, academics, development workers and bureaucrats, supports the programme, bringing in new concepts, ideas and experiences and guides and advises on the programme policies and strategies.

Mahila Samakhya has expanded its coverage to 31 districts in the country, while its approach has influenced several other educational proposals. Under Dutch funding the programme is being implemented in 2,574 villages of 15 districts in the States of Uttar Pradesh, Karnataka, Gujarat, and Andhra Pradesh. The effectiveness of the MS strategy in mobilising women for education has resulted in it being adopted by other basic education projects. Through the IDA assisted UP Basic Education Project, 6 districts have been additionally covered in UP. The programme is being implemented in 7 districts of Bihar as part of the Bihar Education project and in 3 districts of Madhya Pradesh the programme is supported by the District Primary Education Programme.

Over the past several years the MS strategy has been validated in different regional contexts in the country. Womens' capacities and their information base are continually being enhanced, setting in motion a process of collective questioning and action. Vibrant and strong "Mahila Sanghs" or women's collective have evolved at the village level, thereby laying a foundation for women's empowerment at the grass-roots.

The effectiveness of the MS strategy and its impact can be seen both in the rich texture of women's mobilisation and action as well as the various alternatives that the programme has thrown up. "Mahila Samakhya" in all States have engaged with a remarkable range of issues. The spheres of Sangha activity and action are ever expanding, ranging from accessing basic civic amenities; learning to deal with health issues; committing themselves to ensuring learning opportunities for their children, especially girls; doggedly trying to make themselves literate; breaking gender stereotypes in acquiring new skills like even becoming mechanics; learning to manage credit, effectively participating in Panchayati Raj processes; learning legal procedures and understanding how administrative and social structures work; gaining in strength to demand accountability and effective delivery of services; to confidently addressing issues like violence against women, child marriage and the devadasi system.

Women's Sanghas have taken an active lead in the area of children's/girl child education. The needs from pre-school education to adult literacy are being addressed.

In Gujarat, Early Child Care Centres are being run and managed by committees of *sakhis*, *sahayoginis* and *anganwadis*. These committees monitor the centres and mobilise local resources in cash and kind. In UP, the centres picturesquely called Udan Khatola, Hindola or Buransh cater to children who have dropped out, never gone to school and to pre-schoolers. Bal melas and Bal sabhas are periodically organised to enable children from various villages to meet and share their excitement. The teacher's (anudeshikas) skills are continually upgraded through a planned training programme. In Karnataka, some Sanghas are running balwadis with no financial assistance from MS except the initial setting up and training to the workers. These Sanghas are playing an active role in enrolling children into primary school.

Significant interventions have evolved specially in the area of girls/women's education. Bal Mitra Kendras (Non-formal education) for girls have been started in Andhra Pradesh to cater to the needs of girls. An important feature of these kendras is the focus on establishing and creating a sense of partnership and ownership in this activity among the Sangha women, parents and the community. Sanghas and parents play a proactive role in selection of teachers, monitoring the centres and most importantly contribute financially to the teacher's fee.

The Mahila Shikshana Kendra (MSK) is a unique learning opportunity for adolescent girls and young women. This institution has evolved through the Mahila Samakhya programme and there is a major demand for setting up these centres in all MS districts and blocks. A residential programme, it varies in its focus and curriculum as it is designed to meet the specific local needs. There are 8 kendras being run in Uttar Pradesh, Andhra Pradesh, Karnataka and Gujarat. In Bihar 5 MSKs are being run by MS-BEP for school drop-outs and never enrolled adolescent girls. In Karnataka, the MSK helps and prepares school drop-outs to take school leaving examinations. In Andhra Pradesh, a one year curriculum has been evolved to include basic literacy skills, health and environment awareness, mobilisation and vocational skills. In UP, an innovative and gender focused curriculum has been evolved along with the learners, whose ages range from 15 to 35. The duration of the condensed course is about 6 months. It is anticipated that the MSK would facilitate the learning and training of aware young women who will play a decisive role in the development of their communities.

Interventions for literacy have been propelled by the demand and desire of Sangha women to learn to read and write. In almost all instances this demand has emerged when women want to deal with issues like wages, savings, accessing government schemes, skills upgradation, interacting with socio-political structures. MS has responded to this demand by producing gender sensitive and learner friendly materials and through efforts to sustain the literacy efforts through camps/centres. In some cases linking up with on-going Total Literacy Campaigns has also been done. In Karnataka, the Sanghas have awarded the title of "gnana gelathiyaru" or guiding light to women who have learnt to read and write and are now teaching others. The most significant achievement has been the training of neo-literate women in screen printing and production of broadsheets in Banda district of UP. The Mahila Dakhiya which is regularly published by Banda women, received the Chameli Devi National Media Award in March 1996.

To enable women to improve their health status, health awareness and trainings are systematically being imparted particularly in the States of Karnataka and Andhra Pradesh. As part of this training, herbal medicine, which traditionally was in the hands of women is being retrieved, documented and its usage validated. This has resulted in the emergence of Sangha women as health healers. Sanghas themselves are engaged in growing herbariums and keeping alive this indigenous knowledge system. In addition, Sanghas have also in many instances managed to enforce greater accountability from the health system and ensured that ANMs visit villages regularly. A health curriculum for adolescent girls is also being evolved in the States.

Learning to access and control resources has been an important objective of the learning process in Mahila Samakhya. To learn what resources are available, how to develop them or access fresh ones, the procedures involved therein, the bottlenecks likely to be encountered etc. are all part of the education that rural women find exciting and informative.

In Rajkot district of Gujarat, MS in collaboration with the District panchayat and the UNICEF is involved in a major venture for handpump repair and maintenance through women's participation. This has meant training women as mechanics and the constitution of water committees. Discusssions on health and environment have led to a variety of activities. In Banda district in UP Sangha women have been active in the Van panchayats and afforestation programmes. In Andhra Pradesh's Medak district, as a result of health training, 830 women applied for and were sanctioned funds and materials for setting up toilets. An offshoot of this has been the initiation of training in masonry.

Savings and access to credit has been the focus of Sanghas in Bijapur districts of Karnataka. With a savings pool of over Rs.7 lakhs, the Sanghas are now considering starting a rural women's bank. They have been able to negotiate with NABARD for income generation activities of their choice. The savings activities in all the States have led to training in accounts and record keeping and most importantly given a spurt to literacy activity. In all the States, strong Sanghas have now begun to consciously access schemes like DWCRA.

In UP, Sangha women and *sahayoginis* in Banda have formed a women's co-operative VANANGNA, which handles screen printing, handpump maintenance and contract jobs for masonry, as women in the co-operative are well trained to carry out these tasks.

Women across the MS supreme have confidently addressed issues of violence, child carriage and the devadasi system. In Karnataka and Andhra Pradesh the Sanghas have been effective in the prevention of initiation of young girls as devadasis. Legal awareness and education inputs are being run in all States. In UP the Saharanpur district unit provides legal support for registering cases of violence and assists in regular follow-up.

One of the most interesting alternative structures developed to deal with legal tangles issues, has been the setting up of a Nari Adalat in Vaghodia block of Baroda district. Women have received para legal training and are handling cases relating to *stridhan*, maintenance, child custody and property disputes in community counts.

Taking conscious decisions and making informed choices have underlined the participation of Sangha women in all the States. This has logically brought women into the area of political processes especially at the local levels. Extensive dissemination of information on the provisions of the Panchayati Raj Act resulted in many Sanghas putting up women candidates and deciding upon strategies for election. 231 women from the MS programme in Gujarat, 135 in Karnataka, 120 in UP and 51 in Andhra Pradesh have been elected to various Panchayat bodies. Reports particularly from Karnataka indicate that the participation of Sangha women in the working of the panchayats is of a qualitatively higher as they have shown themselves to be more aware, informed and articulate with gender-conscious agendas.

Empowering Women through Education

A corner-stone of the National Policy on Education is the removal of disparities in the field of education and to bring this about a well conceived edge in favour of women is posited

Gender awareness, gender sensitisation and gender weightage are, therefore, ingredients in all educational interventions.

— One of the most successful efforts to link women's empowerment with education has been Mahila Samakhya. The programme is operational in 17 districts spread over the four States of Andhra Pradesh, Gujarat, Karnataka and Uttar Pradesh. The Samakhya approach begins with the understanding that women must identify their problems and evolve solutions at their own pace.

  A critical factor in the process of empowerment has been the Sangha or women's collective. The Sangha is a forum where women can collectively analyse their problems and share their experiences. The Samakhya approach has been successfully adopted by several basic education programmes, including the Bihar Education Project, District Primary Education Programme in Madhya Pradesh and in Assam.

— The Total Literacy Campaign (TLC) has been successful in raising the demand for education especially among women. In most of 417 districts, women made up over 60 per cent of adults enrolled in the programme. The classes have motivated women to fight for minimum wages and launch a crusade against prohibition.

  In campaign mode, the programme actively seeks to attract women and girls to participate in the educational process. In 178 TLC districts, post literacy campaigns have begun and these address the needs of neo-literate learners. TLC is gradually being extended in the educationally backward states.

— In order that illiteracy may be eradicated amongst adult women, it would first be necessary to tackle the problem at the primary stage. Under the scheme of Operation Blackboard, of the 1.47 lakh teachers appointed, 47 per cent or 69,090 were women. In future, at least half of all teachers appointed are expected to be women.

— The Non-Formal Education system is being extended to meet the needs particularly of the girls who are unable to attend formal school. NFE Centres run exclusively for girls get 90 per cent assistance from the Central Government. The number of such centres has been increased from 25 per cent to 40 per cent of the total during the Eighth Plan Period.

— At the other end of the spectrum are the Navodaya Vidyalayas, centres for excellence, where at least one-third of the students would be girls. In both the Kendriya Vidyalaya and Navodaya Vidyalayas, education for girls is free upto Class XII.

— Building on these schemes is the District Primary Education Programme (DPEP) which focuses on improving girls' access to and participation in school. The programme is now operational in 52 districts spread over eleven States: Assam, Haryana, Karnataka, Kerala, Maharashtra, Madhya Pradesh, Tamil Nadu, Andhra Pradesh, Gujarat, Himachal Pradesh and Orissa. It is proposed to cover another 61 districts by the end of the 8th Plan. The attempt is to build in an equity focus from early formal schooling.

DPEP's district focus is a conscious attempt to decentralise the planning process as a strategy to universalise elementary education. Educationally backward districts which have a female literacy rate below the national average have been selected for the programme. As DPEP has a well-defined gender focus which ensures that all interventions and activities are gender-aware, this effort to integrate a gender perspective begins with the planning process.

— In many States, free education for girls is already part of the effort to improve participation rate.

— For girls who complete Class X and then dropout, vocational training programmes which emphasise entrepreneurship have been designed. This is a centrally sponsored scheme which consciously attempts to introduce new and emerging technologies to women.

— Another step in girls' education is the operationalisation of the scheme for assistance to voluntary organisations for strengthening boarding/hostel facilities for girl students of the secondary and higher secondary schools. During the Eighth Plan 3,580 girls are expected to be benefited.

— The efforts of the last four decades and more have resulted in a massive increase in number of women who enter universities.

— In the technical and professional higher education programmes too, there has been marked increase in the participation of women.

— The University Grants Commission has been encouraging institutions to take up research projects in the area of women's studies by providing necessary funds. UGC has also assisted 22 universities and 11 colleges to set up Women's Studies Centres. This is in addition to the 40 positions of part-time research associateships for women.

PART – TWO

DIVERSE FACETS OF EDUCATION

2

Delhi University Committee on Launching of Employment Oriented Courses (1995)

Introduction

University of Delhi appointed the committee under the Chairmanship of Dr. Abid Hussain to review the on-going programmes of vocational education and job oriented programmes at the University of Delhi and suggested newer approaches, programmes and supportive/promotive measures for an effective programme of job oriented courses including self-employment to be implemented by Delhi University.

Observations

On the basis of discussions held with the principals and also interviews with policy makers the Committee makes the following observations:

(i) The traditional role of the University education puts a major emphasis on the acquisition of knowledge. This emphasis on pure knowledge in the various academic disciplines has tended to create a gap between the educational system and the society at large. The changing social environment makes it necessary that our educational programmes should also take into account the need for the development of self-awareness and acquisition of skills that would enable the students to participate in the overall national development.

(ii) A large number of graduates remain unemployed and their number is increasing year after year. The educated unemployed is a serious drag to our development process and the solution lies in evolving appropriate strategies to make our education more meaningful and purposeful. The system therefore needs to be modified in a fundamental way in order to satisfy these needs.

(iii) The New Economic Policy seeks to make structural changes in the patterns and procedures of socio-economic development. The fundamental changes in the social and economic paradigms are exerting their influences on education particularly higher education and there has been a significant change in the prioritisation and resource allocation for educational programmes. The need for a drastic restructuring of courses of study and vocationalisation of higher education has also been felt.

(iv) The Programmes of Action (1992), taking its clue from the National Policy on Education, has suggested that Higher Education Programmes have to be redesigned to meet the growing demands of specialisation, provide flexibility in the combination of courses, facilitate mobility among courses, programmes and institutions; update and modernise curricula; and integrate work/practical experience and participation in creative activities with the learning process.

(v) The scheme of Restructuring of courses was initiated by the University Grants Commission (UGC) during the Fifth Plan period. The crucial concept behind the Restructuring of courses is to replace the existing conventional courses by courses oriented towards field/practical work. The scheme aims at an educational system which is flexible and which helps the students to cultivate self-help skills, subject skills, group and social skills as well as ethical values.

(vi) The University Grants Commission's Committee on the Vocationalisation of the First Degree Education chaired by Dr. Dhar has drawn up a scheme for introducing 35 vocational subjects initially in Universities and Colleges offering first degree courses in arts, science and commerce. The Committee has identified subjects and prepared detailed syllabi for each of them. The emphasis in these courses is on providing knowledge and skills required for entry into gainful employment, particularly self employment.

(vii) Restructuring of courses in higher education and successful implementation of the programmes of vocationalisation of education would be greatly facilitated if proper manpower planning exercises are undertaken by the implementing agencies at the Centre and States.

(viii) Since industry is the user of the products of university institutions, it is imperative that it should share the cost of imparting education to create a reservoir of highly trained professional and technical manpower. So far industrial and commercial houses have contributed little to this process.

It has now become necessary to persuade the industry to contribute towards higher education. This would become possible provided we take steps to establish closer and continuous interaction between the universities and the productive sector who are the users of the products of the university.

(ix) While mobilisation of resources from private sources is an urgent necessity, it should not be forgotten that higher education is integrally related to socio-economic development and no government can afford to allow it to languish for want of funds.

In this context, the suggestion made by Punnayya Committee of the UGC (1994) is worth emphasizing: "State or Government funding must continue to be an essential and mandatory requirement for support of higher education. The Government/State must continue to accept the major responsibility for funding the essential maintenance and development requirements of the Universities."

(x) The need of the hour is to re-orient education in new emergent fields or areas so as to *channelise the manpower into the right direction.*

(xi) Re-orientation or re-restructuring of the educational programmes in higher education system is essential for *providing manpower for economic growth.* Re-orientation of the educational programmes should be undertaken in such a manner so as to produce self-reliant and self-dependent citizens.

(xii) The country has now introduced a *free market economic policy* gearing the Indian Industry to enter into the *Global market* and International Trade. Consequently, a major challenge is now thrown open to the higher and technical education system of the country.

(xiii) Lack of momentum in implementation of restructured courses could be attributed to *non-availability of specialised teachers*, limited opportunities for practical training, course contents and absence of clear linkages between these courses and improving the job prospects.

Recommendations

1. The re-oriented courses should offer facilities and opportunities for the *total development of the students* and should establish link between an institution and the surrounding community/industry.
2. With a view to mounting useful job oriented programmes in a planned manner so as to make the educational programmes more productive and useful, the *major emphasis for re-orientation of courses should be as under:*

   (a) Courses and programmes should be need based, employment oriented and should help in self-employment generation.

   (b) Programmes should ensure higher academic standards with more professional content to attract bright students.

(c) Students to be admitted should have the necessary aptitude and ability to pursue the courses and programmes.

(d) Courses be offered in institutions *having competent faculty* and necessary infrastructural and other facilities.

(e) Suitable teaching and learning materials including audio visual teaching aids shall promote soundness of the programmes.

(f) For each course there should be properly trained core faculty supplemented by competent and qualified visiting faculty to ensure proper blending of theory and practice.

(g) Existing facilities such as buildings, classrooms available with the Institutions/University be optimally utilised and shared.

(h) In the long run the programmes may be self supporting. Some help from the UGC may be required in the initial stages for creating specialised facilities for these programmes.

(i) Association of Business and Industry with the University and their participation as teaching faculty and their involvement in curriculum designing and development shall be necessary for ensuring a two way communication between the University and the Practising Business World or Research Laboratories so as to make the programmes up-to-date and more useful from the practical point of view.

(j) Programmes should be monitored on a continuous basis particularly for identifying need based courses, orientation of teachers and mechanism for evaluation of the various programmes.

(k) Each institution should monitor the programmes as per guidelines of the University. Besides a Central Machinery should continuously monitor the implementation of the programme and suggest corrective measures. After every three years there may be an external evaluation of the programme for identifying weaknesses and for corrective measures to be taken to fulfil the objectives of the scheme.

(l) Some guidelines for giving academic freedom to institutions for developing employment oriented and self-employment programmes under the scheme be formulated for implementation.

(m) University should play a leadership role in developing new programmes, course curriculum, material, training of teachers and for monitoring the programmes etc.

(n) While fullest use be made of the existing facilities, the scheme may not suffer for want of funds.

Strengthening of Popular Courses, Phasing out Unpopular Courses and New Courses and Combinations:

(a) Present restructured courses, which are found to be popular need to be strengthened.
Unpopular courses not in demand need to be phased out.

(b) For example, Data processing could be changed into Computer Applications to provide the students with knowledge and work experience of several software packages.

(c) Similarly Nutrition and Health and Food Technology when offered as an integrated course would be found to be more useful and acceptable in the job market.

(d) Wherever possible, colleges could adopt the *Menu* or *Cafeteria approach* where there is greater flexibility for the student to opt for a group of subjects of his/her choice from among different subjects offered by the college or department. This will help the students to choose the subjects for which they have aptitude and interest instead of being compelled to study subjects in which they do not have much interest. Under this approach students may also be given freedom to offer one more extra subject in addition to the normal three subjects at B.A.(P) and B.Sc.(Gen) if it is going to be of help to them to get better employment opportunities.

(e) *Proper grouping of subjects*: While grouping the subjects-traditional and vocational for the degree programme it has to be done in a meaningful and integrated manner keeping in view the job market opportunities and at the same time not diluting the value of the traditional subjects.

3

National Commission for Women Committee on Development of Female Education among Tribal Women (1995)

Main Observations

While several committees have observed the status of women in tribal societies to be "high and honourable" and one where widow remarriage is not considered a stigma and where there is a very low incidence of child marriage, it has been found that the overall literacy percentage of tribal women is "abysmally low", with Rajasthan accounting for a mere four per cent literacy rate among tribal women.

Andhra Pradesh accounts for a mere seven per cent literacy rate while Orissa and Madhya Pradesh record nine per cent each in the tribal societies. Interestingly, Mizoram records the highest per centage of literacy level among tribal women (77 per cent), followed by Lakshadweep which has a literacy level of 75 per cent according to the report on "Development of Female Education among the Tribal Communities" brought out by the National Commission for Women (NCW).

The report observes that the States which have a high overall literacy level have a low gender differential. While in Rajasthan there is a vast gender differential — as much as 31 per cent points between male and female literacy (35 per cent and four per cent respectively) in Mizoram and Lakshadweep the gender differential is six and nine per cent points respectively.

While the male literacy in Mizoram and Lakshadweep is 83 and 84 per cent respectively, the female level in these two places is 77 and 75 per cent respectively. As against this, Kerala records a difference of 8 per cent points with the literacy level of men being recorded at 60 per cent against 52 per cent among women.

The report also observes that the literacy percentage in States having a large population of Scheduled Tribes has remained at a consistently low level while stating that the gap in the literacy rate between the Scheduled Castes, Scheduled Tribes and non-Scheduled Castes and Tribes continues to widen. This is evident from the literacy rate at an all-India level where the gap between the rest of the population and the Scheduled Castes and Scheduled Tribes rests at 25.24 per cent and 33.05 per cent in 1991 as compared to 17.59 per cent and 19.33 per cent in 1961.

According to the Report while Lakshadweep and Mizoram account for over 70 per cent range of literacy level, States of Andhra Pradesh, Bihar, Madhya Pradesh, Orissa, Rajasthan, and Uttar Pradesh among others have a literacy level which is below 20 per cent. While Maharashtra, Karnataka, Tamil Nadu, Goa and Gujarat are among the States which account for a literacy level which ranges between 20 to 30 per cent, Assam and Himachal Pradesh are the only two States which have a literacy level between 30-40 per cent. There are only four States in the country which have a literacy level as high as 40 to 50 per cent, viz, Andaman and Nicobar Islands, Daman and Diu, Manipur and Meghalaya.

An astounding revelation of this Report is that as per the 1981 census data there is evidence to suggest that there are a few tribal communities where there is not a single literate person in both the rural and urban areas. As per 1991 census there were 11 cases in rural areas and nine in urban areas where there was not a single literate female.

Among the tribal communities, numbering 21, where the population exceeds 5 lakh, the female literacy rate varied from 29.96 per cent among Naga tribes in Nagaland to "Bhil Bhil Garasia" tribe in Rajasthan. Further there were three tribes in the States of Madhya Pradesh, Rajasthan and Andhra Pradesh respectively where the literacy level is recorded below two per cent. As against this the "Bhil Bhil Garasia" tribe in Maharashtra was the only one wherein the literacy level was as "high" as 4.28 per cent.

The report also states that the spread of literacy among the tribal people of the Central belt was perceptibly lower than among the tribal population of the North-East region. Credence is lent to this by the fact that while the overall literacy rate among the tribals of the Central belt ranged from 15 per cent in Andhra Pradesh to 31 per cent in Gujarat, in the North-East region it varied from 33 per cent in Arunachal Pradesh to 80 per cent in the other States, the lowest and highest literacy rate among tribals accounted for 24 per cent in Tamil Nadu and 79 per cent in Lakshadweep.

In addition to literacy, on which there is a major thrust in the Report, other interesting finding relates to the representation of Scheduled Tribes in Central Government services and in public sector undertakings which recorded an increase. As per data available, the representation in central services was recorded at 5.44 per cent in 1991 as against 2.52 per cent in 1971. Of these as much as 2.53 per cent accounted for representation in Class-I services as against 0.41 per cent in 1971, while as much as 6.82 per cent in Class IV services as against 3.65 per cent in 1971.

While the representation in Class III services increased from 1.70 per cent in 1971 to 4.98 per cent in 1991, in Class-II services the representation registered an increase of nearly two per cent.

In the public sector undertakings, however, the representation in all categories in 1989 was 9.68 per cent as against 2.24 per cent in 1971. In Class I and Class II services, however, it was 1.29 per cent and 2.31 per cent respectively as against 0.17 per cent and 0.16 per cent respectively in 1971.

The report while noting that recommendations made by committees, commissions and task forces etc. have drawn a blank and been a "consequence waste of valuable resources" calls for a fresh look at the contents of non-formal education combined with what it terms as the need for a "major offensive" in the field, while stressing the need to equip the tribal women to protect themselves from all kinds of exploitation.

Significant Recommendation

It has been suggested that a tribal language should be the medium of instruction which assumed greater importance in the realm of female education particularly because tribal women and girls have little interaction with the outside world. "If the *status quo* continues, in the years to come one may witness scant progress on tribal females' education front", the report observes.

Source: *Hindustan Times*, January 2, 1996

4

National Seminar on Funding of Higher Education in India (1995)

National Institute of Educational Planning and Administration (NIEPA) organised a two-day seminar on the Funding of Higher Education in India, on January 23-24, 1995, to discuss the problems relating to the financing of higher education in India in the context of (i) UGC report on funding of Institutions of Higher Education (Chairman: Dr. Justice K. Punnayya) and (ii) AICTE Report on Mobilisation of Additional Resources for Technical Education (Chairman: Dr. D. Swaminathan).

Significant Policy Suggestions

(i) The State cannot abandon its responsibility of funding higher education and shift the onus to the market forces. State has to continue to play a dominant role in financing higher education in India.

(ii) There is urgent need for improving the mechanism for the allocation and flow of UGC/government grant to universities and institutions of higher education. Grant mechanisms based on unit cost formulae are the minimum needed reforms in this direction. The change-over to this approach would require detailed estimation of costs of education.

(iii) Efforts can be made to raise resources from non-governmental sources to supplement governmental resources but this should be done without affecting equity and efficiency in education.

(iv) One important measure in this regard would be a modest and gradual increase in fees to cover about 20-25 per cent of the recurring costs of higher education, along with introduction of a well designed scholarship and student loan programmes.

(v) Another important measure would be to generate resources through voluntary donations, and other contributions from corporate sector, through tax incentives on the one side, and incentives in use of these funds by the institutions, on the other side.

(vi) A basic need of the whole system is a strong, reliable and up-to-date statistical information system in the UGC, AICTE, Central and State governments and higher education institutions.

(vii) Lastly, all aspects of financing of higher education — grants, costs, fees, cost recovery, scholarships, other direct and indirect subsidies, generation of other internal resources, etc. — should be completely transparent.

5

NIEPA Workshop on Planning of Higher Education in 21st Century: Role of Management (1995)

A two-day workshop on 'Planning of Higher Education for 21st Century: Role of Management' sponsored by the University Grants Commission was organised by National Institute of Educational Planning and Administration (NIEPA) on March 24-25, 1995.

Objectives of the Workshop

(i) To discuss the planning and management implications of the opening of economy to the world market and also of technological advancement for higher education in 21st Century.

(ii) To focus discussion on the future imperatives of:

- (a) Growth and development of universities;
- (b) Programmes of studies, curriculum and evaluation of students;
- (c) Teachers' recruitment, professional development and their accountability;
- (d) Sources of funding and financial management; and
- (e) Alternative forms of Governance and management.

RECOMMENDATIONS

1. General

Technological advancement and the opening of the world market have far reaching implications for Higher Education in the country.

There is a need for thorough analysis of these implications in order to lay the plans for reforms which would enable the system to face the challenges of the future. The last Commission on Education was set up in 1964-66 and a specific study on Higher Education was made in 1948. In the light of new developments it would be most appropriate to set up another National Commission on Higher Education to provide a vision for the future and help chart a viable course for its realization.

2. Growth and Developments

(a) The gaps among the disciplines of education and between education and societal needs are increasing. The gap between the education, finance and administration has also increased in the past. The policy thrust should be to bridge gaps among the disciplines of education and between society and education, administration and finances.

(b) For competing in the world market, India will have to excel in certain technologies buttressed by a reservoir of high quality human resources engaged in teaching, research and development. This will be a prerequisite for enabling India to have favourable terms of trade and competitive edge among the nation states. Policy thrust should be to increase interdependence and networking between India and the rest of the nations through R&D and the programmes for human resource development. This would enable India to translate knowledge into both soft and hard technologies.

(c) Every State should prepare a perspective plan for 15 to 20 years and this plan should become a guiding document for the development of higher education at the university and State levels. A similar perspective plan for 15 to 20 years, keeping in view the likely changing in knowledge, environment and demand, should be made for the development of higher education at the national level. There is a provision in NPE 1986/1992 to constitute an apex level body comprising UGC, AICTE, Medical Council, Indian

Council of Agricultural Research and Education and other organisations for the integrated and holistic planning of higher education. This apex body should be constituted as early as possible. It will help India to develop a national level perspective plan for the development of higher education for facing the challenges of the 21st Century.

(d) It is clear that in the coming years, technological development is going to be very swift and wide. This will have both positive and negative implications. India should guard against likelihood of dehumanization of society as well as the erosion of its basic values and culture. Therefore, the policy for higher education should make sure that while developing and adopting technologies and opening of the country to the world market, India would maintain its essential character and identity.

3. Sources of Funding and Financial Management

Provision of adequate finances and ensuring their efficient management is pivotal to the system of higher education. It is indeed very unfortunate that higher education is facing resource crunch today. The situation calls for a two pronged strategy. On the one hand, efforts have made to rationalise the cost structure with a view to minimising the cost of education and, on the other hand, avenues for mobilising further resources must also be tapped. Accordingly, steps in the following three areas need to be initiated: (i) Resource allocation/management at the apex level,(ii) Resource mobilisation, and (iii) Cost reduction.

(i) Resource Allocation/Management at Apex Level

(a) In the foreseeable future, the question of resources for higher education shall remain important in a developing country like ours. A welfare state like ours has at least to facilitate the availability of funds for higher education. Higher education, in theory, has always been regarded as an investment. Now is the time when the investment required in this field should be assessed and provided for. To facilitate this, the Government of India must set up a National Educational Development Bank with the two fold objectives of providing long term loans to institutions of higher education for their capital needs and to fund and administer a Student Loan Programme. While the new institution is being created, the scope of the IDBI may be increased to cover Human Resource Development as well. Besides, HUDCO could also be persuaded to extend financial support for the construction of Faculty Residence and Students' hostel in institutions of higher education.

(b) The Punnayya Committee has highlighted the need of continuing State support for higher education. Keeping in view the fact that the State shall continue to play a major role in provision of finances for higher education, it seems reasonable to expect that the maintenance expenditure of higher education would be borne equally by the Centre and the State.

(c) An Educational Finance Commission should be set up to evolve strategies of resource sharing between State governments and Universities.

(ii) Resource Mobilisation

It is increasingly evident that the institutions of higher education have to find alternative sources of finance and they cannot remain totally dependent on the government. Accordingly:

(a) Institutions of higher education should raise fees in a phased manner and thus recover part of their cost from the beneficiaries of higher education. However, to provide for equity as well as merit, it would be appropriate to evolve a differential fees structure, linking fees to economic status and the performance of the students. The deprived sections of the society could be provided higher education free of cost.

(b) Private initiatives in higher education would need to be encouraged with due care to see that these would promote merit and not lead to the commercialization of education.

(c) To facilitate access with equity, students loan programmes should be launched on a large scale. The programme can be implemented through the commercial banks and can be monitored by the National Education Development Bank.

(d) Industry being the employer of technically trained manpower must also bear a part of cost of higher education. An educational cess from industry employing graduates be charged and credited to an educational fund created for the specific purpose of the development of higher education.

(e) The emigrating professional/educated persons should be made to reimburse the cost of their education. This is not with the intention of discouraging trained manpower from going abroad; it is intended really to recover part or the total expenditure incurred on them by the state.

(f) Universities and colleges should launch self financing courses/programmes and in some cases, the fees charged should be aimed at generating substantial surpluses for the institutions.

(g) Universities and colleges should also try to raise funds through better interaction with industries, in areas of common interest.

(h) Export of education should be encouraged. Colleges and Universities of proven merit may provide educational opportunities to students from abroad. In this area, India has a competitive edge. The fees chargeable from such students may, however, be linked with per capita income of the country of origin.

(iii) Cost Reduction

(a) Steps should be taken to remove wastage and improve efficiency.
(b) Some activities of the universities and colleges, like the conduct of examinations and provision of hostel facilities, should be made self supporting.
(c) The supply of higher education should be regulated. Existing non-viable colleges should be revamped to make them viable.
(d) Steps should be taken to avoid duplication and promote resource sharing between departments and institutions. Efforts should be made to make the most optimal utilization of academic and physical resources.

4. Recruitment, Professional Development, Accountability and Curriculum

(i) Recruitment

(a) Heads of institutions must develop a serious concern for ensuring merit-based selection of the faculty members.
(b) The basis of selection should be:

  (i) Strong academic record (emphasis not on grades only).
  (ii) Pedagogical skills (emphasis on communicative skills) and capability for coping with changing technologies and changing students perceptions.
  (iii) Management skills

(c) The Selection Committees would have to be broad based. Selection procedures must include any one of the following besides the interview:

(i) Groups discussions
(ii) Demonstration lecture
(iii) Seminar

(d) The Selection Committee must be empowered to adopt a flexible approach while fixing the pay package of the staff recruited.

(ii) Professional Development

(a) The Heads of the Institutions and the management boards must be sensitized and involved in professional development programmes which include not only the updating of knowledge but also aim at enhancing of various skills needed for becoming effective teachers and researchers.
(b) Professional development of faculty has to be a continuous process. Ultimately it must become a built-in activity of the institutions.
(c) Research in higher education must be given a top priority. The research units of institutions like NIEPA, CPDHE and other must be strengthened to produce high quality research in the context of Indian higher education.
(d) A process of faculty exchange between the institutions and also vis-a-vis R&D establishments must be initiated.

(iii) Accountability

It refers to rendering of accounts to those who pay for higher education and those who are affected by it.

(a) Accountability must be measured in terms of performance of the faculty as assessed by the peers and students.

(b) The principle of accountability must be applicable to all the components of the Higher Education System.

(iv) Curriculum

Curriculum must be understood in broader context especially in view of the changing scenario in technological and economic policies.

(a) Curriculum development has to be a continuous process.

(b) Curriculum must be internally generated by those who teach. It ought to be developed through interactions with the users.

(c) Procedure for change/approval of curriculum must be simplified.

5. Models of Governance, Planning and Management

In planning and management, the emphasis has to be on efficiency and excellence within the framework of general societal welfare. Towards this end the following steps may be taken:

(a) Industry may be involved in the management of higher education. There is a need to build linkages between universities and industries. This will also help in raising the requisite resources;

(b) The large sub-system within the university system, i.e. collegiate education, central facility, administration and estate etc. need to be decentralized;

(c) College education needs to be liberated from the control of the university and must be given academic and administrative freedom in matters such as curriculum restructuring, evaluation procedures, recruitment of staff, disciplinary proceedings, etc. Universities' role must be confined to standard setting and accredition of colleges. Universities, in turn, must also be evaluated periodically. For this purpose suitable mechanisms need to be instituted;

(d) For optimizing the use of research, suitable mechanism for research management must be instituted. The setting up of UGC sponsored State Council of Higher Education is a step in right direction;

(e) The conventional discipline-oriented centres have long been superseded by composite interdisciplinary centres/schools/R&D missions. Such an innovation calls for a reappraisal of the institution of departments and departmental heads. This must give way to the concept of mission oriented leaders/coordinators;

(f) The critical decision-making bodies of the universities such as the academic council, syndicate and executive committee should have a set-up whereby they can effectively discharge their functions without any concession to extra-academic considerations. This can best be achieved through a substantial reduction in their size, as well as by balancing academic and public representation in the membership of decision making bodies.

(g) The Vice-Chancellors/Directors/Principals are critical functionaries whose recruitment and grooming need to be carefully looked into. Procedures for their recruitment must be flexible. Their status and resources support should be commensurate with their functions.

(h) Granting of autonomy to the colleges should be encouraged. Universities and State Government would need to be persuaded to grant autonomy to a large number of colleges. Development Grants to the universities and colleges by the UGC may be linked with the promotion of the concept of autonomy to the colleges.

6

The Private Universities (Establishment and Regulation) Bill (1995)

Be it enacted by Parliament in the forty-sixth year of the Republic of India as follows:-

1. (1) This act may be called the Private Universities (Establishment and Regulation) Act, 1995.
   (2) It extends to the whole of India except the State of Jammu and Kashmir.
   (3) It shall come into force on such date as the Central Government may, by notification in the Official Gazette, appoint and different may be appointed for different States.
2. In this Act, unless the context otherwise requires

   (a) "Commission" means the University Grants Commission established under section 4 of the University Grants Commission Act, 1956;
   (b) "Ordinances" means the Ordinances of a University;
   (c) "Prescribed" means prescribed by Rules, Statutes or Ordinances, as the case may be made by notification in the Official Gazette, under this Act; and
   (d) "Sponsoring body", in relation to a University means—

The text of the Bill introduced in the Rajya Sabha on 25 August 1995 by the Minister for Human Resource Development, Govt. of India.

(i) a society registered under the Societies Registration Act, 1860 or any other corresponding law for the time being in force in a State,

(ii) a public trust; or

(iii) a company registered under section 25 of the Companies Act, 1956:

Provided that no member of such society, author or trustee of such trust or member of such company shall be a person other than a citizen of India;

(e) "Statutes" means the Statutes of a University;

(f) "University" or "the University" means a university established under sub-section (1) of section 10.

3 (1) An application containing a proposal for establishment of a University shall be made to the Central Government by a sponsoring body in such manner and shall be accompanied by such fees as may be prescribed by rules.

(2) On receipt of an application under sub-section (1), the Central Government shall make such inquiries as it may deem necessary and shall consult the Commission seeking its views on the proposal.

(3) The Commission, before furnishing its views to the Central Government, shall notify in the Official Gazette and at least in one daily newspaper having circulation in the State in which the University is proposed to be established the fact of receipt of the application seeking the views of the general public on the proposal.

4 (1) On receipt of the views of the Commission, the Central Government may ask the sponsoring body to furnish a project report.

(2) The project report shall contain the following details, namely:

(a) the objectives of the University alongwith the details of the sponsoring body;

(b) location of the University, extent and availability of land;

(c) the nature and types of programmes to be offered and their relevance to development goals and employment needs and phasing of such programmes over the next ten years with enrolment targets;

(d) the arrangements for academic auditing;

(e) nature of faculties and, in a case where the focus is on a particular discipline, nature of emphasis on instructional inputs in humanities and social sciences would be evidenced in the project report;

(f) ten years perspective of campus development in terms of buildings, equipments and infra-structural facilities;

(g) phasing of capital expenditure over a period of ten years and its source of finance;

(h) phasing of recurring expenditure item-wise, its source of finance and unit cost per student of such expenditure;

(i) resource mobilisation plan including the proposed fee structure;

(j) fee structure proposed with reference to the unit cost and the costs of freeships and scholarships subject to the condition that the number of scholarships and freeships to be not less than thirty per cent of the number of seats and different rates of fee may be specified for non-resident Indians and fee paying foreign students;

(k) track record of the sponsoring body;

(l) the method of selecting candidates for admission and the total number of freeships and scholarships and the admission policy to the disadvantaged classes; and

(m) such other details as may be prescribed by rules.

5. The project report under section 4 shall be submitted by the sponsoring body through the State Government in which the University is proposed to be established and the State Government shall furnish the same to the Central Government along with its comments, if any, within a period of six months from the date of its receipt from the sponsoring body.

6. (1) On receipt of the project report alongwith comments, if any, of the State Government, the Central Government shall refer the same to the Commission seeking its recommendations.

(2) On receipt of the project report under sub-section (1), the Commission shall obtain the views of such other expert bodies, organisations or individuals as it may deem necessary.

(3) The Commission shall furnish its recommendations to the Central Government within a period of six months from the date of receipt of the project report under sub-section (1).

7. If the Central Government is satisfied that it would be advisable to establish a University as recommended by the Commission, it may, subject to such conditions as may be specified in such directions, direct the sponsoring body to establish a permanent endowment fund in the manner provided in Section 8.

8. (1) Every University shall have a fund called the Permanent Endowment Fund which it shall invest and keep invested in securities issued or guaranteed by the Central Government.

(2) The Permanent Endowment Fund shall consist of a sum of ten crores of rupees or a sum equivalent to the recurring expenses for three years for fully operational University, whichever is more, in long term interest bearing securities of the Central Government or any such other securities as the Central Government may approve in this behalf.

(3) The Central Government shall have the power to direct any upward revision of the Permanent Endowment Fund from time to time.

9. Every University shall also have a fund called the General Fund which shall consist of:

(a) fees and other charges received by the University;
(b) income from the Permanent Endowment Fund;
(c) Income from any other source; and
(d) any contributions made by the sponsoring body.

10.(1) The Central Government, having regard to:
(a) the desirability of establishment of a University;
(b) recommendations of the Commission;
(c) the establishment of a permanent endowment fund under section 7;
(d) recognition or authorization as may be required under any other law for the time being in force for conduct of the courses and award of degrees or diplomas, as the case may be made by notification in the Official Gazette, establish a University under such name and having such jurisdiction and location of the campus as may be specified therein.

(2) Every notification under sub-section (1) shall be laid before both Houses of Parliament.

11.(1) Every University established under sub-section (1) of section 10 shall be a body corporate by the name notified under that section having perpetual succession and a common seal and shall by the said name sue and be sued.

(2) A University established under sub-section (1) of section 10 shall have no power to affiliate any college or other institution with it and shall not have more than one campus.

(3) Every University shall, within three years of its establishment, obtain accredition from a body nominated in this behalf by the Commission and shall renew such accredition at an interval of every five years thereafter.

12. A University shall not be entitled to receive grant-in-aid or other financial assistance from the Central Government, any State Government, the Commission or any other authority.

13. Every University shall be open to persons of either sex and of whatever caste, creed, race or class, and it shall not be lawful for a University to adopt or impose on any person any

test whatsoever of religious belief or profession in order to entitle him to be appointed as a teacher of the University or to hold any other office therein or to be admitted as a student in the University or to graduate thereat or to enjoy or exercise any privilege thereof:

Provided that nothing in this section shall be deemed to prevent the University from making special provisions for the employment or admission of women, physically handicapped or of persons belonging to the weaker sections of the society and, in particular, of the Scheduled Castes and the Scheduled Tribes.

14. Every University shall have the following officers, namely:

(a) the Chancellor;
(b) the Vice-Chancellor;
(c) the Registrar;
(d) the Chief Finance and Accounts Officer;
(e) such other officers as may be prescribed by the Statutes.

15.(1) The Chancellor shall be appointed for a term of three years by the sponsoring body with the previous approval of the Central Government in such manner as may be prescribed by the Statutes.

(2) The Chancellor shall, by virtue of his office, be the Head of the University.

(3) The Chancellor shall preside over the meetings of the Board of Governors and if present, preside at the convocation of the University held for conferring degrees or diplomas.

(4) The Chancellor shall have the following powers, namely:-

(a) to call for any information or report;
(b) to appoint the Vice-Chancellor;
(c) such other powers as may be prescribed by the Statutes.

16.(1) The Vice-Chancellor shall be appointed by the Chancellor from a panel of five names to be prepared by the Board of Governors.

Provided that the first Vice-Chancellor shall be appointed by the Central Government from a panel of three names proposed by the Chancellor.

(2) The Vice-Chancellor shall be the principal executive and academic officer of the University and shall exercise general supervision and control over the affairs of the University and give effect to the decisions of all the authorities of the University.

(3) The Vice-Chancellor may, if he is of the opinion that immediate action is necessary on any matter, exercise any power conferred on any authority of the University by or under this Act and shall report to such authority the action taken by him on such matter:

Provided that if the authority concerned is of the opinion that such action ought not to have been taken, it may refer the matter to the Chancellor whose decision thereon shall be final:

Provided further that any person in the service of the University who is aggrieved by the action taken by the Vice-Chancellor under this sub-section shall have the right to appeal against such action to the Board of Management within three months from the date on which decision on such action is communicated to him and thereupon the Board of Management may confirm, modify or reverse the action taken by the Vice-Chancellor.

(4) The Vice-Chancellor, if he is of the opinion that any decision of any authority of the University is beyond the powers of the authority conferred by the provisions of this Act, the rules, the Statutes or the Ordinances or that any decision taken is not in the interest of the University, may ask the authority concerned to review its decision within sixty days of such decision of the authority and if the authority refuses to review the decision either in whole or in part or no decision is taken by it within the said period of sixty days, the matter shall be referred to the Chancellor whose decision thereon shall be final.

(5) The Vice-Chancellor shall exercise such other powers and perform such other duties as may be prescribed by the Statutes or the Ordinances.

17.(1) The Registrar shall be appointed in such manner as may be prescribed by the first Statute.

(2) The Registrar shall have the power to enter into agreements, sign documents and authenticate records on behalf of the University and shall exercise such powers and perform such duties as may be prescribed by the Statute.

18. The Chief Finance and Accounts Officer shall be appointed in such manner and shall exercise such powers and perform such duties as may be prescribed by the first Statutes.

19. The manner of appointment and powers and duties of the other officers of the University shall be prescribed by the Statutes.

20. The following shall be the authorities of a University, namely:

(a) the Board of Governors;
(b) the Board of Management;
(c) the Academic Council; and
(d) such other authorities as may be created by Statutes to be the authorities of the University.

21.(1) The Board of Governors shall consist of the following, namely:

(a) the Chancellor;
(b) the Vice-Chancellor;
(c) three persons to be nominated by the sponsoring body;
(d) one representative of the Central Government;
(e) one representative of the State Government in which the University is situated;
(f) one academician to be nominated by the Commission.

(2) The Chancellor shall be the Chairman of the Board of Governors.

(3) The Board of Governors shall be the supreme governing body of the University with powers:

(a) to review decisions of the other authorities of the University if they are not in conformity with the provisions of this Act, the rules, the Statutes or the Ordinances;
(b) to approve the budget and annual report of the University;
(c) To lay down broad policies to be pursued by the University; and
(d) to take decisions about voluntary winding up of the University.

(4) The Board of Governors shall meet twice in a calendar year.

22.(1) The Board of Management shall consist of the following, namely:

(a) the Vice-Chancellor;
(b) one representative to be nominated by the Commission;
(c) two representatives to be nominated by the sponsoring body;
(d) the senior-most professor of the University.

(2) The Vice-Chancellor shall be the Chairman of the Board of Management.

(3) The powers and functions of the Board of Management shall be such as may be prescribed by the Statutes.

23.(1) The Academic Council shall consist of the Vice-Chancellor and such other members as may be prescribed by the Statutes.

(2) The Vice-Chancellor shall be the Chairman of the Academic Council.

(3) The Academic Council shall be the principal academic body of the University and shall, subject to the provisions of this Act, the rules, the Statutes and the Ordinances, co-ordinate and exercise general supervision over the academic policies of the University.

24. The constitution, powers and functions of the other authorities of the University shall be such as may be prescribed by the Statutes.

25.(1) The Commission shall have powers to inspect the University at any time after giving prior notice of such inspection.

(2) The findings of the Commission shall be communicated to the Central Government which may, if considered necessary, issue a show cause notice to the University as to why it should not be directed to rectify the deficiencies pointed out by the Commission.

(3) If the Central Government is not satisfied with the reply given by the University, it shall direct the University to rectify the deficiencies and the University shall be bound to comply with such directions.

26.(1) Subject to the provisions of this Act and the rules, the first Statutes of a University may provide for all or any of the following matters, namely:

(a) the procedure regarding transaction of business of the authorities constituted by or under this Act and the composition of bodies not specified in this Act;
(b) the terms and conditions of appointment of Vice-Chancellor and his powers and functions;
(c) the terms and conditions of appointment of the Registrar and the Chief Finance and Accounts Officer and their powers and functions;
(d) the method of appointment and the conditions of service of the other officers and the faculty members;
(e) the terms and conditions of service of employees of the University;
(f) the procedure for resolving of disputes between the University and its officers, faculty members, employees and students;
(g) the procedure for conferment of honorary degrees;
(h) provisions regarding grant of freeships and scholarships;

(i) provisions regarding admission policy including regulation of reservation of seats;

(j) provisions regarding fees to be levied from students; and

(k) provisions regarding number of seats in different courses.

(2) The first Statute of a University shall be prepared by its Board of Management and shall be submitted to the Commission through its Board of Governors for approval of the Commission

(3) The Commission shall consider the first Statutes submitted by the University within two months from the date of its receipt and shall communicate its approval to the University with such modifications as it may consider necessary:

Provided that the time limit of two months shall not apply in relation to Statutes in respect of matters specified in clauses (j) and (k) of sub-section (1).

(4) The University shall communicate its acceptance of the first Statute as approved by it and if it desires that the modifications suggested by the Commission under sub-section (3) shall not be given effect to, the reasons thereof shall be communicated within one month to the Commission and the Commission may either accept the suggestions of the University or reject the same.

(5) The Commission shall, by notification in the Official Gazette, publish the first Statute of the University as finally approved by it and the first Statute shall thereupon come into force.

27.(1) Subject to the provisions of this Act and the rules, the Statutes of a University may provide for all or any of the following, namely:

(a) creation of new authorities of the University;

(b) accounting policy and financial procedure;

(c) election of teachers for their representation in the authorities;

(d) creation of new departments and abolition or restructuring of existing departments;

(e) institution of fellowship, scholarship, studentships, freeships, medals and prizes;

(f) procedure for creation and abolition of posts;

(g) revision of fees;

(h) alteration in the number of seats in different courses; and

(i) other matters prescribed by rules to be prescribed by Statutes.

(2) The Statutes of a University other than the first Statute shall be prepared by its Board of Management with the approval of the Board of Governors.

(3) The Statutes made under sub-section (2) shall be furnished to the Commission and the Commission shall within two months from the date of its receipt shall, if considered necessary, suggest modifications therein:

Provided that the time limit of two months shall not apply in relation to the Statute in respect of matters specified in clauses (g) and (h) of sub-section (1).

(4) The Board of Governors shall consider the modifications suggested by the Commission and return the Statutes alongwith its comments on the suggestions of the Commission to the Commission.

(5) The Commission shall consider the suggestions of the Board of Governors and cause publication of the Statutes as finally approved by it in the Official Gazette and on such publication the Statutes shall come into force.

28.(1) Subject to the provisions of this Act, the rules and the Statutes, the Ordinances may provide for all or any of the following matters, namely:

(a) admission of students to the University and their enrolment as such;
(b) the courses of study to be laid down for all degrees, diplomas and certificates of the University;
(c) the award of degrees, diplomas, certificates and other academic distinctions, qualifications for the same and means to be taken relating to the granting and obtaining of the same;
(d) the conditions of award of fellowships, scholarships, studentships, medals and prizes;
(e) the conduct of examinations including the term of office and manner of appointment and duties of examining bodies, examiners and moderators;
(f) the fees to be charged for admission to the examinations, degrees and diplomas of the University;
(g) the conditions of the residence of the students of the University;
(h) arrangements concerning disciplinary action against the students;
(i) the creation, composition and functions of any other body which is considered necessary for improving the academic life of the University;
(j) the manner of co-operation with other Universities or institutions of higher learning; and
(k) all other matters which by this Act, the rules or the Statutes may be provided by the Ordinances.

(2) The first Ordinances of a University shall be made by the Vice-Chancellor who shall submit the same to the Commission.
(3) The Commission shall consider the first Ordinances submitted by the Vice-Chancellor under sub-section (2) within two months from the date of receipt of the same and shall either approve the first Ordinance or suggest modifications therein.
(4) The Commission shall, by notification in the Official Gazette, publish the first Ordinance and if it has suggested modifications, return the first Ordinance to the University for its reconsideration.

(5) The Vice-Chancellor shall furnish his comments on the modifications suggested by the Commission and return the first Ordinance to the Commission and on receipt of the same, the Commission shall either accept the comments of the Vice-Chancellor or reject the same and on the basis of its decision finally notify the first Ordinance as approved by it in the Official Gazette and on such publication the first Ordinance shall come into force.

29.(1) All Ordinances of a University other than its first Ordinance shall be made by its Academic Council with the approval of the Board of Management.

(2) The Commission shall cause publication of all Ordinances made under sub-section (1) in the Official Gazette and on such publication the Ordinances shall come into force.

30.(1) The annual report of a University shall be prepared by its Board of Management which shall include, among other matters, the steps taken by the University towards the fulfilment of its objects and shall be approved by the Board of Governors.

(2) A copy of the annual report as prepared under sub-section (1) shall be submitted to the Commission.

31.(1) The annual accounts and balance sheet of a University shall be prepared under the directions of its Board of Management and shall, once at least every year and at intervals of not more than fifteen months, be audited by an auditor duly appointed by the University.

(2) A copy of the annual accounts together with the audit report thereon shall be submitted to the Board of Governors.

(3) A copy of the annual accounts together with the audit report and the observations, if any, of the Board of Governors shall be submitted to the Central Government.

(4) The directions of the Central Government on matters arising out of the accounts and audit reports of the University shall be binding on it.

32. No act or proceeding of any authority of a University shall be invalid merely by reason of the existence of a vacancy or vacancies among its members.

33.(1) All officers and other employees of a University while exercising any power or performing any duty under this Act shall be deemed to be public servants within the meaning of section 21 of the Indian Penal Code.

(2) No suit or other legal proceedings shall lie against any officer or other employee of a university for anything which is in good faith done or intended to be done in pursuance of any of the provisions of this Act, the rules, the Statutes or the Ordinances.

34. A copy of any receipt, application, notice, order, proceeding, resolution of any authority or committee of a Univer-sity, or other documents in possession of the University, or any entry in any register duly maintained by the University, if certified by the Registrar, shall be received as *prima facie* evidence of such receipt, application, notice, order, proceeding, resolution or documents or the existence of entry in the register and shall be admitted as evidence of the matters and transactions therein where the original threof would, if produced, have been admissible in evidence, notwithstanding anything contained in the Indian Evidence Act, 1872 or in any other law for the time being in force.

35.(1) If the sponsoring body proposes its dissolution in terms of the provisions of the law governing its constitution or incorporation, it shall give a notice of at least six months to the Central Government.

(2) Upon receipt of such notice, the Central Government shall, in consultation with the Commission, make such arrangements for administration of the University from the date of dissolution of the sponsoring body and until the last batch of students in regular courses of the University complete their courses as may be prescribed by rules.

(3) The expenditure for administration of the University during the taken over period of its management shall be met out of the Permanent Endowment Fund.

36.(1) If the Central Government notices violation of any of the directions issued by it to a University under this Act or on receipt of a complaint of mismanagement by a University, it shall issue a notice to the University calling upon the same to show cause within such time not less than forty-five days as to why it should not be ordered to be wound up.

(2) If the Central Government considers it necessary for the proper investigation to suspend the Board of Management, it shall, by notification in the Official Gazette, order suspension of the Board of Management and make such arrangements for the administration of the affairs of the University as may be necessary till the investigation is completed.

(3) If, upon receipt of the reply of the University to the notice under sub-section (1), the Central Government is satisfied that a *prima facie* case of mismanagement or violation of the provisions of this Act or any directions issued thereunder is made out, it shall order such inquiry as it may deem necessary.

(4) For the purposes of any inquiry under sub-section (3), the Central Government shall, by notification in the Official Gazette, appoint an officer or authority as the inquiring authority to inquire into and report upon any of the allegations.

(5) Every inquiring authority appointed under sub-section (4) shall have the same powers as are vested in a civil court under the Code of Civil Procedure, 1908, while trying a suit, in respect of the following matters, namely:

(a) summoning and enforcing the attendance of any witness and examining him on oath;

(b) requiring the discovery and production of any document or other material which is producible as evidence;

(c) requisitioning of any public record from any court or office;

(d) any other matter which may be prescribed by rules.

(6) Every inquiring authority making an inquiry under this Act shall be deemed to be a civil court for the purposes of section 195 and Chapter XXVI of the Code of Criminal Procedure, 1973.

(7) If, upon receipt of the inquiry report, the Central Government is satisfied that the University has been mismanaged or has violated any of the directions of the Central Government or provisions of this Act, it shall, by notification in the Official Gazette, order winding up of the University.

(8) While issuing a notification of winding up under sub-section (7), the Central Government shall make further arrangements for administration of the affairs of the University till its current courses of study are over.

(9) During the period of management of the University under sub-section (8), the Central Government shall utilise the funds available under the Permanent Endowment Fund and forfeit to itself the balance, if any, in such fund.

(10) Every notification issued under sub-section (7) shall be laid before both the Houses of Parliament.

37. The Central Government shall have the following powers, namely:

(a) to approve the appointment of a Chancellor;

(b) to issue directions to do anything required to be done by the University by or under provisions of this Act, the rules, the Statutes or the Ordinances made thereunder or to rectify any violation thereof;

(c) to adjudicate disputes under this Act between the University, the Commission or any other expert body and to issue directions to comply with its decisions on such disputes;

(d) to order winding up of the University in accordance with section 36;

(e) to order framing of Statutes under section 27 on particular subjects;

(f) to generally issue such orders as may be required to be followed by the University under this Act or any other law for the time being in force.

38.(1) The Central Government may, by notification in the Official Gazette, make rules for carrying out the provisions of this Act.

(2) In particular, and without prejudice to the generality of the foregoing power, such rules may provide for all or any of the following matters, namely:

(a) the manner in which an application containing proposal for establishment of a University shall be made by a sponsoring body and the fee payable thereto under sub-section (1) of section 3;
(b) the details which a project report shall contain under clause (m) of sub-section (2) of section 4;
(c) matters to be provided in the Statutes under clause (i) of sub-section (1) of section 27;
(d) arrangements for administration of a University on a dissolution of its sponsoring body under sub-section (2) of section 35;
(e) matters to be specified under clause (d) of sub-section (5) of section 36.

39. Every rule, Statute or Ordinance made under this Act shall be laid as soon as may be after it is made, before each House of Parliament, while it is in session, for a total period of thirty days which may be comprised in one session or in two or more successive sessions, and if, before the expiry of the session immediately following the session or the successive sessions aforesaid, both Houses agree in making any modification in the rule, Statute or Ordinance or both houses agree that the rule, Statute or Ordinance should not be made, the rule, Statute or Ordinance shall thereafter have effect only in such modified form or be of no effect, as the case may be; so however, that any such modification or annulment shall be without prejudice to the validity of anything previously done under that rule, Statute or Ordinance.

40.(1) If any difficulty arises in giving effect to the provisions of this Act, the Central Government may, by order published in the Official Gazette, make such provisions, not incosistent with the provisions of the Act, as appear to it to be necessary or expedient for removing the difficulty;

Provided that no such order shall be made under this section after the expiry of three years from the commencement of this Act.

(2) Every order made under this section shall be laid, as soon as may be after it is made, before each House of Parliament.

STATEMENT OF OBJECTS AND REASONS

1. Of late, considerable interest has been generated in establishment of self-financing universities not requiring any financial support from the Government. Such universities can play a subsidiary but supportive role to the State run universities in the tertiary education sector. In emerging areas of science and technology, especially, these universities may provide useful instructional inputs by making available additional finances.
2. Establishment of universities requires either a specific or enabling legislation. As the establishment of such universities would require a broadly uniform set of guidelines for ensuring academic standards, prevention of commercialization and mismanagement, etc., enactment of an enabling legislation of general applicability is considered expedient. It has, therefore, been decided to provide for establishment of self-financing private universities in the country and to regulate their functioning by enacting an enabling law on the subject.
3. The Bill seeks to achieve the above objects.
4. The notes on clauses appended to the Bill explain its various provisions.

New Delhi   Madhavrao Scindia
The 22nd August, 1995.

NOTES ON CLAUSES

Clause 2 The clause seeks to define certain words and expressions used in the Bill.

Clause 3 This clause provides for a preliminary application for establishment of self-financing universities and action to be taken thereon.

Clause 4 This clause lays down the format and procedure for a comprehensive application in the form of a project report.

Clause 5 This clause provides for transmission of the project report through the State Government.

Clause 6 This clause provides for examination of the project report by the Universities Grants Commission (UGC) and its recommendations thereon.

Clause 7 This clause gives power to the Central Government to direct the sponsoring body for creation of a Permanent Endowment Fund.

Clause 8 This clause provides for the manner of creating the Permanent Endowment Fund and prescribes the size of the corpus of such fund.

Clause 9 This clause provides for creation of a General Fund for the University.

Clause 10 This clause provides for establishment of the Universities through notification and subject to certain conditions specified therein.

Clause 11 This clause gives legal personality to the Universities established and lays down that such Universities shall be single campus Universities with mandatory academic accredition.

Clause 12 This clause prohibits receipt of grant-in-aid or any other financial assistance from Government by the Universities.

Clause 13 This clause provides for the Universities to be open to all in the matter of admission and employment.

Clause 14 This clause defines the offices of the University.

Clause 15 This clause provides for appointment of the Chancellor and specifies his certain powers.

Clause 16 This clause provides for appointment and powers of the Vice-Chancellor.

Clause 17 This clause provides for appointment and power of the Registrar.

Clause 18 This clause provides for the appointment of Chief Finance and Accounts Officer.

Clause 19 This clause enables the University to appoint other officers and define their powers under the Statutes.

Clause 20 This clause defines the authorities of the University.

Clause 21 This clause lays down the composition of the Board of Governors and its powers and responsibilities.

Clause 22 This clause lays down the composition of the Board of Management and its powers and responsibilities.

Clause 23 This clause provides for the Academic Council and defines its powers and responsibilities.

Clause 24 This clause enables the Universities to create other authorities and to define their powers and responsibilities under the Statutes.

Clause 25 This clause provides for the power of the University Grants Commission to inspect and the power of the Central Government to require the universities to rectify deficiencies noticed in the inspection.

Clause 26 This clause describes subjects to be covered by the first Statute of the University and how such Statutes may be made and approved.

Clause 27 This clause describes the subjects to be covered by subsequent Statutes and how such Statutes may be made and approved.

Clause 28 This clause describes the subjects to be covered by the first Ordinance and how such Ordinances may be made and approved.

Clause 29 This clause provides for subsequent Ordinances and how they may be made and approved.

Clause 30 This clause provides for the annual report of the University.

Clause 31 This clause provides for the preparation and audit of the annual accounts and balance sheet of the University.

Clause 32 This clause provides for not invalidating any act or proceedings of any authority of a University by reason of any vacancy.

Clause 33 This clause provides for all officers and other employees of the Universities to be public servants and immunity from suit, etc., to them in respect of their actions in good faith in their official capacity.

Clause 34 This clause provides for certified copies of documents of the Universities as admissible in evidence in courts of law.

Clause 35 This clause provides for voluntary winding up of the University.

Clause 36 This clause empowers the Central Government to order winding up of the University in case of mismanagement, etc.

Clause 37 This clause defines the powers of the Central Government in relation to the Universities.

Clause 38 This clause confers powers upon the Central Government to make rules for the purposes of carrying out the provisions of the Bill, when enacted.

Clause 39 This clause provides for laying of rules, Statutes and Ordinances made under the enactment on the table of both the Houses of Parliament.

Clause 40 This clause empowers the Central Government to remove difficulties in giving effect to the provisions of the Bill and for laying the orders issued in this behalf before each House of Parliament. This power is exercisable only for three years from the date of commencement of the Act.

MEMORANDUM REGARDING DELEGATED LEGISLATION

1. Sub-clause (1) of clause 26 of the Bill enumerates the matters in respect of which the Board of Management of a University may make the first Statute, Sub-clauses (3) to (5) of the said clause lay down the procedure for making of the first Statute. The first Statute shall be finally approved and published in the Official Gazette by the University Grants Commission (UGC).
2. Sub-clause (1) of clause 27 of the Bill specifies the matter in respect of which the subsequent Statutes of a University may be prepared by the Board of Management with the approval of the Board of Governors. Sub-clauses (2) to (5) of the said clause lay down the procedure for making such subsequent Statutes.
3. Sub-clause (1) of clause 28 enumerates the matters in respect of which the first Ordinance of a University shall be made by the Vice-Chancellor with the approval of the UGC.
4. Clause 29 of the Bill provides that the Academic Council of a University, with the approval of the Board of Management, may make the subsequent Ordinances and the same shall be published by the UGC.
5. Clause 38 of the Bill empowers the Central Government to make rules for carrying out the provisions of the Bill.
6. Clause 39 of the Bill provides that every rule, Statute or Ordinance under the enactment shall be laid before both the Houses of Parliament. The matters in respect of which the rules. Statutes or Ordinances may be made are generally matters of procedure and administrative detail and it is not practicable to provide for them in the Bill itself. The delegation of legislative power is, therefore, of a normal character.

7

Sixth All India Educational Survey (1995)

Introduction

For the proper planning of schooling facilities at the grassroot level, and for ensuring a balanced growth in all areas, rural and urban, Ministry of Education and Social Welfare (Erstwhile), Government of India, conducted the first survey in 1957. Thereafter the Second, Third, Fourth, Fifth and Sixth surveys have been conducted by the National Council of Educational Research and Training in 1965, 1973, 1978, 1986 and 1993 respectively.The date of reference of the Sixth Survey was September 30, 1993.

Objectives

(i) To create a database on different variables of Sixth AIES that can be shared by different agencies.

(ii) To develop Computerised Management Information System (CMIS) and update it on annual basis at various levels of administration.

(iii) To assess the present position of educational facilities at various school stages and the distance at which available, enrolment in general, and of Scheduled Castes (SC) and Scheduled Tribes (ST) and girls in particular, with special reference to UEE.

(iv) To assess the availability of physical facilities, like school building, play ground, furnitures, etc.

(v) To assess the availability of basic amenities, like medical check-up, drinking water, urinals, etc.

(vi) To identify incentive schemes and the number of beneficiaries.

(vii) To assess the position of educational inputs, like blackboard and chalk, library, laboratory, textbooks bank, etc.

(viii) To know about the academic and professional qualifications of working teachers with special reference to teaching of science and mathematics and to determine attrition rate in the teaching profession.

(ix) To assess availability of other educational facilities like non-formal education, for disabled children and pre-primary education.

SUMMARY

A. Educational Facilities within Rural Habitations

	1986	1993	Increase (%)
1. Total Number of Habitations	98,186	10,59,191	7.88
2. Number of Habitations having Primary stage in them	5,02,343	5,32,962	6.10
3. Number of Habitations having Upper Primary stage in them	1,28,951	1,45,824	13.08
4. Number of Habitations having Secondary stage in them	43,541	53,175	22.13
5. Number of Habitations having Higher Secondary stage in them	8,940	11,955	33.72

B. Gross Enrolment Ratio (GER)

		1986		1993		Increase (%)	
		Total	Girls	Total	Girls	Total	Girls
(i)	GER (I-V)	91.69	77.75	95.90	85.02	4.2	7.47
(II)	GER (VI-VII)	47.95	35.03	59.07	47.91	11.12	12.88

C. Schools

		1986	1993	Increase (%)
1.	Total Number of Schools			
	(i) Rural	6,34,908	6,99,616	10.19
	(ii) Urban	1,00,863	1,26,091	25.01
	(iii) Total	7,35,771	8,25,707	12.22
2.	Primary Schools			
	(i) Rural	4,75,823	5,11,849	7.57
	(ii) Urban	52,907	63,286	19.62
	(iii) Total	5,28,730	5,75,135	8.78
3.	Upper Primary Schools			
	(i) Rural	1,13,087	1,27,863	13.07
	(ii) Urban	25,929	33,046	27.45
	(iii) Total	1,39,016	1,60,909	15.75
4.	Secondary Schools			
	(i) Rural	38,862	48,262	24.19
	(ii) Urban	13,698	17,877	30.51
	(iii) Total	52,560	66,139	25.84
5.	Higher Secondary Schools			
	(i) Rural	7,136	11,642	63.14
	(ii) Urban	8,329	11,882	42.66
	(iii) Total	15,465	23,524	52.11

D. Enrolment

		1986		1993		Increase (%)	
		Total	Girls	Total	Girls	Total	Girls
1.	Classes I-V						
	(i) Rural	6,58,00,799	2,59,76,138	7,34,35,414	3,08,01,248	11.60	18.58
	(ii) Urban	2,01,12,679	90,83,369	2,43,06,324	1,13,30,734	20.85	24.74
	(iii) Total	8,59,13,478	3,50,59,507	9,77,41,738	4,21,31,982	13.77	20.17
2.	Classes VI-VIII						
	(i) Rural	1,77,29,718	56,40,427	2,15,98,278	78,37,997	21.82	38.96
	(ii) Urban	95,42,618	39,91,553	1,24,55,038	55,85,598	30.52	39.94
	(iii) Total	2,72,72,336	96,31,980	3,40,53,316	1,34,23,595	24.86	39.36
3.	Classes IX-X						
	(i) Rural	64,68,750	17,67,367	84,86,169	27,12,756	30.88	53.49
	(ii) Urban	50,51,246	18,85,745	67,91,531	28,03,075	34.45	48.65
	(iii) Total	1,15,19,996	36,53,112	1,52,57,700	55,15,831	32.45	50.99
4.	Classes XI-XII						
	(i) Rural	17,07,494	4,13,144	24,84,220	7,16,633	45.49	73.46
	(ii) Urban	34,99,320	12,02,380	46,86,546	17,70,749	33.93	47.27
	(iii) Total	52,06,814	16,15,524	71,70,766	24,87,382	37.72	53.92
5.	Classes I-XII						
	(i) Rural	9,17,06,761	3,37,97,076	10,59,84,081	4,20,68,634	15.57	24.47
	(ii) Urban	3,82,05,863	1,61,63,047	4,82,39,439	2,14,90,156	26.26	32.96
	(iii) Total	12,99,12,624	4,99,60,123	15,42,23,520	6,35,58,790	18.71	27.22

E. Teachers

		1986	1993	Increase (%)
1.	Total Number of Teachers	2531300	2860539	13.01
	(i) Rural	1113381	1342249	20.56
	(ii) Urban	3644681	4202788	15.31
	(iii) Total			
2.	Teachers in Primary Schools			
	(i) Rural	1179920	1301800	10.33
	(ii) Urban	312801	359142	14.81
	(iii) Total	1492721	1660942	11.27
3.	Teachers in Upper Primary Schools			
	(i) Rural	720087	774746	7.59
	(ii) Urban	282049	331067	17.38
	(iii) Total	1002136	1105813	10.35
4.	Teachers in Secondary Schools			
	(i) Rural	469466	534399	13.83
	(ii) Urban	254159	304432	19.78
	(iii) Total	723625	838831	15.92
5.	Teachers in Higher Secondary Schools			
	(i) Rural	161827	249594	54.24
	(ii) Urban	264372	347608	31.48
	(iii) Total	426199	597202	40.12

F. Percentage of Female Teachers

		1986		1993	
		Total	Rural	Total	Rural
(i)	Primary Schools	28.20	20.94	31.41	23.45
(ii)	Upper Primary Schools	32.80	23.47	35.08	24.66
(iii)	Secondary Schools	31.27	22.42	33.92	18.10
(iv)	Higher Secondary Schools	27.79	12.92	31.57	18.10

G. Percentage of Girls Enrolment

		1986		1993	
		Total	Rural	Total	Rural
(i)	Classes I-V	40.81	39.48	43.11	41.94
(ii)	Classes VI-VIII	35.32	31.81	39.42	36.29
(iii)	Classes IX-X	31.71	27.32	36.15	32.04
(iv)	Classes XI-XII	31.03	24.20	34.69	28.85
(v)	Classes I-XII	38.46	36.85	41.21	39.69

8

Synergy Sub-Group on IITs and RECs (1995)*

The Ministry of Human Resource Development, Government of India appointed a 14-member group, headed by Vinay Kumar Modi.

Terms of Reference

Finding out ways and means of developing interface between training and end-users (industry and trade) and suggesting measures for improving the quality of training at IITs and Regional Engineering Colleges so as to bring it closer to the high standards prevailing outside.

Recommendations

Chapter 9

9.1 IITs have established a reputation as institutions of excellence. It is now incumbent upon them to play a larger role by acting as "change agents" for higher technical education in the country. For a start, one REC in each region should be affiliated to an IIT. A close relationship needs to be developed with the next level of technical institutions, i.e., Regional Engineering Colleges (RECs). However, if this synergy is to be meaningful, greater operational freedom needs to be accorded to them. For this, the Central Government needs to relieve the State Government from contributing towards their budgetary support. This would not only relieve the pressure on State Government finances but also permit the relevant portions of the IIT Act to be extended to the RECs.

---

*Ministry of Human Resource Development, Department of Education, New Delhi, 1995.

9.2 Synergy with industry requires its greater involvement in the running of IITs. This would not only make industry more aware of the potential for collaboration but also urge it to avail of it fully. Board of Governors of IITs should be more representative of industry with alumni, in particular, who now occupy positions of considerable importance in industry playing an important role. A beginning has been made in improving linkages with alumni associations. More needs to be done. Their apprehensions of being only fund raisers needs to be dispelled by involving them in all important issues.

9.3 To foster inter-IIT and IIT-Industry interaction, Government has sponsored seven Technology Development Missions, each involving a group of IITs and leading industrial houses in the core areas of information technology, genetics, etc. This has generated keen participative interest and promoted collaborative effort. This initiative should now be extended by IITs to cover other technological areas of concern.

9.4 Presently, undergraduate students receive only limited industry exposure. As a result, they are unable to relate themselves to real life situations. It is necessary that students spend at least one full semester with industry as this would prepare them better, to accept operational responsibility after graduation. As this would relieve industry of burden of imparting additional training, it should compensate both the institution and the student in equal proportion, commensurate with prevailing wage levels.

9.5 To develop an on-going relationship with industry, methodologies successfully developed by institutions abroad should be incorporated in IIT synergy programmes. Specifically, the IITs should work towards: (i) an industry liaison programme which would associate industry units on an annual membership basis; (ii) a direct research programme on a cost reimbursement basis;

(iii) 'consortium' programme which would be supported by groups of companies having common research interests, and (iv) consultancy on an individual basis involving faculty members directly.

9.6 'Hi-Tech Parks' should be set up in the IITs. This would provide industry units or associations easy and on-going access to IIT laboratory facilities for research and development, which could also be used for other related activities. These Parks may be named after an Industrial House if it funds acquisition of new equipment of a certain minimum value.

9.7 Government subsidy presently amounts to about 75 per cent of operating costs of IITs. This dependence should be reduced to not more than 30 per cent within the next three years and complete self-sufficiency attained by the end of the decade. In order to do so, IITs should budget that around 35 to 50 per cent of their resources to be raised through fees and the balance by income generated through new revenue streams emerging from innovative industry interaction.

Consistent with the emphasis on autonomy, each IIT should eventually evolve its own fee structure taking into account its institutional strength and recognition which society accords to it. However, Government should ensure that scholarships are provided to the meritorious underprivileged. For the others, it would be incumbent on IITs to work out merit-cum-means scheme by which students would be in a position to have access to soft bank loans.

9.8 As IITs move towards financial self-reliance, an increase in the enrolment of foreign students beyond the present limit of 10 per cent would be desirable. The fees structure for these students should be in keeping with the pattern prevailing in institutions of similar excellence in other countries. A fee of around US $ 10,000 per student per year would seem reasonable as against the present fee of US $ 4,000 per year. The selection of students should be the exclusive prerogative of the IITs and the term 'foreign students' should include wards of NRIs provided they have not gone through the Indian academic system within the country.

9.9 The prevailing student-teacher ratio is indicative of sub-optimal utilisation of resources. Increasing student intake would provide IITs within additional resources and industry with an urgently required large pool of first-rate engineers to draw upon. A doubling of the student intake should be possible with marginal inputs in infrastructure and faculty. Modalities for this enhanced student intake should be put in place before 1997-98 scholastic year.

9.10 The research effort in IITs should increasingly focus on areas where world-wide technological advances are most rapid. This would not only enable IITs to maintain their unique position as technological leaders but also enable them to provide industry with a view of new areas to concentrate upon.

Patent searchers, participation in seminars by both faculty and students, and a greater involvement of IITs in documentation and dissemination of state-of-the-art technological activity would not only serve industry but enable IITs to earn substantial additional income.

9.11 IITs have a vast reserve of research experience. A serious effort needs to be made to disseminate this information to industry through workshops, technology capsules and news letters.

In addition, IITs should work in close association with other R&D organisations in the country, to enhance their contribution to technological developmental at the national level.

9.12 There is urgent need to shift the focus of the research activity in the IITs from generation of new knowledge to applied research. IITs need to concern themselves with areas of immediate application, i.e. process parameters for the chemical industry and manufacturing processes for the engineering industry.

9.13 To evolve a direction of future activity, the Group recommends that a high level body be constituted and designated as the "Perspective Technology Group". This Group would comprise: (a) captains of industries, (b) eminent academics from the IIT system, and (c) heads of major R&D groups, drawn both from the private and public sectors. This group would review, evaluate and determine the thrust for the future research nationally. IIT Delhi could serve as the Group's secretariat in view of its convenient location.

9.14 The existing IITs were set up in association with overseas universities acting in "consortium", with financial support from their respective governments. A new IIT at Guwahati has just come into being and needs support for the development of both infrastructure and faculty in its formative years. As in the past, a "consortium approach" needs to be structured where the existing IITs would pool resources and take on this task as a "consultancy assignment" so that normal institutional constraints do not cause delays and act as a distinctive in the involvement of appropriate faculty.

9.15 The emerging industrial scenario with its emphasis on global competitiveness calls for managers with ability to analyse the situation beyond the confines of technology. It is imperative that a Business School of world standard be available to provide IIT student with an on-campus facility for career development. The Sloan School of Management attached to MIT is an example which could be emulated.

The Business School would offer a standard two-year MBA programme as well as a post-experience modular programme for students who intend to remain in full employment. In addition, the School would provide Advance Management Programmes for senior managers and captains of industry.

The burden of setting up the Business School, which should include a Convention Centre and residential facilities of an appropriate standard, should be borne by industry as it stands to benefit directly and significantly. IITs should pursue this with industry and alumni as has been done by IIT, Kharagpur.

9.16 The existing four years B. Tech. programme does not provide for an internship with industry. The duration of the course should be suitably extended to provide for this.Internship placement should begin well before the end of the academic course so that students know what would be expected of them by industry. They can thus choose 'electives' accordingly. The onus of practical training should be shared by IITs and industry both in its structure and supervision.

The Master's programme also needs to be restructured and extended to two years with the student spending a semester on a "specific project" in industry. Here again, industry should provide suitable compensation to both the student and the institution.

A joint B. Tech./MBA programme has found wide acceptance overseas. A double degree programme should be structured by extending the B. Tech. course by a year. Admission to this course should be through a separate competitive examination.

9

Synergy Sub-Group on Primary Education and Literacy (1995)*

A synergy sub-group was appointed in 1995 by Ministry of Human Resource Development, Government of India, with a view to making an assessment of the existing scenario and making recommendations for achieving the objectives of Primary Education as envisaged in the revised NPE.

RECOMMENDATIONS

PRIMARY EDUCATION

MLLs

While consideration progress is recorded in the last few years, much remains to be done in terms of improving real access, ensuring retention and achievement of MLLs. The focus in the coming years will be to accelerate and strengthen the processes which have already been set in motion and have demonstrated their success. New strategies will have to be evolved for the unresolved issues particularly those related to the quality improvement programmes and the education of the needy children in difficult circumstances.

That the private schools are intrinsically and uniformly better is a myth that deserves to be laid to rest. Some are among the best

---

Ministry of Human Resource Development, Department of Education, New Delhi, 1995.

in the country, others are mediocres and sub-standard. The distance between the best and the average, be the Government or private schools, is too big to one's comfort. The State should or would continue to play a predominant role but the Government's role would be a departure from the past tradition of regulation and control. Government should be more open and receptive to the participation of other actors in civil society like NGOs and industry in the opening of schools, management of existing schools and teacher training institutions and in experimenting with a variety of alternatives in the teaching-learning process. We would recommend a review of the existing regulations in the country.

Educational discourse in the country has too often been exclusively devoted to pedagogic issues; while these are vital, the locus of discussions should shift to the logic of how to ensure the management of change.

Community Awareness and Mobilisation

— We cannot have islands of school excellence in a sea of community indifference. Parents, teachers and students constitute what may be called the Golden Triangle, the civic foundations of education reform. Students should learn, teachers should teach and parents take on the responsibilities of sending children to school and facilitating the teaching-learning process in the school. While we do not favour a legalistic approach to compulsory primary education we would strongly urge societal and peer pressure being exerted by the community so that all children go to school.

— The three R's, while perhaps outdated elsewhere, are still accepted by a vast majority as accepted learning goals.

We only add that while three R's are for a teacher, the fourth R is for parents. It is to emphasise their responsibility. Though family life is hectic and harassing, diminishing guidance from parents to children, yet it has to be emphasised that solution to students' unsatisfactory motivation and performance lies at home. Structuring of extra help at school would not suffice. A co-ordination between home and school is required. We need a forum and process for this. Caring and knowledgeable adults/parents are indispensable.

— The shared vision of educational responsibility must emphasise not only goals for learning but also the responsibility that parents must accept for developing children's future. Community must start talking of "our children", instead of talking about "those children" and "my children".
— There is a need to adopt a more flexible approach for involvement of community leaders and should not be limited to merely PR bodies. The model could vary from one state to another. The VECs must have representation of parents of children attending primary schools alongwith other representatives.
— The enthusiasm and awareness generated by the total literacy campaigns need to be sustained through systematic environmental building efforts and effective management of the demand which is largely emerging from the hitherto uncovered segments of the society. The role of NGOs in this context needs to be further encouraged.
— An analysis of the reasons for the large number of children being out-of-school needs to be made and its correlation with the economic development studied in the village specific situation. The evidence should be used for micro-planning.
— Women empowerment programmes should be accorded high priority and implemented through an integrated rather than compartmentalized approach. Lessons learnt from successful programmes like *Mahila Samakhya* should be disseminated widely.
— Comprehensive and need based programmes for the development of community leadership should be undertaken by the resource institutions like DIETs/SCERTs/SRCs etc.

Role of Industry

— The industry should be willing to share the social responsibility for educating their workers and children in the school going age-group. The industry should arrange classes for illiterate workers and open and fund primary schools in the large residential colonies/complexes used for residential purposes for their workers. Other possibilities to share this responsibility should be explored.

— The industrial houses should be encouraged to financially support the strengthening of primary schools, DIETs and other resource institutions particularly those located in educationally backward areas.

— The financial contributions made by the industrial houses and individuals to the cause of primary education should be eligible for tax relief.

Education of the Girl Child and Special Groups

— The education of the girl child must be given high priority and concerted efforts must be made to ensure that the enrolment, retention and achievement of girls in primary education are improved. Incentive schemes like free textbooks, free uniforms, mid-day meals should be pursued and implemented more vigorously.

— Necessary support in terms of basic facilities and security arrangements needs to be provided to encourage women teachers to work in rural and backward areas.

— Extensive use of the media should be made to educate the community, create necessary awareness and provide appropriate role models to encourage the girls to join the mainstream of education.

— As progress towards Education for All is attained, it will be necessary to reach marginal groups of population through local specific approach. Specific disadvantaged groups like pavement dwellers and communities in violence prone areas, should be given special attention through identification of their educational needs. Research should be initiated and action plans drawn accordingly.

— ICDS scheme should be expanded to include creches for younger children to prevent drop-out of older children, particularly girls.

Curriculum Development

— To develop a child into a creative and contributing member of society, the school should link the quest for knowledge through instruction with a quest for improving life around the child through well thought out activities. How tedious and time consuming tasks done in dull surroundings could be easily done in much more delightful form should be the dictum of the new approach. This would equip her/him with an inner confidence to be creative and useful in later life. Skills are liberating and can only be acquired by learning through work. Similarly, the effort to familiarise students with their past should not be at the expense of dwelling on elements of modern scientific life located in time and place familiar to the child.

— The learning process should also instil in the child an inquisitive mind, a joy and zest for discovery, a love and respect for nature. The school calendar should adequately provide for extra-curricular and after school activities including games and sports.

— To encourage fuller participation and utilisation of primary education facilities at the field level, the school programme should be adapted to a more flexible mode which can attract children and is convenient in terms of timings, curriculum, school climate, etc.

— The school climate must be made joyful and interesting for children through an attractive school environment, activity based child centred pedagogy and a nurturant rather than intimidating school ethos for which the basic resources and appropriate staff preparation are critical inputs.

— The curriculum for Grades I and II should be reviewed to ensure that it matches with the developmental status of the children and is able to provide a proper foundation for later learning.

— The relationship between higher education and primary education should not become so close as to let the primary school lose its identity and its purpose. In the name of good relationship and partnership there is a temptation to lose the critical place of primary education and reduce the latter to a preparatory stage of higher stages of education.

— While the national statement of MLLs provides the necessary framework, the content of the curriculum should be adapted to suit district/state specific context. Children should be emancipated from the back breaking load of books; the curricular and textual overload should be realistically assessed.

— We will have to drive out fear of education from the children, instead put confidence in them to achieve a drive towards meeting further learning challenges. The present system of examination, wherever it exists, derails the process. As a tool of assessment it measures neither the breadth of understanding nor the sharpness of skills of small kids and should therefore go. Assessment is not an end in itself but a means of enhancing student achievement. "Assessment is an advocacy process." Teachers should find less fearsome, more reliable and loving ways of diagnosing impediments to learning. We must not threaten (burden) the child with assessments that frustrate rather than facilitate learning.

— The system of continuous and comprehensive evaluation must be implemented in schools to ensure reasonable learning outcomes in the primary grades with greater accountability.

— The issue of mother tongue being different from the medium of instruction for a large percentage of children has serious implications for learning and achievement. Bridge materials should be developed to facilitate transition to the standard language for the initial grades.

— Classroom is not an oasis but part of the world, closely intertwined and intimately interdependent on surrounding socio-economic conditions that do not offer a means of escape from the spiral of despair. Our students inhibit a world that extends beyond classroom. They will perform better when we will perform better as architects of a just and compassionate social order. We will have to rediscover some aspects of erstwhile schools which prided in imparting moral (religious) teaching. Education has a role in developing well adjusted and creative adults with right moral values.

Teacher Preparedness and Motivation

— We must empower teachers to evolve ways of working appropriate, with State continuing to provide "Scaffolds" of support. Standardised teaching tasks and greater routinisation of teaching work with less reliance on innovative methods of communication reduce teaching to the status of 'semi-skilled' labour. Changing educational demands would require more flexible teaching forms and problem solving responses more contextual to the needs of the students and realities of local situation/ surroundings, more freedom than what current educational bureaucracies allow.

— For years to come we have no option but to live with schools of sub-optimal size; a teacher in a typical rural primary school world have to simultaneously teach more than one class. The issue of multi-grade teaching has not been adequately addressed. The achievement of satisfactory levels of learning in disadvantaged schools depends on ability to master the challenge of multi-grade teaching.

— Recruitment of women teachers for primary schools is necessary to facilitate the girls enrolment and retention. Teachers are overwhelmingly male. Major efforts to recruit and train women teachers ought to be initiated. Teaching will be substantially transformed by infusion of women teachers. A leaf can be taken from the new Tamil Nadu policy of appointing only women as primary school teachers.

— There is continuing under-investment in teacher training. We will never have better schools until we have better teachers. Teachers training, accountability and reward system is critical for improving the quality of education. This should be accompanied by confidence building and motivation enhancement.

— Schools require support and pressure. Both are needed in ample proportion. Without close supervision, education could become peripheral. There must be rigorous appraisal of school and teachers' performance. Failing schools and incompetent teachers should be weeded out. Indeed there should be zero tolerance of half baked and ineffective teaching. Simultaneously, there should be a battery of measures to encourage more effective schooling. Local authorities should also have the authority of supervision and providing local support. Dual control by local authority and school inspectorate should not be an exercise in teacher bashing. In fact community must give them esteem and respect.

— Teachers' guilds, forums and associations have a role since they exercise a mix of support and pressure which should be listened to. While teachers and parents are targeted, "Teachers' trade unions" are sometimes shunned.

— Machinery for the redressal of teachers' grievances should be created in a manner that quick decisions in matters of pensions, allowances and service conditions are taken.

— Local teachers should be involved in the development of school curriculum and teachers training materials so that the content of the educational programme emanates from the living conditions of the target group and make it relevant and need based. This will also enhance motivation of teachers.

- Special problems like large class sizes, multi-grade teaching, inadequate facilities, etc. being faced by teachers in the school situation should be examined and solutions provided to facilitate the classroom teaching and learning.
- Teachers competency in use of materials and equipment supplied under various schemes like Operation Blackboard, should be fully developed through in-service training programmes.
- Primary school teachers have little chances of promotion and vertical mobility. New avenues for their professional advancement for horizontal and vertical mobility should be explored through distance education. Professionally qualified and competent primary school teachers could be recruited/inducted as DIET faculty.
- Training institutions should be adequately strengthened and they should be able to adopt a group of schools and develop them into model institutions in their area of operation. The NGOs which have established themselves should be involved as resource institutions.

Planning and Management of Primary Education

- Block should become the unit of educational planning. all programmes like teacher training, curriculum development and evaluation should be attempted at the block level instead of at the district level.
- The SCERTs and DIETs should provide necessary support for block level planning.
- The DIETs and SCERTs should be strengthened as resource institutions so that these become outward looking and should work in close co-operation with NGOs and the community.
- A long-term development plan based on micro-planning should be evolved for each block/district. The plans should be such that these take into account the social, economic

and other considerations while suggesting strategies to achieve the national goals.

- The quality of educational statistics, particularly on enrolment needs to be improved and if necessary should be revalidated by independent surveys.
- The states should ensure that devolution of powers to VECs takes place as recommended by the CABE committee.
- Particular emphasis should be given to those efforts which develop methodologies of micro-planning and aim at capacity building at the district and lower levels for undertaking micro-planning experiments.
- The inter-linkages between ECE, NFE and primary school programmes need to be viewed and strengthened in a holistic perspective in terms of mid-day meals, timings, location, infrastructural facilities, etc.
- While there is no optimum size of a school, we should advance towards the ideal of having at least one separate section for each class with a headmaster who can provide the much needed administrative and academic leadership. Small schools tend to be children-friendly and particularly in urban areas, large schools may need to be reorganised as a cluster of children-friendly and viable schools.
- Since most of the primary schools have now two teachers, the staff provision in primary schools must, therefore, include a head teacher for whom necessary training in institution building could be organised by the resource institutions.
- The offices of the education department require a comprehensive training in educational planning, monitoring, evaluation, supervision and developing linkages with the community.
- Minimum specifications for primary education in terms of staffing, resources, infrastructure must be worked out and provision for primary education made in conformity with these.

Resources for Education

— The Prime Minister has made a commitment to raise the resource allocation to 6 per cent of GNP during the Ninth Five Year Plan. A greater share of GNP is welcome but usually additional funds lead to proliferation of bureaucracy and expansion of administrative and supervisory cadres. It should be ensured that the additional resources flow for improvement of the teaching-learning process; it should also be ensured that disparities among states of per capita education expenditure are reduced.

— While there is a need to have increased allocations for education as a whole, the intra-sectorial allocations could be re-examined and pre-primary and primary education should be accorded highest priority.

— The early childhood years are crucial as foundation for human development and as feeder programmes for primary education. We must develop a national children policy. A connection has to be built between provision of minimal base of support for health care, nutrition and support for development of cognitive skills through primary education. It is time that we invest in the future of our children. We have the examples of a few states where such investment has paid rich dividends.

— A trust be setup at the block level to extend support to the extra-curricular activities of the school-going children.

ADULT LITERACY

Issues

The Synergy Sub-Group on Primary Education and Literacy considered the following issues and made recommendations on them.

1. Need to differentiate between the Total Literacy Campaigns (TLCs) and the Post-Literacy Campaign (PLCs) in terms of approach, funding and management.

2. Question of voluntarism versus payment of cash incentives in literacy programmes.
3. Need to ensure greater participation of local self-governing institutions in literacy campaigns.
4. Need to involve industry in literacy campaigns.
5. Need for strengthening the monitorium mechanisms.

RECOMMENDATIONS

Voluntarism

— The total literacy campaigns should be a purely voluntary effort. The motivations of volunteers should be sustained through refresher courses and providing recognition to their contribution. The volunteers involved in post-literacy could be paid volunteers. The feasibility and modalities for such payments need to be carefully examined.

— There is a need for conscientisation wherever the demand for literacy has not emerged from people. Particular attention should be paid to include vulnerable groups like mine workers, pavement dwellers and fishermen in the fold of adult literacy programmes.

— The curriculum of the literacy primers need second look to ensure that these are relevant for the adult illiterates and also of the special groups in the regional context. India's rich tradition of folklore could be used to improve the quality of primers. The emphasis should be on learners attaining life long literacy rather than giving importance to quantitative targets achieved.

Involvement of Panchayati Raj Bodies

— There is a need to increase the participation of Panchayati Raj institutions, voluntary agencies and other community organisations in the planning and organisation of TLCs.

Role of Industry

— The industry has a major role to play in literacy programmes. The industry must come forward to arrange literacy classes for their own workers.

— The industry should also provide skill development training in their establishments to that neo-literates benefit from the skill formation at the post-literacy campaign stage. The developments in Maharashtra are heartening where the industries are contributing by providing infrastructural facilities for TLC and PLC programmes.

Post-Literacy Campaigns

— There is a need to formulate a strategy for post-literacy efforts especially in view of its prolonged duration. The post-literacy campaigns have to be timed in a manner that these take off soon after the TLC work is completed. This is essential to prevent neo-literates again relapsing into illiteracy.

— The post-literacy campaigns should be inter-linked with the working and living conditions of the masses and involve income generations and skill orientation activities.

— In order to ensure that adequate literature is available to neo-literates, local and regional newspaper houses should be actively involved in TLCs and should be persuaded to devote space for neo-literates in their newspapers.

Monitoring of TLC/PLC

— While the TLC is making considerable progress, the monitoring of the programme is weak. Computerised flow of information and its sharing at various levels will facilitate the timely interventions. It is also necessary to monitor the fund flows in relation to the achievements. Steps should be initiated so that an integrated system of monitoring is established.

10

Workshop on Industry-University Partnership (1995)

All-India Council for Technical Education in collaboration with Department of Higher Education, Government of Uttar Pradesh, organised the workshop on Industry-University partnership in Lucknow on March 22, 1995. Industries, representatives of important industrial organisations, senior officers of U.P. Administration, Vice-Chancellors of the State University and representatives of All India Council for Technical Education and industries organisations participated in the workshop. The workshop was held under the chairmanship of Shri Bhola Nath Tiwari, Commissioner for Agricultural Production, U.P. Administration.

THE FOCUS

A. The Conceptual Framework

While it is truism that research contributes to technological innovation and that technological innovation contributes to industrial development, which in turn, contributes to competitive advantage. The observers are of the opinion that a simple linear model is inadequate to describe this complex process. This aims to give an overview of the conceptual framework.

B. Role of Government

As the education and research are becoming increasingly expensive and industrial technologies are becoming increasingly knowledge based, the Government is attempting to frame policies for encouraging fruitful knowledge between the knowledge producers in research and higher education institutions on the one hand and wealth producers in industry on the other. This issue attempts to examine the rationale which lies behind the Government policies.

C. Role of University Authorities

Academics sometimes work under severe constraints of different kinds. There is a resource crunch and old, stale and unimaginative procedures are rigorously imposed. Thus the academics acquire an uncanny skill to steer through a myriad of impediments and get on with their research to compete internationally. Unlike industry, academics do not enjoy any tariff barriers. The mechanism has to be evolved to give operational flexibility to operate their programmes effectively.

D. Interaction Mechanism

A variety of different mechanism may be developed to facilitate the transfer of knowledge from Research and Educational Institutions to Industry. The interaction mechanism may also be looked from the point of view of industrialists, how can they get, what they want from universities?

SUMMARY OF THE RECOMMENDATIONS

1. To create more opportunities for employment universities should start vocational courses. The courses and research works should be linked with industry and trade. The importance may be given to such courses as are self-financed and job-oriented.
2. At the time of starting the courses the universities , through various chambers should interact with members to obtain the information regarding the need of the industries with regard to the qualifications of the personnel they require. Accordingly, such type of courses should be prepared in

cooperation with U.G.C./All India Council for Technical Education and various chambers to obtain information regarding industries and other informations. The chambers of various industrial organisations should be made the focal point. The cooperation of various chambers should be sought for. The informations with regard to every unit member industry can be obtained from the chamber.

3. For continuous interaction, coordination and monitoring on Industry-University cooperation, immediate steps should be taken to establish a cell at university level which would work as coordinating cell for all the faculties/subjects of the university. For this purpose monetary help should be sought for from All India Council of Technical Education. From time to time this cell would organise meetings of University Industry for the concerned faculties/subjects of the university. This would also coordinate (networking) the work of regular Teaching-Training Exchange Programme, Research-Development, Third Party Projects etc.

4. There should be exchange of Teaching Training between Industry and University. For some time university teachers in Industries and Industrial experts in university should be appointed. If the expert working in the Industry does not have prescribed minimum qualifications for the appointment as teacher, he may be invited as Visiting Faculty Resource Person. The question of establishing the 'Floating Faculty' alongwith University Core Faculty can also be considered.

5. The Government have decided to nominate the representative of the Industry in Work Councils of the universities. This will not only increase the coordination with the industries but will also provide opportunities for the revision of courses with their help.

6. A regular "Think Tank" may be provided at state level so that time and again need to organise seminars does not arise. Regular interaction should be maintained. The institutions such as CCI, PHD Chamber of Commerce, Indian Industries Association, FICCI etc. are permanently based in Lucknow.

In this "Think Tank" the representatives of Industry, Government and university should be included. The meetings should be held regularly. This can be established as a state level cell so that contact and exchange of information of courses/services amongst universities, Industry and Government may be maintained.

7. Today the employment opportunities in government sector are few whereas in other sectors these are increasing. It has not been possible to cope with increasing demand of desired trained personnel for Industry, Private Sector and Public Sector. Therefore, the changes in courses should be done keeping in view the present day needs. This should also be ensured as to how many persons in various subjects are to be given training at different levels. Availability should be consistent with the requirement of personnel.
8. The deficit of the university should be settled once for all so that a new beginning may be made by the university. The work of sanctioning the block grants to the universities may be started from the year 1995.
9. For the human resource development, the universities/ institutions may be provided with necessary infrastructure. Besides, for organising Research-Development Programmes sophisticated appliances would be required for which help should be provided by Industry and Government.
10. The university/institutions after making agreement with the industries can develop definite Programmes/Courses. The non-recurring expenditure for the development of necessary infrastructure and facilities required for running the courses as per the requirement of the industry, should be borne by the industry. The rest of the recurring expenditure should be borne by the university.
11. It needs to send the students for apprenticeship to the various industries. For such students the arrangement for scholarship may be made. This scholarship may be provided by the concerned industry. If the industry does not agree then request may be made to the U.G.C./AICTE.

12. The Industrial establishments in U.P. should provide assistance to the universities for establishing a Chair/Foundation instead of establishing a separate institute in their own establishment.
13. As per the requirements the universities can start consultancy services. The State Government will provide matching grant equivalent to the amount of income earned through such consultancy services.
14. The pressure of Higher Education is increasing every year. In order to maintain quality of Higher Education it is essential to exercise control over the number of students. In view of liberalization of economic policy and competition, it is necessary that more stress is laid on high level specialization and research development programmes.
15. In National Policy of Education 1986 after 10+2 level, recommendations has been made for vocational education. It is necessary that the students be provided consultation as regards the choice of vocational courses in accordance with their qualifications and capabilities. For this, regular arrangements may be made in university/college so that the students are able to get employment as per their qualifications and capabilities.
16. A nominal fee is charged for university education in the state. The rates of various types of fees may be reviewed and revised.
17. The continuing educational programmes may be conducted for the people working in industries and as per requirements day/evening training programmes may be conducted.

11

46th All India Adult Education Conference (1996)

Indian Adult Education Association in collaboration with Centre for Continuing/Adult Education, M.S. University of Baroda organised 46th All India Education Conference in Vadodara on March 9, 1996. The theme was Strategies for Post Literacy in the Next Decade.

Recommendations

1. The 46th All India Education Conference organised by the Indian Adult Education Association and the Department of Continuing/ Adult Education and Community Services, MS University of Baroda notes with satisfaction that post-literacy programme has been expanded considerably during the last 3-4 years and about 140 districts at present are in the post-literacy phase.
2. The Conference notes that at many a time there is a wide gap between the literacy and post-literacy phase. This it feels results into relapse into illiteracy and wastage of efforts and resources. It, therefore, recommends that the gap between the TLC and PLC should be reduced. The functionaries both at the top level and at the grass-root level should adopt suitable strategies to achieve it.
3. The Conference notes with satisfaction that Continuing Education Centres in every village on experimental basis are to be started soon. But it feels that the part-time Prerak would not be in a position to deliver the goods. It urges that Prerak should be a full time person with an honorarium of not less than minimum wages prevalent in the State.

4. The Conference recommends that Jan Shikshan Nilayams/ Continuing Education Centres should be provided adequate space and other infrastructural facilities to make them effective centres. There should be at least two rooms for the centre as recommended by Ghosh Expert Group.
5. The Conference notes that no concerted effort has been made to make adult literacy programme for women effectively linked with development plans. It urges that after completing the post-literacy phase the women should be provided competitive skills for employment or self-employment so that they forge ahead in the next decade as responsible agents for social change.
6. The Conference urges that post-literacy programme to be effective must be linked with economic development through active cooperation of other training institutions for vocational and technical skills. It should be closely linked with job oriented skills such as TRYSEM, IRDP, JRY and DWARCA.
7. The Conference recommends that village institutions particularly Panchayats should be entrusted with the responsibility for the conduct of the post-literacy programme. It feels that involvement of school teachers, extension workers, health workers and other important village leaders is also essential for its success.
8. The Conference recommends that the neo-literates should be encouraged to continue their education and undertake open school examination so that they could get gainful employment.
9. The Conference notes with satisfaction that some districts have started newsletter to stabilise the knowledge of reading and writing of neo-literates and to provide current information to them and to the members of the family. But, it feels that all PC/CE districts should bring out the newsletter so that neo-literates get opportunities for self education. But, before bringing out the newsletter the persons involved with newsletter should be oriented in editing, production and distribution so that the right message reaches the people at the right time.

10. It feels that studies at grass-root level are necessary to identify the specific needs of the target group so that the teaching/learning process gets strengthened. For this the Conference feels that research institutions and universities could play a leading role in conducting such studies.
11. The Conference feels that Universities are playing an effective role in continuing education of the masses. But, uncertainty regarding their continuation beyond March 1997 is considerably effecting their programmes. It urges upon the University Grants Commission (UGC) to announce its policy regarding continuation of the Department/Centres of Adult and Continuing Education beyond March 1997 so that adult and continuing education becomes a permanent system in the university structure.

12

NCTE Curriculum Framework for Teacher Education (1996)

National Council for Teacher Education (NCTE) was given a statutory recognition on August 17, 1995 (Gazette Notification No. 484) by Ministry of Human Resource Development (Department of Education). In pursuance of the National Council for Teacher Education, 1993 (No. 73 of 1993), NCTE published a discussion paper seeking a country wide debate on the document to develop a national consensus on guidelines for improving teacher education, designing futuristic programmes, developing curriculum and evolving transactional strategies to meet the demands of the 21st century.

Main Considerations in the Discussion Document

1. Teacher education as an integral part of educational and social system.
2. Teacher education and national and social goals.
3. Plural society and national integration.
4. Homogeneous curriculum in a heterogeneous society.
5. Nature of the State and nature of polity.
6. Human resource and economic development.
7. Migration from rural to urban areas and application of educated youth.
8. Unemployment.
9. The philosophy of equality and the ramification of teacher education.
10. The philosophy of social justice.

11. Role of teacher education values and nation building.
12. The scientific philosophy and nature.
13. Panchayati Raj and traditional power structure.
14. Teacher in the community.
15. Teachers for the 21st century.
16. Education: Theory and practice.
17. Changes in schools demand concomitant changes in teacher education.
18. Competencies and skills in education of teachers unrelated to work situation.
19. Clarity in curriculum.
20. Universalisation of elementary education.
21. Facing the challenges of science and technology.
22. Manpower planning in teacher education.
23. Mismatch between the training and nature of work in teaching.
24. Education as a life-long process and need for in-service education.
25. Institutional autonomy.
26. Teaching as a profession.
27. Towards evolving a culture-sensitive pedagogy.
28. Research and innovation.
29. Need for a fresh outlook.
30. Critical concerns.

13

National Seminar on Educational Development in India: The Future Perspectives (1996)

National Seminar on Educational Development in India: The Future Perspectives was organised by UGC sponsored Department of Special Assistance in Education, Himachal Pradesh University, Shimla in September, 1996.

Recommendations

(i) The specific causes for not achieving the target of universalisation of elementary education (UEE) among the specific groups, namely, SCs, STs including nomadic tribes, rural girls, children drawn from coastal and desert areas, need to be analysed in the perspective of their socio-cultural milieu;

(ii) Strategies need to be evolved for providing *Mass Movement Support* to the cause of universalisation of elementary education so that common citizens are involved to strengthen and support the movement;

(iii) Mass media should be utilised effectively and meaningfully to make the average citizen's attitude more receptive so as to encourage his involvement in UEE;

(iv) The disturbing phenomenon of *Educational Zamindari,* existing in certain parts of country wherein teachers contract out their jobs to others on much lower salary, needs to be curbed at the earliest;

(v) Teachers should be motivated and encouraged to be accountable to themselves and criteria of self-accountability need to be developed at the earliest;

(vi) More funds especially in Elementary Education sector should be made available and suitable strategies evolved to ensure optimal utilisation of allotted funds and check their wastage and leakage;

(vii) A harmonious blend of General Education and Vocational Education must be made at the secondary stage. However, the students who intend to follow vocational stream after tenth grade should pursue vocational component seriously;

(viii) Keeping in view the rapidly changing technology there is a need to survey the world of work so that the concept of vocationalisation at secondary level is modified accordingly;

(ix) For the success of vocationalisation of education at +2 level there is need for joint collaboration and active involvement of higher secondary schools, polytechnics and other technical institutions. The concept of sponsoring by the industries should be encouraged by universities;

(x) The educational process at the school and college/university levels should be restructured so that 'Education' can serve as an instrument of empowerment for the disadvantaged sections of Indian Society;

(xi) The interlinkages between school, college and university education systems need to be evolved in a new paradigm to make the educational system as catalyst of change so that the future generations are equipped with abilities for facing the post-modern era in the wake of technological advancement, globalisation and privatisation;

(xii) Equity, equality and fraternity should be watch words in the pyramid of higher education;

(xiii) Keeping in view the overall deterioration in the educational standards and indiscipline in the institutions of higher learning there is a need to design the curricular framework in such a way that the teachers and student community can be motivated and involved jointly in nation building activities. This step will also help in developing creativity and leadership qualities among the students which are essential for nurturing democratic secular values;

(xiv) Research and development at university level need to be focussed on the immediate needs and long-term goals of Indian masses keeping in view the globalisation and privatisation of Indian economy;

(xv) There is a need for encouraging 'action research programmes' especially at grassroot levels so that basic educational needs of the ruralites and people living in remote, far flung, hilly snow-bound areas, and desert and coastal regions of the country are identified;

(xvi) Distance/open learning system should be developed in such a way that it can serve as a supplementary system to formal system of education. The open and distance learning system needs all encouragement in terms of funds, trained manpower, technological support so that the fruits of the system can reach to each and every corner of the country, especially the hill, coastal and desert areas;

(xvii) Teacher is the focal point of social transformation and hence the teacher training and orientation programmes undertaken by teacher-training institutes (for school teachers) and Academic Staff Colleges (for college and university teachers) need restructuring so that teachers are made fully conversant with innovative techniques and strategies of brain storming, quiz, think tank, simulation and role playing, fish bowl, SWOT analysis, action research, self evaluation, etc.;

(xviii) Human rights should be made a subject of study at the primary, secondary and university levels for developing awareness among the students from the beginning of educational process be-cause even after four decades of independence Human Rights still remains a teasing illusion for a vast majority of Indian masses especially the disadvantaged and the deprived.

(xix) The programme for sensitizing and creating awareness about Human Rights among special groups—police and prison personnel, workers working at the grassroot levels, namely, patwari, village level worker, forest guard, etc. and administrators, should be developed so that Human Rights can become a major component in the extension education programmes. Such programmes will be helpful in development of strategies for bringing about an attitudinal change among people and law enforcement agencies towards Human Rights.

14

National Seminar on Modernisation of Teacher Education (1996)

National Seminar on Modernisation of Teacher Education was held at Centre for Advanced Study in Education (CASE), Faculty of Education and Psychology, M.S. University of Baroda, Vadodara.

Recommendations

1. There is a need of manpower planning in the field of teacher education in India.
2. Admissions to teacher education be done on the basis of carefully developed entrance test.
3. In-service teacher education programmes be strengthened for micro specialisation.
4. There should be uniformity of core courses in teacher education programme at pre-primary, primary, secondary, and higher-secondary levels offered through different modes such as distance, correspondence, formal, regular and part-time, summer.
5. There should be a networking of teacher training programmes through different modes.
6. In view of the problems of vertical mobility and employability of the products of teacher education programme with micro specialization, some foundation courses, viz., pedagogy of education, philosophical, psychological and sociological foundations of education, Research and Statistics in Social Science should be incorporated into such programmes.

7. The teacher education institutions should work in close collaborations with schools, community and the other institutions of teacher education around them.
8. Teacher education should give more weightage to practical than theory and at the end of the programme, there should be internship with stipend facilities from the state government for student-teachers.
9. The duration of teacher education programme be extended to minimum of two years as one year was insufficient to prepare quality graduates.
10. The teacher education programme should include people at all levels in its planning for total quality management and match its programme to customer's expectations.
11. There should be specific curricular inputs in the teacher education programmes at all levels to sensitize the student teacher to the needs of the disabled children.
12. Teacher education programmes should be personalized and activity based. The approach should be child-centred. Learning should be without burden and joyous as visualised in *Divaswapna* of Gijubbhai.

15

Seminar on Privatization of Universities and Role of University Administrators in the Changing Scenario (1996)

Association of University Administrators organised the Seminar at Gurukula Kangri University, Hardwar in December 1996. It was attended by the university Registrars, Controllers of Examinations, Finance Officers, Deputy Registrars, Assistant Registrars and some Deans and Vice-Chancellors from all over the country.

Significant Recommendations

1. There is a lot of scope of better management of human and physical resources of these universities by way of internal economies, generation of funds through consultancies, research, hiring of infrastructure, floriculture, and Horticulture, etc, International marketing of higher education in the global market particularly among the developing countries needs to be pursued vigorously.
2. It is necessary that adequate precautions and safeguards are incorporated in the Private Universities Bill before its enactment. Only those people or private organisations be permitted to establish private universities who have an established reputation of promoting high quality education and good track record of contribution to social, cultural and economic welfare of the society.
3. Adequate steps need be taken for the professional development of university administrators by way of establishment of

National Institute of Training with Regional Centres throughout the country to take care of the present pressing requirements of professional growth of lakhs of personnel (about 6 lakh) involved in the administration and management of our Universities, colleges and institutions of higher learning.

Resolutions

1. The Ministry of Human Resource Development, the University Grants Commission and the State Governments should ensure parity of pay scales and service conditions between the teachers and university administrators for efficient and effective implementation of policies and programmes of universities and also for a better management of university administration.
2. University administrators should also be provided travel grant facilities and other opportunities similar to academic staff for participation in national and international conferences for their professional development and to equip them for better management of university affairs and administration.
3. University administrators should also be granted study/sabbatical leave for publishing their administrative experience and expertise as professional research work, on the same pattern as it is permissible to academic staff to ensure parity in professional development of teaching and administrative staff of the universities.

16

Thiruvananthapuram Declaration on Quality of Secondary Education in India (1996)

The Preamble

Council of Boards of School Education in India (COBSE) and the Department of Education, Government of Kerala organised a National Conference on Quality in Secondary Education on September 5–6, 1996 at Thiruvananthapuram, Kerala.

The conference was attended by Chairmen and Secretaries of Boards of Secondary and Higher Secondary Education, from various States representatives of national institutions like the National Institute of Educational Planning and Administration and National Open School, COBSE, eminent academicians from all over the country, Vice-Chancellors of Universities, non-governmental organisations, people's representatives and Presidents of District Panchayats in Kerala.

Noting with great interest that country is in the process of formulating its Ninth Five Year Plan, which will usher us to the next millennium, the Conference found further justification in presenting these ideas and recommendations duly endorsed by the participants in the Conference as the "Thiruvananthapuram Declaration".

Tenets of the Declaration

The Conference identified the following areas for reorientation while considering the conceptual and operational aspects of quality in Secondary Education.

— Structures at the macro and micro levels.
— Curriculum renewal: competency based and mastery oriented curriculum.
— Teacher Training: pre-service, in-service and recurrent training of teachers and school principals.
— School based evaluation and external examination.
— Processes and materials of teaching and learning at the level of excellence.

Structures at the Micro and Macro Levels

The unprecedented extent of technological changes and the pace with which they influence our lives, coupled with the far reaching socio-economic implications, make it imperative to critically examine the effectiveness and adequacy of the different structures in the field of Secondary Education. The Conference took note of this techno-economic and social milieu and felt that there is an urgent need to strengthen the existing structures and create new structures and processes with a sense of futuristic realism. This has become all the more urgent in view of the 73rd and 74th Constitutional amendments which is translating the idea of decentralisation into reality.

The function of the Boards of most of the States is confined to the pressing responsibility of conducting the examinations. However in the light of the new needs as aspirations, it is necessary to develop a full-fledged academic wing which should be made functional by developing appropriate and effective structures for developing competency based and mastery oriented curriculum, training and re-training of teachers, preparing remedial and enrichment material for quality teaching and learning, conducting operational research and maintaining a documentation centre.

At the micro level, strategies need to be evolved for school level programmes by forming Secondary and High School clusters to impart recurrent orientation of teachers and for strengthening individual schools and class room practices so as to maximise the quality and minimise wastage and failures. The ultimate concern has to be the creation of competent individuals to carry on the ever diversifying tasks of our society both in the urban and the rural areas.

Whereas primary education has been able to attract a fair amount of attention at the National and State levels, as reflected in the structures and curriculum, the Conference noted with concern that there has been no institutions corresponding to DIETs or National Programmes like MLL for the Secondary Education covering the classes from 8th to 12th. This lacunae has to be covered and effective institutions created to accomplish the task of achieving the objective of socially relevant Secondary Education.

Teacher Training

Teacher's training in Secondary Education has been grossly neglected. It has been the view of the Conference that this area should receive national attention. At a time when the Ninth Five Year Plan is being drawn up and priorities are being refixed, this concern for new structures in Secondary Education and the imminent need to initiate initial and in-service training has to be necessarily taken up as a Centrally Sponsored Programme in the Ninth Plan.

The special skills required of a School Principal have received scant attention. Considering the significant contribution that a Principal makes towards quality, this is a major lapse, which the Conference considers as a key area for intervention. At the national and state-levels, this should receive adequate attention with more training modules with emphasis on management skills for the principals.

Better linkages with Colleges of Education and University Departments of Education and even outstanding Secondary Schools with the initial training of teachers have to be established. This will not only make the training more effective but also indirectly enrich the colleges. Moreover, there should be realistic assessment of the requirement of teachers checking overproduction and the consequent devaluation of the profession of teaching.

Curriculum Renewal

It has been observed by the Conference that the conceptualisation of quality and curriculum renewal has not so far taken into account the cognitive, affective and psycho motive aspects of learning. In order that education is able to truly illuminate, enlighten and empower the child, curriculum renewal should take into account the need for integration of all these three aspects.

A situation where the opportunities after the Higher Secondary level are narrow and stereotyped is not uncommon in many parts of the country. Regular interaction with industries will open new opportunities and alternatives. This feedback should then form the basis for manpower planning to produce skilled personnel and enhancing their employability.

Vocational development has to be viewed in this context with a new perspective. Vocational orientation should commence from the primary classes which would become vocational exploration at the upper primary stage. Secondary Education should concentrate on vocational training with emphasis on retraining and updating skills.

Evaluation

While acknowledging the unhappy fact that the number of students who fail in the 10th class is shamefully high, even in states with good record in the field of education, the consensus in the Conference is that it would be unfair to blame the child for this. Students with different levels of capabilities should be appropriately helped. The outstanding should be given special tasks commensurate with their capability, while those with different aptitudes should be given remediation and reinforcements. Even while ensuring that the core minimum level is attained there could be flexibility for combining subjects and allowing the student to develop his skills and aptitudes.

At the national level the Council of Boards of School Education in India (COBSE) has to be strengthened. The task of monitoring and providing inputs to maintain international compatibility should be key responsibility of COBSE. Preparing the personnel for academic work is another area where it should work in close conjuction with COBSE.

Global Trends clearly indicate that Secondary Education has to expand with socio-economic developments. With rapid economic progress taking place in India as a whole and with a few states and provinces having progressed well beyond the national averages in literacy and primary education, universalisation or near universalisation of Secondary Education will have to be aimed sooner than later. In a developing and modernising economy, Secondary Education has the responsibility to provide trained manpower to meet the needs of the society. The Conference considers that eventually universalisation of Secondary Education will have to be taken up as a National Goal.

In order to fulfil the ideas and vision of this Declaration, the Planning Commission has to accept and appreciate the pivotal importance Secondary Education ought to get as against its present stage of inadequate attention.

This Declaration has been adopted unanimously after due deliberations by the participants of the National Seminar on Quality in Secondary Education at Thiruvananthapuram on this Sixth Day of September, 1996 with an appeal to:

(a) *National Planning Commission* to accord due place for the development of Secondary Education which otherwise remains the weakest link and to develop Centrally Sponsored Schemes to address the issues of teacher training curriculum and research and establishment of Secondary Boards with a view to enhancing the quality of Secondary Education.

(b) *Ministry of Human Resources Development, Government of India* to extend support to COBSE to undertake appropriate schemes to strengthen local institutes and provide financial and technical support to the new structures for improving quality.

(c) *State Governments* to reorganise or establish Boards of Secondary Education covering both Secondary and Higher Secondary and Vocational Education.

(d) *Boards of Secondary Education* to take up remediation and enrichment programmes with regard to pupil performance and upgrade the quality of Secondary Education.

17

UNDP Action Plan to Development Strategies for a University-Industry Cooperative Programme in Science, Technology and Engineering in India (1996)

UNDP Technical Support Services Programme, on request of the Government of India, prepared an Action Plan to develop strategies for strengthening university-industry linkages in the country. The Action Plan included the following six core areas:

(i) Motivating and enabling facility;
(ii) Improving curricula;
(iii) Identification of R&D needs and capabilities;
(iv) Interface for interaction;
(v) University of management reforms;
(vi) Promotion of indigenous R&D through university-industry collaboration.

MOTIVATING AND ENABLING FACULTY

Faculty of universities lacks entrepreneurial spirit and motivation to take up industrial projects. Adequate monetary as well as promotional incentives are missing. In general faculty is evaluated on the basis of contributions like research papers and notes on R&D consultancy work for industry.

Existing Policies/Mechanisms

(i) UGC scheme of job protection for faculty: not may takers;

(ii) Faculty Consultancy Earning Scheme (a proportion of Institutional earnings paid to faculty members taking up consultancies)

Recommendations	*Actions*
1. Ensure payment of at least 50 per cent of the consultancy earnings to the concerned faculty/support staff.	Amend University Rules through Academic Councils
2. Raise upper limit on consultancy earnings of faculty and introduce tax exemption on earnings upto the equivalent of one year's salary.	Ministry of Human Resource Development to propose to Ministry of Finance.
3. Provide consultancy-linked advanced increments/promotions, and include patents in evaluation of academic performance.	Academic Councils of Universities
4. Promote staff mobility between industry and universities. Raise the number of persons from industry for the higher degrees studies through sponsorship. Make industrial training (optimally one year or more) for lecturers indispensable.	Academic Councils of Universities Ensure support from CII/FICCI/ PHDCII
5. Introduce linked industrial professorship scheme through flexible mode of appointing adjunct faculty from industry. Give less emphasis to academic qualifications and greater emphasis to industrial/commercial expertise.	Ensure support from CII/FICCI/ PHDCII.

IMPROVING CURRICULA

The capabilities (skills) of new graduates and postgraduates (B.Tech., M.Sc., M.Tech.) do not conform to the requirements/ expectations of industrial employers.

Existing Policies/Mechanisms

No clear-cut policy on active involvement of industry in developing industry-oriented curricula.

Recommendations	*Actions*
1. Suitably designed and well monitored industrial training for a duration of at least one Semester at post-graduate level should be at least part of curricula.	Academic Councils of Universities
2. Make at least 50 per cent of student projects (M.Sc./B.Tech./ M.Phil./M.Tech./Ph.D.) liable to support from industry and/or agencies concerned with development.	CII to work out scheme and disseminate among member industries AICTE/UGC to work out scheme and disseminate among member institutes
3. Ensure more practical courses (40 per cent of curricula) and update laboratory/ workshop programmes to include industry-oriented problem solving exercises.	Academic Councils of Universities. AICTE/UGC
4. Conduct entrepreneurship training programmes in universities, particularly at science departments (at least once a year).	University Departments, DST
5. Curricula of colleges located in rural areas should suit the needs of local industries/development agencies.	UGC Academic Councils of Universities.

IDENTIFICATION OF R&D NEEDS AND CAPABILITIES

The prevailing awareness gap regarding the R & D needs of industry and the ability of universities to meet these needs is a major obstacle in the process of universities becoming an important source of R&D inputs/technology for industry.

Existing Policies/Mechanisms

Initiatives have been taken by AICTE, CII, PHDCII.

Recommendations	*Actions*
1. Develop a region-wise database of present and future R&D needs of industry for selected fields and identify specific university departments for each field (in terms of expertise of faculty/R&D facilities).	Local Universities to coordinate with regional offices of CII/ FICCI/PHDCII/DSIR/ Technology Forecasting & Assessment Council of DST to initiate with support from UGC/ AICTE/CII/FICCI and others Disseminate by CII/FICCI and others.
2. Generate common-interest R&D programmes and develop need-based infrastructure jointly with industry by concentrating on specific areas of capabilities of universities (taking up 5 universities in each region including less prominent ones).	Research Councils of Universities CII/FICCI/PHDCII and others DST AICTE/UGC
3. Initiate full-fledged industrial collaboration programmes at science departments by identifying the R&D needs of specific industrial and development sectors.	University Departments

INTERFACE FOR INTERACTION

Universities and industrial companies have failed in evolving a dynamic two-way interface to co-ordinate/promote various aspects of their interaction.

Existing Policies/Mechanism

Institutions-Industry Interaction cells in different institutes are being set up by AICTE and UGC.

Recommendations	*Actions*
1. Set up Industrial Liaison Centres at each university (headed by an expert with the rank of a professor with independent charge and staffed by professionals from a variety of backgrounds: technical, industrial, commercial, legal etc.	AICTE/UGC
2. Facilitate Universities to set up a market-oriented Industrial Consultancy Company to provide a corporate approach towards taking up R&D consultancy work.	Governing bodies of Universities with approval from Ministry of Human Resource Development
3. Promote local and regional university-industry get-togethers (at least once a quarter) to obtain/provide information on industry's needs/new products/processes/ continuing education courses/curricula etc.	Universities Departments Regional Offices of CII/FICCI/ others and local industrial associations.
4. Publicise university activities with relevance to industry (e.g. on available R&D expertise of faculty/specialised R&D facilities/patents held by universities).	University Departments through Liaison offices.

UNIVERSITY MANAGEMENT REFORMS

Excessive red-tape in the universities and a lack of flexibility in the execution of outside funded projects are major obstacles for the faculty to collaborate with industry. Lengthy procedures and stringent norms set by university administrations hamper the execution of industrial projects and progress in other areas of collaboration.

Existing Policies/Mechanisms

No evidence of any action.

Recommendations	*Actions*
1. Give greater functional autonomy to institutions in matters of resource allocation and use; creation and filling of positions; and determining payment terms.	Amend University Act, 1981
2. Provide autonomy to faculty to conduct projects and expenditure of budget.	Amend University Administration procedures
3. Institute a system of nomination of industrialists to university management and academic bodies (at every level), to utilize entrepreneurial expertise and to make university education and R&D systems more productive and accountable.	Governing bodies of Universities.
4. Encouraging establishment of corpus fund with matching funds from Government and industry.	

PROMOTION OF INDIGENOUS R & D THROUGH UNIVERSITY-INDUSTRY

Indian industry prefers to buy ready-made technology from abroad or to do R&D with foreign collaboration. In India industrial investment in R&D is comparatively low in comparison with (newly) industrialized countries.

Existing Policies/Mechanisms

Tax incentives are provided to industry (100 per cent for grants to universities; 125 per cent for sponsored research); no clear impact is visible.

Recommendations	*Actions*
1. Provide package of generous tax incentives for companies that provide resources to universities for industry linked activities and facilitate these companies to use university facilities and expertise on a regular basis.	Ministry of Finance through Ministry of Industries UGC
2. Introduce MOU's between universities and industry, particularly for creating joint R&D facilities and initiating technology development programmes.	Ministry of Finance through Ministry of Industries UGC
3. Facilitate industrial organizations (FICCI /CII/PHDCII/Others) to set up permanent units at national and regional level for conducting regular coordination with universities.	FICCI/CII/PHDCCI/others.

18

AICTE Committee to Review Scales of Pay of Teachers of Technical Institutions (1997)*

All India Council of Technical Education (AICTE) Committee to Review Scales of Pay of Teachers of Technical Institutions, (called Shukla Committee) submitted the report on July, 31 1997.

SIGNIFICANT RECOMMENDATIONS

1. Cadre Structure

1.1 *Recommended Cadre Structure*

The Cadre Structure recommended for Degree level institutions is given in Table 18.1. The Structure recommended for Diploma level institutions is given in Table 18.2. The total number of faculty positions in an institution would be determined by the staff/student ratio prescribed by AICTE for various categories of programmes. The ratio of the substantive positions amongst the various Cadres (levels) of purely academic positions is also given in above mentioned tables. The actual number of incumbents at each level may vary somewhat depending on the number of persons advanced to higher levels under Flexible Staff Structure Scheme (see section 2.7).

---

* Since this article includes only the Sixth Chapter of the Report of the Committee in question. all the references to other Chapters and Sections of the Report that have been made in it have been deleted.

1.2 *New Cadres Recommended*

As far as Degree level institutions are concerned, it may be noted that the cadre of Associate Professor is not a new creation as it is already existing in some institutions. The recommendation is only to extend this to all institutions. As such only one additional cadre has been recommended, viz, that of Dean/Deputy Director, and that too only in large size National and Post-graduate institutions.

Similarly, for large technician level institutions, offering many advance post-diploma level programmes, creation of post of a Vice-Principal is recommended, with the Post of Principal being in a Senior Scale.

Table 18.1: Cadre Structure for Institutions Conducting Degree Level Programmes

(a) Centrally Funded (including RECs and TTTIs) and other Autonomous Advanced Post-graduate Institutions*			(b) All Degree level Institutions other than at (a)	
Level	Cadre	Ratio	Cadre	Ratio
1.	Lecturer	3	Lecturer	3
2.	Assistant Professor#	2	Assistant Professor#	2
3.	Associate Professor	1	Associate Professor	1
4.	Professor	1	Professor	1
5.	Dean/Deputy Director	@	Principal	single post
6.	Director	Single post		

$ The higher grades under the Career Advancement Scheme are not shown here.

* There are institutions with annual intake of 400 and above offering at least 6 full-time UG programmes and 10 full-time Master's programmes as well as regular Doctoral programmes, and are Administratively Autonomous.

@ Number of positions in this category to be determined by the appropriate authority of the institution based on the individual needs of the institution.

\# The workshop Superintendent's post in Degree level institutions is a teaching post with qualifications, salary scales and other conditions identical to those of Assistant Professor.

TABLE 18.2: Cadre Structure for Institutions Conducting Diploma Level Programmes

	(a) Large Size Institutions with several advanced Post-Diploma programmes.@		(b) all Degree level Institutions other than at (a)	
Level	Cadre	Ratio	Cadre	Ratio
1.	Lecturer	3	Lecturer	3
2.	Sr. Lecturer	1	Sr. Lecturer	1
3.	Head of Department.	One per deptt.	Head of Department. #	One per deptt.
4.	Vice-Principal	Single post #		
5.	Principal (Sr. Scale)	Single post	Principal	Single post

$ The higher grades under the Career Advancement Scheme are not shown here.

@ These are institutions with 8 of more regular, 3-year full-time diploma programmes, 5 or more Advanced Post-diploma level full-time programmes, an intake of 400 or more, and are Administratively Autonomous.

In departments with 5 or more faculty members.

1.3 *Non-faculty Positions in Institutions and Administrative Cadres in the Directorates of Technical Education*

In some institutions there are non-faculty cadres such as Research Associate/ Assistant drawing salary comparable to those of certain Faculty positions. Review and revision of their scales of pay is not within the mandate of the AICTE Pay committee. Where their pay scales are not covered by any other guidelines (such as those of CSIR, UGC, etc.) the Committee feels that the appropriate authorities of the institutions concerned may decide on the revisions to be implemented.

Similarly, in Polytechnics there are cadres such as Training and Placement Officer, Workshop Superintendent etc. Because of the varying practices followed in different States regarding their cadre level and qualifications, their salary scales are not included in these recommendations. However, such of those posts, which are designated by AICTE or Academic posts at any level and which have specified qualifications and experience requirements identical to the academic post at that level, may be given the corresponding salary scales.

There are also cadres in the Directorates of Technical Education drawn from the Faculty. It is also recommended that the Cadre of Director of Technical Education in those States where both degree and diploma level education comes under the Directorate's purview be equated to the Director given in Table 18.1. For the other cadres drawn from faculty positions, the respective States may decide on the parity of those cadres with corresponding faculty cadre positions. Where the State Government has declared any such post (filled by persons drawn from faculty) as equivalent to a teaching post and has qualifications and experience requirements identical to those of the latter (teaching post), the salary may also be fixed at the same level as that of the equivalent teaching post.

1.4 *Term Appointment and Visiting Professors*

The Committee feels it is essential to have the services of outstanding experts from the Industry and Professions made available to the educational institutions. There should be a provision to appoint such persons on Term basis at appropriate levels. To facilitate this, the institutions may earmark a certain percentage of the total number of their faculty positions and reserve them for such term appointments. Such eminent professionals may have to be given exemption from the formal qualification requirements prescribed for the posts they occupy.

There should also be a provision to appoint experienced professional of high calibre including Faculty members from other institutions in India or abroad as Visiting Professors and such persons should be paid adequate compensation. These appointments also would be a part of the percentage earmarked for term appointments.

1.5 *Teacher Trainee/Probationary Lecturer*

The Committee strongly feels that a major scheme for recruitment, training and placement of bright young technical graduates as teachers must be taken up by the Government of India. An upgraded and improved version of the erstwhile Technical Teachers' Training Scheme is recommended for this. Such persons are to be trained in the Post-Graduate Institutions of Excellence where they will be placed in the category of "Teacher Trainees". A Teacher Trainee will concurrently be on the rolls of the institution where he is to be placed on completion of training, falling in the category "Probationary Lecturer". The posts of "Probationary Lecturer" will be supernumerary, over and above the regular cadre strength. A Probationary Lecturer will be automatically placed as Lecturer at the Appropriate level on successful completion of training. The period of service as Probationary Lecturer will count for all service and retirement benefits also.

1.6 *Department of Applied Science and Humanities*

The number of teachers in individual subjects like Physics, Chemistry, Mathematics and Humanities in most technical institutions is quite small. With such low numbers and fixed ratio between cadre levels (such as 1:1:2:3) in these subject areas it is quite likely there will be hardly any senior positions if they are treated as separate entities. The committee recommends that these subject areas to be grouped together as a single "Department of Applied Sciences and Humanities" and senior positions instituted in this combined department as per norms. The Committee recognises that this pattern already exists in some institutions.

1.7 *Flexible Staff Structure*

The Committee recommends that this scheme, already approved by the Government along with the 1986 Pay Revision be implemented forthwith.

1. 8 *Professor of Eminence*

The Committee recommends that AICTE introduce a scheme of Professor of Eminence. The selection and placement in selected institutions of these Professors and providing the necessary financial and infrastructure support should be the responsibility of AICTE.

2. Pay Scales

2.1 *Pay Scales of Teaching Staff*

The Committee has kept various considerations in view as well as the necessity of attracting and retaining talented technical persons while recommending the pay scales for technical teachers. These are given in Table 18.3 for Degree level technical institutions and Table 18.4 for Diploma level technical institutions.

TABLE 18.3: Scales of Pay of Teachers in Engineering Colleges and Other Institutions at Degree Level*

S. No.	Designation of Post	Pre-revised Scale (Rs.)	Revised Pay Scale (Rs.)	Remarks
1	2	3	4	5
1.	Lecturer	2200-75-2800-100-4000	9375-275 -13500	See note 1
2.	Assistant Professor/ Workshop Superintendent	3700-125-4950-150-5700	13875-375 -18000	See Note 2
3.	Associate Professor	4500-150-5700-200-6300	16300-400 -20300	See Note 3
4.	Professor	4500-150-5700-200-7300	16550-450 -22400	See Note 4
5.	Deans/Deputy Director	Not existing	18400-500 -22400	See Note 5 and 8

Table 18.3: (Contd.)

1	2	3	4	5
6.	Principal	6300-200-7300	20400-500 -22400 + Rs. 1000 Admn. Allowance	See Note 6
7.	Director	7300-100-7600	22400-525 -24500	See Note 7

* Pay scales for posts under Career Advancement Scheme are presented in Table 18.4.

Notes:

1. This is V CPC Scale No. S-15 with a higher start.
2. V CPC scale has been adapted with a higher start. Scale S-23 is the exact equivalent of the prerevised scale of Assistant Professors.
3. The scale is an adoption of V CPC Scale S-24. The prerevised scale had to start at the minimum of SG (Rs. 4500) and went upto Rs. 6,300 which is beyond the maximum of the SG (Rs. 5,700). The grade proposed is the equivalent of this, with a higher start. V CPC Scale S-24 has been extended to reach near equivalent of Rs. 6,300 in the revised scales.
4. V CPC Scale S-28 has been adapted with a higher start. This scale is the exact equivalent of the prerevised scale of Professors.
5. V CPC Scale S-29 has been adapted.
6. V CPC Scale S-29 has been adapted with a higher start nearly equivalent to the higher start (Rs. 6300) for Principals in the prerevised scales. An allowances of Rs. 1,000 has been proposed taking into account the additional administrative responsibilities for Head of the Institutions has to shoulder, and as encouragement for Professor to accept the responsibilities of this position.
7. The V CPC Scale S-30 has been adapted. This is the exact equivalent of the prerevised scale for this post.
8. Only in Centrally funded and large sized institutions meeting specified criteria.
9. There may be a few teachers who are occupying the Posts of Reader or Professor under the Merit Promotion Scheme. For these the pre-revised pay scales are Rs. 3000-5000 and 4500-5700 respectively. The scale Rs. 3000-5000 is the same as that of Lecturer (Sr. Scale), which the Committee has recommended to be revised as Rs. 11625-325-16500 (see Table 3B) and the same may be adapted for promotees as Reader/Assistant Professor under MPS. The scale of Professors (MPS) is revised to Rs. 14300-400-19500 which is at par with the proposed scale for Assistant Professor (Senior Scale) (See Table 3B).

Table 18.4: Scales of Pay for Teaching Positions under Career Advancement Scheme for Degree Level Institutions.

S. No.	Designation of Post	Pre-revised Scale (Rs.)	Revised Pay Scale (Rs.)	Remarks
1.	Lecturer (Sr. Scale)	3000-100-3500-125-5000	11625-325 -16500	See Notes 1, 4
2.	Lecturer (selection grade)	3700-125-4950-150-5700	13875-375 -18000	See Notes 2, 4
3.	Assistant Professor (Sr. Scale)	Not existing	14300-400 -19500	See Note 3

Notes:

1. The pre-revised scale was a merger of Senior Time Scale and Junior Administrative Grade of Central Service (Grade-A). Parity is maintained by adopting V CPC Scale S-19 and extending it to the maximum of the revised of JAG Scale.
2. The prerevised scale is identical to the scale of Assistant Professors. Parity is maintained by adopting the same scale.
3. This is a new grade created for career advancement. The scale of pay adopted for this post is S-24 of V CPC with the upper end and extended by 3 increments,
4. The higher start is only notional as there is no direct recruitment to this post and normal pay fixation rules will apply.

2.2 *Pay Scales of Librarians and Physical Education Personnel*

The Committee recommends that Librarians and Physical Instructors in technical institutions be given revised pay scales as approved for corresponding positions in the University system.

3. Qualifications and Experience Requirements

The Qualifications and experience requirements are given in Annexures.*

4. Recruitment and Training

4.1 *Recruitment Procedure*

In keeping with the strong views of the Committee of the need to bring about a distinct qualitative improvements in technical education it is emphasised that recruitment to all cadre posts of technical teachers listed in Table 1 and 2 should be by open selection following advertisement in National papers and merit should be the sole criterion in making the selection.

Major initiatives are to be taken to avoid delay in the recruitment of teachers and of Lecturers in particular. The Committee recommends 2 initiatives in this direction, viz, (a) *Permitting Staff Selection Committees of Institutions to resort to campus selection process and (b) the reintroduction at the National level of Technical Teachers' Training Scheme* as detailed below.

4.2 *Technical Teachers' Training Scheme*

The objective of the Scheme should be to attract and recruit bright young technical students right at the final year level prior to graduation, give them training over a period of 2 years in pedagogical skills as well as subject advancement leading to a Master's degree and then place them as Lecturers with 2 increments in predetermined institutions. While details of the Scheme can be worked out by MHRD/AICTE, some of the elements that should be included, in the opinion of the Committee, are given below:

(i) The Scheme should be operated by MHRD/AICTE.

(ii) Recruitment and training of Lecturers in all Centrally funded institutions, including Regional Engineering Colleges, should be through this scheme.

(iii) State Governments and Government aided institutions may be persuaded to join this scheme.

---

* Annexures have not been included.

(iv) Those institutions which participate in the Scheme would place indents based on the requirements of lecturers needed 2 years into future, with a responsibility to absorb the recruit on completion of training. For such trainees, salary and allowances during training period would be paid by the concerned Government/MHRD/AICTE. At the time of selection for training itself, the trainee will be allotted the institution where he will be posted on completion of training. The allotment will be based on his choice, his merit position and the availability of posts as per indents from the various institutions.

(v) The period of training will be treated as service as "Probationary Lecturer" in the institute where he will be posted on successful completion of training. The period will count for increments and all service and pensionary benefits. Placement after successful completion of training will be automatic, without any further selection procedure.

(vi) Private institutions may be encouraged to join the Scheme, by deputing probationary lecturers selected by them for the training, on condition that they will pay the salary and allowances during the training period through the training institution.

(vii) All QIP Centres and large Post-graduate institutions may be designated as training centres with relaxation in intake capacity to accommodate the trainees.

4.3 *Selection through Campus Interview*

Recruitment through campus selection is an efficient procedure for selection of Lecturers which can be effectively resorted to by the administratively autonomous managements. Even those institutions coming under the TTT Scheme may resort to campus selection for (a) filling up vacancies in the interim period, and (b) for recruiting lecturers in areas where availability of qualified personnel is extremely low and competition from competing sectors very high. Personnel recruited through campus selection should also be required to go through the training scheme detailed above under TTTs.

4.4 *Training of Faculty*

It should be mandatory for every newly recruited lecturer (except those who come through the TTTs) to undergo 8 weeks of induction training and 8 weeks of industrial training within 2 years of joining service, and as a requirement for satisfactory completion of probation. Idealy, such training could be arranged during vacation periods. The MHRD/AICTE should institute facilities for such training and also for the short-term training in all IITs, RECs, IIMs and selected institutions in other disciplines for staff of degree level institutions and in TTTs and selected Degree level institutions for teachers of Diploma level institutions.

5. Career Advancement

The 1986 pay revision introduced Career Advancement Scheme for Lecturers to advance to Lecturer (senior scale) and Lecturer (selection grade) subject to certain conditions. Lecturer (selection grade) has the same scale of pay as that of an Assistant Professor. This Committee recommends the continuation of this Scheme with the following changes/clarifications, all other conditions remaining the same.

(i) The minimum period of regular service as Lecturer required for eligibility to be considered for selection and placement in the senior scale should be 7 years with relaxation of 2 years and 4 years respectively for those holding M.Tech and Ph.D. degrees in Engineering/Technology (1 and 3 years in Humanities and Science for M.Phil and Ph.D. degree holders).

(ii) The minimum period of regular service as Lecturer (senior-scale) required for eligibility to be considered for selection and placement as lecturer (selection grade) should be 6 years, with relaxation for M.Tech/Ph.D. degrees holders in Engineering and Technology (M.Phil/Ph.D. degree holders in Humanities and Science) as in (i) above.

(iii) The relaxation in service period for M.Tech/M.Phil/Ph.D holders given in (i) and (ii) above is limited to a maximum of 4 years for Engineering/Technology and 3 years for Humanities/Science in the entire service.

(iv) Requirement of participation in 2 refresher courses or summer institutes each of approximately 4 weeks duration may be replaced by "participation in 2 relevant and approved (by AICTE/ISTE/Government) refresher courses or summer institutes each of 2 weeks duration and training/placement in a relevant industry for a period of 3 months (in not more than 3 stretches)".

(v) Out of the 7 years of service required in (i) above, a minimum of 4 years shall be in the institution/service where he is currently employed and the balance may include outside the institution provided:

(a) Such previous service was without any break, and was at the level of lecturer or equivalent in a Higher Technological Institute. University, College (polytechnic or equivalent institution also admissible for lecturers in Diploma level institution), National Laboratory or other such Scientific/Technological organisation (such as CSIR, DRDO, AR&DC, BARC, etc) or in a relevant major industrial unit,

(b) the post was at least in an equivalent grade/scale of pay to the post of lecturer,

(c) The qualifications for the post were not lower than the qualifications prescribed by AICTE for the post of lecturer and the person concerned possessed such qualifications while holding that post,

(d) the post was filled in accordance with the prescribed selection procedures laid down by the UT/State/Central Government/relevant appointing authority,

(e) the appointment was not ad hoc or in a leave vacancy of less than one year duration.

(vi) Lecturer (selection grade) in Degree level institutions should be re-designated Assistant Professor in Degree level institution as given under:

Every Assistant Professor should be placed in the grade of Assistant Professor (senior scale) of Rs. 14,300-400-19,500 if he has:

— completed 8 years of service as Assistant Professor after regular appointment in that post or re-designation as Assistant Professor under clause (vi) above

— participated in 2 relevant and approved refresher courses or summer institutes each of 2 weeks duration during the above period.

— undergone placement in a relevant industry for a period of 6 months (in one or at least 2 stretches) after appointment/re-designation as Assistant Professor

— has consistently good performance appraisal reports.

Placement in the grade of Assistant Professor (Sr. scale) should also be through a process of selection by a Selection Committee set up by the appointing authorities and should be related to the performance appraisal reports and not be automatic and time bound.

For those placed in the higher grade under the scheme, the post held by the individual will be upgraded for the duration that it is held by him. However on the individual vacating the upgraded post, it will revert back to its original grade/scheme.

6. Merit Promotion Scheme

Prior to placement of the 1986 pay revision orders, some institutions had implemented a Merit Promotion Scheme. The 1986 pay revision gave an option to the then existing teachers in such institutions to continue to be governed by the provisions of the Scheme. However, they were given scales of pay lower than those recommended for regular appointees. As a result, it is learned, that very few, if any, have opted for this scheme and, as such, the scheme is believed to be non-existent in most institutions. With the introduction of the career advancement scheme and flexible staff structure, and the insignificant number of optees for this scheme, there is no justification left for continuing with this scheme. The AICTE may take appropriate action.

7. Job Responsibility

7.1 *Job Description*

The Committee recommends that just one responsibility list each be prescribed to describe the job responsibilities of technical teachers in Degree and Diploma level institutions. All teachers naturally can nnot be expected to be active, let alone excel, in all components of the job responsibility spectrum. However, all of them must participate in, contribute to and excel in a combination of several activities and extension segments, in addition to regular teaching work. The job responsibility list for degree and diploma level institutions are given in Annexures* 6.3 and 6.4.

It should be noted that these lists are not "all inclusive". Naturally, any other work relevant to the goals and objectives of the institution, assigned to a teacher by the Head of the institution will qualify as a job responsibility of the teacher.

7.2 *Work Load*

The Committee feels that a teacher should put in a minimum of 40 hours of work per week in the college related to his duties and responsibilities. AICTE should prepare rational norms for the teaching load (contact hours) of various level of teachers. Till

---

* Annexures have not been included.

such time, the hours of contact teaching per week should be a minimum of 10, 12, 14, and 16 for Deans and Heads of Departments, Professors, Associate and Assistant Professors, and Lecturers including Lecturer (senior scale) and Lecturer (Selection Grade) respectively. The Director/Principal/Deputy Director may have a minimum of 4 hours of contact teaching. These are essentially as per the Madan Committee norms presently in vogue. The work plan of the teachers should plan, in the most productive manner, for the utilisation of the stipulated 40 working hours per week, with regard to the roles, jobs and targets assigned to him by the Department/Institution. Teachers should be present in the institution during working hours unless engaged in official work outside.

Further, every institution should have at least 180 full working days per year (or 90 per semester) and any loss of regular working day for whatever reason should be made up by working extra hours or extra days. Since the input would be compensatory in nature, there should be no expectation of overtime or other remuneration to the faculty for this.

8. Service Conditions and Work Environment

Recommendations were made in Section 2 and 8 in respect of several critical components to the salary and service conditions of teachers. These, in particular the salary scales, qualifications and experience requirements, mode of recruitment to regular post by open selection through advertisement, training, career advancement schemes, job responsibilities and work load should be mandatory in nature and should be implemented by the State/institutions without any dilution. There are several more items pertaining to the service conditions and work environment which need improvement if the objectives of the pay revision are to be achieved. As indicated earlier, recommendations on these are presented below under 2 categories, viz, (a) other mandatory conditions and (b) additional conditions on which the state governments/institutions may have the freedom to adjust/adapt in tune with local conditions.

8.1 *Other Mandatory Conditions*

(i) DA and Other Allowances:

Centrally Funded Institutions including Regional Engineering Colleges: Dearness allowance (DA), City Compensatory Allowance (CCA), House Rent Allowance (HRA), Special Compensatory Allowance (SCA), Training Allowance, Transport Allowance and Educational Assistance should be admissible to teachers in Centrally funded institutions at the rates applicable to Central Government employees.

Similarly, teachers in Centrally funded institutions should be given Pension and other Retirement Benefits, Medical facilities, Group Insurance, all leaves and Leave encashment facilities, Leave Travel Concessions (LTC), etc. on the pattern of similar benefits available to corresponding categories of Central Government employees.

State Government/Aided institutions: Teachers in State level institutions (Government and aided) should be paid these allowances at rates applicable to Central Government Employees in the corresponding categories of the State Government employees.

Self Financing Institutions: Self financing institutions should provide DA and other Allowances, Medical Facilities/Group Health insurance, Leaves and Leave encashment facilities, Pension and other retirement Benefits (GPF-cum-Pension-cum-Gratuity Scheme or CPF-cum-Gratuity Scheme) and Group Insurance at rates not lower than those available to teachers (or corresponding employees) in the respective State Government Service.

(ii) Superannuation and Re-employment

The age of superannuation of all teachers in technical institutions should be 62 years, with provision of re-employment up to 65 years in deserving cases after careful evaluation of individual merit and institution's requirements. For this purpose strict, transparent and comprehensive evaluation criteria should be prescribed.

(iii) Advance increments

The provision for granting of 2/4 advance increments to Lecturers who possess Master/Doctorate Degrees in Engineering/Technology (1/3 increments for MPhil/PhD Degrees in Science and Humanities) respectively at the time of their recruitment as Lecturer (both in Degree level and Diploma level institutions) should be continued. Similarly, the provision for giving service weightage of 2/4 years (1/3 years for Science and Humanities stream) for Lecturers for placement in Lecturer (Senior Scale) and Lecturer (Selection Grade) should be continued.

(iv) Reimbursement of Expenditure on Books and Journals, Professional Society Membership Fee and TA/DA for attending Conferences:

Teachers should be reimbursed:

(a) 85 per cent of the cost of books/journals relevant to the work of the teacher up to a maximum reimbursement limit of Rs. 3000 per annum.

(b) 85 per cent of annual membership fee of one International/National professional society in their field of specialization/work, and

(c) 100 per cent of expense for registration and TA/DA for presenting papers in one national conference every year and one international conference every 3 years.

(v) TA Rules

TA/DA rules should be in accordance with Central/State Governments rules for Central/State level institutions respectively.

(vi) Sabbatical Leave

Teachers should be eligible for one year of sabbatical leave after every 6 years of service, for carrying out academic or industry related work outside the institution. Alternatively they should be eligible for deputation for appointments outside the institution for a maximum of one year for every completed 5 years of service.

(vii) Consultancy and Testing Services

Consultancy and testing services by faculty should be encouraged with liberal norms for sharing of income therefrom.

(viii) Remote Area Allowances

Many of the newer technical institutions are located in remote and/ or rural areas where teachers are generally reluctant to serve. To attract teachers to such institutions and to partly offset their hardships, teachers in such institutions should be given a suitable Remote Area Allowances. The nature and quantum of such allowance may be worked out by the respective State Governments depending on local conditions. Such allowances should be in lieu of Special Compensatory allowance as recommended by V CPC.

8.2 *Additional Conditions*

The following benefits should be applicable for Central Government institutions and are suggested for adoption by State level and other institutions also unless similar or better benefits are already existing.

(i) House Building Advance and advance for Purchase of Vehicles at rates applicable to Central/State Government employees.

(i) Reimbursement of 50 per cent of cost of purchase of a Personal Computer, limited to a maximum reimbursement of Rs. 20,000 once in the entire service. Should the teacher leave the institution within 3 years of the receipt of this amount, the same would have to be paid back to the institution.

(iii) Housing within or near the campus at rates of rent and norms applicable to Central/State Government employees.

(iv) Easy access to communication facilities such a Telephone, Fax, e-mail and Internet connection, and secretarial assistance with facilities for word processing, DTP, etc.

(v) Reasonable opportunities to better their qualifications. The Madan Committee norms have been worked out on the basis of provision of 10 per cent of cadre strength as leave and training reserve. The Committee therefore recommends that at any time, up to 10 per cent of the faculty strength be deputed for higher studies/training and qualification improvement. Such deputees should be paid their full salary and allowances during the period of such deputations, subject to appropriate conditions/bonds.

9. Performance Appraisal and Accountability

The Committee recommends that the following steps be implemented as an integral and essential part of the pay revision package.

1. The institution should define its mission, long-term and short-term goals and objectives, and corresponding operational plans.
2. Each individual teacher should prepare a work plan at the beginning of each year in respect of the various roles assigned to him by the Department/Institution in consultation with him. In assigning roles, it should be ensured that (i) each teacher has a judicious mix of jobs from all of the major sectors of job spectrum, viz, Instruction related, Research and Consultancy related. Extension service related and Administration and Management related, (ii) all projected activities of the Department and Institution are fully covered collectively by the faculty as a whole, and (iii) a teacher puts in a minimum of 40 hours of work per week.

3. The department/Institution should assign attainable targets in respect of various roles/jobs and associated activities included in the work plan. Wherever possible, the targets should be quantified.
4. A simple system of reporting at the end of every academic year in the form of feedback should be introduced. The format for this should include all components of the role spectrum, the assigned targets in respect of each item and the targets actually achieved (with reasons for shortfall, if any).
5. A suitable system for an objective Instructor and Course Evaluation (ICES) by the students towards the end of every semester (twice in a year where the annual system is followed) should be introduced.
6. A peer group consisting of at least 3 members including the Head of the Department concerned (the 2 other members being from faculty, nominated by the Head of the Institution/ Vice-Chancellor in the case of University) should evaluate at the end of year feedback data and the student evaluation (ICES) summary result, have discussions with the teacher concerned and record their assessment. They should also assign a Performance Evaluation Score (PES) on a 10 point scale, which will be shown to the teacher concerned. Based on this evaluation the group should also advise the teacher concerned and the Department/Institution regarding follow-up/corrective actions, if any, to be taken.

   [*Note*: in the case of Heads of Departments/Deans, the peer group may consist of the Head of the Institution and 2 Heads of other departments/ Deans, nominated by the Head of the Institution, provided that such nominees are rotated from year to year].

7. The Institution should set up a suitable grievance redressal mechanism to examine and settle complaints, if any.
8. The performance appraisal score should be used to take decisions regarding the Staff Development needs, rewards

and advancement. This score should be one of the components considered in the matter of selection of staff, both by open selection and through career advancement schemes.

It is recognised that there may have to be slight variations in the appraisal formats depending on the type and stage of development of the institution. However, the principles behind the process should be made uniformly applicable.

10. Consultancy

The Committee makes the following recommendations:

1. Institutions should actively encourage and support the faculty in taking up consultancy (and testing) work. The teachers should actively liaise with industry to attract projects, particularly those which have elements of industry problem-solving, student involvement and educative values.
2 There need not be any limit on the quantum of consultancy work a teacher can take up or the remuneration he can earn, so long as this is done with the concurrence of the Competent Authority and without prejudice to the other duties and, responsibilities of the teacher or to the interest of the institution and the students. While working out the fees/charges for carrying out the consultancy project, suitable methods of estimation should be used. These would include either:

 (a) Fixing a percentage of the total cost of the project, as in the case of Architectural projects, Structural Engineering design projects, etc., or
 (b) Estimates worked out on the basis of required man-hour input at different levels and expenditure to be incurred on purchase of materials, use of outside labour, use of outside consultants, computer charges, etc.

Suitable charges for overheads up to 10 per cent should be added to the cost estimated as above, to cover indirect costs such as use of electricity, building space, stationery, etc. This amount should go to the revenue account of the institution.

3. There are 2 major types of consultancy assignments generally undertaken by faculty. Type-I involves participation of a teacher or group of teachers who use institutional infrastructure facilities such as workshop, laboratories, computers, etc. for the work. Type-II involves participation of teacher(s) without using any institutional infrastructure. In both cases, there generally is some direct expenditure involved consisting of purchase of material, use of outside labour/expertise, etc.

4. A suggested pattern for the sharing of the net revenue (after meeting all expenses and remitting the 10% overhead to the revenue account of the institution) from consultancy work is as given below:

Consultancy Project of Type-I

(a) 50 per cent to the Development Fund of the Institution

(b) 50 per cent to be shared by the team involved with the work including supporting staff

Consultancy Project of Type-II

(a) 30 per cent to the Development Fund of the Institution

(b) 70 per cent to be shared by the team involved with the work

5. The Development Fund share should be placed at the disposal of the Head of the Institution for use towards the development of the institution and its facilities, subject to normal procedures.

6. The disbursement of all the remuneration should be the responsibility of the Head of the Institution. To facilitate

this, the requirement in some Government Institutes to have the revenue deposited in the treasury first should be done away with. Such a requirement should be only with respect to the 10 per cent share going to the revenue account.

11. Special Benefits to Women Teachers

The V CPC has recommended a series of measures to benefit women employees. This Committee fully endorses these. In particular, the Committee recommends that women teachers in technical institutions be extended the special benefits as given below:

11.1 *Part-time Employment*

Option may be given for a woman teacher to work half-time for a maximum period of 6 years in her career, connected with 2 child-rearing periods, at half the salaries, with such period counting for all service benefits.

11.2 *Day-Care Centres*

Day-Care Centres may be provided in the Campus to take care of very young children of working parents. Such services should be run on a shared cost basis jointly by the beneficiaries and the institution.

11.3 *Interrupted Career*

Provision may be made for a woman teacher to interrupt her career for a minimum of 5 years for the purpose of child-caring and to come back to the profession, without the period being counted as a break in service.

11.4 *Accommodation*

In providing campus accommodation, some quarters/rooms in faculty hostels may be earmarked for women teachers.

11.5 *Other Benefits*

Apart from the above, all other special benefits extended to women employees in the Government as recommended by the V CPC may be extended to women teachers in technical institutions.

12. Tax on Income

We have brought out in earlier Chapters, *the need for a significantly better package for technical teachers.* However, for practical reasons, we have had to recommend pay scales which are much more modest than what the industry pays for comparable personnel. The Committee feels that the effective way to offset the differential is to offer tax concessions. Hence, the Committee recommends that *all allowances, consultancy revenue and pensions of teachers of technical institutions be made tax exempt.* In this, the Committee was guided by the same principles which have been followed by V CPC in recommending tax concessions for Central Governments employees.

13. Corpus Fund

Many of the activities related to maintaining excellence in the institutions suffer due to the very common problem of imbalance between Grants and Revenue and Expenditure. In such situations, naturally, unavoidable expenses such as salary get priority and items such as sponsorship for conferences and technical presentations, reimbursement of cost of books, etc. get abandoned. To protect academic interests and provide some flexibility in such situations, it is desirable that institutions build up a Development Fund or Corpus Fund to fall back on. Various models do exist for such Funds in this country. The Committee recommends that AICTE take necessary steps for the building up of such funds in all technical institutions.

14. Effective date for Implementation

The Committee recommends that the dates of implementation of the revised pay scales and associated conditions of service of Technical Teachers, as recommended above, be synchronized with those of V Central Pay Commission recommendations.

15. Quality Improvement Scheme

The MHRD/AICTE should substantially increase the number of positions available for higher studies under QIP, particularly for the PhD degree. The QIP should be extended to cover polytechnics (for MTech or equivalent programme) and also the disciplines not presently covered such as Management, Pharmacy, etc.

16. Monitoring of Implementation

The desired results of the pay revision will not be achieved if the crucial recommendations are not implemented on a time-bound basis and without dilution. This has been demonstrated by the review of the 1986 pay revision implementation. In order to ensure that some mistakes are not repeated again, the Committee feels that a formal mechanism should be set up by the MHRD/AICTE for monitoring and enforcing the implementation. This set-up can also resolve the anomalies, doubts and problems which are bound to crop up in the process of implementation of any pay revision.

***Source**: University Today*, November, 1997.

19

Committee of Ministers on Making Elementary Education a Fundamental Rights (1997)

A Committee headed by Minister of State for Human Resource Development Muhi Ram Saikia, was constituted by the Ministry of Human Resource Development to examine and consider the legal, academic, administrative and financial implications of the proposal to amend the Constitution to make the right to free and compulsory elementary education a fundamental rights, presented its report to the Government on January 24, 1997.

Significant Recommendations

State Governments should consider levying an education cess so as to raise revenues and augment their resources for education and improving facilities in schools.

This recommendation comes in the light of the Committee's estimate that an additional Rs. 40,000 crore will be required to implement the proposal to amend the Constitution as to make free and compulsory elementary education a fundamental right.

The Committee also suggests that an explicit provision should be made in the Constitution to make it a fundamental duty of every citizen who is a parent to provide opportunities for educa tion of all children up to 14 years.

Since the education is a State subject, the report said there is no need to enact a Central legislation making elementary education compulsory. Instead states should either amend their existing legislation or else the Centre should issue guidelines providing a broad framework for enactment of fresh legislation on compulsory elementary education.

As regards the additional funding, the report suggests the Finance Ministry and the Planning Commission evolve an appropriate formula with the State Governments to share the additional resources needed to implement the proposal. It also said that the Centre and the State Governments allocate 50 per cent of budgetary allocations for education to elementary education and ensure that the funds so allocated are not reappropriated or diverted to any other sector.

While suggesting that each state formulate its own approach on education in keeping with the local situation, the report says to ensure uniformity, free elementary education may include exemption from tuition fee, provision of free textbooks for all primary school children and girls upto upper primary level and provision of essential stationery to all children in primary classes.

According to the Committee, the legislation to be enacted by the States should provide for "permissive compulsion to enable state governments and local governments to enforce the law selectively in a phased manner."

Source: The Times of India, January 27, 1997

20

Delhi University Committee on Law Admissions (1997)

The 5-member Executive Council Committee on admissions to the 1st year of LL.B. course at Delhi University headed by Om Prakash, submitted the report on August 28, 1997.

Excerpts

The committee noted that the Prospectus of the Law Faculty for 1997 stipulated that "subject to other provisions of this Prospectus, all admissions, except foreign nationals covered under rule (ii)..., will be strictly accordingly to the merit.....keeping in view the preference of the Law Centre given by the candidates....The Committee also noted that the Prospectus did provide for a change at any stage in the candidates' preferences as originally given.... This means that once the candidate has indicated his/her preference ranking, it cannot be changed.....

"....The Committee notes that its suggestions were not acceptable to the relevant officers of the Faculty of Law. On August 5, 1997, Prof. S.N. Singh writing on behalf of the Admission Committee wrote back saying that the "allotment of a Law Centre falls squarely within the jurisdiction of the Admission Committee which has statutory powers and no other body/Committee has any power to interfere with the decision of the Admission Committee". He further states, "the Admission Committee is under no obligation to consult any external authority about the admissions and it will take its own decisions".... A letter was also received from the Professor-in-charge of Law Centre dated August 4, 1997.... A letter from the Dean, Faculty of Law, dated August 5, 1997 noted that " I hope the decisions of the Committee will be honoured by all concerned" but at the same time added that "as regards the Admission Committee of the Faculty of Law, there is not much that it has to do"....

Since the students' complaints continued, the Committee decided that it could examine the changes in order of preferences and other matters only by looking at the original Application and Entrance Test Application Forms and other documents in the possession of Dean, Faculty of Law...

Nature of Grievances Received till July 29, 1997

1. Cases where admission slips were denied to candidates otherwise eligible for admission because:

   (a) the students' last qualifying degree was from a university hitherto recognised by the University of Delhi, but which changed its name; or

   (b) the results of the qualifying degree from Delhi University had not been declared.

2. Students had been issued the admission slips but in whose cases the Professor-in-charge concerned had refused to let them deposit their fees on the ground that their preferences as per the Entrance Test Application Form had been altered. This meant that they automatically missed the last date for payment of fees. Such candidates claimed that many other candidates in a similar situation had been allowed to deposit their fees...

Findings

Application Forms

The Committee was shocked to note that the Entrance Test Application Form... and the Main Law Faculty Application Form...

had been treated in an extremely casual and cavalier fashion by both the Candidates and the authorities of the Faculty of Law. Candidates had often not supplied the information required in the two forms...

Though information could with some effort be gathered from other places...., the office never cared to fill it in where it should have been... What is striking is that.... the form is not signed by any member or the convenor. It simply bears the fascimile rubber stamp of the signatures of the Dean. This stamp (or often even the signatures elsewhere of various Law Faculty functionaries – a very rare phenomenon) rarely indicates the date on which it was put. The Main Application Form provides column where the eligibility and choice of the candidate have to be verified. It also provides columns for the cashier and section officer where details of class roll number, amount of fees received and receipt number and date should be filled in. Once again, in most cases this has not been done and it is very rare that a cashier or a section officer has signed at the appropriate places. Given the above facts, it is impossible for the Committee to match the date of admission of a given student with the publication of the cut-off marks. In these circumstances, how does one determine whether a student was not admitted before the date he should have been?

Irregularities

We examined in detail 1398 forms. The centre-wise breakdown is given below:

Law Centre I :	581
Law Centre II:	354
Campus Law Centre:	463
Total:	**1398**

The nature of irregularities may be seen in Table 20.1 below:

Table 20.1: Irregularities (Faculty of Law Admissions, 1997)

Irregularity	LC-I	LC-II	CLC	Total
Preferences changed	234	21	28	283
Preferences violated	16	1	5	22
Preferences repeated	7	14	6	27
Preferences repeated and changed	6	5	2	13
Preference sheet missing	–	–	2	2
Rank-related problem	–	–	2	2
Photographs different (?)	–	–	1	1
Photo and sign different (?)	1	–	–	1
Result awaited but admitted	4	–	7	11
Total	268	41	56	365

The magnitude of irregularities noticed in the above table is indeed enormous. In addition to the problem already enumerated ... 365 (above 26%) of the 1398 forms examined showed the kind of irregularities listed in the above Table 20.1. The 22 cases listed under 'preference violation' category could have easily gone to the centre of their choice. Yet they were admitted to another centre without any authorization from the Dean, Faculty of Law. In 323 cases, the choice has been changed and/or repeated. In some cases, these alterations are signed by the candidate. The question is: why and by whom were changes allowed and what are the implications of these changes in terms of causing disadvantage to some other students in the process? Further, most changes of preference are from CLC to LC-I or LC-II. CLC admits candidates who are not employed. Most candidates who opt for LC-I or LC-II initially may have been employed persons. To the extent CLC candidates were shifted to LC-I or LC-II, the employed candidates who gave LC-I or LC-II as their first choice may have failed to secure a place and pursue a professional course while working. The question-marks in Table 20.1 against certain categories indicate that they should perhaps be examined by experts in the relevant field e.g. handwriting experts. In 2 cases, how could admissions be made when the Entrance Form showing preferences, rank, marks, etc was missing? The 2 cases involving rank-order problems could also be serious. For example, in one case if we are to believe the rank order clearly written on both the forms, the candidate concerned gets an advantage of 80 ranks.

Observations

We feel that the admission procedure adopted by the Faculty of Law had not been clear, consistent and uniform and it may have resulted in avoidable discrimination against some students. We have noticed a variety of incosistencies, e.g.

(a) It is not clear to us what were the motivations and rationale for deciding cut-off points for different centres.

(b) If both merit and order of preference were to be respected simultaneously as laid down in the Faculty Prospectus, how could it be achieved without actually announcing a detailed Merit List separately for each centre? No Merit List was ever published. Only the cut-off points were announced.

(c) How could students be admitted without the signatures of the Dean? A fascimile rubber stamp is likely to be misused.

(d) Most of the forms from LC-I and LC-II do not bear the details of fee received and the signatures of the cashier.

(e) The change of centre appears to have been allowed in the most arbitrary manner. According to the prospectus, there is no provision for change in the order of preference originally given. Even if at any stage, a decision to allow the change of preference was taken by the Faculty, this inform-ation should have been notified for the benefit of all the candidates so that nobody would have been discriminated against. A change of centre, given limited number of seats at each centre, may result in serious discrimination and violation of individual rights. If a student with a higher merit is allowed to change to a centre with a lower merit cut-off, the student who was otherwise eligible for that centre and had marked it as his 1st preference may not find a place there at all. This process will also automatically create a vacancy at the centre with the higher cut-off marks which might eventually lead to lowering of the cut-off marks at that centre.

(f) It is not clear to us why the change of centre bearing the stamp of the Dean was accepted by the Centre Incharges in some cases but not in others.

Source: *University Today,* 15 September, 1997.

21

UGC Committee to Review the Pay Scales of University and College Teachers (1997)

CHAPTER 1

Constitution

The University Grants Commission appointed a Pay Review Committee vide Office Memorandum No.3-1/94 (PS) dated 24th August, 1994 with the following members:

1.	Prof. R.P. Rastogi, Former Vice-Chancellor Banaras Hindu University, Varanasi.	Chairman
2.	Prof. V.C. Kulandaiswamy Former Vice-Chancellor Indira Gandhi National Open University New Delhi.	Member
3.	Prof. D.P. Barooah Former Vice-Chancellor Guwahati University, Guwahati.	Member
4.	Prof.(Mrs.) Kanta Ahuja Former Vice-Chancellor Maharshi Dayanand Saraswati University Ajmer	Member

5. Sh. N. Parthasarthy, IARS — Member
Joint Secretary and Financial Adviser
DARE and ICAR
Representative of Ministry of Finance,
New Delhi.

6. A representative of Deptt. of — Member
Education, Ministry of Human
Resource Development
New Delhi (Not below the rank of
joint Secretary)

7. Secretary, UGC — Member Secretary

The Committee was expanded vide Office Memorandum No. 3-1/94(PS) dated 30th August, 1994, by including the following members:

8. Sister Romana Fernandes — Member
Principal
St. Francis College for Women
Begumpet
Hyderabad - 500 016.

9. Dr. Prithipal Singh Kapur — Member
Formerly Pro Vice-Chancellor
of Guru Nanak Dev University and Principal
Gujranwala Guru Nanak Khalsa College
Ludhiana - 141 001, Punjab.

10. Sh. Q.A. Saeed — Member
Principal
Burhani College of Commerce and Arts
Neisbit Road, Mazagaon, Bombay-400 010

Terms of Reference

(i) To review the implementation of the previous decisions of the Government/University Grants Commission under the scheme of Revision of Pay Scales approved for University and college teachers, Librarians, Directors of Physical Education and Registrars of Universities and in the process, to evaluate the extent to which the earlier recommendations in relation to qualifications, service conditions, pay scales, etc. have been implemented.

(ii) To examine the present structure of emoluments and conditions of service of university and college teachers, Librarians, Directors of Physical Education and Registrars of universities, taking into account the total package of benefits available to them (such as superannuation benefits, medical, housing facilities, etc.)

(iii) To make recommendations on the above having regard to the need for improving the quality of education, the necessity of attracting and retaining talented persons in the teaching profession and advancement opportunities to the above categories of persons. It was also stated that the Committee should make its final recommendations in the light of the recommendations of the Fifth Central Pay Commission and the advice of the Pay Review Committee should be in harmony with the recommendations of the Central Pay Commission.

Time Schedule

The Committee was initially appointed for a term of one year but its term was extended till 31st May, 1997, since the recommendations of the Fifth Central Pay Commission were finalised only on 30th January, 1997.

Pay Scales and Service Conditions:
A Retrospective Overview

CHAPTER III

3.1 Introduction

The subject of pay scales and service conditions of teachers in universities and colleges has been receiving due attention of the Government of India ever since Independence. Teachers deservedly constitute the most important component of any educational structure. Providing emoluments and service conditions commensurate with the role of teachers in the development process has, therefore, been a major policy concern of the University Grants Commission – an institution established in 1956 for the promotion and coordination of university education as well as for the determination and maintenance of standards of teaching, examination and research in the universities across the country. Successive Education Commissions and Committees appointed by the Government of India and UGC have, therefore, gone into these aspects in detail. This chapter provides a brief overview of the recommendations made by various Commissions and Committees on different aspects of recruitment.

3.2 Qualification of Teachers

3.2.1 The Radhakrishnan Commission was appointed in 1948 by the Government of India to report on "Indian university education and suggest improvements and extensions that may be desirable to suit the present and future requirements of the country." In doing so, the Commission also dealt with qualifications of teachers. According to the Commission, the gradation of university teachers should be based on experience, scholarship, research and teaching ability. A professor who was given the highest grade among the academics was expected to have a combination of all these at the highest level. In the opinion of the Commission, a Professor should have taught the higher classes for a considerable number of years and established reputation for scholarship. Not just that, he should have wide interest and a broad outlook to inspire and stimulate his colleagues in the department and effectively contribute to the solution of academic problems of the university. It was pointed out that the expected age when these qualifications are fulfilled is likely to be 48 years. For the post of the Reader, the Radhakrishnan Commission recommended a research degree and published research work in recognised well-established journals as the required qualifications. A person of 35 years should be able to fulfil these conditions. For the post of the Lecturer, the Commission recommended a first-class academic record as a necessary qualification with some teaching experience as a desirable qualification. Further, a Lecturer should have started as a research scholar or a fellow and preferably should have completed his Ph.D. He should be able to command the respect of his pupils and should have empathy, tact and sense of vocation.

3.2.3 The Education Commission appointed in 1964 under the Chairmanship of Prof. D.S.Kothari, Chairman, UGC was expected to advise the Government on the national pattern of education and on the general principles and policies for the development of education at all stages and in all respects.

The Sen Committee (1973) on the governance of universities and colleges, recommended that 'a Master's degree alone would not suffice for the selection of a Lecturer.' It, therefore, recommended higher teaching/research/ advanced study beyond Master's degree as essential qualifications for recruitment. This was considered basic to improvement of standards. An M.Phil or a Ph.D was, therefore, recommended for appointment.

3.2.4 The National Commission on Teachers for Higher Education (NCT, 1983) under the chairmanship of Prof. Rais Ahmed endorsed the minimum qualifications of teachers prescribed by the UGC in 1973, on the basis of the Sen Committee recommendations with further insistence on good academic record, evidence of research capabilities in addition to a research degree and pedagogic skills to be added to the qualifications for appointment. The NCT was of the view that the candidates' academic performance should be given greater weightage than any other factor at the time of their first appointment.

3.2.5 The Mehrotra Committee, constituted in 1983 by the UGC was specifically asked to examine and recommend a structure of emoluments and conditions of service of university and college teachers "keeping in view the necessity of attracting and retaining talented persons in the teaching profession." The Committee found that the stipulation of M.Phil/Ph.D as an essential qualification for Lecturers had neither been followed faithfully nor did it necessarily contribute to the raising of teaching and research standards. In fact, it was of the view that, if at all, it had led to the dilution of research standards on account of the rush to get a research degree in the shortest possible time. In view of this as well as of the fact that 10+2 pattern of schooling had led to an additional year of college study, the Committee recommended a good M.A./M.Sc./M.Com. or equivalent degree as the minimum qualification for a Lecturer. A research degree should be necessary only for career advancement.

3.2.6 The Mehrotra Committee recommended that additional increments be sanctioned to research degree holders at the time of selection as Lecturers to give due recognition to their research experience. It is expected that this could attract bright young persons to the teaching profession. However, in view of the diversity of standards among universities, the Mehrotra Committee recommended that passing a national qualifying examination before recruitment be made an essential pre-condition.

3.3 Process of Recruitment

3.3.1 The process of recruitment and selection is a crucial aspect of ensuring the appointment of competent persons as teachers. Implicit in the recommendations of the Radhakrishnan Committee is the view that all appointments will be through a process of selection laid down by the universities.

3.3.2 The Kothari Commission made explicit recommendations about the process of recruitment/selection. The suggestions of the Commission merit mention in some detail.

3.3.3 It made a general suggestion about qualification by saying that, it should search for talent among the most outstanding and promising Ph.Ds, M.A.s and M.Sc.s; it was also suggested that even brilliant nascent graduates be identified and groomed for appointment as university teachers. The Commission also recommended the selection of teachers at national or even international level instead of being limited to the state or the region and proposed advance increments for deserving candidates besides giving them assistance for research and opportunities for study-leave to enable them achieve higher professional excellence. It suggested that while making appointments and deciding on promotions, there should be room for flexibility to take care of persons of exceptional promise and performance. It is only inspired teachers – found, rewarded and planted firmly in the class-rooms – who could and undoubtedly would give the universities and colleges a new lustre, "built on the mysterious moments when mind confronts mind and a student suddenly senses the power and richness of his own intellect".

3.3.4 The Sen Committee visualised the following three modes of appointment:

(a) Open recruitment where the vacancies are advertised and the selection is made on all-India basis.

(b) Appointment after at least 6 years of service on the basis of outstanding work.

(c) Promotion after reaching the maximum of the scale.

The selection under categories (b) and (c) above is to be made through a centralised machinery in each state, to be set up for all the universities on a statutory basis.

The Mehrotra Committee did not make specific recommendations in this regard excepting appointment through a process of career advancement. These are discussed in the next section.

3.4 Career and Professional Development

3.4.1 The Radhakrishnan Commission (1948) in its recommendations emphasised that security of tenure and reasonable prospects of advancement are essential to maintaining the health and tone of a service. It was of the opinion that the ratio between the senior and junior positions of teachers, viz, of Professors and Readers on the one hand and Lecturers and Instructors on the other should be 1:2. A teacher entering the profession at the age of 22 or 23 as an Instructor or a Fellow could become a Lecturer at the age of 25-26 after he obtained some training as a teacher and also got an opportunity for scholarship and acquired a research degree. By the time he reached the maximum of the Lecturer grade, he would have acquired sufficient experience and standing to be eligible for a Readership and could rise to a Professor's position at about 48 years of age provided that he accepted the challenge of open competition. In short, the view was that in the interest of the university as well as of the teacher, there should be opportunities for career advancement but only through selection in open competition.

3.4.2 The Sen Committee recommended that a Lecturer/Reader after completing six years of service should be permitted to offer himself for higher position on the basis of his qualification and work. The higher scale of a Reader/

Professor should be given to him only after his assessment by a duly constituted selection committee of the university. The promotion in such a case should be regarded as personal promotion. If not selected at the time of first assessment, he could offer himself again for assessment but only after a lapse of three years. This proposal envisaged that there should be no limit to the number of posts of Readers and Professors within the total sanctioned strength of the department. The Committee, however, recommended that the workload should be so arranged that it would not involve the appointment of any additional staff while making possible the promotion of the existing staff.

3.4.3 Although the Committee was not in favour of introducing the system of confidential report as in Government services, it recommended annual evaluation of a teacher through an assessment of academic programmes proposed by the teacher himself or herself in the beginning of the session and of the work done by him or her by the end of the session. A suitable procedure for proper evaluation of the teacher would have to be evolved by the UGC. The most significant recommendation of the Committee was that teachers having similar qualifications, whether working in a university or a college, should have similar scale of pay. It also recommended sanctioning of posts of Readers and Professors in selected colleges on the basis of prescribed criteria with the provision that the persons appointed to these posts would have the same criteria as those applicable to the university teachers.

3.4.4 The National Commission on Teachers in Higher Education (NCT) while reiterating the importance of adequate and suitable opportunities for professional and career development, cautioned against using seniority as a proxy for merit. Instead, it suggested that the merit of the teacher should be assessed in terms of func-tions defined for teachers. To enable such an assessment to be made, the focus would be on maintaining a continuous record of the work of a teacher, and for this, a suitable proforma to be filled in by the teacher himself would be devised which took into account the various functions performed by a teacher. These would include teaching, research, extension and administration. This self-evaluation record should be a record for every semester/academic year and submitted to the head of the department who would record his assessment on the same proforma. Other sources of evaluation such as student assessment and peer assessment should also be recorded in the same record. The NCT emphasised that professional development be linked to career advancement. For this, facilities needed to be increased and a better coordination among organisations like UGC, Indian Council for Social Science Research, Indian Council of Agricultural Research, Department of Science and Technology and the Indian Council for Historical Research was to be achieved so that facilities provided by them were optimally utilised. Leave and travel facilities were to be made available to teachers for participation in various programmes of professional development.

3.4.5 The Mehrotra Committee for the first time proposed a comprehensive scheme of career advancement along with creation of facilities for the professional development of teachers. This was to be achieved through orientation programmes for new teachers and refresher courses for teachers in general. New courses to be introduced by the Indira Gandhi National Open University to encourage continuous self-learning process amongst teachers, participation of teachers in seminars, symposia and conferences and provision of adequate facilities to teachers for study leave to pursue M.Phil./ Ph.D programmes formed part of the comprehensive recommendations of the Committee. Various modes of performance evaluation of teachers which would assist them in self improvement and career development were suggested. The suggested modes were evaluation by the students, self-appraisal by the teachers themselves and evaluation by seniors in the institutions and peers in the discipline.

3.5 Quality of Education

3.5.1 All the Commissions/Committee have stressed the need for continuously maintaining highest standards of teaching and examination. At the same time it was required that the teacher and the academic system should be made accountable. In this context, emphasis was laid on maintaining a suitable academic calendar providing for a specified minimum number of working days. The Radhakrishnan Commission (1948) suggested that a minimum number of 180 working days, exclusive of examination days, be ensured in every university and college. Further, each day of work should be utilised to its maximum. It also advocated some check on teachers who did not fulfil their obligations to engage in research to keep themselves up-to-date knowledge wise. Further, tutorials and seminars must be given as much importance as class-room lecturers.

3.5.2 The Kothari Commission on the other hand advocated reduction in formal teaching and library hours and increase in guided, independent study by the students in the form of writing of essays, solving problems and undertaking of small research projects in which the students would seek out and learn how to use books and documents on their own. The content and quality of lectures in general also needed to be improved. One way of monitoring the level of class work was to ensure that one hour of class-room instruction required from the student about 3-4 hours study for proper understanding and grasp of the subject. Improvements in teaching methods and techniques of evaluation were also to receive attention through a composite programme of seminars, discussions and workshops.

3.5.3 The Sen Committee recommended that the period of probation for teachers in no case should be more than 24 months. The workload of all university and college teachers should be the same and not less than 40 hours a week of work that should include preparation for teaching, actual class-room teaching, correction and examination work, research, tutorials and guidance to students, as well as co-curricular activities, administrative and professional work, etc.

3.6 Accountability

3.6.1 The Mehrotra Committee acknowledged that in order to attain excellence in the sphere of teaching, research and extension work, an environment of autonomy and freedom was essential for the universities. An average workload of approximately 15 hours of formal teaching per week was expected from them. It was assumed that besides the regular teaching, the teachers would devote their working hours to preparation for teaching assignments, research towards advancement of knowledge and participation in extension work. However, taking into account those teachers who were taking their work rather lightly and not working for prescribed hours, the Committee was of the view that adequate ways and means should be evolved for professional and career development of teachers along with the systematic evaluation of their performance. The Committee endorsed the UGC's decision regarding working days and workload of the teachers (like 180 days per year and 40 hours a week). It recommended that, "eighteen periods a week including tutorial classes is the minimum that any teacher should be required to do. Those who are in charge of Master's degree classes and have to guide research students should have between 12 and 15 periods".

3.7 Pay Scales of Teachers

3.7.1 The Radhakrishnan Commission (1948) recommended a three-tier structure for each of three different levels namely, the universities, postgraduates colleges and undergraduate colleges. Higher scales of pay were recommended for the university teachers. The designation of Reader and Professor was limited to university teachers only.

It suggested that the multiplicity of scales of pay should be reduced to the minimum and that an attempt should be made to adopt uniform scales of pay for the entire category of teachers engaged in higher education.

The Commission also recommended that Special Professors might be appointed for a definite term not exceeding five years on a fixed pay of Rs. 1,500 p.m.

3.7.2 During the Second Plan period (1956-61), UGC introduced higher pay scales and recommended the schemes for government colleges. While forwarding its recommendations to Government of India, the Commission proposed that the increased cost be shared between the Centre and State Government in the ratio of 80:20 in the case of universities and 50:50 in the case of colleges. However, these were introduced only in a few places as the State Governments in General did not accept the UGC recommendations.

3.7.3 During the Third plan period (1961-66), the scales of pay were once again revised and recommended for introduction at the university level provided that they agreed to take over the its responsibility at the end of the plan period. For college teachers, no further revision was recommended. However, the benefits of Second Plan scheme were extended to those colleges which had not been covered earlier.

3.7.4 The Kothari Commission's recommendations retained the three-tier structure as well the distinction in pay scales of college and university teachers and the distinction in the designations of college and university teachers.

3.7.4.1 The Kothari Commission strongly affirmed the critical role of teachers in maintaining and improving the standard of higher education. It expressed the view that the "remuneration of teachers should be broadly comparable with that of the senior services of the Government so that a fair proportion of the top talent in the country is attracted to the profession of teaching and research; and that the maximum salary of a University Professor should be the same as the maximum in the senior scale of the IAS and for outstanding

Professors, higher salaries comparable to super-time scale of pay of the IAS should be available."

3.7.4.2 The Commission recommended that the proportion of Lecturers in the senior scale to those in the junior scale should be progressively improved. By the end of the Fifth Plan, this proportion should on an average be raised to about 75 per cent.

3.7.4.3 Further, the Commission noted that proportion of junior (i.e. Instructor and Lecturer) to senior posts (i.e. Reader to Professor) was about 3:1 (the corresponding ratio for affiliated colleges was 5:1). It recommended that this ratio should gradually move to 2:1.

3.7.4.4 One-third of the Professors who were exceptionally meritorious persons, should be placed in the senior scale and in selected centres of advanced studies.

3.7.4.5 The Kothari Commission recommended that the teachers' salaries be reviewed every five years and that the dearness allowance paid to teachers should be the same as paid to government servants.

3.7.4.6 During the Fourth Plan period (1969-74), the Government accepted the recommendation made by the UGC on the basis of the Kothari Commission regarding revision of scales of pay for teachers and agreed to provide assistance from non-plan funds. The pay scales were made effective from 1st April, 1966.

3.7.4.7 After the Fourth Five-Year Plan, the question of pay revision was taken up by the Sen Committee and the Mehrotra Committee. A brief account of their recommendations is as follows:

3.7.5 The Sen Committee made for reaching recommendations on the pay structure. The recommendations made earlier by the UGC to the State Government were not implemented uniformly in all states. Disparities in dearness allowance and pay scales between the Central and the State Universities continued to persist. The Sen Committee's recommendations are important not only because of the improved scales recommended by it but because of its emphatic recommendation that there should be no difference in the pay scales of university and college teachers. A three-tier structure was recommended for universities. For colleges, there was only one scale of a Lecturer and scales equivalent to that of a University Reader or Professor were recommended for Principals of colleges only.

3.7.5.1 The scales were to be implemented with effect from January 1, 1973. The Central Government was to provide 80 per cent of the additional cost involved in pay revision. To provide promotional avenues to teachers, it was recommended that the proportion of senior posts (Professor and Reader) to Lecturer be kept at 1:2.

3.7.5.2 In the light of the recommendations made by the Sen Committee and the UGC, the Government of India, in 1974 determined the scales of pay for the universities and affiliated colleges.

3.7.5.3 On the recommendation of the Third Pay Commission, the pay scales prevalent in the institutions of scientific research and training such as CSIR, Indian Council of Medical Research, Bhabha Atomic Research Centre, Indian Council of Agricultural Research etc. had also been revised.

3.7.5.4 *Professors of Eminence*

The Committee recommended that eminent Professors in the country ought to be given the scale of pay applicable to the Directors of National Laboratories. The UGC was requested to evolve a suitable and credible machinery for an all-India selection of Professors of Eminence.

3.7.6 *Mehrotra Committee: 1983-1987*

Salaries of teachers at different levels were to be at levels comparable to the salaries of the All India Civil Service officers. This was the underlying principle of pay revision. It recommended that it be ensured that the teachers of universities and colleges were not put to any financial disadvantages and the parity envisaged by the Committee in its recommendations be maintained.

3.7.6.1 *Pay Scale of Principal*

The Principal should be placed either in the grade of a Reader or in the grade of a Professor. The criteria in this regard were to be decided by the respective State Governments.

3.7.6.2 *Professor (UGC)*

A provision should be made to award UGC Professorships on the lines of the Indian National Science Academy Award to some Professors who have shown outstanding merit in their field work. They should be given the pay of Rs. 3.500 (in the existing framework) and the usual allowances available to the university teachers. The selection for such awards should be done at the national level. The UGC may evolve a suitable mechanism for such awards.

3.7.6.3 The Mehrotra Committee had also recommended revised pay scales for Librarians and Directors of Physical Education in universities and colleges. Subsequently the pay scale of Registrars were also revised.

3.8 Conditions of Service and Service Benefits

3.8.1 The University Education Commission, 1948, recommended provisions of Provident Fund for each teacher to which the teacher would contribute eight per cent of this salary and the university another eight per cent. It was felt desirable for teachers to live either on the campus of the university or as near to it as possible. It also recommended setting apart a room for each teacher in the university building.

3.8.1.1 Regarding the age of retirement, the Commission observed that the university teachers as a class belonged to the longest-lived group of any community and had a more disciplined life-style having more congenial surroundings. Even though their physical vigour declined, the intellectual capacity was expected to remain unimpaired. The Commission, therefore, recommended that the superannuation age for teacher should be 60 years but for a Professor who possessed good health, it could be extended till 64 years. However, no extension was to be allowed for more than two years at a time.

3.8.1.2 The Commission also recommended setting up of a tribunal composed of the representatives of the teacher, the university and an umpire to settle any dispute arising between the university authorities and teachers.

3.8.1.3 In addition to every type of leave like casual leave; leave without pay; leave on quarter, half or full pay; it also recommended the provision for study leave which could be for a duration of one year at a time and three years in entire service. These periods could be spent abroad or in India according to the nature of the study undertaken with the advice of the Professor. A teacher should receive half pay during the period of study leave.

3.8.1.4 The Commission also suggested that since a large number of teachers could not afford to buy books or subscribe to journals to keep themselves up-to-date, the teachers of lower grades should be given a grant of Rs. 100 a year for buying books on the condition that they would supplement it by an equal amount.

3.8.2 The National Commission on Teachers in Higher Education under the chairmanship of Prof. Rais Ahmed observed that there was a general shortage of housing owing to rapid urbanisation, nuclear family system and lack of investment in the housing sector. They recommended that to encourage teachers to have their own houses, schemes of investment on houses should be re-formulated. Since the traditional method of promoting investment in housing had not helped the teachers because they were not able to provide the initial capital, the Committee suggested that a revolving loan fund for each institution should be provided and 20-30 per cent of the money provided by the financial institutions might be earmarked for teachers. Land should also be earmarked by State Governments for construction of private houses by teachers.

3.8.2.1 Regarding medical facilities, the Committee recommended that in the absence of free medical facilities in colleges and universities, a medical allowance of Rs. 20 per month might be given to the teachers for spending on minor ailments. For major diseases like cancer, tuberculosis, heart ailment etc., where hospitalisation was required, the full cost must be met by the institutions and leave on full pay should also be given for such period as necessary. The Committee also recommended the necessity of providing retirement benefits like contributory provident fund, gratuity, pension and group insurance to teachers. Leave facilities including study leave, sabbatical leave, maternity leave, travel facilities such as home travel concession and leave travel concession should also be uniformly available to all teachers on the lines of the central universities. They recommended that a subsidy to teachers should be given and if they bought up to Rs. 500 worth of books every year, they should be given 50 per cent of the cost as subsidy. The Committee recommended higher non-practising allowance (NPA) to teachers in all medical institutions where private practice was not allowed so that the differential in earnings was reduced and there was greater satisfaction and mobility. The Commission also recommended higher start for the Lecturers in view of their late entry into the service. One increment for an M.Phil entrant and three for a Ph.D entrant were recommended. A Typist should be available in every college or a university department for every 10 or 15 teachers working there. The Commission also recommended a higher age of retirement for the teachers in view of their late entry into the service. It was also considered desirable that since considerable investment was made on education and professional development of teachers, the society would benefit from this investment for a longer period if service period of teachers be increased.

3.8.3 The Sen Committee recommended that for creative work like teaching and research, provision of proper conditions of service was extremely important as it played a very significant role in helping to attract and retain in the profession the right type of persons. Hence, it recommended that the University Act should make provisions for framing statutes with regard to the security of service. They were also of the opinion that an aggrieved teacher in an affiliated college should have the opportunity to appeal to the university. The university might appoint a tribunal comprising one representative of the Vice-Chancellor who would be Chairman of the tribunal.

3.8.3.1 It recommended the extension of the scheme introduced by UGC regarding pension-cum-gratuity-cum-general provident fund and, contributory provident fund-cum-gratuity in the central universities, to the employees of the other universities and affiliated colleges. To encourage mobility among universities, other organisations and the government, they considered having a uniform superannuation scheme as desirable.

3.8.3.2 It recommended 60 years as the age of superannuation with no provision for extension. If a university/college required the services of a teacher after the age of superannuation, he should be appointed on a contract basis for a period not exceeding five years. During this contract period, the teacher should not be given any administrative responsibility, for example, that of the Head of the Department or a Dean of a Faculty, etc., and he should be made to devote himself entirely to teaching and research.

3.8.3.3 The Committee was of the view that the provision of medical facilities for teachers in universities and colleges was very essential to attract talented people to the teaching profession. It recommended that the UGC should explore the possibility of extending the Group Insurance Scheme to teachers.

3.8.3.4 Yet another recommendation made by the Committee was that adequate housing facilities should be provided for teachers where land was available. Advantage should also be taken of the loan schemes available for construction of houses. The Sen Committee gave a detailed write-up on the rules governing leave of absence to teachers of the universities and colleges.

3.8.4 The Mehrotra Committee in its recommendations regarding conditions of service recommended the following:-

3.8.4.1 At the time of recruitment, every teacher should be required to sign a contract to be lodged with the Registrar/ Principal with a copy to the teacher concerned. These forms of contract should reflect the need of the university and the college concerned and should contain other service conditions and rules of service. To encourage mobility of teachers, a scheme should be worked out so that the periods of service of a teacher in several institutions could be added up for purposes of superannuation benefits.

3.8.4.2 Regarding provision of housing facilities and house rent allowance, the Committee recommended that a concerted effort should be made to find resources to satisfy at least 25 per cent of the housing requirements in the Eighth Plan period. The rest could be provided in future. It also recommended review and scaling up of house rent allowance so that the teachers in different cities were able to rent suitable accommodation without being required to contribute at a rate higher than 10 per cent of their salaries.

3.8.4.3 The Mehrotra Committee recommended a tentative scheme suggested by National Insurance Company Limited exploring the possibility of medical insurance under the schemes of nationalised General Insurance Companies. An annual premium of Rs. 800 to Rs. 1,000 was suggested to take care of all medical problems of a family of four.

3.8.4.4 In the matter of leave rules, the Committee recommended that the types of leave at present available to the central university teachers should also be made available to those working in other universities and colleges. The Committee was of the view that the teachers should utilise their vacations to update their knowledge, participate in curricular, extra-curricular, extra-mural and extension activities.

3.8.4.5 The Committee also recommended that teachers should be free to exercise all civic rights and should be eligible for public offices but that the leave for such purposes should be without pay protecting his service benefits and increments so that when he returned to the institution, his interests did not suffer.

3.8.4.6 Regarding the age of superannuation the Committee recommended that the age of superannuation of teachers might continue to be 60 years. However, if on the recommendation of the Fourth Pay Commission, the Central Government agreed to increase the age of retirement of its employees beyond 58 years, the age of retirement of teachers should be correspondingly increased beyond 60 years. At the same time, the Committee expressed the view that in special circumstances it might be necessary to have the benefit of the services of the distinguished teachers even after superannuation. In such, cases the Committee recommended that the universities/colleges might appoint such persons on contract basis after superannuation. For this purpose, supernumerary posts might be created in the universities. However, it was pointed out that those positions would be personal to the persons concerned.

3.8.4.7 The Committee was of the view that the rate of dearness allowance payable to all teachers in the universities and colleges should be at par with that of the central universities. The Committee recommended that every teacher should be given a professional allowance of Rs. 1,000 per annum to enable them to get the research papers typed, duplicating the articles and in getting the journals or books which were not available in the library. The facilities of leave travel concession as available to Central Government employees and central university teachers, should be made available to all university/college teachers. The Committee also recommended that a suitable conveyance allowance be given to the teachers depending upon the type of vehicle. Provision of a suitable conveyance allowance for teachers living outside the campus might also be given due consideration.

3.9 Summary of the Principal Recommendations of the Mehrotra Committee

3.9.1 The principal recommendations of the Mehrotra Committee could be summarised as under:

(i) Salaries of teachers at different levels were to be comparable to the salaries of the All India Civil Service officers. This was the underlying principle of pay revision.

(ii) Career advancement of Lecturers was provided through the recommendation to introduce two more scales: one, a senior scale; and two, a selection grade to be given after completing well-defined steps in the process of professional development and after performance assessment.

(iii) Fast-track promotions were suggested even though the details of the scheme were not worked out. Open selections for higher posts (if held regularly) could be treated as fast-track as the number of years of service required to fulfil the eligibility conditions was less than the required service under the career advancement scheme.

(iv) No promotions from Lecturer to Reader or Reader to Professor were recommended. Readers and Professor were to be appointed only after a process of all-India open selection. The Committee made critical comments on attempts being made to introduce time-bound promotions for teachers. The merit promotion scheme introduced by the UGC in 1983 came in for critical comments by the Committee. Incidentally, the National Commission on Teachers-II also arrived at similar conclusions. In short, the Mehrotra Committee recommended that career advancement might provide for higher scales of pay, but the higher designation might not be given without careful selection.

(v) Performance assessment was recommended as an essential component in career advancement. Other conditions were: obtaining higher degree such as M.Phil or Ph.D. and participation in at least two refresher courses. Evaluation of teachers in the refresher courses was also suggested as a component of the process of performance assessment.

(vi) Qualifying in a national eligibility test (NET) was recommended as an essential condition for recruitment to the post of Lecturer in any university or college throughout the length and breadth of the country. This recommendation replaced the provision introduced by the Sen Committee in 1973, which had made M.Phil or Ph.D. as essential qualification for appointment to the post of Lecturer. The recommendations of a national eligibility test was aimed at removing disparities in standards of evaluation and teaching that prevailed among large number of institutions.

3.9.2 In arriving at the above set of recommendations, the objectives of pay review spelled out explicitly by the Committee were, first, to ensure that teachers were remunerated in keeping with their role in nation building and upgrading of human skills; to enable them to live in moderate comfort and concentrate on teaching and research; secondly, the scales of pay and conditions of services should be such that a talented person who had to choose from a number of competing careers, might be attracted towards teaching; thirdly, merit should be rewarded; and lastly, stagnation in service should be relieved.

3.9.3 The above summary has been recapitulated because of recommendation of Mehrotra Committee formed the basis of the Government of India notifications issued in 1987 and 1988. Having regard to the first term of the reference of the present Pay Review Committee, viz, revision of pay scales of teachers in universities and colleges and other measures for maintenance of standards in higher education, it is being discussed in the next session.

3.9.4 Revised pay scales had since been made applicable also to Registrars (including Deputy Registrars and Assistant Registrars), Librarians (including Deputy Librarians and Assistant Librarians) and Directors of Physical Education (including Deputy Directors and Assistant Directors).

3.10 The Recommendations of the Mehrotra Committee as accepted by the Government of India

3.10.1 The Mehrotra Committee submitted its recommendations to the UGC on 21st May, 1986. Thereafter, the recommendations were placed before the Commission and were then sent to the Government of India for its approval. The Government of India notified the revision of pay scales of teachers in universities and colleges and other measures for maintenance of standards of higher education with effect from 1st January, 1986 (vide its letter dated the 17th June, 1987). The scheme as contained in the above-mentioned letter was to be implemented in the central universities and other institutions fully financed by the Central Government. The Government of India also decided to assist the State Governments which might in their discretion decide on introducing the scheme of revision of pay scales subject to the following terms and conditions.

(i) The Central Government would provide assistance to the State Governments to the extent of 80 per cent of the additional per cent expenditure involved in giving effect to the revision of scales of pay.

(ii) The Central Assistance to the extent indicated above would be available for the period ranging from January 1, 1986 to March 31, 1990.

(iii) The State Governments would meet the remaining 20 per cent of the exependiture from their own resources and would not pass on the liability or any portion thereof to the universities or the managements of private colleges.

(iv) The State Governments would take over the entire responsibility for maintaining the revised scales of pay with effect from April 1, 1990.

(v) Central assistance would be restricted to the revision of pay scales of the posts which were in existence on January 1, 1986. Some of the recommendations to the Government of India which were notified on the 17th June, 1987 were later modified vide another notification dated the 22nd July, 1988. The main features of these two notifications are listed below:-

1. **Recruitment and Qualifications**

(i) Recruitment to the posts of Lecturers, Readers and Professors in universities and colleges shall be on the basis of merit through all-India advertisement and selection, provided that a Lecturer who fulfilled the criteria prescribed in this scheme would be eligible for the promotion to the post of Reader.

(ii) The minimum qualifications required for appointment to the posts of Lecturers, Readers and Professors would be those prescribed by the UGC from time to time. Generally, the minimum qualifications for appointment to the post of Lecturer in the scale of pay of Rs. 2,200 – 4,000 shall be Master's degree in the relevant subject with at least 55 per cent marks or its equivalent grade, and good academic record.

(iii) Only those candidates who, besides fulfilling the minimum academic qualifications prescribed for the post of Lecturer, had qualified in a comprehensive test to be specially conducted for the purpose, would be eligible for appointment as Lecturers. The detailed schemes for conducting the test including its design, the agencies to be employed in the conduct of tests, content, administration, etc., would be worked out by the UGC, keeping in view the requirements of the media of instruction as followed by the different states, universities and colleges, as also other relevant considerations.

(iv) In order to encourage research, in continuation of post-graduate studies, candidates who, at the time of their recruitment as Lecturers, possessed Ph.D. or M.Phil degree would be sanctioned three and one advance increments respectively, in the scale of Rs. 2,200 – 4,000 along with the benefit of corresponding years of service for purposes of promotion. The existing Lecturers without research degrees, and those similarly situated, and recruited in future would be eligible for a similar benefit in service for purposes of promotion as and when they acquired research degrees but would not be eligible for advance increments. Existing Lecturers with research degrees would also be eligible for a similar benefit.

2. **Career Advancement**

(i) Every Lecturer would be placed in the senior scale of Rs. 3,000 – 5,000 if he or she had:

(a) Completed eight years of service after regular appointment;
(b) Participated in two refresher courses or summer institutes, each of which approximately of four weeks' duration or engaged in other appropriate continuing education programmes of comparable quality as might be specified by the UGC; and
(c) Consistently satisfactory performance appraisal reports.

(ii) Every Lecturer in the senior scale would be eligible for promotion to the post of Reader in the scale of pay of Rs.3,700 –5,700 if he or she had:

(a) Completed eight years of service in the senior scale, provided that the requirement of eight years would be relaxed if the total service of the Lecturer was not less than 16 years;

(b) Obtained a Ph.D. degree, or equivalent published work;

(c) Made some mark in the areas of scholarship and research as evidenced by self-assessment, reports of referees, quality of publications, contribution to educational innovation, design of new courses and curricula, etc.;

(d) Participated in two refresher courses or summer institutes each of approximately four weeks' duration and engaged in other appropriate continuing education programmes of comparable quality as might be specified by the UGC, after placement in the senior scale; and

(e) Consistently good performance appraisal reports.

(iii) The existing teachers in universities and colleges where the merit promotion scheme formulated by the UGC in 1983, or any other similar schemes were in operation would have an option to continue to be governed by the provisions of those schemes provided that they exercise their option in writing prior to their pay fixation under this scheme. They would also be entitled to the designations envisaged for various categories of teachers in those schemes. The scales of pay would be as follows:

Lecturer	—	Rs. 2200–4000
Reader/Lecturer (selection grade)	—	Rs. 3000–5000
Professor	—	Rs. 4500–5700

Promotions made before the announcement of the revised scale on June 17, 1987, would not be reopened. However, in such cases, the benefit of revision would be available to teachers only from the date of their promotion.

3. Other Conditions of Service

(a) Probation

The period of probation of a teacher would not exceed a period of 24 months. A Lecturer appointed on probation would ordinarily be confirmed only after he or she has completed appropriate short-term orientation programmes and his or her performance appraisal reports are satisfactory. The UGC was required to make arrangements to ensure that facilities were available for organising orientation programmes to cover all Lecturers appointed in and after 1988-89.

(b) Superannuation and Re-employment

The age of superannuation for teachers would be 60 years and thereafter no extension in service would be given. However, it would be open to a university or college to re-employ a superannuated teacher according to the existing guidelines framed by the UGC up to the age of 65 years.

(c) Grievance Redressal Mechanism

Appropriate mechanism for the redressal of teachers' grievances would be established in all universities and colleges in respect of which guidelines would be issued separately.

(d) Code of Professional Ethics

The UGC would prepare a code of professional ethics for teachers in consultation with the representatives of national level associations of teachers; and all concerned should see that this code was observed.

(e) Formula for Pay Fixation and Career Advancement to Other Categories

A formula and some examples for fixing pay were also given.

The notification also provided for revised scales of pay of Librarians and Physical Education personnel in universities and colleges. A career advancement scheme was also given for Assistant Librarians and Assistant Directors of Physical Education on the patterns on Lecturers.

RECOMMENDATIONS

CHAPTER VI

6.1 Introduction

Pay scales, service conditions and work environment are the conditions that enable a teacher to contribute to the system of education which, in turn, contributes to national development. These conditions help in attracting and retaining talented persons in the teaching profession.

Keeping this objective in view and in order to improve the quality of education, the Committee examined the present structure of emoluments and conditions of service of university and college teachers, Librarians (including Deputy Librarians and Assistant Librarians). Directors of Physical Education (including Deputy Directors and Assistant Directors of Physical Education) and Registrars (including Deputy Registrars and Assistant Registrars) of universities. In making its recommendations, the Committee took into consideration the recommendations of the Fifth Central Pay Commission on such matters as covered by its own terms of reference.

6.2 Recruitment

6.2.1 *Minimum Qualifications for Lecturers*

The UGC on September 19, 1991 had issued regulations setting out minimum qualifications for the recruitment of Lecturers, Readers and Professors for various subjects. For the post of a

Lecturer the minimum qualification is a good academic record with at least 55 per cent marks or an equivalent grade obtained at the Master's level in the relevant subject and qualifying eligibility test for recruitment of Lecturers, conducted by the UGC, CSIR or any other similar tests accredited by the UGC.

The Committee deliberated on several dimensions and difficulties expressed by the teaching community as well as by those concerned with the system of higher education across the country. There are two issues on which, a considerable number of representations were received by the Committee, both from the associations of teachers as also the university/college authorities. These issues are:

(i) the requirements of a minimum of 55 per cent marks in the Master's degree programme; and
(ii) qualifying in the NET/SLET examination so as to be able to become eligible for the post of a Lecturer in a college or university.

It was argued that opportunities for scoring high marks vary from subject to subject, representing a wide spectrum, with certain subjects in humanities and social sciences, say, like languages and history at one end and those like physics and mathematics at the other. Again, the method of examination and evaluation as well as the standards vary from university to university in the country. Then, there are candidates who otherwise happen to be well-qualified, as evidenced from a good research record and ample promise to be good academicians, but who do not fulfil the basic requirement of 55 per cent marks for various reasons. It was also pointed out that, in certain regions of the country, candidates with 55 per cent marks were not generally available in sufficient number. It was not, therefore, logical to prescribe one common, minimum percentage for all, without taking into account these variations. This, by and large, is the essence of these representations.

The Committee deliberated on this issue and carefully considered the points made. Its considered view is that while no doubt variations are there for scoring high marks in different subjects, the requirements of 55 per cent marks by itself is nevertheless not very exacting in respect of any subject. Hence, to ensure certain academic excellence on the part of those who seek to enter the academic profession, the modest minimum of 55 per cent marks needs to be insisted upon. In addition, the national eligibility test (NET), as conducted by the UGC as well as the state-level eligibility test (SLET) as conducted by a few states on the basis of accreditation given by the UGC, have also been generally very well accepted.

However, the Committee sees the validity of some points made in the representations. The UGC already has a provision to grant exemption in deserving cases. The UGC may, from time to time, regulate the use of this provision, whether for individuals or in respect of certain regions of the country as the case may be. The relaxations, however, should be within a minimum 50 per cent marks and every candidate must have necessarily qualified in the NET/SLET or be eligible for exemption from NET as per the UGC regulations.

Regarding NET, exemption exists for those who had qualified for M.Phil or submitted the thesis for award of Ph.D before December, 1993. The plea is to extend this provision for doctorate degree-holders without any time limit. The points for consideration are as follows:

We need to promote research in various areas of knowledge in the country. Promotion of research is crucial for the university system. The employment opportunities for doctoral candidates exist mainly in teaching institutions and research centres. If opportunities for doctoral candidates into academic institutions are made difficult, it will adversely affect the research activities in the higher education system. Not many will opt for full-time research. It must also be conceded that a candidate with a doctoral degree develops abilities to formulate a problem, set out the objectives of investigation, gather data from journals, books and experiments, analyse them properly and finally draw valid conclusions. This means that he/she would have also enquired deeply into a subject and developed an appreciation for scholarly pursuits. All these are valuable assets for an academic. We also have cases where Indian candidates who have qualified for Ph.D abroad seek placements in teaching institutions in India. Certainly, they would not have passed NET. Hence, by insisting upon it, we would be losing such talent for our education system. The Committee has taken into account all these aspects and recommends that those candidates who have 55 per cent marks in the Master's degree and have obtained a Ph.D after 1993 should also be exempted from qualifying in the NET/SLET to be able to become eligible for the post of Lecturer.

Subject to the above, the Committee recommends that good academic record, 55 per cent at the Master's level and clearance of NET/SLET shall remain necessary conditions in order to determine eligibility for appointment as Lecturer.

6.2.2 *Minimum Qualifications and Selection Committees*

Minimum qualification and composition of Selection Committees for posts, namely Reader, Professor, Principals of Colleges, Librarians, Deputy Librarians, Assistant Librarians, Registrars, Deputy Registrars, Assistant Registrars, Physical Education Directors, Deputy Directors of Physical Education, Assistant Directors of Physical Education as adopted, modified and recommended by the Committee.

6.3 **Period of Probation for Teachers**

The Committee deliberated on the issue of probation and is of the view that one year is too short a period for observing the performance of a teacher. He/She should have at least two academic sessions to adjust and give evidence of performance. Therefore, the Committee recommends that the probations should normally be for a period of 24 months. In case, the performance is not up to the mark, the teacher shall be informed well in time, and asked to improve his/her performance. If there is no satisfactory improvements, his/her probation may be terminated or the period of probation extended upto a further period of 12 months. A teacher should be confirmed on his/her successful completion of probation, subject to successful completion of one short-term orientation course/diploma in Higher Education (from the Indira Gandhi National Open University) as is the case at present.

6.4 **Pay Scales**

6.4.1 The guiding principle of deciding the pay scales is to attract the talented people as well as to retain them in the system. Accordingly, the scheme of pay scales, keeping in view the revision as suggested by the Fifth Pay Commission and the relative position of the teacher vis-a-vis other professions, are recommended.

6.4.2 *Principals of Colleges*

The position of College Principals is not very ambiguous as far as the pay scales are concerned. In some of the states, Principals are in the pay scale equivalent to that of a Professor. But in other states the pay scale is equivalent to that of a Reader. Still in other states, Principals are given some allowance and a scale of pay equivalent to that of a Professor. The Committee having considered these variations felt that the Principals of an institution occupied a very important academic and administrative position. The person occupying this post is expected to play a key role in the management and development of the college. It is, therefore, recommended that a separate cadre of Principals of colleges should be created. Also there are wide ranging variations in the size and level of colleges which warrant three types of scales for Principals for different categories of colleges. The scales are, therefore, recommended based on the number of faculties, undergraduate/postgraduate programmes, autonomy and enrolment of students.

6.4.3 *Professor of Eminence*

The University Grants Commission has formulated a scheme of Professor of Eminence. The Committee recommends that the scheme be implemented at the earliest.

6.4.4 *Establishment of Chairs*

Of late, many Chairs in specialised subjects are being established in different universities of the country with endowments from various quarters. The Committee recommends that while the selection of persons for these Chairs should be even more rigorous than usual, the delimiting of emoluments to the UGC scales may not be insisted upon when a recommendation to this effect is made on a case by case basis by the Selection Committee on grounds to be stated formally. Appropriate guidelines for establishment of such Chairs may be laid down by the UGC.

6.4.5 *Pay Fixation*

The formula governing pay fixation as suggested by the Central Pay Commission may be made applicable to the teachers or universities and colleges and other categories of staff recommended above.

6.4.6 *Pay Scales for Inter-University Centres, etc.*

In case of Inter-University Centres, Department of Adult Education, etc. the pay scales recommended by the Central Pay Commission for equivalent categories may also be given to different categories of Scientists, Directors and other similar positions.

6.4.7 *Pay Scales for Other Organisations*

Representations have been received from organisations such as Indian Council of Agricultural Research (ICAR), and state agriculture universities which have adopted the UGC scales of pay in respect of their staffs. Since in our deliberations and recommendations we have generally taken note of universities coming under the purview of UGC as per our terms of reference and not other institutions which have adopted these scales of pay, it is only logical that these organisations are given sufficient flexibility by the Central/State Governments at the time of change over to the new scales of pay, subject of course, to their keeping the broad framework of the recommendations of this Committee as well as the Central Pay Commission.

6.5 **Career Advancement Scheme**

We learn that at present the upward movement of Lecturer to Senior Lecturer and Senior Lecturer to the Selection Grade Lecturer and then redesignating them as Reader on acquisition of Ph.D. degree has become a matter of routine. Those who satisfy the condition of required period of service take it for granted that they will automatically move to the next higher level. Even the requirement of having to attend two refresher courses of one-month duration each, has not been insisted upon because of the simple reason that we have not been able to provide enough opportunities for all teachers/subjects.

Further, the scheme for career advancement requires consistently good performance appraisal reports. However, it was found during the course of visits and discussions that a viable and functioning system of personal assessment has not been in operation in most places. Even where personal assessments are required formally, these are not taken seriously by the universities as well as by the teachers. A performance appraisal system is absolutely crucial and basic if merit were to be rewarded and encouraged. It is more so in the case of teachers in whose case quantification becomes a really formidable task. It is because of the importance attached to the performance-appraisal that the NPE 1986 (National Policy on Education) made the following observations:

A system of teacher evaluation – open, participative and data-based – will be created and reasonable opportunities of promotions to higher grades provided. Norms of accountability will be laid down with incentives for good performance as well as disincentives for non-performance.

The last Pay Committee of the UGC recommended teacher evaluation as part of the package. Inquiries made by us and the evidence collected as a result, indicate that the UGC recommendation notwithstanding, a well-designed system of performance appraisal of teachers has not been developed so far. Some institutions have an annual appraisal in a prescribed form. Some have it only once when the upward movement of Lecturer to Senior Lecturer and Senior Lecturer to Selection Grade Lecturer is on the anvil. In the case of Readers and Professors, there seems to be very little evidence of performance-appraisal aimed at evaluating the contribution made by them, either teaching or in research or in institution-building or in the development of education material and/or any other related matter. It has, therefore, become necessary to address ourselves to this question and lay down a reasonable method of performance appraisal. Accordingly, the method and format of performance appraisal including student evaluation of teaching have been discussed under the section on Accountability. The same may be used for performance appraisal of teachers. The Committee is of the view that maximum efforts be made to put in place an effective and well functioning system of performance appraisal. Subject to the basic requirements that a system of performance appraisal is put in place, the Committee recommends the following Career Advancement Scheme for teachers:

6.5.1 *Lecturers*

It is recommended that for placement in the senior scale, a Lecturer may offer himself/herself for review after four years if holding a Ph.D degree; after six years if holding an M.Phil degree; after seven years if not holding M.Phil/Ph.D.

The Committee further recommends that a Lecturer (senior scale) can offer himself/herself for review after six years of experience as Senior Lecturer for placement in the selection grade.

A Lecturer at the point of joining will be eligible for one advance increment if he/she possesses the M.Phil degree. With a Ph.D. he/she will be eligible for three advance increments. If a person acquires the above qualification while in service, then he/she will get the service benefit for career advancement but not the advance increments.

When an individual fulfils the minimum requirements in terms of years of service, attendance in courses and has good performances, he/she becomes eligible for consideration for placement in the senior scale. The performance-appraisal forms, students' evaluation records as well as records of academic achievements by the candidate may be forwarded to two external experts. The reports of the external experts along with the records of the candidates may be placed before the Selection Committee, the composition of which will be the same as that for a Lecturer. The candidate will be interviewed by the Selection Committee and on the basis of its recommendations, his/her movement to the next higher grade will be decided upon. The same procedure will be followed for placement in the selection grade or in the position of a Reader in the case of candidates having Ph.D. The composition of the Selection Committee will be the same as in the case of Reader.

6.5.2 *Reader*

There has been a uniform and pervasive demand that there should be room for performance appraisal of a Reader for elevation to the post of a Professor after one fulfils certain basic requirements as well as the desired level of performance at the level of a Reader. It has been represented to us by the members of the various faculty associations that there are a large number of Readers who have excellent record both with regard to teaching and research and hence are eminently qualified to be appointed as Professors. However, for want of vacancies they continue to stagnate as Readers and this creates frustration among them. It was suggested that a method must be established for offering positions of Professors on the basis of assessment of the contribution made and academic excellence achieved by an individual as Reader. It is a major issue. If the request is conceded, it would, by and large, mean, in practice, that in the case of any individual, open competition will be restricted to the entry-point only. It is not an ideal situation for maintaining certain vibrancy, vitality and introduction of fresh talent. Any system worth the name ought to have provision for lateral entry. This may be taken as a pre-requisite for the health of the education system as well. In order to fulfil this requirement, some tend to suggest that the appointment to sanctioned positions may be through open recruitment. As for promotion by performance-appraisal, it may be considered personal to the individual.

The problem in performance-appraisal and promotion has been the credibility of implementation of the system and the discouraging factor is the experience we so far have had in the operation of the merit promotion scheme. While the lack of opportunities for upward movement for the really qualified candidates because of the absence of vacancies is quite real and the consequent grievance cannot but be appreciated, the remedy for such a situation does present formidable problems. These really arise out of the fact that a system of peer review has not been well developed in this country and we have reasons to feel that many extraneous considerations enter into the field in the case of career advancement of an individual on the basis of performance-appraisal, as in operation. The Committee gave due consideration to this representation with regard to all its implications. The Committee had in mind the merit promotion scheme and the way it happened to be implemented, resulting in the lowering of standards of the institution of Professor which is one of the highest academic positions that we have. The Committee was not convinced that we would be able to find a fool-proof method. However, after due consideration of all aspects of the matter, the Committee recommends as follows:

(a) Sanctioned position of Professors must remain to be filled in through direct recruitment. This is absolutely necessary to maintain the efficiency and vibrancy of the system.

(b) For appointment of a Reader as Professor on the basis of assessment of performance and level of academic excellence achieved, the following parameters are to be weighed in the case of one who becomes eligible for consideration:

(i) A minimum of 10 years' service as Reader;

(ii) Publication of research papers or standard text books, since appointment as Reader;

(iii) Annual performance-appraisal forms for the entire service as Reader, if for any reason, appraisal forms for the earlier years are not available in the present situation, the assessment will start from the time the appraisal-forms actually become available. To begin with, the appraisal forms must pertain to the last three consecutive years. However, in all future cases the forms must be available for the full period of Readership;

(iv) Student-evaluation record for each year; and

(v) Contribution made by the individual for institutional development.

The personal file of the candidate who becomes eligible for consideration shall be sent to the UGC for placing the same before a Panel of Readers to be specially constituted by the UGC for each subject. The observations of the Referees will form an important input to be considered by the duly constituted Selection Committee of the university concerned. Negative findings by the UGC Referees may normally disqualify the candidate for promotion for two years after which he/she may offer himself/herself again for promotion. All subject-specific applications may be considered periodically. Positions offered on performance appraisal should be regarded as personal but the teacher should get every other privileges in the university system that a Professor is entitled to.

The Selection Committee shall have the same composition as is necessary for the selection of Professors under open recruitment.

Detailed guidelines may be worked out by the UGC in this regard. Attempts may be made to qualify the assessment as far as possible.

In order to enable the UGC to perform the responsibility assigned in this regard, it may need a complement of staff for which separate assistance may be made available by the Government of India.

6.5.3 *Merit Promotion Scheme and Dual Emoluments*

In order to reward merit and relieve stagnation, the University Grants Commission introduced in 1983 a merit promotion scheme. This scheme was mainly for rewarding the merit of the deserving teachers. However, the Mehrotra Committee observed that owing to mal-implementation arising out of accumulated pressure, the scheme had, by and large, failed to achieve its primary objective of rewarding merit. It had virtually culminated in time-bound promotions with the result that pursuit of excellence had fallen by the way-side. The edge of the incentive for hard work had got blunted. Not just that, the assumption attached to senior positions in the teaching hierarchy too got blurred. Therefore, the Mehrotra Committee recommended a considerable improvement in the merit promotion scheme.

The Government of India notification of 1987 eventually came out with a merit promotion scheme under which the existing teachers in universities and colleges, where the merit promotion scheme formulated earlier by the UGC or some other similar scheme was in operation, had an option to continue to be governed by the provisions of those schemes provided that they exercised their option in writing prior to their pay fixation. They were also entitled to the designation envisaged for various categories of teachers but the scales of pay in case of teachers promoted under merit promotion scheme were lower. The following scales were given:

Lecturer	—	Rs. 2200–4000
Reader/Lecturer (selection grade)	—	Rs. 3000–5000
Professor	—	Rs. 4500–5700

The concept of dual emoluments between the merit-promotees and direct recruits led to a lot of litigation in various courts. Some of the High Courts like the High Court of U.P. and High Court of Rajasthan decided that equal pay should be given for equal work and hence, the merit-promotee teachers should be treated at par with the directly recruited ones in the matter of pay scales. Many court cases also came up regarding seniority of a merit-promotee teacher vis-a-vis the directly recruited one. The Supreme Court in the case of Rashmi Srivastava vs. Vikram University decided that merit-promotees and direct recruits formed two distinct categories of teachers and hence, two separate seniority lists should be maintained.

The Committee feels that the merit promotion scheme or, for that matter, any similar scheme has really become a scheme of time-bound, automatic promotion and is not exactly a scheme to reward merit. Therefore, the merit promotion scheme, having dual emoluments or, for that matter, any such scheme should be dispensed with. Henceforth, the career advancement scheme as recommended above may be implemented to reward the meritorious teachers. The Committee notes with deep concern that some of the universities have deviated from the Government announcement on this subject without the concurrence of the Government or the UGC and also just before the submission of the report of this Committee. The Committee recommends that the Government and the UGC may take appropriate action in this matter to avoid recurrence of such things in the future. The UGC may also take a policy decision, after detailed analysis about the abolition of dual emoluments system and the *inter-se* seniority of merit-promotees vis-a-vis direct recruits, in the event of the dual emoluments system being abolished.

6.5.4 *Administrative Positions*

The administrative positions in the university, namely, the Registrars, the Deputy Registrars and the Assistant Registrars have been kept at par with academic positions keeping in view the academic and administrative experience of the incumbents of these positions. The Committee is of the view that the existing parity may continue to be maintained. The position of a Registrar should be the same as that of a Professor, and that of Deputy Registrar the same as Reader. The career advancement scheme which already exists for this category of staff may continue.

However, the review of the work of the persons at these levels in administration should include a quantitative statement of number of cases settled, annual average handling of files, handling of meetings, handling of staff and students, innovations and development carried out by them by way of professional development. The Committee, therefore, recommends that the present system of annual confidential report as per established procedure may continue to be followed. However, the form may be modified on the pattern of the form now in use in the Central Services. Reports may be placed before the Selection Committees constituted for purpose of career advancement.

6.5.5 *College Librarian*

Most of the College Librarians are found to be in the scale of a Lecturer or in a still lower scale. This scale of pay also varies from institution to institution. The library system in colleges needs to be upgraded. The Committee, therefore, recommends that there should be at least one post of College Librarian in every college. The college library should now be developed into a library of information system and it should, besides having books and journals, have audio and video materials and should be computerised. It should closely interact with university library and national libraries. The Librarian should also be able to engage students in a workshop–like situation with a view to training them regarding information retrieval and resourcing of material for their studies. For performing these newer tasks, the position of Librarian in the colleges should be that of a Lecturer in the colleges. It should be a non-vacant job and have the qualification equivalent to that of a Lecturer in the colleges. It should have career advancement up to level of a Librarian (senior scale). An incumbent with eight years of service should be eligible to offer himself/herself for review and present before the Selection Committee. The review should include extent of modernization, development of library information system, relationship with students and faculty members and professional development. Achievements of the incumbents should be sent for peer review and the report of the peer review be placed before the Selection Committee.

6.5.6 *University Librarians*

Librarian, Deputy Librarian, Assistant Librarian in the universities are non-vacation posts and should have pay scales equivalent to those of Registrar, Deputy Registrar and Assistant Registrar. The path of career advancement as existing at present for this category should continue. However, the method of selection should involve review of work and achievement. The parameters of this review should include: professional development, innovations and development carried out, modernisation of library development, interaction with other university libraries with and outside the country, development of library into information and resource centre, lectures delivered to the students about information-retrieval and resourcing of material, skill in dealing with students and faculty members, etc.

6.5.7 *Directors of Physical Education*

The role and responsibilities of the Directors of Physical Education need to be redefined so as to enable them to act as health, hygiene, yoga, sports and body-fitness teachers. They should engage themselves in imparting these skills to a great extent. They have also to devote a part of their time in creating awareness about body/physical fitness. They should be well-versed with modern methods of body fitness and yoga. The Committee recommends that there should be at least one position of Director of Physical Education in the pay scale equivalent to that of a Lecturer in every college. The position should be non-vacation post and he/she should hold coaching camps during the vacations for such students as are interested in sports and body development. The college Director of Physical Education should be eligible to offer himself/herself for review after a period of eight years of service for the position of a College Director of Physical Education (senior scale). The review should incorporate professional development, numbers of games/sports programmes developed, performance of the students, rate of participation of students, handling of students, number of awards secured, etc. There need be no position in this category at the college level.

At the university level, however, the position of Assistant Directors, Deputy Directors and Directors of Physical Education should continue to exist.

6.6 **Creation of Posts**

The Kothari Commission recommended that the proportion of positions of Professors, Readers and Lecturers should be in the ratio of 1:2:3 respectively. The Mehrotra Committee had also recommended creation of more posts of Professors and Readers. This was reiterated by the Government of India vide its notification dated July 22, 1988 in the interest of broadening the channel of open selection. The UGC was to evolve suitable criteria for the purpose. The Committee recommends that this be done and universities be given freedom to seek out brilliant people, providing them opportunities for joining the teaching profession at appropriate levels. It is recommended that the proportion of teaching positions as suggested by the Kothari Commission be achieved. At present there are no positions of Readers or Professors in the colleges in general. The Committee recommends that posts of Professors be provided in the post-graduate colleges. No college should be allowed to undertake post-graduate teaching in a discipline without providing for the post of a Professor in that discipline. In addition, at least one post of Reader should be created for each discipline being taught in under-graduate and post-graduate colleges.

6.7 **Faculty Development Programme**

The Committee noted the progress made in the scheme of training of teachers as initiated by the UGC through its academic staff development programmes and operated by Academic Staff College (ASC). The scheme has provided opportunity to a good proportion of teachers to complete orientation and subject-refresher programmes. However, this facility still falls short of requirement as a large number of teachers have not been able to attend such programmes. As per the UGC regulations, a teacher is required to attend one orientation programme and one subject-refresher programme to become eligible for placement in the senior scale and is required to complete at least two more refresher programmes in his/her career for placement in the selection grade. Usefulness of such programmes has also been appreciated by the teaching community as a whole. The Committee recommends that there is need for introducing the concept of induction-training programmes for the teachers through Academic Staff Colleges. The training should be imparted soon after recruitment.

The Committee further recommends that Academic Staff Colleges may continue to conduct such programmes at the beginning of the academic session as well as some time after the winter break so as to provide opportunity to newly-recruited teachers for attending orientation programmes. There is need for strengthening these programmes and making the opportunity available to a large number of Lecturers so as to help them update their knowledge and skills. Diploma course in Higher Education of the Indira Gandhi National Open University has already been recognised as equivalent to an orientation programme by the UGC. This may continue.

The Committee also felt that for faculty development at all levels, subject-refresher programmes of advanced nature should be made available. Details of these programmes may be worked out by the UGC.

Special training programmes/refresher courses for Librarians, Deputy Librarians, Assistant Librarians, Registrars, Deputy Registrars, Assistant Registrars and Directors, Deputy Directors of Physical Education and Assistant Directors of Physical Education may also be conducted regularly. The UGC should come out with a detailed scheme in this regard.

6.8 Teaching Days

The UGC regulations provide for universities and colleges to have minimum of 180 teaching days. The data obtained from various universities and colleges indicated that the actual number of teaching days was not more than 140 in a large number of cases and there were very few institutions which were observing 180 days as actual teaching days. The Committee feels that this is a matter of great concern. A reasonable and disciplined academic calendar is necessary in any system of quality education. It is also the single most transparent parameter in terms of which society judges teachers and academic institutions. No activity – academic or co-curricular – is possible without the presence of teachers and students in an institutions. One of the reasons for the decline in the number of teaching days is the large number of holidays being observed. Another reason is the demands on the institutions due to examinations. These further reduce the time available for smooth conduct of teaching work. In short, ensuring adequate teaching days would require vacations to be reduced by about a fortnight. This would encourage a University to change over to a two-semester academic calendar with each semester being of 90 days. We recommend that:

— in lieu of reduction in vacation, teachers be given additional earned leave of 5 days, say, equivalent to one third of the reduced vacation days. If an institution is not able to observe 180 teaching days, the provision of additional 5 days earned leave may not be applicable;

— a six day working week in institutions, may be enforced;

— the UGC may monitor the enforcement of a calendar of 180 days in a systematic manner.

The copy of the calendar thus worked out should be sent by the colleges to the universities and the universities to the UGC, every year.

6.9 **Workload**

The UGC guidelines regarding minimum number of actual teaching days, programme of examination reform and workload for teachers in universities and colleges issued in 1989 prescribe that the workload of a teacher in full employment should not be less than 40 hours a week for 30 working weeks in an academic year.

Actual teaching/contact hours with the students constitute 55 per cent of the prescribed workload for undergraduate teachers and about 35 per cent for the postgraduate teachers. The teachers are expected to spend the rest of the time in various activities like research, preparation for teaching, administration work, supervision of extra-curricular activities and self improvement.

The Committee endorses this workload pattern and further recommends as follows:

(i) Workload of a Lecturer on promotion to the post of Reader under the career advancement scheme will remain unchanged.

(ii) Colleges are being advised to include job-oriented programmes which involve field work/project work. It is being recommended that three hours per week be allocated to such activities and counted towards the work load of a teacher; and

(iii) In case of autonomous colleges, teachers have to take part in curriculum formation/setting and evaluation of assignments, conducting examinations, etc. Two hours may be counted for these towards the workload of a teacher.

6.10 Problems of Part-time Teachers

The Committee noted that a large number of teachers are employed on part-time or on per lecture basis. The Committee is of the view that such teachers must also fulfil the minimum eligibility criteria for being appointed as teachers. The practice of appointing part-time teachers should be sparingly used and the remuneration given for such work must be based on realistic norms. The UGC should take steps to evolve suitable guidelines and recommend revised remuneration for them. The Committee also noted that in some cases such part-time appointments have met with legal difficulties. It would, therefore, be necessary to provide a legally sustainable contract for such appointments. At the same time, this method should not become a means for avoiding the appointment of regular teachers against vacancies.

6.11 Age of Superannuation

The age of superannuation has been the subject of many representations received by the Committee. At present there is considerable diversity among institutions in this respect. While most universities observe 60 years as the age of retirement, Government colleges in most part of the country, have 58 years as the age of superannuation. Government-aided colleges, on the other hand, follow the universities in some places and the Government colleges in other. Kerala continues with 55 years as the age of superannuation for its college teachers. The Committee, therefore, recommends that the age of superannuation be uniformly 60 years in all colleges and universities. This gives an additional two years in most of the states and in Kerala, 5 years, to teachers as compared to employees in the Government sector. The Fifth Pay Commission has recommended 60 years as superannuation age for Government employees. If this is accepted by the Government, the age of superannuation for teachers should be 62 years.

6.12 Re-employment of Teachers after Superannuation

A provision for re-employment beyond 60 years of age was suggested by the UGC through a circular of 1988. Re-employment was to be given in two phases of three years and two years, respectively. This provision was not meant to be a provision for extension up to the age of 65 years for all teachers. It was to be used selectively and was to be justified in terms of specific institutional needs. This provision is not used generally in most of the state universities. Only a few central universities are using the provision to give re-employment to all teachers upto 65 years. The Committee is of the view that while the provision may be retained, the UGC should ensure that the practice of re-employment as a routine is not allowed to be followed by any institution. UGC may issue appropriate instructions in this regard.

6.13 Pension and Superannuation Benefits

Pension schemes have been introduced in the universities during the 90s replacing the earlier Contributory Provident Fund Schemes. A few universities had introduced pension scheme even before 1990. In 1995, the Employees Provident Fund Scheme under the Employees PF and Miscellaneous Provisions Act of 1952 was replaced by an Employees Pension Scheme by the Government. This pension scheme is applicable to all establishments that were covered by the earlier scheme. This implies that all private colleges would be covered. Government colleges would be covered by Government pension schemes and the universities that were allowed to operate their own provident funds would have to formulate their own pension schemes in line with the Government schemes. This has given rise to the problem of counting of qualified service for pension. This problem is inherent in the teaching profession as there is much greater institutional mobility in the service. Often the mobility entails moving from private to Government or from Government to university as well as from one state to another. Some State Governments e.g. Gujarat and Rajasthan have framed rules in this regard which permit counting of qualified service within the state. However, the service rendered outside the state is excluded. In the case of the Employees Pension Scheme, 1995, the problem is obviated as the pension would be determined by the number of years of participation in the scheme. In the case of universities, unless specific provisions are made along the lines of Central Government Rules in this respect, counting of qualified service rendered in parts would continue to remain a problem. The Committee recommends that the UGC issue guidelines to all universities so that uniform rules be followed by them.

The University Grants Commission had earlier considered the issue of counting of past service for purposes of senior scale/selection grade under the career advancement scheme for Lecturers.

A circular in this regard was also issued to all universities and colleges. The Committee is of the view that the same principle be adopted.

The Fifth Pay Commission has introduced special provision for all pre-1986 pensioners in order to ensure that the disadvantage of the older persons vis-a-vis the relatively recent retirees are reduced to some extent. In this regard, as teachers were not earlier covered by pension schemes, there is considerable economic distress among the older persons, due to the erosion caused by inflation in the value of the PFs as received by them. It is, therefore, suggested that for university teachers covered by CPF before the introduction of the pension scheme, an amount equivalent to the DA permissible at the pension level at the minimum of the present (i.e. pre-revised) pay scale be given as relief in DA to them. This would be a small gesture of goodwill for our older generation of teachers who were not given their rightful share for many years. They deserve our gratitude. Hence this small token.

The Committee recommends that a waiver may also be provided up to a maximum of five years due to late entry in service of the teachers having Ph.D. degree so that almost all teachers get full retirement benefits, which are available after 33 years of service.

6.14 **Facilities for Women Teachers**

The Fifth Pay Commission has suggested special facilities for women employees and officers. The Committee also feels that since the working women have to bear dual responsibilities in our society, there is need for provision of special facilities to women teachers. The following provisions are recommended by the Committee in this regard:

6.14.1 *Family Commitment*

A woman teacher may be allowed to work half-time for a maximum period of six years in her career when the children are young and family commitments are at the maximum. She may be given half of the pay plus half the allowances during this flexitime period. But she should not be deprived of other benefits such as LTC, housing and pension benefits, etc. during the same period.

6.14.2 *Day-care Centres*

The Committee recommends that quality day-care centres may be opened in universities and colleges with adequate equipment and staff to take care of the children of working parents. Such services should have adequate contribution from the users themselves for all programme-related costs and food, as also proportionate contribution to the salaries of the staff.

6.14.3 *Interrupted Career*

A woman teacher may have sometimes to interrupt her career for child-caring. The Committee recommends that there should be a provision for allowing women teachers to come back to the profession (not necessarily the same job) after an interruption of a maximum of five years and this period should not be considered as causing break in service.

6.14.4 *Leave-sharing Arrangement*

The Committee recommends that where both husband and wife are teachers in the same institution, the creation of an earned leave bank to be availed of by women teachers may be considered only for the period of rearing of very young children (such period should not exceed six years in all), provided that a woman teacher has exhausted the earned leave at her credit and there is earned leave lying at the credit of her husband.

6.14.5 *Accommodation*

The Committee recommends that while providing residential accommodation in the universities and colleges, some rooms may be earmarked for women teachers. Also construction of hostels and quarters should be undertaken specially for single-woman teachers. Apart from the above, the special facilities as recommended by the Central Pay Commission may be introduced for teachers, taking into account the specific requirements of higher education sector.

6.15 **Conditions of Service**

6.15.1 *Service Agreements*

Appointment of teachers is usually done through appointment letters which specify some of the important terms and conditions of employment. In many universities/colleges, at time of recruitment, every teacher is required to sign a service agreement to be lodged with the Registrar/Principal, with a copy to the teacher concerned. The Committee recommends that this should be made uniformly applicable to all the universities/colleges. Universities/colleges may draw up service agreements designed to reflect their particular needs. The agreement should indicate that performance assessment and evaluation would form an essential part of the terms of appointment and career advancement.

Some of the essential points to be covered in the service agreements are as follows:

(i) period of appointment;
(ii) period of probation and mode of confirmation;
(iii) pay scale and allowances;
(iv) rules for lien or deputation;
(v) leave facilities;
(vi) age of superannuation and superannuation benefits;
(vii) resignation, termination of service, retirement;
(viii) nature of appointment, duties and responsibilities;
(ix) disciplinary procedure; and
(x) code of professional ethics.

A teacher has to abide by and conform to the relevant provisions of the rules and regulations and code of conduct for teachers as laid down by the concerned university and as amended from time to time. It is essential that those rules be made part of the University Statutes/Ordinances. The new entrant should be provided with the above rules and regulations.

6.15.2 *Mobility*

The need for mobility in the academic profession arises because of well recognised factors. Open selections for the higher posts result in movement, and , the need to avoid inbreeding for generat-ing healthy and vibrant academic environment requires that mobility be consciously encouraged, It is , therefore, sometimes suggested that a minimum of 20 per cent appointments be made of persons from outside the state/university. We reiterate the importance of the need to encourage mobility especially because mobility is being reduced rather than being encouraged as a result of several factors that are outside the control of the universities. How this will be done will have to be decided at the level of individual universities. We feel that facilities like provision of adequate housing and rules about carrying service benefits (pensions, leave etc.) will go a long way in achieving the objective of encouraging mobility. Recommendations about these matters have been made separately.

6.15.3 *Medical Facilities*

There are variations in provision of medical facilities according to the types of institutions. Universities have the facility of medical reimbursement, etc. but the rates and facilities vary. Central Universities and state universities have different schemes. Government colleges are governed by Government rules and have access to medical facilities. Private colleges – aided as well as unaided– have very limited facilities and in many cases none are available at all. Therefore, efforts should be made at all levels to extend medical benefits to teachers, either through medical insurance or through state assistance. The UGC may set up a Committee to examine different aspects of medical facilities for teachers to work out a scheme with the advice of financial institutions like the General Insurance Corporation and Unit Trust of India.

6.16 **Dearness Allowance and Other Benefits**

6.16.1 *Dearness Allowance*

The Committee is of the view that the rate of dearness allowance payable to all teachers in the universities and colleges should be uniform and at par with those available to Central/State Government employees.

6.16.2 *Incentives for Professional Development*

The faculty should be encouraged to become members of a maximum of two professional national associations and the cost of the membership should be subsidised by the university/college to the extent of 50 per cent. Also, to help teachers to subscribe to journals, the committee recommends that every teacher should get a subsidy to the extent of 50 per cent of the cost of the journal subscribed, subject to the maximum of Rs. 500 per year. In addition, to encourage the teachers to be able to make use of E-mail facilities, the Committee recommends that the expenditure incurred on installation of e-mail facilities and annual charges excluding actual usage charges may be subsidised to the extent of 50 per cent.

6.16.3 *Computer Advance*

The Committee recommends that computer advance of Rs. One lakh may be given to the teachers, as per Central/State Governments rules.

6.16.4 *Leave Travel Concession*

The facility of leave travel concession to visit home town and any place in the country, as available to Central/State Government employees should be made available to all university/college teachers.

6.16.5 *Group Insurance Scheme*

Group Insurance Scheme is available to the employees of Central Government, autonomous organisations, Government undertakings, and central universities. The concerned authorities should take steps to make this facility available to the teachers.

6.16.6 *Housing*

6.16.6.1 Housing is one of the main areas of discontent and dissatisfaction among the teaching community. Many representations have been made to the Pay Committee at different places, highlighting the woefully inadequate facilities with the universities and colleges for providing housing to the staff members. While problems are more acute in the metropolitan cities, these are not very much less in other areas as well. This also seriously hampers the mobility of the teaching community and leads to the growth of vested interests in different places.

6.16.6.2 It is noted by the Committee that subsequent to the recommendations of the Fourth Central Pay Commission in respect of Central Government employees, the Central Government had taken certain positive steps to alleviate the sufferings of the staff on this account. Some of these initiatives are:

(i) Setting up of welfare society called the Indian Railway Welfare Organisation (IRWO) by the Ministry of Railways to look after the housing needs of railwaymen. This society is patterned after the Armymen's Welfare Society. IRWO, with its head office in New Delhi and under the control of the Ministry of Railways, has branches in different parts of the country and undertakes efforts pertaining to land acquisition, development, building of houses of different types for different categories catering to the needs of the people with different levels of purchasing power and allots these houses to the members on certain rational basis. Thus, a member of the society while being relieved of the botheration of purchase of land, construction, etc. has the choice to select a house within his/her means and in a place of his/her choice.

The Ministry of Urban Development has also constituted a similar society for meeting the housing needs of employees working in different Central Government departments other than the Ministry of Railways. Thus, by and large, different segments of the Central Government like Army, the Railways and other departments have been covered by these societies.

(ii) As a sequel to the Fourth Central Pay Commission recommendations, the Central Government has also liberalised the quantum of house-building advance and the eligibility criteria as well as the building cost ceilings.

(iii) Some of the State Governments have also taken steps in similar direction by encouraging the formation of employees' cooperatives housing societies and giving these societies suitable concessions, facilities, etc. But these mainly relate to State Government employees.

(iv) Some of the banking and other public sector undertakings have also extended housing facilities to their employees.

6.16.6.3 Several measures are being taken to increase the available housing stock including cooperative housing, state launched housing schemes and availability of financial housing, which may be reinforced further. There is, however, one avenue which has not been explored. This is the avenue of mobilising institutional finance from housing finance companies and banking institutions for house building on university land. If this is to be done, it would require the setting up of autonomous university housing agencies with an initial corpus contribution from the budget. This will enable mobilising institutional finance. Houses will be let out to teachers only and the rent, determined on a fair market basis, will be paid back to the agencies. The rental income will repay the loan and provide for maintenance. The police departments of Gujarat and Haryana have done so and the corporate sector raises such finances in a routine manner. Details will have to be worked out by a Committee specially set up for this purpose. We recommend that:

(i) A Committee be set up by the UGC in this regard; and
(ii) adequate provision may be made during the Ninth Plan period for the setting up of a University Housing Agency.

6.16.6.4 *House-Building Advance and House-Rent Allowance:* In the paras on housing, the Committee has given its recommendation about the provision of housing facilities to the university and college teachers. Further to this, the Committee recommends that house-building advance and house-rent allowance be made available to all university/college teachers, as per the Central/State Government rules.

6.16.7 *Conveyance Advance and Conveyance Allowance*

The Committee is of the view that conveyance advance and

conveyance allowance may be given to teachers as per the Central/ State Government rules.

6.17 Allowance for Teachers of Universities and Colleges in the Hilly Areas

It has been represented to us that considering the backwardness of hilly areas and high cost of living there, coupled with lack of ready means of communication, it is desirable to extend the benefit of some compensatory allowance to attract good teachers to the universities/colleges in the hilly areas of the country (North East, Sikkim, Himachal Pradesh, etc.). We recommend that such allowances as are applicable to the Central/State Government employees in the hilly areas may also be given to the university and college teachers.

6.18 Leave Rules

The Committee took note of the Leave Rules as recommended by Sen Committee and the Mehrotra Committee. It feels that the leave rules as laid down by these Committees may be followed except for some changes as necessitated by the recommendations of the Central Pay Commission.

6.19 Leave Encashment

The Committee recommends that leave encashment facilities be extended to teachers of universities and colleges as per Central/ State Government rules.

6.20 City Compensatory Allowance

The Committee recommends that the City Compensatory Allowance as applicable to Central/State Governments be made applicable to the teachers in universities/colleges.

6.21 **Resource Mobilization**

The Committee realises the necessity of greater Government funding for supporting Higher Education. It is aware of the National Policy on Education, 1986 which recognised that concurrency in education required a new sharing of responsibility – a meaningful partnership – between the Union Government and the states in this vital area of national life. The number of universities and colleges have considerably increased over the years and further, higher education is an important source for providing trained and skilled professional for Industry, Agriculture, Trade, Commerce and other socio-political sectors. Nevertheless, as additive to resource mobilization, the institutions should take adequate steps for resource generation by promoting (i) self-financing courses, (ii) greater interaction with industry (iii) greater involvement in consultancy; and (iv) contract research work. At the same time, it will be useful: (i) to promote ingenious optimisation of library and laboratory resources available in various institutions of the country; and (ii) to encourage the ingenuity in fabrication of low-cost laboratory equipment and indigenous fabrication of instruments.

The UGC has already started a scheme to encourage the resource mobilization by the universities in the form of giving bonus grant to the extent of 25 per cent of the resource mobilized. In addition, donations to the universities are exempted from income tax. However, all these facilities do not exist for colleges and the Committee recommends extension of both these facilities to the college sector. In addition, the individuals who mobilise resource for their universities/colleges should be suitably rewarded. Appropriate guidelines may be formulated by the UGC in this regard.

6.22 **Civic Rights**

In this context, the Kothari Education Commission (1964-66) recommended as follows:

Teachers should be free to exercise all civic rights and should be eligible for public offices at the local, district, state or national level. No legal restriction should be placed on their participation in elections, but when they do so, they should be expected to proceed on leave.

The latest circular of UGC, issued in this respect in 1987, envisages that the teachers who are elected/nominated to Parliament or State Legislature would be required to take leave of absence during their term as members. However, in this process they would not be losing their seniority or increments. The Committee endorses this recommendation.

Thus, the above provisions should continue. Leave in this regard should mean extraordinary leave.

6.23 Code of Professional Ethics

The UGC, with the participation of All India Federation of University and College Teachers' Organisations, prepared a code of professional ethics for university and college teachers which included responsibilities of the teachers, do's and don'ts for teachers with respect to their relations with students, colleagues, authorities, non-teaching staff, guardians and even society. It was sent to all the universities and colleges in February, 1989. However, the Committee feels that despite its recognized usefulness, it is not being followed in actual practice by the teaching community. The Committee, therefore, recommends that instead of being advisory in nature, it may be made part of the regulation of UGC and incorporated in the Statutes/Ordinances of the universities. It may form part of the service agreement to ensure implementation.

6.24 Grievance-Redressal Machinery

The Kothari Commission examined the issue of redressal of grievances of teachers and made certain recommendations.

The National Policy on Education, 1986 (with modification undertaken in 1992) specifically mentioned the creation of a machinery for redressal of grievances of teachers. The Ramamurti Committee (1990) also examined the matter on the basis of recommendations made by the Law Commission. But all these await implementation. The Committee recommends the implementations of the Law Commission's recommendations regarding tribunalisation of justice after due examination by the UGC, Government of India and the State Governments. The university may also consider appointing an ombudsman to deal with grievances of students and others affected by the university functioning. Details may be worked out in consultation with the National Law School at Bangalore.

6.25 **Date of Implementation and Review**

The date of implementation of the pay scales should be January 1, 1996, or the same as decided by the Central Government in respect of its employees. However, the recommendations regarding age of superannuation and other conditions, including new provision for advancement from Reader to Professor may be implemented from a prospective date to be decided by the UGC. The UGC may take up quinquennial review of the implementation of the pay scales and other recommendations of the Committee in all relevant aspects.

6.26 **Accountability**

Better pay scales and service conditions are important requirements for ensuring the quality of higher education. However, these do not reflect the quality of teaching-learning process and the contribution made by teachers in teaching, research and extension, in other words, the accountability of the teaching profession. Concern for the accountability of the profession had been expressed by the Radhakrishnan Commission, the Kothari Commission and the National Commission for Teachers in Higher Education as also by the Pay Review Committees headed by Professors Sen and Mehrotra. The last named Committee had even spelt out the methodology of introducing the concept of accountability in the teaching profession and pressed for its implementation.

The National Policy on Education (1986) contemplated three requirements for the measurements/evaluation of accountability. According to it, the evaluation must be:

(i) Open;
(ii) Participative;
(iii) Data-based.

(a) Precisely speaking, evaluation becomes open when:

(i) The components evaluated have clearly defined objectives;
(ii) indicators of performance regarding the achievement of objectives are prescribed in advance; and
(iii) the teacher has knowledge of the job he/she is expected to perform along with the details of each specific role.

(b) Evaluation becomes participative if the indicators of good performance and relative weightages to be given to the components of evaluation are decided upon in consultation and collaboration with the users of the system. This clearly permits the involvement of students in the evaluation process. As users of the system, they are entitled to playing this role.

(c) Coming to the third aspect, namely, making performance appraisal data-based, we realise that this is perhaps the most formidable component in the entire scheme of performance appraisal. It may be useful to discuss at some length as to how we lay down possible quantitative/qualitative criterion that will go towards generating the necessary data. From our discussions, it appears that students' evaluation must constitute one of the main indicators in-so-far as the performance of the individual teacher is concerned.

Further, we may have to prescribe suitable criteria for research, institutional development, preparation of instruction material and general contribution to the building up of the academic atmosphere on the campus.

In this connection, the Mehrotra Committee requires to be quoted. It had said, ..."A reliable and credible system of evaluation by students of teachers' performance should be worked out carefully and meticulously and introduced gradually and selectively." Had this been done, there would not have been any problem. Now it has become necessary that the instruments of accountability are introduced without further delay and all over the country.

6.26.1 *Self-Appraisal of Teachers*

In regard to self-appraisal by teachers, the Mehrotra Committee recommended that it be "introduced immediately in all institutions of higher learning." It was also suggested that the self-assessment report should include "factual information about the total workload, the average number of hours spent by the teacher per day in the institution, the number of periods for which he conducted actual teaching/practicals/tutorials: and the number of days for which leave of any kind was availed of, etc."

But, except in a few cases, the State Governments/universities did not evolve a system or frame regulations so as to ensure assessment and accountability of teachers. The UGC did some follow-up work by bringing forth a self-appraisal proforma and code of professional ethics for university and college teachers with the help of AIFUCTO. The overall impact in both cases has been far from noticeable.

The Committee reiterates that the self-appraisal proforma as in force (with modifications) should be made an annual feature of the review of teachers' performance as also an essential component for the grant of any type of incentive or upward movement in the career of a teacher.

6.26.2 *Students' Assessment of Teachers*

The Committee examined in detail the concept of students' assessment of teachers' performance in the light of frequent objections raised and apprehensions expressed in this regard. The Committee has come to the conclusion that limitations notwithstanding, the students' evaluation of the teacher, has to be accepted as one of the components for assessing a teachers performance. The Committee recommends that students' assessment be made a part of the evaluation procedure in all colleges and universities. A proforma has been designed to initiate the process.

6.26.3 *Maintenance of Attendance Registers*

The Mehrotra Committee reiterated the following recommendations concerning the maintenance of Attendance Registers and their submission by teachers as made by the National Commission on Teachers-II.

> *It is suggested that every teacher should maintain a register in which he/she records his/her activities for each working day. This is particularly important for the teaching function.*
> *Procedures relating to the maintenance of attendance registers need to be strictly observed. It is suggested that registers may be submitted to the Principal's office, preferably at the end of the day, but certainly on every Saturday, and information contained therein may be made use of to remove lacunae and inadequacies during the week itself.*

It should be ensured that the above requirement is strictly fulfilled. In addition, details about invigilation and examination work should also be provided. Guidelines in this regard should be framed and incorporated in the proposed Statute. This would ensure uniformity of approach.

6.26.4 *Implementation*

During the discussions with the officers of the universities, Ministries and the State Governments, references were frequently made to the decline of work culture in educational institutions. The Committee is aware of the fact that a lapse on the part of a few tends to become a reflection on the entire teaching community. The Teachers' Associations with whom we have had discussions in different states took the view without exception that they were in favour of ensuring accountability and submission of appraisal forms as contemplated in the Mehrotra Committee Report. It is our considered opinion that this aspect of the accountability procedure deserves the highest consideration. The recommendations of the Committee concerning performance appraisal and students' assessment of teachers, therefore, should be treated as an integral part of the package of recommendations on pay scale and service conditions and should not be viewed as detachable in any way. The committee therefore recommends as follows:

1. The universities may have to make necessary amendments in their Statutes and Ordinances to take into account these recommendations and implement them effectively. Likewise the State Governments may also frame appointment rules and regulations to give effect to these recommendations in accountability.
2. It is necessary that the appraisal form by each individual teacher is submitted annually. Universities/colleges should lay down a definite time-schedule for the submission of appraisal forms, their review and communication of comments, as and when required. Non-submission of appraisal forms has to be viewed seriously and considered as a lapse which should invite action as per rules, to be framed in an appropriate manner.
3. There may be provision for review of the appraisal form by a Committee constituted by the Executive Council/Syndicate/Board of Management, as the case may be. The

composition of the Committee must be such as to ensure objectivity and credibility, both on the part of the faculty and the management.

6.26.5 *Generation of Appropriate Environment*

Teachers' discontent is sometimes related to problems of selection. The administration should see to it that selections are made in time and in a transparent manner. Transparency instils confidence among teachers, students and all others concerned. It is desirable to give encouragement to good teachers. Further, efforts should be made to provide facilities to all teachers, thereby making room for enhancing their professional efficiency.

A proper, congenial, and encouraging atmosphere for academic activities can certainly be created in universities and colleges. Vice-Chancellors, Principals of colleges and Heads of Departments including Professors of the departments and, indeed, all teachers have to play a vital role in this regard.

Teacher-emoluments and career opportunities are indeed very important motivating factors for the teachers to play their role effectively. Another equally important aspect is the academic environment of our institutions. Unfortunately, while emoluments have significantly improved, the institutional environment has deteriorated almost across the board. A few islands of healthy environment in the system are exceptions. We are of the view that unless conscious steps are taken at all levels – political (Centre and the States), administrative and, academic – it would be rather difficult to arrest the decline. Teachers can and must perform better. They can do so only if the environment in which they function is improved. This could be achieved by having a common minimum agenda for higher education with a perspective view and an accepted code of institutional behaviour involving all concerned. The Higher Education sector, along with the Defence sector and the Judiciary needs to be treated as a pillar of healthy democracy by taking appropriate steps to free the sector from political interference and possible manipulations which have unfortunately become a common feature of our social life in the present times.

Certain other steps for generating the proper academic environment in colleges as well as in universities may also be thought of. Academic activities involving a cluster of colleges, whether in rural or urban areas, all over the district or towns around the universities should be organised. Frequent seminars by the parent university departments may be organised with the help of the departments of the affiliated colleges. All efforts should be made to encourage development of teaching and research capability.

In the context of accountability for all, a combination of administrative skills and academic will be combined with transparency in action and real and sincere academic attitude would certainly improve matters. This will go well with the Indian psyche as reflected in the following verse of the *Gita*.

> " The way in which persons of the higher order act, ordinary persons also act in the same way. The example which they set is followed by others".
>
> — *Shrimad Bhagwad Gita* 3.2.1

In fact, nothing is more infectious than an example.

22

World Bank Report on Primary Education in India: Summary (1997)

India's primary education glass is two-thirds full, one-third empty. Having steadily raised primary enrolment rates over the past four decades, India now has 67 million children aged 6-10 who are attending primary school, but 28 million to 32 million primary school-age-children who are not.

The result is that many of the huge returns to primary education are forgone. Primary education leads to better family health, lower fertility, and thus slower population growth. It helps workers to take advantage of technological change, which raises their productivity and earnings. Increasing the labour force's average primary schooling by even one year can increase output substantially. And because educated parents are more likely to send their children to school, primary education perpetuates the benefits from one generation to the next.

These benefits of primary education launched the takeoff of the rapidly growing economies of East Asia. But India's low average educational attainment has not yet reached the critical threshold where benefits are greatest and high economic growth rates are sustained. Reaching that threshold will take some time. At the current rate of growth in schooling, some of the largest states in India will not reach an average of four to five years of primary education until well into the next century.

Nor can education be measured solely in years of enrolment. What matters is what students learn, retain, and apply in life. Teachers are critical in students' learning, but with teachers' salaries consuming 97 per cent of the primary education budget, little is left for anything else, including instructional materials and teachers' in-service training. Textbooks are also critical in students' learning, but the instructional and physical quality of textbooks in India is often poor.

Another important part of the primary education story is the great diversity in performance. Almost all students — 97 per cent— are in the 15 major states. Two of these states are doing very well, providing almost all their children with a primary education. But several are far behind, and six account for 25 million of the 32 million primary-school-age children not in school. Progress in the other states falls somewhere in between. Within states, too, there is diversity, with some districts faring poorly even in states that are otherwise doing well, and vice-versa. There also are gaps between groups of children, with education outcomes differing between girls and boy, between the poor and the better-off, and between the tribal and scheduled caste children and others.

India's goal of universal primary education of good quality points to three main challenges: expanding access, raising learning achievement, and reducing gaps in education outcomes across states and among groups. Four actions will be key in meeting these challenges:

— Increasing the financing for primary education;
— Improving the preparation, motivation, and deployment of teachers;
— Improving the quality of textbooks and the efficiency of their production; and
— Building managerial and institutional capacity.

The decentralization of authority and financing — to the states today and the districts tomorrow — makes the task of ensuring the required levels of funding problematic, the improvement of teaching and textbooks easier, and the building of local capacity essential. In all this, the Central Government's leadership will be more important than ever for guiding policy, sponsoring national initiatives, and transferring resources to the states while devising incentives for states to increase their education budgets.

CHALLENGES FOR PRIMARY EDUCATION

India has achieved high gross enrolment rates, but low attendance and high dropout rates mean that many fewer children complete the primary cycle than enrol in primary school. If all children are to complete a primary education of good quality, the Indian governments (national, state, and local) must create accessible schools, increase the efficiency of student flows (by reducing repetition), and provide the resources needed to improve quality. For the most difficult-to-reach children, this education may be provided through non-formal or alternative education programmes.

Finding the money for this will not be easy because primary education is particularly vulnerable to today's fiscal problems, especially at the state level. Of all services that state governments provide, education invariably consumes the largest part of the budget. Primary education in turn consumes the largest part of the education budget — as it should, because as well as producing benefits directly, it also increases the effectiveness of investments in such other services as health and nutrition.

The main challenge for central, state, and district education authorities is to improve the supply, quality, and holding power of education in rural primary schools. Cost-effective strategies must be found for increasing the percentage of children aged 6 to 10 who complete primary school, improving their general levels of learning, and reducing gaps associated with gender, poverty, and tribal or caste affiliation. The scale and complexity of the necessary changes require that authorities and civic society at all levels continue to play a role in planning and implementation.

Expanding Access

Accommodating all children aged 6 to 10 in primary schools by 2007 (the final year of the Tenth Plan) could require building as many as 1.3 million class-rooms and hiring 740,000 new teachers.

Building schools using professionally supervised community construction and local materials can be cost-effective. Also required will be temporary measures to accommodate the primary school participation of overage students who enroll late and sustained measures to reduce repetition. Local efforts by village education committees to monitor student enrolment and school attendance could help to ensure that children who enroll in school complete their education without repeating grades or dropping out.

Enrolment data and age-specific literacy rates suggest that India has made much progress in expanding access to education: in 1993 about 100 million children were enrolled in primary school, up from 85 million in 1987. But school attendance is often irregular, and primary school dropout rates are high. About 32 million of the 105 million children aged 6 to 10 were out of school in 1993. About 75 per cent of the children who are out of school live in six states: Andhra Pradesh, Bihar, Madhya Pradesh, Rajasthan, Uttar Pradesh and West Bengal.

Reaching full enrolment of the age group 6 to 10 remains a major challenge in all states of India and a distant goal in some. Although there is considerable uncertainty about the reliability of the available data on India's education system, the following picture emerges. On the positive side,

— More than 80 per cent of 6 years old enrol in school.
— Enrolment by girls increased by 20 per cent between 1986 and 1993.
— About 70 per cent of children aged 6-10 attend school regularly.

And on the negative side,

— Growth in enrolment between 1986 and 1993 was modest (13.8 per cent), and the official gross enrolment rate increased only 4.2 percentage points to reach 95 per cent in 1993-94.

— There are severe shortages of teachers and classrooms, especially in the most populous states.
— About 15-20 per cent of the children enrolled do not attend school regularly.
— About 35 per cent of those who enroll drop out before completing the primary school cycle.

To address this situation, the Indian government has made a commitment to the goals of the 1990 World Conference on Education for All, held in Jomtien, Thailand. It has set a goal of providing education of good quality to all primary-school-age children. And it has committed itself to ensuring that the necessary resources are available, indicating that the allocation to education will increase from less than 4 per cent of Gross Domestic Product (GDP) to 6 per cent by the end of the Ninth Plan in 2002.

Improving the quality of primary education and using available resources more efficiently are priorities that no state can ignore. Several of India's states – for example, Kerala, Orissa, and Tamil Nadu – now have the capacity to enrol all children ages 6 to 10 and, by improving efficiency, could reach the Jomtien goals in the near future.

Other states – and districts within states – will require special attention if India wishes to make real progress toward achieving the Jomtien goals. National progress will critically depend on making progress in the six states that have three-quarters of the children who are out of school. Almost half the additional classrooms and teachers required to enroll all children aged 6 to 10 are needed in Bihar and Uttar Pradesh. Rajasthan has the lowest female literacy rate and the second lowest (after Bihar) proportion of children aged 6 to 10 attending school. Andhra Pradesh, Madhya Pradesh, and West Bengal are populous states with below-average school attendance rates. It is in these six states that the key challenges of educational development lie and that the success of the government's policy goals will be determined.

Demand-side interventions may be needed to encourage the regular attendance of children in school. One possible approach is to enforce compulsory attendance laws in states where enrolment rates are relatively high. Another is to create demand for attendance, through midday meal programmes, attendance scholarships, or awareness campaigns. Researchers have found that the midday meal programme has positive effects on learning achievement in Madhya Pradesh, and attendance scholarships have been effective in Kerala. Although more research is needed to assess the effects of these benefits and more selective targeting may be necessary to improve their cost-effectiveness, these strategies could help poor families meet the costs of schooling. Probably more important, however, is to provide schools that parents perceive to be of sufficient quality to be worthwhile.

Enhancing Learning Achievement

Learning achievement in India is low. Children who reach final year of lower primary school (grade 4 in some states and grade 5 in others) often have mastered less than half the curriculum. Studies around the world show that parents' investing in their children}s education may be the most effective way to boost learning achievement. But poverty limits the ability of many Indian parents to make the necessary investments, such as purchasing books and supplies and forgoing their children's labour. So, for the foreseeable future, strategies for raising learning achievement will need to focus on improving the quality of education in schools. What is most effective in doing this varies across states and districts, making it important to enable states, districts, and even schools to make their own decisions about which inputs to invest in.

Increasing learning achievement requires building on knowledge about the factors that affect learning and their costs in India.

— Most important is the opportunity to learn: time spent in school, with the teacher present and providing instruction, and time spent doing homework.

— Teachers' subject knowledge is the most critical factor in teacher quality.

— Teaching practices matter.
— School factors associated with higher learning achievement vary by location.
— Good school facilities and sufficient classroom space are associated with higher achievement.
— Even modest teaching tools — such as textbooks, libraries, and classroom instructional materials — are significant determinants of achievements.
— Some popular investments do not boost achievement.

Supply-side (school-level) interventions to increase instructional time, provide a physical facility for learning, provide better-educated teachers, and ensure that students teachers have appropriate instructional materials deserve the highest priority in developing strategies to raise learning achievement. Cost-effectiveness analysis can help identify specific inputs appropriate for different local conditions. Because teachers' attendance is a strong predictor of students' learning, strategies that more closely link teachers' salaries to their work performance could also be considered. The new *panchayati raj* institutions at the district, subdistrict, and village levels could play a role in such strategies.

Considerable variation across states, districts, and schools means, however, that packages of interventions identified locally to meet the needs of specific schools are more likely to be cost-effective that are uniform packages. What is effective in a state with a higher level of educational development may differ from what is effective in a state with a lower level of development. Recognising this, the Government of India has established a programme, now being implemented in most of the major states, to support the local development of primary education.

Particularly important is the need to improve the quality of rural primary schools, where more than 78 per cent of children are educated. Providing better services should not only directly improve learning achievement, it should also increase the schools' attractiveness to children and parents alike and thus increase enrolment and attendance.

Achieving acceptable levels of quality will require strategies that take into account variation in access, completion, and learning achievement in primary education within and among states. Strategies also need to take account of the fact that girls, the poor, and students from Scheduled Castes and tribes tend to stay in school for the shortest period and to score below average.

Reducing Gaps in Enrolment, Retention, and Achievement

Gaps in education outcomes persist in India between girls and boys, between the poor and the better-off, and between children from Scheduled Castes and Tribes and other children. Poverty partially explains the gaps between genders and between caste and tribal groups, and poverty-reducing interventions would probably help to narrow them. But such interventions have been insufficient and poorly targeted; it would be more efficient to target them to all poor students, regardless of gender or caste or tribal status. Other constraints contributing to gaps in education are more cultural than economic. These constraints — and appropriate strategies for addressing them — vary among disadvantaged groups and, for tribal students, within them.

In India the gender gap is due to a mix of cultural and economic constraints and could be reduced through awareness campaigns, child-care centres, direct incentives, and the hiring of more female teachers. Although the caste gap is due largely to poverty, welfare-based interventions may be more efficiently directed at the poor, regardless of case status. To close the tribal gap, which stems from a complex combination of economic and cultural factors, non-welfare-based interventions focusing on cultural factors will continue to be appropriate.

International evidence shows that education gaps narrow for two main reasons: enrolment gaps close as the education system expands to provide access to all, and achievement gaps (including differences in attendance and retention) close when the education system targets interventions selectively.

FIVE ESSENTIAL ACTIONS FOR EXPANDING ACCESS AND IMPROVING LEARNING

Five actions are crucial for expanding access and improving learning in India's schools: providing more financing for primary education; improving the preparation, motivation, and deployment of teachers; improving the quality of text-books and the efficiency of their production; strengthening management and institutional capacity; and strengthening the leadership of the Central Government.

Increasing Financing for Primary Education

Over the past two years, the Indian authorities—at both the centre and the state level—have frequently reiterated their intention to ensure that public resources for education increase to 6 per cent of GDP over the period of the Ninth Plan (1997-2002). In 1993-94 total spending on education by Central and State departments of education was 3.5 per cent of GDP, down from 3.8 per cent in 1989-90. As a share of GDP, spending on elementary education was 1.6 per cent in 1993-94. So, both the centre and the states need to increase significantly their allocations to education. This will be very difficult unless the fiscal performance of the public sector improves substantially.

Nevertheless, providing all children with a better primary school education is within India's grasp. Many states have identified and applied successful strategies for providing schools, classrooms, teachers, textbooks, and other instructional materials to reach this objective, and these strategies could be adapted and used in other states. Many states have found avenues for cooperation between public and private institutions in training teachers, constructing and managing schools, and producing and distributing text books; these lessons too could be applied in other states.

With conservative assumptions about economic growth, 80 per cent of the resources required for universal primary education would be available a decade from now if past trends continue. But three problems must be resolved before universal primary education can be reached. First, states need to learn more from one another about successful strategies. Second, a means needs to be found for transferring resources to the states with the highest share of children out of school. Third, strategies for increasing the demand for primary education need to be explored to ensure that the places created in primary schools are used.

The trends in revenue deficits in the major states and the falling share of development expenditures suggest that boosting budgetary resources for education will require significant changes in the conduct of fiscal policy, such as increasing revenues, restructuring expenditures, and providing schooling cost-effectively. A combination of strategies could be considered. In line with agreements reached with the Government of India as reflected in the 1995 country economic memorandum (published as World Bank 1995), these include:

— Developing a wider revenue base to improve resource mobilization.
— Allocating at least the share of plan expenditure for primary education projected for the Eighth Plan period and preparing for significant increases (as planned) in the share under the Ninth Plan beginning in 1997.
— Increasing the spending on education through a general restructuring of total expenditures. (There is a scope for such restructuring: losses by the state electricity corporations are two and a half times the total state plan expenditures on education).
— Developing financial arrangements for the planned third tier of government, the district level, to ensure that adequate financing is developed for these governments' responsibilities in education and that there are incentives not to divert such funds. Inequalities within states will have to be addressed through policies that effect differential transfers from the state to lower levels of government. And local governments will have to be enabled to raise additional revenues from taxes that may be less available to state governments.

In addition,

— Focusing on reducing repetition and dropout rates to reduce the cost per graduate. Lowering repetition rates would make it possible to accommodate many more students for marginal increases in expenditure.
— Reviewing the efficiency and effectiveness of incentive programmes. Even without the school programmes, twice as much is spent on incentive programmes as is spent on all non-teacher school inputs. The little evidence that exists suggests that several of the major components of incentive and scholarship programmes tend to be inefficiently administered and have no real effect on enrolment and retention. More effective might be the free distribution of higher-quality textbooks.

Overall, governments of educationally backward states may be able to increase the growth rate of expenditures on primary education if economic growth rates are buoyant and public finances are restructured. But growth rates in these states would need to double, which is probably not realistic. To augment the efforts of the state governments, the central government could increase its support to these states.

Improving the Preparation, Motivation, and Deployment of Teachers

Improving teachers' performance is the most important challenge in primary education in India. Teachers' salaries claim by far the largest share of state education budgets. Teachers are the principal instructional instrument in most schools, and their performance falls short of what is needed to ensure that all children complete primary school with adequate learning.

India's governments have done much to improve the quality of the teaching corps. They have raised pre-service education requirements, improved teacher training, and increased the diversity of the teaching force (although not enough to match the diversity of the students). As a result of historical deficiencies in teachers' education and training and poor performance incentives, however, many teachers still have little understanding of the material they teach, have few teaching skills, and are poorly motivated. Teachers are frequently absent from school, because of poor motivation or competing administrative demands on their time. Thus, in the next decade an essential task will be to improve the preparation, motivation, and deployment of teachers.

What will it take to improve the performance of teachers? Here are five strategies that could have high payoffs:

— Implementing teacher qualification standards that extend the length of pre-service general education and increase teachers' knowledge.
— Shortening the duration of pre-service teacher training and shifting its emphasis to building teaching skills.
— Sustaining state-level and district-level provision of continuous, school-based in-service training
— Improving the conditions of teaching and making career advancement and promotion contingent on performance.
— increasing the share of female teachers and teachers who speak local languages, which is especially important for girls and students from scheduled tribes.

Improving the Quality of Textbooks and the Efficiency of their Production

India supplies textbooks to almost all its primary students—often at no cost—but the quality of the textbooks leaves something to be desired. The instructional quality and readability of many are low. The physical quality is often poor. And in many states children carry too heavy a load (both physical and cognitive) of textbooks. Improving textbooks is critical: they are the main instructional aid in India's primary schools, they carry the curriculum for both students and teachers, and for most students they are the only available reading material. There also is a need for increased efficiency in the production and distrubution of textbooks. For many of the quality and efficiency issues, the solutions can be found within India. Studies have found good practices in one or several states in most aspects of textbook development and publishing.

Among the examples are the good use of the private sector for printing and distribution in Uttar Pradesh, better pay for textbooks writers in Karnataka, simpler and more readable texts in Maharashtra, Tamil Nadu, and Assam, and limitations placed on the number of pages assigned and printed in Kerala. Each state will need to select combinations of reforms that suit local circumstances, building on present strengths and changing practices in key areas. The changes called for should be feasible for each state, given that a large share of improved practices have been put in place in other Indian states.

As could be expected, new practices are also called for. Some are needed to take advantage of the potential for improved efficiency that is emerging with the adoption of minimum levels of learning standards by all states and is making cross-border sales more feasible. Others are needed to help the textbook publishing industry evolve toward international standards of practice. The three most promising areas are: adopting strategies to improve quality, establishing autonomous textbook corporations, and reducing the cost of providing textbooks as the result of heightened involvement of the private sector.

Three relatively straightforward actions would do much over time to produce more readable, more effective textbooks:

— Setting standards for vocabulary and for sentence complexity and length
— Conducting simple trials of readability and comprehension with students and teachers
— Investing more in research, writing and design.

In many states the fragmentation of authority for textbook publishing raises costs and lowers effectiveness. Financially autonomous textbook corporations such as the one in Tamil Nadu offer three key advantages:

— Instituting financial controls
— Improving quality control
— Using flexible staffing strategies.

In India, as elsewhere, there has been a tendency to manage the costs of textbooks by reducing the quality of manufacturing. Six alternative strategies may prove more fruitful:

— Increasing the financial accountability of textbook corporations
— Reducing the number of pages in each textbook
— Increasing the amount of competition in printing
— Letting printers purchase paper
— Encouraging cross-border sales
— Expanding the private sector's role in distribution.

Strengthening Management and Institutional Capacity

Strengthening the managerial and institutional capacity of the education system typically requires improving organizational structures, developing institutional capacity, and strengthening information systems. Although progress on all these is still needed. India has made significant strides in addressing them in four ways:

— Establishing, through the 73rd and 74th amendments (enacted in 1992) to the Constitution, panchayati raj institutions in all states and devolving responsibility for primary education to district-level panchayats.
— Training district-level planners, village education committee members, and school headmasters and head teachers involved in the District Primary Education Programme.
— Strengthening state and district education institutions to provide support at the block and village (school) level.

— Establishing a management information system to provide more accurate and timely education data for use at all levels.

The management of education in India should soon change dramatically as responsibility is devolved to panchayati raj institutions. This devolution is likely to lead to much uncertainty as states sort out which responsibilities they should transfer to these institutions and which they should retain. It will also create new needs in training and technical support for the *panchayati raj* institutions many of which have little experience in managing education.

Institutions at all levels will see their functions change, and district-level personnel, school headmasters, and village education committees will acquire many new responsibilities or receive formal authority to carry out complex tasks that they already perform. These shifts in responsibility need to be accompanied by careful planning to prevent the administrative weaknesses that arise when managers lack sufficient authority or resources to do their jobs effectively, when lines of communication are blocked, when roles and responsibilities are unclear, or when managers' time is consumed by routine tasks.

Strengthening the Central Government's Leadership

India's Central Government is responsible for developing many aspects of policy and for funding centrally sponsored plan schemes in primary education, and it provides general financial transfers to states. Its allocations to education under the Ninth Plan are slated to increase significantly, particularly for elementary education.

The Central Government has increased its role in support of primary education since 1986, mainly by supporting interventions to improve learning achievement. It has employed both uniform and specially tailored interventions. First, centrally sponsored schemes to strengthen basic education have supported such relatively standard interventions as Operation Blackboard for small rural schools, a national research and development programme to help states establish minimum levels of learning in core subjects, district institutes of education and training to provide professional support to teachers, state-level programmes of non-formal education, and total literacy campaigns. Second, recognizing the role of location-specific factors in educational achievement, the central government launched the District Primary Education Programme in 1993 to increase enrolment, retention, and the quality of primary education through district-designed activities and performance-based resource allocation specially tailored to meet local needs.

The analysis in this book suggests that the Central Government will need to expand its role in primary education in the medium term for three reasons; the low level of resources devoted to primary education by many State Governments and the large number of children out of school; the importance at this stage of the country's educational development of capacity-building in states and districts to plan and manage education more effectively; and the need for substantial research to select cost-effective strategies.

Gradually expanding the District Primary Education Programme, paying careful attention to cost-effectiveness, will be essential during the medium term to provide a bridging mechanism as states undergo fiscal reforms. Untied grants to states for educational development might also be considered under terms that do not allow substitution and that require a commitment by the State Government either to increase the growth of its education spending (for low-spending states such as Haryana) or to maintain the share of education in total spending (for high-spending states such as Kerala) and generally to shift expenditures toward the social sectors.

The Central Government might also wish to address educational inequality across states more broadly. It could focus the criteria for distributing general transfers more on need, balanced by an increased emphasis on equal fiscal effort across states. And it could target grants for the centrally sponsored schemes to ensure that states which have made strong efforts to raise revenues and allocate expenditure toward the social sectors are not penalized and that those which have not tried to raise revenues or which have expenditure patterns biased against the social sectors are not rewarded.

India faces these challenges with four assets. The first is an expanded primary education system that has put the basic elements of schooling within reach for many children. The second is a strong policy framework with significant commitment from the central and state governments. The third is an innovative and initially well-financed reform programme aimed at strengthening primary education, with a strong focus on quality. And the fourth is an educational research and development community increasingly engaged with the problems of primary education.

Source: Reproduced from UPA Mailing 97/2 July, 1997, World Bank, Washington D.C.

PART — THREE

EDUCATIONAL STATISTICS

EDUCATIONAL STATISTICS

Table 23.1: Basic Indicators of Human Development

Year	Life Expectancy at birth+ (Years)	Literacy rate @ (per cent)	Birth rate*	Death rate* (Per thousand)	Infant Mortality rate*	Per Capita NNP at 1980-81 prices** (Rs.)
1951	32.1	18.3	39.9	27.4	146	1127
1961	41.3	28.3	41.7	22.8	146	1350
1971	45.6	34.5	36.9	14.9	129	1520
1981	50.4	43.6	33.9	12.5	110	1630
1982	NA	NA	33.8	11.9	105	1693
1983	55.4	NA	33.7	11.9	105	1691
1984	NA	NA	33.9	12.6	104	1790
1985	NA	NA	32.9	11.8	97	1811
1986	NA	NA	32.6	11.1	96	1841
1987	NA	NA	32.2	10.9	95	1870
1988	57.7	NA	31.5	11.0	94	1901
1989	58.3	NA	30.6	10.3	91	2059
1990	58.7	NA	30.2	9.7	80	2157
1991	59.4	52.2	29.5	9.8	80	2222

(*Contd.*)

Table 23.1 : (*Contd*)

1992	60.8	NA	29.2	10.1	79	2175
1993	NA	NA	28.7	9.3	74	2243
1994	NA	NA	28.7	9.3	74	2334
1995P	NA	NA	28.3	9.0	74	2449

NA = Not Available
P = Provisional

+ Data for 1951, 1961,1971, 1981 relate to the decades 1941-50, 1951-60, 1961-70, 1971-80 respectively, centred at mid-point of the decade i.e. 1946, 1956, 1966, 1976. For 1983, data relate to 1981-85 centred at 1983. The estimates centred at 1988, 1989, 1990 and 1991 refer to the periods 1986-90, 1987-91, 1988-92 and 1989-93. For 1992, it is based on the extrapolated values of the Standing Committee of Experts on Population Projection, centred at June, 1992.

@ Data for 1951, 1961 and 1971 relate to population aged 5 years and above and those for 1981 and 1991 relate to population aged 7 years and above. Data exclude Assam for 1981 and Jammu and Kahsmir for 1991.

* Data for 1951, 1961 relate to the decades 1941-50, 1951-60 respectively and the estimates for 1971 and 1981 onwards are based on the Sample Registrations System (SRS).

** Relate to financial years 1950-51, 1960-61 and so on.

Source: Economic Survey 1996-1997, Ministry of Finance, Economic Division, Government of India, New Delhi

Table 23.2: Selected Indicators of Human Development for Major States*

	States	Life expectancy at birth (Years) @ (1989-93)	Literacy rate** 1991			I.M.R. + Death rate + Birth rate (Prov. estimates of SRS - 1995)		
			Total	Male (per cent)	Female	(Per thousand)		
1.	Andhra Pradesh	60.6	44.9	55.13	33.72	66	8.3	24.0
2.	Assam	54.9	52.89	61.87	43.03	77	9.6	29.3
3.	Bihar	58.5	38.48	52.49	22.89	73	10.5	32.1
4.	Gujarat	60.1	61.29	73.13	48.64	62	7.6	26.7
5.	Haryana	62.9	55.85	69.10	40.47	68	8.0	30.0
6.	Karnataka	61.9	56.04	67.26	44.34	62	7.6	24.2
7.	Kerala	72.0	89.81	93.62	86.17	16	6.0	17.7
8.	Madhya Pradesh	54.0	44.20	58.42	28.85	99	11.1	33.0
9.	Maharashtra	64.2	64.87	76.56	52.32	55	7.4	24.5
10.	Orissa	55.5	49.09	63.09	34.68	103	10.8	27.7
11.	Punjab	66.4	58.51	65.66	50.41	54	7.3	24.7
12.	Rajasthan	58.0	38.55	54.99	20.44	85	9.1	33.2
13.	Tamil Nadu	62.4	62.66	73.75	51.33	56	7.9	20.2

(Contd.)

Table 23.3 : *(Contd)*

14.	Uttar Pradesh	55.9	41.60	55.73	25.31	86	10.4	34.7
15.	West Bengal	61.5	57.70	67.81	46.56	59	7.7	23.6
	All India	59.4	52.21	64.13	39.29	74	9.0	28.3

* Major States include States with population of 10 million and above as per 1991 Census.

@ Data relate to average over 1989-93 as estimated by the SRS and centred at 1991.

** Relate to population aged 7 years and above for 1991 and excludes Jammu and Kashmir for All India.

\+ Infant Mortality Rate.

Source: Economic Survey 1996-97, Ministry of Finance, Economic Division, Government of India.

Table 23.3: Percentage of Sectorwise and Statewise Approved Outlays to Total Outlays on Education, Eighth Five Year Plan, 1992-97

(Rs. in Crores)

S.No.	States/UTs	Elementary	Adult	General	Technical
1.	Andhra Pradesh	63.03	6.13	79.78	20.22
2.	Arunachal Pradesh	75	1.84	100.0	0
3.	Assam	61.8	2.00	95.07	4.93
4.	Bihar	64.55	6.61	79.69	20.31
5.	Goa	35	1.42	83.33	16.67
6.	Gujarat	47.26	7.09	71.61	28.39
7.	Haryana	39.44	1.25	79.29	20.71
8.	Himachal Pradesh	36.36	0.65	84.56	15.44
9.	Jammu and Kashmir	47.16	2.14	94.32	5.68
10.	Karnataka	42.85	1.96	94.77	5.23
11.	Kerala	12.6	0.44	46.67	53.33
12.	Madhya Pradesh	61.5	2.82	87.86	12.14
13.	Maharashtra	36.64	2.3	76.43	23.57
14.	Manipur	55.51	2.79	92.52	7.48
15.	Meghalaya	69.95	3.66	98.51	1.49
16.	Mizoram	50.76	2.76	92.28	7.72
17.	Nagaland	38.93	1.52	90.52	9.48
18.	Orissa	39.76	7.36	86.42	13.58
19.	Punjab	11.42	2.62	52.52	47.48
20.	Rajasthan	59.12	3.18	89.57	10.43
21.	Sikkim	62.98	1.18	95.16	4.84
22.	Tamil Nadu	52.91	8.38	92.22	7.78
23.	Tripura	57.28	1.93	98.77	1.23
24.	Uttar Pradesh	49.33	1.80	80.86	19.14
25.	West Bengal	58.33	4.45	83.33	16.67
Union Territories					
26.	A and N Islands	37.42	0.61	76.18	23.82
27.	Chandigarh	24.01	1.20	79.11	20.89
28.	D and N Haveli	54.77	0.47	84.35	15.65
29.	Daman and Diu	31.26	1.76	59.02	40.98
30.	Delhi	57.46	1.14	80.36	19.64
31.	Lakshadweep	29.93	2.28	100	0
32.	Pondicherry	31.72	0.7	65.23	34.77
All States/UTs		49.82	3.24	83.86	16.14
	Centre	38.69	18.81	88.93	11.07
Total (Centre and States)		45.59	9.16	85.78	14.22

Table 23.4: Outlays and Expenditure of Seventh and Eighth Plans and Annual Plans, 1992-93 to 1996-97. *(Rs. in crore)*

Sector/Major Scheme	Seventh Plan Exp.	Eighth Plan Outlay	Annual Plan 1992-93	
			Outlay	Exp.
1	2	3	4	5
1. Elementary Education				
i) Other than Ext. Aided	655.15	2350.0	261.10	293.84
a) NFE (State+VAs)	126.28	704.0	90.10	55.36
b) Others	528.89	1646.0	171.0	238.48
c) Mid-day-meal	-	-	-	-
ii) Externally Aided	8.62	530.00	22.90	13.65
Total:	663.77	2880.0	284.0	307.49
2. Secondary Education				
a) Navodaya Vidyalayas		650.0	75.0	92.09
b) Vocational Education		410.0	79.0	77.52
c) Others		459.0	55.0	54.52
Total:	596.01	1519.0	209.0	224.13
3. University and Hr. Edn.*	659.96	701.55	150.01	151.99
4. Adult Education	313.04	1400.0	120.0	97.58
5. Language Development				
i) Hindi		29.40	5.18	4.94
ii) MIL		14.25	3.05	1.44
iii) English		3.80	0.72	0.68
iv) Sanskrit		21.00	3.74	8.11
Total:	43.58	68.45	12.69	15.17
6. Scholarships	9.13	10.0	2.50	1.52
7. Book Promotion	5.74	8.0	2.0	1.49
8. Planning and Admn.	3.34	32.0	1.8	1.15
9. Technical Education				
i) Schemes under AICTE		365.4	79.48	73.97
ii) Schemes of Dep. of Edn.		458.6	90.52	88.87
Total:	610.96	824.0	170.0	162.84
BADP	120.50			
TOTAL	3026.03	7443.0	952.0	963.36

* The schemes of Hindi University and Urdu University have been transferred from Language Development to U&HE.

Table 23.4 : (*Contd.*)

Annual Plan 1993-94		Annual Plan 1994-95		Annual Plan 1995-96			1996-97
Outlay	Exp.	Outlay	Exp.	Outlay	RE	Exp.	Outlay
6	7	8	9	10	11	12	13
358.77	356.81	439.57	425.52	559.00	1145.05	974.64	1959.00
108.67	106.69	131.32	131.27	158.50	153.50	153.50	158.25
250.10	250.12	301.25	294.25	400.50	379.76	379.76	400.75
-	-	-	-	-	611.79	441.38	1400.00
83.43	29.76	83.43	122.33	92.04	297.98	228.27	299.70
442.20	386.57	523.00	547.85	651.04	1443.03	1202.91	2258.70
131.71	132.00	152.63	152.63	200.00	177.00	177.0	186.00
85.00	85.00	33.46	75.26	82.00	82.00	69.07	82.00
89.16	86.54	93.91	92.83	127.11	105.10	93.85	113.11
305.87	303.54	335.0	320.72	409.11	364.10	339.92	381.11
161.31	157.91	220.0	264.35	244.50	245.41	246.84	238.04
177.97	166.39	214.0	206.90	234.00	170.35	144.13	224.50
5.93	8.77	6.79	6.79	8.53	8.54	8.43	6.79
3.74	1.56	4.22	2.04	4.94	2.47	1.89	4.22
0.75	0.69	0.75	0.75	0.83	0.83	0.66	0.75
4.24	3.95	5.19	5.10	7.65	6.72	6.20	5.19
14.66	14.97	16.95	14.68	21.95	18.56	17.18	16.95
2.65	0.91	2.15	0.92	2.15	1.37	1.10	2.15
1.98	1.87	1.98	1.96	2.98	2.59	2.42	1.98
5.36	6.32	5.36	3.80	5.36	4.45	4.11	5.36
58.65	59.64	58.65	62.92	71.89	71.89	71.36	71.89
139.35	133.92	164.35	175.74	182.02	181.32	169.62	182.02
198.0	193.56	223.00	238.66	253.91	253.21	240.98	253.91
1310.00	1232.04	1541.46	1599.84	1825.00	2503.07	2199.59	3382.70

Source: Annual Financial Statistics of Education Sector 1996-97. Ministry of Human Resource Development, Deptt. of Education, Planning and Monitoring, New Delhi.

Table 23.5: Statewise Approved Outlays for Eighth Five Year Plan, 1992-97

(Rs. in crores)

S. No.	States/UTs	Elementary Education	Adult Education	General Education	Technical Education	
	1	2	3	4	5	6
1.	Andhra Pradesh	176.13	17.12	222.95	56.50	279.45
2.	Arunachal Pradesh	113.92	2.79	151.90	0.00	151.90
3.	Assam	568.35	18.36	874.38	45.33	919.71
4.	Bihar	588.83	60.34	726.95	185.22	912.17
5.	Goa	27.30	1.11	65.00	13.00	78.00
6.	Gujarat	149.82	22.47	227.00	90.00	317.00
7.	Haryana	202.44	6.40	407.04	106.30	513.34
8.	Himachal Pradesh	98.90	1.77	230.00	42.00	272.00
9.	Jammu & Kashmir	157.65	7.16	315.30	19.00	334.30
10.	Karnataka	409.50	18.70	905.55	50.00	955.55
11.	Kerala	22.21	0.77	82.25	94.00	176.25
12.	Madhya Pradesh	432.68	19.84	618.12	85.38	703.50
13.	Maharashtra	350.00	22.00	730.07	225.18	955.25
14.	Manipur	40.80	2.05	68.00	5.50	73.50
15.	Meghalaya	64.33	3.37	90.60	1.37	91.97
16.	Mizoram	23.02	1.25	41.85	3.50	45.35
17.	Nagaland	18.47	0.72	42.95	4.50	47.45
18.	Orissa	242.66	44.91	527.52	82.86	610.38

Table 23.5: (*Contd.*)

1		2	3	4	5	6
19.	Punjab	47.15	10.80	216.78	196.00	412.78
20.	Rajasthan	567.75	30.50	860.23	100.18	960.41
21.	Sikkim	36.40	0.68	55.00	2.80	57.80
22.	Tamil Nadu	252.47	40.00	440.00	37.14	477.14
23.	Tripura	69.60	2.34	120.00	1.50	121.50
24.	Uttar Pradesh	663.53	24.26	1087.75	257.40	1345.15
25.	West Bengal	350.00	26.72	500.00	100.00	600.00
Union Territories						
26.	A & N Islands	20.74	0.34	42.22	13.20	55.42
27.	Chandigarh	10.62	0.53	35.00	9.24	44.24
28.	D & N Haveli	7.00	0.06	10.78	2.00	12.78
29.	Daman & Diu	2.67	0.15	5.04	3.50	8.54
30.	Delhi	321.80	6.37	450.00	110.00	560.00
31.	Lakshadweep	1.68	0.16	7.02	0.00	7.02
32.	Pondicherry	18.04	0.40	37.10	19.78	56.88
	All States/UTs	6056.44	394.44	10194.35	1962.38	12156.73
	Centre	2880.00	1400.00	6619.00	824.00	7443.00
Total (Centre & States)		8936.44	1794.44	16813.35	2786.38	19599.73

Source: Analysis of Annual Plan 1992-93, (Education Sector), Planning Commission, New Delhi.

Table 23.6: Sectorwise and Statewise Approved Plan Outlays, 1995-96

(Rs. in Crores)

S.No.	States/UTs	Elementary	Adult	General	Technical	Total
1.	Andhra Pradesh	62.30	11.00	100.00	12.00	112.00
2.	Arunachal Pradesh	33.00	1.05	48.05	0.00	48.05
3.	Assam	166.00	0.00	298.05	14.73	312.78
4.	Bihar	93.00	9.99	118.99	61.92	180.91
5.	Goa	4.45	0.38	14.35	15.38	29.73
6.	Gujarat	14.51	3.95	33.90	30.00	63.90
7.	Haryana	38.34	1.00	86.02	38.54	124.56
8.	Himachal Pradesh	36.44	0.50	86.30	12.00	98.30
9.	Jammu and Kashmir	42.05	0.92	89.00	4.40	93.40
10.	Karnataka	176.15	7.19	287.95	19.00	306.95
11.	Kerala	6.05	0.00	32.70	30.50	63.20
12.	Madhya Pradesh	100.28	5.83	203.58	53.70	257.28
13.	Maharashtra	99.18	6.31	224.00	72.69	296.69
14.	Manipur	5.96	0.61	17.36	1.20	18.56
15.	Meghalaya	19.50	1.00	28.83	0.60	29.53
16.	Mizoram	.5.00	0.00	10.70	0.80	11.50
17.	Nagaland	5.58	0.07	9.78	1.10	10.88
18.	Orissa	26.98	4.34	126.52	25.57	152.09
19.	Punjab	14.71	1.43	57.13	53.00	110.13
20.	Rajasthan	156.92	4.50	282.96	22.43	305.39
21.	Sikkim	7.85	0.15	18.73	0.59	19.32
22.	Tamil Nadu	54.13	19.43	98.17	10.64	108.81
23.	Tripura	24.00	0.00	40.55	0.38	40.93
24.	Uttar Pradesh	69.45	11.04	320.25	62.74	382.99
25.	West Bengal	31.90	5.26	80.40	25.24	105.64
Union Territories						
26.	A and N Islands	10.28	0.09	20.69	1.82	22.51
27.	Chandigarh	3.47	0.00	11.45	2.20	13.65
28.	D and N Haveli	2.50	0.05	4.06	1.80	5.86
29.	Daman and Diu	1.79	0.04	2.25	1.50	3.75
30.	Delhi	82.14	0.50	139.40	34.17	173.57
31.	Lakshadweep	0.77	0.03	1.62	0.00	1.62
32.	Pondicherry	5.12	0.01	13.89	3.51	17.40
	All States/UTs	1399.80	96.67	2907.73	614.15	3531.88
	Centre	651.04	234.00	1571.09	253.91	1825.00
	Total (Centre and States)	2050.84	330.67	4478.82	868.06	5346.88

Table 23.7: Eighth Plan Yearwise Approved Allocation for Schemes of Adult Education, 1992-93 to 1996-97.

(Rs. in crores)

S.No.	Name of the Scheme	Approved Allocation (1992-93)	Approved Allocation (1993-94)	Approved Allocation (1994-95)	Approved Allocation (1995-96)	Approved Allocation (1996-97)
1.	Special Projects for Eradication of Illiteracy (TLS/PLC)	58.65	120.00	154.75	120.00	100.00
2.	Voluntary Agencies (VAs)	18.00	15.00	10.00	10.00	10.00
3.	Directorate of Adult Education (DAE)	2.50	5.70	6.00	12.00	12.00
4.	Shramik Vidyapeeth (SVP)	1.30	1.75	2.00	4.35	4.95
5.	Strengthening of Administrative Structure (SAS)	7.00	10.00	14.00	14.00	18.00
6.	Rural Functional Literacy Project (RFLP)	15.00	6.00	6.00	6.00	0.90
7.	Post Literacy & Continuing Education (PL&CE)	10.00	13.50	18.00	66.00	75.50
8.	Mass Programme of Functional Literacy (MPFL)	3.75	2.50	0.75	0.00	0.10
9.	Technology Demonstration	0.50	0.47	0.30	0.15	0.05
10.	Cultural Exchange Programme	0.05	0.05	0.25	0.25	0.25
11.	National Literacy Mission (NLM)	0.25	0.50	0.75	0.75	2.00
12.	National Institute of Adult Education (NIAE)	1.50	2.00	1.20	0.50	0.75
13.	Nehru Yuvak Kendras (NYK)	1.50	0.50	0.00	0.00	0.00
	Total	120.00	177.97	214.00	234.00	224.50

Table 23.8: Eighth Plan Approved Outlay, Actual Allocation and Expenditure for Adult Education, 1992-97.

(Rs. in crores)

	Name of the Scheme	Approved Outlay (1992-97)	Actual Allocation (1992-97)	Actual Expenditure (1992-97)
1.	Special Projects for Eradication of Illiteracy (TLS/PLC)	1000.00	553.40	496.09
2.	Voluntary Agencies (VAs)	115.00	63.00	35.04
3.	Directorate of Adult Education (DAE)	14.50	38.20	42.91
4.	Shramik Vidyapeeths (SVP)	17.00	14.35	13.95
5.	Strengthening of Administrative Structure (SAS)	28.00	63.00	53.84
6.	Rural Functional Literacy Project (RFLP)	25.00	33.90	15.26
7.	Post Literacy and Continuing Education (PL & CE)	132.00	183.00	53.31
8.	Mass Programme of Functional Literacy (MPFL)	25.00	7.10	3.83
9.	Technology Demonstration	8.00	1.47	0.38
10.	Cultural Exchange Programme	0.50	0.85	0.156
11.	National Literacy Mission (NLM)	2.50	4.25	1.81
12.	National Institute of Adult Education (NIAE)	17.50	5.95	1.35
13.	Nehru Yuvak Kendras (NYK)	15.00	2.00	0.00
	Total	1400.00	970.47	717.926

Table 23.9: Eighth Plan Yearwise Actual Expenditure for Schemes of Adult Education, 1992-93 to 1996-97.

(Rs. in crores)

S.No.	Name of the Scheme	Actual Expenditure (1992-93)	Actual Expenditure (1993-94)	Actual Expenditure (1994-95)	Actual Expenditure (1995-96)	Actual Expenditure (1996-97)
1.	Special Projects for Eradication of Illiteracy (TLS/PLC)	71.40	120.92	155.26	100.00	48.51
2.	Voluntary Agencies (VAs)	3.50	6.51	11.00	6.43	7.60
3.	Directorate of Adult Education (DAE)	3.26	9.61	5.87	11.86	12.31
4.	Shramik Vidyapeeth(SVP)	1.24	1.72	2.80	4.15	4.04
5.	Strengthening of Administrative Structure (SAS)	8.54	10.00	12.40	11.00	11.90
6.	Rural Functional Literacy Project (RFLP)	1.37	6.00	7.30	0.27	0.32
7.	Post Literacy & Continuing Education (PL&CE)	6.20	9.02	11.05	9.33	17.71
8.	Mass Programme of Functional Literacy (MPFL)	1.44	1.40	0.75	0.19	0.05
9.	Technology Demonstration	0.02	0.30	0.06	0.00	0.00
10.	Cultural Exchange Programme	0.00	0.07	0.04	0.06	0.04
11.	National Literacy Mission (NLM)	0.16	0.34	0.37	0.50	0.44
12.	National Institute of Adult Education (NIAE)	0.45	0.50	0.00	0.20	0.20
13.	Nehru Yuvak Kendras (NYK)	0.00	0.00	0.00	0.00	0.00
	Total	97.58	166.47	206.90	143.936	103.12

Table 23.10 : Eighth Plan Funds Released to States for Adult Education, 1992-93 to 1996-97

(Rs. in lakhs)

States/UTs	1992-93	1993-94	1994-95	1995-96	1996-97	Grand Total
1	2	3	4	5	6	7
Andhra Pradesh	839.64	1846.70	1370.68	884.21	1081.06	6022.29
Arunachal Pradesh	8.59	28.73	71.56	25.63	20.72	155.23
Assam	111.50	125.21	1159.04	361.09	194.29	1951.13
Bihar	299.67	1109.93	1628.87	1997.84	1062.52	6078.83
Goa	5.29	15.37	11.59	5.95	3.32	41.52
Gujarat	659.44	1079.70	884.50	262.98	458.78	3345.40
Haryana	426.79	181.05	243.01	175.31	57.12	1083.28
Himachal Pradesh	214.69	80.07	109.15	26.43	49.18	479.52
Jammu & Kashmir	—	84.47	190.40	132.70	50.47	458.04
Karnataka	698.32	1683.64	1041.84	319.58	350.16	4093.54
Kerala	21.46	122.71	57.32	7.00	537.97	746.46
Madhya Pradesh	289.45	1455.12	2821.52	977.67	548.58	6092.34
Maharashtra	838.71	1453.16	1024.55	1153.63	432.83	4902.88
Manipur	7.55	28.18	72.67	17.62	20.63	146.65
Meghalaya	14.16	19.47	29.08	127.74	112.45	302.90
Mizoram	1.66	2.66	16.42	2.29	0.57	23.60
Nagaland	16.37	26.31	39.73	47.81	56.90	187.12

Table 23.10: (*Contd.*)

1	2	3	4	5	6	7
Orissa	589.51	614.12	606.36	801.36	310.13	2921.48
Punjab	5.29	25.00	277.61	370.34	135.00	813.24
Rajasthan	501.90	784.58	1745.00	1681.76	1304.62	6017.86
Sikkim	—	5.25	11.22	—	11.22	27.69
Tamil Nadu	1232.01	1200.00	1594.58	1212.48	261.21	5500.28
Tripura	—	224.18	6.77	0.10	4.73	235.78
Uttar Pradesh	897.09	2555.48	2805.58	1888.01	943.27	9089.43
West Bengal	1094.58	719.86	1583.69	308.40	728.11	4434.64
Union Territories						
Chandigarh	28.11	28.66	25.62	20.12	41.37	143.88
Delhi	50.42	117.17	120.77	322.58	158.57	769.51
Pondicherry	—	—	—	—	—	—
Daman & Diu	—	1.96	0.56	0.50	—	3.02
Andaman & Nicobar	5.82	9.81	12.15	8.12	12.56	48.46
Dadra & Nagar Haveli	0.58	0.84	0.83	—	—	2.25
Lakshadweep	2.57	1.57	7.41	1.62	4.32	17.49
Total	8,861.17	15,630.96	19,570.08	13,120.87	8,952.66	66,135.74

Table 23.11: Funds Released for Centrally Sponsored Scheme of Pre-Vocational Education at Lower Secondary Stage, 1987-88 to 1996-97.

(Rs. in Lakhs)

S. No.	Name of State	1987-88	1988-89	1989-90	1990-91	1991-92	1992-93	1993-94	1994-95	1995-96	1996-97	Total
1.	Andhra Pradesh	–	–	–	–	–	–	–	–	–	–	–
2.	Arunachal Pradesh	–	–	–	–	–	–	–	–	–	–	–
3.	Assam	–	–	–	–	–	–	3.30	–	–	–	3.30
4.	Bihar	–	–	–	–	–	–	–	–	–	–	–
5.	Goa	–	–	–	–	–	–	–	–	–	–	–
6.	Gujarat	–	–	–	–	–	–	–	–	–	–	–
7.	Haryana	–	–	–	–	–	–	–	–	–	–	–
8.	Himachal Pradesh	–	–	–	–	–	–	–	–	–	–	–
9.	Jammu & Kashmir	–	–	–	–	–	–	–	–	–	–	–
10.	Karnataka	–	–	–	–	–	–	18.2	41.52	–	–	59.72
11.	Kerala	–	–	–	–	–	–	–	–	–	–	–
12.	Madhya Pradesh	–	–	–	–	–	–	23.94	–	–	–	23.94
13.	Maharashtra	–	–	–	–	–	–	–	–	–	56.94	56.94
14.	Manipur	–	–	–	–	–	–	2.30	–	9.77	–	12.07
15.	Meghalaya	–	–	–	–	–	–	–	–	–	–	–
16.	Mizoram	–	–	–	–	–	–	–	–	–	–	–
17.	Nagaland	–	–	–	–	–	–	–	–	–	–	–

Table 23.11: *(Contd.)*

S. No.	Name of State	1987-88	1988-89	1989-90	1990-91	1991-92	1992-93	1993-94	1994-95	1995-96	1996-97	Total
18.	Orissa	–	–	–	–	–	–	–	–	–	–	–
19.	Punjab	–	–	–	–	–	–	7.58	19.24	–	–	26.8
20.	Rajasthan	–	–	–	–	–	–	7.28	1.89	2.25	–	11.4
21.	Sikkim	–	–	–	–	–	–	–	–	–	–	–
22.	Tamil Nadu	–	–	–	–	–	–	–	–	–	–	–
23.	Tripura	–	–	–	–	–	–	–	–	–	–	–
24.	Uttar Pradesh	–	–	–	–	–	–	44.61	–	–	–	44.61
25.	West Bengal	–	–	–	–	–	–	–	–	–	–	–
Union Territories												
26.	A & N Islands	–	–	–	–	–	–	–	–	–	–	–
27.	Chandigarh	–	–	–	–	–	–	–	2.10	–	–	2.10
28.	D & N Haveli	–	–	–	–	–	–	–	–	–	–	–
29.	Daman & Diu	–	–	–	–	–	–	–	–	–	–	–
30.	Delhi	–	–	–	–	–	–	5.62	–	–	–	-
31.	Lakshadweep	–	–	–	–	–	–	–	–	–	–	–
32.	Pondicherry	–	–	–	–	–	–	–	–	–	–	–
	Total	–	–	–	–	–	–	112.83	70.37	12.02	*56.94	252.16

* Released till January, 1997

Table 23.12: Funds Released to States/UTs for Centrally Sponsored Scheme of Vocationalisation of Secondary Education 1987-88 to 1996-97

(Rs. in Lakhs)

S. No.	Name of State	1987-88	1988-89	1989-90	1990-91	1991-92	1992-93	1993-94	1994-95	1995-96	1996-97	Total
1.	Andhra Pradesh	562.63	730.32	177.06	886.85	1010.23	1584.91	640.58	327.45	–	-	5920.03
2.	Arunachal Prad.	–	–	–	–	6.35	–	–	–	–	–	6.35
3.	Assam	30.1	82.61	–	42.62	140.28	100.25	291.54	164.42	108.52	–	960.34
4.	Bihar	136.09	–	7.41	558.61	0.75	–	408.51	157.87	415.39	–	1684.63
5.	Goa	68.53	28.47	64.59	80.63	49.65	92.56	56.93	100.42	115.04	–	656.82
6.	Gujarat	–	236.64	1173.31	778.03	879.37	1070.74	781.73	–	–	–	4919.82
7.	Haryana	276.12	353.04	129.87	184.83	155	131.44	228.18	379.14	621.85	239.28	2698.75
8.	Himachal Prad.	30.9	1.86	98.06	177.47	56.86	59.42	–	–	1.33	–	425.9
9.	Jammu & Kashmir	–	–	–	16.5	15.8	–	22.55	–	–	–	54.85
10.	Karnataka	93	244.70	49.21	156.8	325	727.47	1012.69	729.55	328.32	–	3666.74
11.	Kerala	–	226.42	223.44	353.23	346.9	410.78	352.4	885.23	929.35	–	3727.75
12.	Madhya Pradesh	57.16	745	1121.48	1221.42	3.00	–	–	20.80	–	–	3168.86
13.	Maharashtra	495.9	469.66	509.38	267.2	1230.25	2195.33	2035.74	2449.69	3134.44	–	12787.59
14.	Manipur	–	11.68	–	–	44.00	7.18	7.40	40.24	35.24	–	145.74
15.	Meghalaya	–	–	–	20.75	–	–	–	–	13.67	4.63	39.05
16.	Mizoram	21.42	7.12	–	16.68	–	24.85	21.92	–	8.80	–	100.82
17.	Nagaland	8.00	–	–	14.84	–	–	1.40	–	–	–	24.24
18.	Orissa	156.49	600	83.72	510.4	–	1.22	650	102.2	–	–	2104.03
19.	Punjab	211.59	–	50.25	371.71	222.25	320.62	253.74	265.02	434.53	–	2129.71

Table 23.12: (*Contd.*)

S. No.	Name of State	1987-88	1988-89	1989-90	1990-91	1991-92	1992-93	1993-94	1994-95	1995-96	1996-97	Total
20.	Rajasthan	58.34	159.22	72.35	561.54	323.56	340.39	385.19	556.54	–	617.49	3074.62
21.	Sikkim	–	–	–	5.32	0.04	5.32	7.15	–	–	–	17.83
22.	Tamil Nadu	112.56	225	358.11	279.56	727.9	–	700.16	706.55	–	–	3109.84
23.	Tripura	–	–	–	–	–	–	4.12	–	–	–	4.12
24.	Uttar Pradesh	829.88	800	203.69	707.25	99.15	581.39	258.42	265.39	502.4	473.74	4721.14
25.	West Bengal	40.69	–	–	–	–	–	–	–	–	–	40.69
	Union Territories											
1.	A & N Islands	–	–	3.24	3.24	–	–	–	–	–	–	6.48
2.	Chandigarh	–	*42.70	*42.70	12.34	20.77	8.65	22.77	*23.99	26.86	23.99	224.77
3.	D & N Haveli	–	–	–	–	–	5.25	2.79	–	–	–	8.04
4.	Daman & Diu	–	–	–	–	–	–	3.09	2.66	5.06	4.65	15.46
5.	Delhi	*36.52	–	4.18	*42.86	0.30	*46.38	–	105.00	50.23	–	285.47
6.	Lakshadweep	–	–	–	–	–	–	–	–	–	–	–
7.	Pondicherry	–	–	16.63	–	–	17.44	16.26	14.06	–	64.39	
	Total (UTs)	36.52	42.7	50.12	75.07	21.07	60.28	46.09	147.91	96.21	28.64	604.61
	Total (States)	3189.4	4921.74	4321.93	7212.24	5636.34	7653.9	8120.35	7151.01	6648.88	1335.14	56190.93
	Grand Total	3225.92	4964.44	4372.05	7207.31	5657.41	7714.18	8166.44	7298.92	6745.09	1363.78	56795.54

* Not Claimed ** Released till January, 1997

Table 23.13: Funds Released to States/UTs for Centrally Sponsored Scheme of Improvement of Science Education in Schools, 1996-97

S. No.	Name of State/UT	Amount Released*
1.	Daman & Diu Admn.	504200
2.	Himachal Pradesh	7703400

* Released as on January 31, 1997.

Table 23.14: Grants Released in Respect of Total/Post Literacy Campaigns, 1992-93 to 1996-97.

(Rs. in lakhs)

	State/UT	1992-93	1993-94	1994-95	1995-96	1996-97
1.	Andhra Pradesh	7,01.66	17,19.74	11,06.93	6,11.50	1,28.41
2.	Assam	65.00	25.00	10,14.67	2,48.70	1,06.55
3.	Bihar	1,25.00	8,74.08	13,11.00	16,76.73	7,43.45
4.	Chandigarh	15.00	18.00	–	–	11.50
5.	Daman & Diu	–	1.40	–	–	–
6.	D & N Haveli	–	–	17.00	–	–
7.	Delhi	18.35	55.43	56.53	2,98.44	–
8.	Goa	–	–	–	–	–
9.	Gujarat	4,95.00	8,35.55	5,83.30	35.00	3,59.91
10.	Haryana	2,95.00	1,81.05	2,32.42	1,41.43	35.44

Table 23.14: (*Contd.*)

	State/UT	1992-93	1993-94	1994-95	1995-96	1996-97
11.	Himachal Pradesh	2,11.00	64.67	92.87	11.14	35.79
12.	Jammu & Kashmir	–	–	25.00	1,00.00	30.00
13.	Karnataka	6,27.90	14,94.83	8,16.45	1,40.83	1,91.49
14.	Kerala	–	1,00.00	–	–	–
15.	Madhya Pradesh	1,40.00	11,60.99	25,11.99	6,90.20	3,43.84
16.	Maharashtra	6,30.00	6,77.27	5,58.03	71,7.77	2,77.54
17.	Manipur	–	–	–	–	–
18.	Meghalaya	–	–	–	94.65	1,01.00
19.	Orissa	4,68.00	4,32.38	4,22.95	6,27.05	1,93.42
20.	Pondicherry	–	–	–	–	–
21.	Punjab	–	25.00	2,61.34	3,44.47	1,35.00
22.	Rajasthan	2,20.00	5,01.97	13,37.24	14,23.36	11,15.86
23.	Tamil Nadu	11,46.00	9,26.00	11,51.53	9,64.82	1,01.22
24.	Tripura	–	222.45	–	–	–
25.	Uttar Pradesh	6,85.00	22,12.88	23,44.43	15,04.44	6,28.38
26.	West Bengal	10,69.00	5,83.65	13,53.12	2,38.00	1,75.25
	Total	69,11.91	1,21,12.34	1,51,96.80	98,68.53	47,14.05

Table 23.15: Funds Released to States/UTs/VOs Under the Scheme of Yoga in Schools (Plan)

(Rs. in lakhs)

S.No.	States/UTs	1991-92	1992-93	1993-94	1994-95	1995-96	1996-97*
1.	Andhra Pradesh	–	–	24.24	1.76	–	–
2.	Arunachal Pradesh	–	–	2.35	–	–	–
3.	Bihar	–	–	–	6.17	2.76	–
4.	Jammu & Kashmir	8.00	13.00	–	–	–	–
5.	Karnataka	–	1.00	9.00	–	0.79	–
6.	Madhya Pradesh	5.94	–	–	–	–	–
7.	Maharashtra	–	–	7.66	8.38	2.5	–
8.	Orissa	–	–	–	–	0.83	–
9.	Punjab	3.36	–	–	–	–	–
10.	Tamil Nadu	–	1.65	–	–	–	–
11.	Tripura	–	0.26	1.13	–	–	1.27
12.	Uttar Pradesh	8.05	–	3.70	–	3.00	–
13.	Chandigarh	–	–	–	–	0.35	0.35
14.	Delhi	–	1.69	5.50	2.5	–	–
15.	KSMYN Samiti, Lonavala	35.3	12.37	5.00	5.00	–	–
16.	R. K. Instt. of Moral & Spiritual Edn, Mysore	4.05	–	1.40	1.50	–	–
		64.70	29.97	59.98	25.31	10.23	1.62

* As on November 29, 1996.

Table 23.16: Allocation of Foodgrains under National Programme of Nutritional Support to Primary Education, in EAS and LFL Blocks, 1996-97[1]

S. No.	States/UTs	Mode*	No. of Dists.	No. of Blocks	No. of Beneficiaries	Foodgrains allocated for the period 1.4.96 to 31.03.97 (in Qtls)			Basis of Alloca--tion $
						Wheat	Rice	Total	
1	2	3	4	5	6	7	8	9	10
1.	Andhra Pradesh	FG	22	**330	4913832	0	1474149.60	1474149.60	S
2.	Arunachal Pradesh	FG	12	56	96934	0	29080.20	29080.20	E
3.	Assam	FG	23	157	2093846	0	628153.80	628153.80	S
4.	Bihar	FG	50	715	6125567	1108098.00	729572.10	1837670.10	E
5.	Goa	FG	2	@3	3508	0	1052.40	1052.40	E
6.	Gujarat	CM	18	138	1753695	210443.40	210443.40	420886.80	E
7.	Haryana	CM	16	88	1172399	140687.88	140687.88	281375.76	E
8.	Himachal Pradesh	FG	10	33	303895	0	91168.50	91168.50	S
9.	Jammu & Kashmir	CM	14	121	620364	0	148887.36	148887.36	E
10.	Karnataka	FG	18	147	3701781	395504.70	715029.60	1110534.30	E
11.	Kerala	CM	7	21	314576	0	75498.20	75498.20	S
12.	Madhya Pradesh	CM	45	453	7429866	1051917.36	731250.40	1783167.76	S
13.	Maharashtra	FG	27	200	4297718	0	1289315.40	1289315.40	S

Table 23.16 : (*Contd.*)

1	2	3	4	5	6	7	8	9	10
14.	Manipur	FG	7	25	137631	0	41289.30	41289.30	S
15.	Meghalaya	FG	7	32	218581	0	65574.30	65574.30	S
16.	Mizoram	FG	3	20	96748	0	29024.40	29024.40	S
17.	Nagaland	FG	7	28	97335	0	29200.50	29200.50	S
18.	Orissa	CM	27	235	2220702	0	532968.40	532968.40	E
19.	Punjab	FG	7	40	545284	163585.20	0.00	163585.20	S
20.	Rajasthan	FG	31	237	3636521	1090956.30	0.00	1090956.30	S
21.	Sikkim	FG	4	8	62122	0	18636.60	18636.60	S
22.	Tamil Nadu#	CM	20	185	1163122	0	279149.28	279149.28	S
23.	Tripura	FG	4	27	379028	0	113708.40	113708.40	E
24.	Uttar Pradesh	FG	66	889	9909644	1927741.20	1045152.00	2972893.20	E
25.	West Bengal	FG	17	216	3637813	16412.7	1074931.20	1091343.90	S
26.	A & N Islands	FG	1	2	5483	0	1644.90	1644.90	E
27.	Chandigarh	FG	1	1@	64770	0	19431.00	19431.00	E
28.	D & N Haveli	FG	1	1	24456	0	7336.80	7336.80	E
29.	Daman & Diu	FG	2	2	8150	0	2445.00	2445.00	E
30.	Delhi	PR	1	1@	600000	144000.00	0.00	144000.00	E
31.	Lakshadweep	FG	1	9	8786	0	2635.80	2635.80	E
32.	Pondicherry	CM	4	6@	46996	0	9399.20	9399.20	E
	India		475	4426	55691153	6249346.74	9536815.92	15786162.66	

* FG = Foodgrain,
CM = Cooked Meals,
PF = Processed Food ,
@ = Urban Slums are covered in these blocks,
** = Covers 982 Mandals in Andhra Pradesh,
$ = VI AIES Enrichment,
E = Enrolment Data furnished by States/UTs,
# = Enrolment in respect of LFL Blocks is awaited,
1 = for ten academic months.

NB: (i) In case of foodgrains, the allocation @ 3 kg. per month for 10 academic months during 1996-97

(ii) In case of cooked meals, 240 school days have been taken as the basis @ 100 grams per child per day (200 days in case of Pondicherry)

(iii) In case of J&K and Himachal Pradesh, the allocations have been made from June, 1996 to May 31, 1997 for 37 blocks in J&K, and 7 blocks in Himachal Pradesh being remote and inaccessible areas.

Table 23.17: Budgetary Expenditure on Education as Per Cent of Total Budget (Revenue Account), 1985-86 and 1990-91 to 1995-96

(Per cent)

S. No.	States/UTs	1985-86	1990-91	1991-92	1992-93	1993-94	1994-95 (RE)	1995-96 (BE)
	1	2	3	4	5	6	7	8
1.	Andhra Pradesh	19.06	17.96	17.41	18.36	17.81	17.40	17.13
2.	Arunachal Pradesh	11.06	14.27	15.29	14.76	13.68	14.63	13.53
3.	Assam	22.57	22.93	24.76	26.01	26.78	23.31	24.23
4.	Bihar	24.41	24.51	21.97	20.14	19.00	21.63	22.09
5.	Goa	17.65	24.00	21.15	21.03	19.22	18.16	15.95
6.	Gujarat	23.88	21.76	19.87	17.78	19.56	21.04	22.97
7.	Haryana	17.72	16.40	15.57	17.61	13.19	7.02	10.50
8.	Himachal Pradesh	17.89	18.71	18.29	19.97	17.47	18.30	17.67
9.	Jammu & Kashmir	15.10	14.80	11.33	11.33	26.73	27.32	29.36
10	Karnataka	17.72	19.66	18.85	19.07	20.01	19.44	18.93
11.	Kerala	28.44	26.95	25.53	24.54	26.23	26.20	27.21
12.	Madhya Pradesh	17.49	18.44	18.04	17.69	16.18	17.63	16.44
13.	Maharashtra	17.79	19.49	20.45	19.88	18.02	17.44	15.64
14.	Manipur	22.90	18.67	22.58	26.27	24.66	25.45	26.26
15.	Meghalaya	15.34	17.99	18.34	18.45	19.10	18.13	19.70
16.	Mizoram	14.88	13.28	15.22	14.89	15.33	13.56	14.78
17.	Nagaland	13.48	11.15	10.12	10.88	12.16	12.24	12.81
18.	Orissa	16.84	20.29	20.43	20.03	19.47	19.45	19.08
19.	Punjab	20.05	19.79	13.18	17.10	16.49	12.84	11.04

Table 23.17: *(Contd.)*

1	2	3	4	5	6	7	8
20. Rajasthan	21.99	22.90	21.25	20.81	20.55	20.79	20.80
21. Sikkim	13.91	18.61	17.22	16.30	16.31	7.24	7.59
22. Tamil Nadu	21.46	22.37	16.49	18.01	19.53	21.15	21.25
23. Tripura	21.13	20.62	21.10	22.33	20.85	20.61	18.98
24. Uttar Pradesh	20.75	21.81	19.09	19.48	17.46	18.95	16.85
25. West Bengal	23.57	26.43	23.42	23.81	23.30	21.61	24.24
26. A & N Islands	11.86	23.10	10.67	12.20	13.27	13.28	11.57
27. Chandigarh	27.95	21.86	19.53	19.70	19.47	20.41	20.53
28. D & N Haveli	22.84	11.98	13.72	10.83	11.13	11.44	9.99
29. Daman & Diu		19.26	19.24	19.98	14.22	14.80	12.63
30. Delhi	35.79	28.36	28.23	29.36	25.91	28.76	26.70
31. Lakshadweep	13.62	11.77	12.77	10.03	8.16	9.79	8.39
32. Pondicherry	16.45	16.79	16.11	15.12	14.72	14.78	13.77
State/UTs Total	20.55	21.25	19.35	19.62	19.14	18.82	18.72
Centre	1.68	2.20	2.10	1.94	1.94	2.03	1.98
Centre + States/UTs	11.11	11.70	11.00	11.01	10.66	10.77	10.67

Source: *Annual Financial Statistics of Education Sector 1996-97*. Ministry of Human Resource Development, Department of Education, Planning, Monitoring and Statistics Division, New Delhi.

Table 23.18: Plan and Non-Budgetary Expenditure on Education by Education Department, 1993-94 to 1995-96.

(Rs. in crores)

	State/UT	1993-94 (Accounts)			%age to Total Budget	1994-95 (RE)		
		Plan	Non-Plan	Total		Plan	Non-Plan	Total
	1	2	3	4	5	6	7	8
1.	Andhra Pradesh	77.61	1350.22	1427.82	17.81	95.39	1526.32	1621.71
2.	Arunachal Pradesh	22.78	31.86	54.64	13.68	29.32	34.56	63.88
3.	Assam	227.62	549.46	777.08	26.78	253.99	501.59	755.57
4.	Bihar	61.66	1328.64	1390.29	19.00	123.54	1548.77	1672.31
5.	Goa	13.51	73.67	87.18	19.22	15.83	80.57	96.39
6.	Gujarat	34.07	1322.05	1356.11	19.56	40.01	1501.81	1541.81
7.	Haryana	59.73	389.01	448.74	13.19	89.74	421.91	511.65
8.	Himachal Pradesh	62.95	191.09	254.04	17.47	74.56	227.50	302.0(
9.	Jammu & Kashmir	62.66	263.19	325.85	26.73	56.26	276.73	332.99
10.	Karnataka	195.60	1046.37	1241.97	20.01	284.28	1203.38	1487.66
11.	Kerala	33.38	1092.85	1126.23	26.23	47.35	1311.00	1358.35
12.	Madhya Pradesh	140.03	1076.17	1216.20	16.18	210.29	1252.40	1462.68
13.	Maharashtra	157.42	2464.95	2622.37	18.02	252.15	2707.43	2959.58
14.	Manipur	14.31	93.60	107.91	24.66	16.95	115.58	132.52
15.	Meghalaya	29.63	62.60	92.24	19.10	33.73	66.49	100.22
16.	Mizoram	14.39	49.83	64.22	15.33	12.39	53.75	66.14
17.	Nagaland	7.87	74.93	82.80	12.18	10.26	78.12	88.37

Table 23.18: *(Contd.)*

1		2	3	4	5	6	7	8
18.	Orissa	89.08	589.00	678.08	19.47	201.61	689.72	891.33
19.	Punjab	56.78	609.90	666.68	16.49	114.55	654.70	769.25
20.	Rajasthan	179.14	1032.81	1211.95	20.55	284.93	1139.68	1424.60
21.	Sikkim	9.70	22.92	32.62	16.31	13.68	25.13	38.82
22.	Tamil Nadu	76.71	1633.30	1710.02	19.53	105.79	1836.87	1942.65
23.	Tripura	26.25	107.84	134.09	20.85	33.50	112.74	146.25
24.	Uttar Pradesh	120.20	2198.47	2318.67	17.46	301.42	2620.77	2922.20
25.	West Bengal	68.40	1540.83	1609.23	23.30	117.40	1706.44	1823.84
26.	A & N Islands	4.04	22.84	26.87	13.27	5.61	25.99	31.60
27.	Chandigarh	4.86	53.18	58.04	19.47	9.16	57.98	67.14
28.	D & N Haveli	1.24	3.75	4.98	11.13	1.66	3.98	5.64
29.	Daman & Diu	0.87	4.59	5.46	14.22	1.52	5.00	6.52
30.	Delhi	39.71	91.86	131.58	25.91	83.72	334.44	418.15
31.	Lakshadweep	0.48	6.21	6.69	8.16	1.18	8.65	9.83
32.	Pondicherry	10.69	35.42	46.12	14.72	14.85	38.35	53.21
	All States/UTs	1903.36	19413.41	21316.77	19.14	2936.62	22168.32	25104.94
	Centre	1217.37	878.96	2096.33	1.94	1568.80	920.24	2489.04
Total (Centre & States)		3120.74	20292.37	23413.10	10.66	4505.42	23088.56	27593.98

Table 23.18: (*Contd.*)

(Rs. in crores)

S. No.	State/UT	%age to Total Budget	1995-96 (BE)			% age to Total Budget
			Plan	Non-Plan	Total	
	1	9	10	11	12	13
1.	Andhra Pradesh	17.40	195.36	1670.00	1865.35	17.13
2.	Arunachal Pradesh	14.63	28.24	37.09	65.33	13.53
3.	Assam	23.31	356.78	543.86	900.64	24.23
4.	Bihar	21.63	173.70	1684.28	1857.98	22.09
5.	Goa	18.16	21.16	81.65	102.81	15.95
6.	Gujarat	21.04	33.27	1663.14	1696.41	22.97
7.	Haryana	7.02	101.13	428.78	529.91	10.50
8.	Himachal Pradesh	18.30	88.67	254.41	343.08	17.67
9.	Jammu & Kashmir	27.32	69.89	288.05	357.94	29.36
10.	Karnataka	19.44	384.71	1336.42	1721.14	18.93
11.	Kerala	26.20	79.06	1492.65	1571.71	27.21
12.	Madhya Pradesh	17.63	224.87	1365.65	1590.52	16.44
13.	Maharashtra	17.44	239.31	2651.90	2891.21	15.64
14.	Manipur	25.45	17.28	116.36	133.64	26.26
15.	Meghalaya	18.13	49.77	68.51	118.28	19.70
16.	Mizoram	13.56	10.81	52.75	63.56	14.78
17.	Nagaland	12.24	10.56	87.78	98.34	12.81
18.	Orissa	19.45	162.52	717.71	880.23	19.08

Table 23.18: *(Contd.)*

1	9	10	11	12	13
19. Punjab	12.84	126.75	702.11	828.85	11.04
20. Rajasthan	20.79	344.01	1259.78	1603.79	20.08
21. Sikkim	7.24	16.94	26.00	42.94	7.59
22. Tamil Nadu	21.15	111.17	1994.56	2105.73	21.25
23. Tripura	20.61	43.15	127.08	170.23	18.98
24. Uttar Pradesh	18.95	324.01	2716.22	3040.23	16.85
25. West Bengal	21.61	155.32	2125.20	2280.52	24.24
26. A & N Islands	13.28	7.47	26.86	34.33	11.57
27. Chandigarh	20.41	10.08	61.49	71.57	20.53
28. D & N Haveli	11.44	2.41	4.04	6.45	9.99
29. Daman & Diu	14.80	2.11	5.06	7.17	12.63
30. Delhi	28.76	140.23	363.02	503.26	26.70
31. Lakshadweep	9.79	1.40	8.25	9.65	8.39
32. Pondicherry	14.78	15.58	38.30	53.88	13.77
All States/UTs	18.82	3547.72	23998.96	27546.88	18.72
Centre	2.03	1823.34	880.23	2703.57	1.98
Total (Centre & States)	10.77	5371.06	24879.19	30250.25	10.67

Source: *Annual Financial Statistics of Education Sector 1996-97*. Ministry of Human Resource Development, Department of Education. Planning, Monitoring and Statistics Division, New Delhi.

Table 23.19: Plan and Non-Plan Budgetary Expenditure on Technical Education (Education Department), 1993-94 to 1995-96.

(Rs. in crores)

S. No.	State/UT	1993-94 (Accounts)			% age to Total Budget	1994-95 (RE)		
		Plan	Non-Plan	Total		Plan	Non-Plan	Total
	1	2	3	4	5	6	7	8
1.	Andhra Pradesh	7.42	37.12	44.55	3.12	6.92	43.33	50.25
2.	Arunachal Pradesh	0.00	0.00	0.00	0.00	0.00	0.00	0.00
3.	Assam	6.56	6.61	13.17	1.69	9.18	7.73	16.91
4.	Bihar	7.16	14.34	21.50	1.55	5.28	14.93	20.21
5.	Goa	1.53	2.51	4.04	4.64	2.86	2.99	5.85
6.	Gujarat	8.44	31.04	39.48	2.91	9.71	33.43	43.13
7.	Haryana	4.76	7.60	12.36	2.75	12.42	8.42	20.84
8.	Himachal Pradesh	2.40	1.13	3.53	1.39	4.39	1.22	5.60
9.	Jammu & Kashmir	0.77	7.03	7.80	2.39	1.69	10.50	12.19
10.	Karnataka	6.72	24.29	31.01	2.50	14.16	27.60	41.76
11.	Kerala	12.65	36.01	48.66	4.32	17.08	39.35	56.44
12.	Madhya Pradesh	7.91	34.95	42.86	3.52	23.29	41.89	65.18
13.	Maharashtra	23.00	87.66	110.67	4.22	59.44	94.01	153.45
14.	Manipur	0.36	0.33	0.69	0.63	0.65	0.17	0.82
15.	Meghalaya	0.18	0.50	0.67	0.73	0.61	0.49	1.10
16.	Mizoram	0.31	0.45	0.76	1.18	0.45	0.35	0.80
17.	Nagaland	0.54	0.47	1.01	1.22	0.73	0.48	1.21
18.	Orissa	7.46	7.29	14.75	2.18	17.80	8.55	26.35

Table 23.19: (*Contd.*)

1	2	3	4	5	6	7	8
19. Punjab	10.49	8.13	18.62	2.79	27.95	8.17	36.12
20. Rajasthan	11.08	8.08	19.16	1.58	13.87	9.56	23.44
21. Sikkim	0.15	0.00	0.15	0.46	0.15	0.00	0.15
22. Tamil Nadu	7.66	50.88	58.55	3.42	9.03	54.71	63.74
23. Tripura	0.17	1.30	1.47	1.10	0.11	1.54	1.65
24. Uttar Pradesh	21.99	45.91	67.90	2.93	31.60	49.30	80.91
25. West Bengal	5.38	26.48	31.86	1.98	11.50	32.31	43.81
26. A & N Islands	0.59	0.36	0.95	3.53	0.80	0.44	1.24
27. Chandigarh	0.38	5.85	6.23	10.74	0.87	6.53	7.40
28. D & N Haveli	0.10	0.00	0.10	2.01	0.15	0.00	0.15
29. Daman & Diu	0.51	0.15	0.66	12.15	0.55	0.15	0.70
30. Delhi	4.63	3.46	8.09	6.15	7.69	10.90	18.59
31. Lakshadweep	0.00	0.00	0.00	0.00	0.00	0.00	0.00
32. Pondicherry	0.70	0.63	1.33	2.89	2.43	0.77	3.19
All States/UTs	162.03	450.54	612.57	2.87	293.36	509.83	803.19
Centre	183.45	221.70	405.16	19.33	232.02	232.07	464.09
Total (Centre & States)	345.48	672.25	1017.73	4.35	525.38	741.90	1267.28

Table 23.19: (*Contd.*)

(*Rs. in crores*)

S. No.	State/UT	%age to Total Budget	1995-96 (BE)			% age to Total Budget
			Plan	Non-Plan	Total	
	1	9	10	11	12	13
1.	Andhra Pradesh	3.10	6.90	45.68	52.58	2.82
2.	Arunachal Pradesh	0.00	0.00	0.00	0.00	0.00
3.	Assam	2.24	10.58	7.78	18.36	2.04
4.	Bihar	1.21	12.19	16.24	28.43	1.53
5.	Goa	6.07	7.79	2.95	10.74	10.44
6.	Gujarat	2.80	8.91	35.28	44.20	2.61
7.	Haryana	4.07	18.41	8.75	27.16	5.13
8.	Himachal Pradesh	1.86	4.07	1.56	5.63	1.64
9.	Jammu & Kashmir	3.66	2.58	11.47	14.05	3.93
10.	Karnataka	2.81	15.43	29.24	44.67	2.60
11.	Kerala	4.15	20.19	42.50	62.69	3.99
12.	Madhya Pradesh	4.46	29.65	47.10	76.75	4.83
13.	Maharashtra	5.18	20.61	92.27	112.88	3.90
14.	Manipur	0.62	0.91	0.17	1.08	0.81
15.	Meghalaya	1.10	0.65	0.51	1.16	0.98
16.	Mizoram	1.21	0.45	0.35	0.80	1.28
17.	Nagaland	1.37	0.86	0.53	1.39	1.41
18.	Orissa	2.96	12.37	9.12	21.49	2.44

Table 23.19: (*Contd.*)

1	9	10	11	12	13
19. Punjab	4.70	34.98	7.23	42.21	5.09
20. Rajasthan	1.65	15.61	10.62	26.23	1.64
21. Sikkim	0.39	0.29	0.00	0.29	0.68
22. Tamil Nadu	3.28	8.95	57.03	65.98	3.13
23. Tripura	1.13	0.19	1.72	1.90	1.12
24. Uttar Pradesh	2.77	24.84	54.41	79.25	2.61
25. West Bengal	2.40	16.49	35.87	52.36	2.30
26. A & N Islands	3.92	0.79	0.47	1.26	3.67
27. Chandigarh	11.02	1.12	6.87	7.99	11.16
28. D & N Haveli	2.58	0.25	0.00	0.25	3.88
29. Daman & Diu	10.74	0.65	0.16	0.81	11.25
30. Delhi	4.45	18.06	12.92	30.98	6.16
31. Lakshadweep	0.00	0.00	0.00	0.00	0.00
32. Pondicherry	6.00	3.51	0.80	4.31	8.00
All States/UTs	3.20	298.27	539.60	837.87	3.04
Centre	18.65	253.41	213.37	466.78	17.27
Total (Centre & States)	4.59	551.68	752.97	1304.65	4.31

Source: *Annual Financial Statistics of Education Sector 1996-97*. Department of Education, Ministry of Human Resource Development, Planning, Monitoring and Statistics Division, New Delhi.

Table 23.20: Expenditure on Education (Revenue Account) as Percentage of GNP, 1951-52 to 1994-95.

Year	Education Departments	Other Departments	All Departments
1	2	3	4
1951-52	0.68	0.03	0.68
1961-62	1.63	0.09	1.63
1971-72	2.37	0.23	2.41
1981-82	2.65	0.45	3.00
1986-87	3.27	0.53	3.67
1987-88	3.57	0.64	4.04
1991-92	3.47	0.69	3.99
1992-93	3.39	0.89	4.70
1993-94	3.30	0.69	3.99
1994-95 (RE)	3.29	0.68	3.97

Source: Annual Financial Statistics of Education Sector, 1996-97, Department of Education, Planning, Monitoring and Statistics Division, Ministry of Human Resources Development, New Delhi.

Table 23.21: Budgetary Expenditure on Education by Education Department (Revenue Account), 1995-96

(Rs. in crores)

S. No.	States/UTs	Budget of Education Department			Total State Budget	%age of Education Budget to Total State Budget
		Plan	Non-Plan	Total		
1	2	3	4	5	6	7
1.	Andhra Pradesh	195.36	1670.00	1865.35	10888.16	17.73
2.	Arunachal Pradesh	28.24	37.09	65.33	482.15	13.55
3.	Assam	356.78	543.86	900.64	3717.16	24.23
4.	Bihar	173.70	1684.28	1857.98	8410.12	22.09
5.	Goa	21.16	81.65	102.81	617.67	16.64
6.	Gujarat	33.27	1663.14	1696.41	8195.35	20.70
7.	Haryana	101.13	428.78	529.91	5048.50	10.50
8.	Himachal Pradesh	88.67	254.41	343.08	1852.32	18.52
9.	Jammu & Kashmir	69.89	288.05	357.94	2295.56	15.59
10.	Karnataka	384.71	1336.42	1721.14	9093.63	18.93
11.	Kerala	79.06	1492.65	1571.71	5861.19	26.82
12.	Madhya Pradesh	224.87	1365.65	1590.52	9677.03	16.44
13.	Maharashtra	239.31	2651.90	2891.21	16765.70	17.24
14.	Manipur	17.28	116.36	133.64	508.94	26.26
15.	Meghalaya	49.77	68.51	118.28	600.35	19.70
16.	Mizoram	10.81	52.75	63.56	430.05	14.78
17.	Nagaland	10.56	87.78	98.34	767.41	12.81

Table 23.21: (*Contd.*)

1	2	3	4	5	6	7
18.	Orissa	162.52	717.71	880.23	5115.26	17.21
19.	Punjab	126.75	702.11	828.85	7507.64	11.04
20.	Rajasthan	344.01	1259.78	1603.79	7988.20	20.08
21.	Sikkim	16.94	26.00	42.94	565.43	7.59
22.	Tamil Nadu	111.17	1994.56	2105.73	10060.61	20.93
23.	Tripura	43.15	127.08	170.23	897.11	18.98
24.	Uttar Pradesh	324.01	2716.22	3040.23	18041.00	16.85
25.	West Bengal	155.32	2125.20	2280.52	9633.90	23.67
26.	A & N Islands	7.47	26.86	34.33	296.59	11.57
27.	Chandigarh	10.08	61.49	71.57	348.69	20.53
28.	D & N Haveli	2.41	4.04	6.45	64.53	9.99
29.	Daman & Diu	2.11	5.06	7.17	56.72	12.63
30.	Delhi	140.23	363.02	503.26	1884.70	26.70
31.	Lakshadweep	1.40	8.25	9.65	115.04	8.39
32.	Pondicherry	15.58	38.30	53.88	391.26	13.77
	All States/UTs	3547.72	23998.96	27546.68	148177.95	18.59
	Centre	1823.34	880.23	2703.57	138328.00	1.28
	Total (Centre + States/UTs)	5371.06	24879.19	30250.25	284505.95	10.67

Table 23.22: Per Capita Budgetary Expenditure on Education of Major States, 1985-86 to 1995-96

(in Rs.)

S.No.	States	1985-86	1991-92	1992-93	1993-94	1994-95	1995-96
1.	Andhra Pradesh	89	167	193	205	229	259
2.	Assam	96	234	275	328	312	364
3.	Bihar	65	144	148	152	179	195
4.	Gujarat	123	249	260	313	350	378
5.	Haryana	102	212	246	257	267	292
6.	Karnataka	91	206	231	265	313	357
7.	Kerala	148	280	301	373	444	507
8.	Madhya Pradesh	63	146	159	174	206	219
9.	Maharashtra	113	257	282	316	350	335
10.	Orissa	58	168	187	204	264	256
11.	Punjab	125	270	282	316	360	382
12.	Rajasthan	85	195	228	261	300	331
13.	Tamil Nadu	100	255	271	298	336	360
14.	Uttar Pradesh	62	141	173	159	197	202
15.	West Bengal	88	190	193	226	252	310

Source: *Annual Financial Statistics of Education Sector 1996-1997*, Department of Educational Planning, Monitoring and Statistics. Ministry of Human Resource Development, Government of India, New Delhi

Table 23.23: Statewise Anticipated Expenditure under Operation Blackboard, 1996-97 *(Rs. in lakhs)*

	State/UT	Salary of Addl. Teacher	Salary of 3rd Teacher	Addl. Teachers Upper Primary School	Total
1.	Andhra Pradesh	2835.00	1025.32	1065.54	4925.86
2.	Arunachal Pradesh	40.95	—	—	40.95
3.	Assam	2871.96	—	—	2871.96
4.	Bihar	8548.75	—	—	8548.75
5.	Goa	10.32	0.63	—	10.95
6.	Gujarat	—	—	—	—
7.	Haryana	14.00	62.68	—	76.68
8.	Himachal Pradesh	164.67	—	72.87	237.54
9.	Jammu and Kashmir	461.82	872.23	560.28	1400.1
10.	Karnataka	—	—	2018.1	2890.33
11.	Kerala	—	—	—	—
12.	Madhya Pradesh	4993.38	—	153.93	4993.38
13.	Maharashtra	—	—	—	153.93
14.	Manipur	123.48	—	—	123.48
15.	Meghalaya	—	—	—	—
16.	Mizoram	5.42	—	—	5.42
17.	Nagaland	2.97	—	—	2.97
18.	Orissa	—	—	—	—
19.	Punjab	294.00	—	284.13	578.13
20.	Rajasthan	—	532.98	—	532.98
21.	Sikkim	—	—	—	—
22.	Tamil Nadu	375.9	1453.09	—	1828.99
23.	Tripura	13.12	—	8.4	21.52
24.	Uttar Pradesh	291.72	—	—	291.72
25.	West Bengal	569.52	—	—	569.52
26.	A and N Islands	—	0.63	—	0.63
27.	Chandigarh	—	—	—	—
28.	D and N Haveli	26.46	—	—	26.46
29.	Daman and Diu	—	—	—	—
30.	Delhi	—	—	—	—
31.	Lakshadweep	—	—	—	—
32.	Pondicherry	1.68	—	—	1.68
	Total	21645.12	4325.56	4163.25	30133.93

Table 23.24: Sexwise and Stagewise Enrolment at School Level, 1950-51 to 1995-96.

(In Millions)

Year	Primary			Upper Primary			High/Hr. Sec.		
	Boys	Girls	Total	Boys	Girls	Total	Boys	Girls	Total
1950-51	13.8	5.4	19.2	2.6	0.5	3.1	1.3	0.2	1.5
1955-56	17.1	7.5	24.6	3.8	1.0	4.8	2.2	0.4	2.6
1960-61	23.6	11.4	35.0	5.1	1.6	6.7	2.7	0.7	3.4
1965-66	32.2	18.3	50.5	7.7	2.8	10.5	4.4	1.3	5.7
1970-71	35.7	21.3	57.0	9.4	3.9	13.3	5.7	1.9	7.6
1975-76	40.6	25.0	65.6	11.0	5.0	16.0	6.5	2.4	8.9
1980-81	45.3	28.5	73.8	13.9	6.8	20.7	7.6	3.4	11.0
1985-86	52.2	35.2	87.4	17.7	9.6	27.3	11.5	5.0	16.5
1990-91	57.0	40.4	97.4	21.5	12.5	34.0	12.8	6.3	19.1
1991-92	59.6	42.3	100.9	22.0	13.6	35.6	13.5	6.9	20.4
1992-93	57.9	41.7	99.6	21.2	12.9	34.1	13.6	6.9	20.5
1993-94*	61.8	46.4	108.2	24.2	15.7	39.2	15.3	8.0	23.7
1994-95*	62.3	46.8	109.1	24.5	15.8	40.3	16.0	8.4	24.4
1995-96*	62.4	47.4	109.8	25.0	16.0	41.0	16.1	8.8	24.9

* Provisional

Table 23.25: Sexwise, Stagewise and Statewise Enrolment, 1995-96*

State/UTs		Primary			Middle	
	Boys	Girls	Total	Boys	Girls	Total
1	2	3	4	5	6	7
1. Andhra Pradesh	4105438	3534964	7640402	1315299	920098	2235397
2. Arunachal Pradesh	78782	63122	141904	21974	16215	38189
3. Assam	2024781	1791822	3816603	774281	530223	1304504
4. Bihar	5875144	3211216	9086360	1665207	708337	2373544
5. Goa	66082	60927	127009	41370	35666	77036
6. Gujarat	3571059	2627671	6198730	1239445	881597	2121042
7. Haryana	1019107	894735	1913842	468915	333565	802480
8. Himachal Pradesh	387620	341250	728870	224780	175630	400410
9. Jammu & Kashmir	492080	331173	823253	212536	126279	338815
10. Karnataka	3450182	3058299	6508481	1206887	973796	2180683
11. Kerala	1461062	1385666	2846728	952583	897848	1850431
12. Madhya Pradesh	5186227	3783534	8969761	2378654	1039703	3418357
13. Maharashtra	6084787	5461111	11545898	2567911	2007246	4575157
14. Manipur	146270	129730	276000	58990	50890	109880
15. Meghalaya	148366	146913	295279	40823	35636	76459
16. Mizoram	61641	55440	117081	21357	20330	41687

Table 23.25: *(Contd.)*

1	2	3	4	5	6	7
17. Nagaland	115201	105871	221072	29235	27051	56286
18. Orissa	2279000	1608000	3887000	818000	460000	1278000
19. Punjab	1097346	984212	2081558	529958	422995	952953
20. Rajasthan	4049000	2183000	6232000	1440000	532000	1972000
21. Sikkim	42415	40146	82561	10827	10482	21309
22. Tamil Nadu	4389141	3806531	8195672	2102030	1680399	3782429
23. Tripura	232170	194740	426910	68862	55367	124229
24. Uttar Pradesh	10063991	6200706	16264697	3941480	1687208	5628688
25. West Bengal	5302000	4815000	10117000	2481000	2122000	4603000
Union Territories						
26. A & N Islands	22463	20572	43035	11620	10427	22047
27. Chandigarh	22558	19918	42476	12561	11140	23701
28. D & N Haveli	12953	9042	21995	3439	2085	5524
29. Daman & Diu	7255	6648	13903	3608	3051	6659
30. Delhi	509247	447845	957092	292350	233063	525413
31. Lakshadweep	4763	4010	8773	2129	1544	3673
32. Pondicherry	52621	49726	102347	33135	31019	64154
India	62360752	47373540	109734292	24971246	16042890	41014136

* As on September 30, 1995.

Table 23.25: (*Contd.*)

	State/UTs	Sec./Hr. Sec.			Hr. Education		
		Boys	Girls	Total	Boys	Girls	Total
	1	8	9	10	11	12	13
1.	Andhra Pradesh	1073790	625116	1698906	229929	124215	354144
2.	Arunachal Pradesh	14175	8188	22363	2841	862	3703
3.	Assam	460533	323619	784152	117142	59803	176945
4.	Bihar	777774	262815	1040589	433453	100487	533940
5.	Goa	33753	31096	64849	7139	8895	16034
6.	Gujarat	793750	563180	1356930	223165	173857	397022
7.	Haryana	243692	146140	389832	62451	46667	109118
8.	Himachal Pradesh	141865	86580	228445	34170	19310	53480
9.	Jammu & Kashmir	124359	64601	188960	27540	16547	44087
10.	Karnataka	836638	493674	1330312	282019	139052	421071
11.	Kerala	618924	665593	1284517	67506	97932	165438
12.	Madhya Pradesh	1518092	617057	2135149	182652	75468	258120
13.	Maharashtra	1917438	1235655	3153093	606737	356896	963633
14.	Manipur	45194	37730	82924	12309	9584	21893
15.	Meghalaya	21774	19281	41055	5979	5638	11617
16.	Mizoram	13701	12886	26587	3356	2358	5714
17.	Nagaland	16126	13235	29361	3411	2165	5576

Table 23.25: *(Contd.)*

	1	8	9	10	11	12	13
18.	Orissa	847801	397559	1245360	99739	33823	133562
19.	Punjab	398186	307071	705257	74141	82985	157126
20.	Rajasthan	852000	206000	1058000	93857	41436	135293
21.	Sikkim	5955	5671	11626	872	573	1445
22.	Tamil Nadu	1219919	842354	2062273	201551	153194	354745
23.	Tripura	48055	33017	81072	8347	4797	13144
24.	Uttar Pradesh	2658212	839244	3497456	480764	223495	704259
25.	West Bengal	1154126	727100	1881226	196157	134837	330994
26.	A & N Islands	7369	6459	13828	1113	901	2014
27.	Chandigarh	9042	11312	20354	3494	8060	11554
28.	D & N Haveli	1804	1195	2999	0	0	0
29.	Daman & Diu	2558	1902	4460	412	259	671
30.	Delhi	228050	175406	403456	79342	58068	137410
31.	Lakshadweep	1083	745	1828	0	0	0
32.	Pondicherry	21481	19872	41353	4778	4468	9246
	India	16107219	8781353	24888572	3546366	1986632	5532998

Table 23.26: Sexwise Enrolment Ratio in Classes I-V and VI-VIII of Schools for General Education, 1995-96

S. No.	States/UTs	Class (I-V) (6-11 Age Group)			Class VI-VIII (11-14 Age Group)		
		Boys	Girls	Total	Boys	Girls	Total
1	2	3	4	5	6	7	8
1.	Andhra Pradesh	99.6	89.9	94.9	57.3	41.8	49.7
2.	Arunachal Pradesh	115.5	103.9	110.0	61.3	45.2	53.3
3.	Assam	133.4	124.0	128.8	91.6	65.9	79.1
4.	Bihar	93.0	55.4	75.1	47.5	21.9	35.3
5.	Goa	90.6	100.5	95.1	95.1	84.1	89.6
6.	Gujarat	158.3	106.8	131.4	81.1	61.5	71.6
7.	Haryana	86.4	84.8	85.6	70.9	56.7	64.2
8.	Himachal Pradesh	108.4	113.7	110.8	112.7	90.5	101.8
9.	Jammu & Kashmir	88.6	72.2	81.2	73.3	46.8	60.5
10.	Karnataka	131.1	123.5	127.4	78.1	66.8	72.6
11.	Kerala	98.4	95.4	96.9	105.1	101.5	103.3
12.	Madhya Pradesh	112.9	88.9	101.4	91.6	43.3	68.4
13.	Maharashtra	125.5	120.2	122.9	92.4	77.2	85.0
14.	Manipur	93.1	100.3	96.4	69.4	63.2	66.4
15.	Meghalaya	105.3	125.4	114.4	51.6	45.5	48.6
16.	Mizoram	112.6	124.8	118.1	67.3	67.7	67.5

Table 23.26: (*Contd.*)

1	2	3	4	5	6	7	8
17.	Nagaland	120.6	135.5	127.3	52.5	51.2	51.9
18.	Orissa	113.4	78.2	95.6	73.0	39.8	56.2
19.	Punjab	92.4	90.7	91.5	74.0	65.0	69.7
20.	Rajasthan	129.3	75.3	103.4	79.9	32.0	56.9
21.	Sikkim	104.2	118.4	110.6	50.5	50.8	50.7
22.	Tamil Nadu	159.3	145.6	152.6	118.2	99.5	109.1
23.	Tripura	122.7	124.4	123.5	66.8	57.0	62.0
24.	Uttar Pradesh	104.3	72.0	89.1	72.3	34.9	54.7
25.	West Bengal	128.6	122.3	125.5	102.8	91.5	97.2
26.	A & N Islands	76.6	69.2	72.9	73.5	68.6	71.1
27.	Chandigarh	36.4	40.4	38.2	36.4	34.9	35.6
28.	D & N Haveli	121.0	102.7	112.7	59.2	40.8	50.6
29.	Daman & Diu	93.0	88.6	90.8	92.5	84.7	83.7
30.	Delhi	67.7	77.8	72.1	71.1	67.3	69.3
31.	Lakshadweep	125.3	125.3	125.3	112.0	81.2	96.6
32.	Pondicherry	117.2	133.3	124.5	113.0	109.6	111.3
	India	114.5	93.3	104.3	79.5	54.9	67.6

Table 23.27 : Female Students per Hundred Male Students in Universities, 1950-51 and 1995-96

Year	Total Enrolment ('000s)	Enrolment per Hundred Men
1950-51	40	14
1995-96	2191	52

Source: Annual Report 1995-96, University Grants Commission, New Delhi.

Table 23.28: Stagewise Percentage of Women Enrolment to Total Enrolment in Universities, 1986-87 and 1995-96

Year	Graduate	Post-Graduate	Research	Diploma Certificate
1986-87	29.9	31.6	31.7	24.4
1995-96	34.1	34.0	39.2	26.6

Source: Annual Report 1995-96, University Grants Commission, New Delhi.

Table 23.29: Facultywise Women Enrolment in Universities, 1995-96

Year	No. of Women Colleges	Faculty	Enrolment
1986-87	780	Arts	11,91,774
1987-88	786	Commerce	3,09,830
1988-89	824	Science	4,40,354
1989-90	851	Education	85,699
1990-91	874	Law	39,551
1991-92	950	Engineering and Technology	26,368
1992-93	994	Others	97,562
1993-94	1033	(including Medicine,	
1994-95	1107	Agriculture, Vet. Science,	
1995-96	1146*	Music/Fine Arts, Social	
		Work, Physical	
		Education, etc).	
Total			21,91,138

* Provisional

Source: Annual Report 1995-96, University Grants Commission, New Delhi

Table 23.30: Enrolment Ratio of Students of Scheduled Castes, 1995-96

S. No.	States/UTs	Class (I-V) (6-11 Age Group)			Class VI-VIII (11-14 Age group)		
		Boys	Girls	Total	Boys	Girls	Total
1	2	3	4	5	6	7	8
1.	Andhra Pradesh	140.68	121.73	131.4	67.03	42.63	55.08
2.	Arunachal Pradesh	25.33	27.50	26.2	21	13	17
3.	Assam	257.62	239.07	248.5	190.13	161.51	176.16
4.	Bihar	102.04	51.39	77.8	38.2	14.03	26.62
5.	Goa	105.31	116.77	110.4	69.5	55.33	62.79
6.	Gujarat	213.43	155.06	182.9	117.32	76	97.32
7.	Haryana	108.12	105.84	107	65.81	47.85	57.36
8.	Himachal Pradesh	115.15	115.75	115.4	90.14	63.06	76.80
9.	Jammu & Kashmir	96.14	83.93	90.6	80.24	59.68	70.34
10.	Karnataka	158.59	137.96	148.5	81.78	57.60	70.04
11.	Kerala	107.64	102.45	105	118.31	114.56	116.46
12.	Madhya Pradesh	129.68	93.48	112.2	80.98	35.62	59.19
13.	Maharashtra	268.31	257.96	263.3	180.15	137.47	159.53
14.	Manipur	153.65	179.19	165	93.64	92	92.86
15.	Meghalaya	—	—	—	—	—	—
16.	Mizoram	—	—	—	—	—	—
17.	Nagaland	—	—	—	—	—	—

Table 23.30: *(Contd.)*

1	2	3	4	5	6	7	8
18.	Orissa	152.85	95.29	123.7	71.82	43.17	57.29
19.	Punjab	134.77	129.98	132.4	79.75	64.83	72.65
20.	Rajasthan	121.53	48.62	86.5	78.13	21.44	50.93
21.	Sikkim	103.75	114.00	108.4	50.83	43.17	47.00
22.	Tamil Nadu	176.76	154.02	165.6	111.26	84.74	98.34
23.	Tripura	147.05	144.14	145.7	63.43	66.69	65.01
24.	Uttar Pradesh	88.94	42.05	68.8	53.34	15.82	35.70
25.	West Bengal	129.79	116.93	123.5	72.03	69.0	70.59
26.	A & N Islands	—	—	—	—	—	—
27.	Chandigarh	82.85	92.93	87.3	68.33	59.02	68.83
28.	D & N Haveli	74.67	87.00	79.6	99.00	93.0	96.00
29.	Daman & Diu	—	—	—	—	—	—
30.	Delhi	83.49	91.76	87	72.66	68.66	70.83
31.	Lakshadweep	—	—	—	—	—	—
32.	Pondicherry	141.29	170.18	154.4	147.36	154.87	151.03
	India	127.56	95.12	111.91	74.88	46.77	61.33

Table 23.31: Sexwise, Stagewise and Statewise Enrolment of Scheduled Castes, 1995-96*

	State/UTs	Primary			Middle		
		Boys	Girls	Total	Boys	Girls	Total
	1	2	3	4	5	6	7
1.	Andhra Pradesh	861802	711386	1573188	228642	139539	368181
2.	Arunachal Pradesh	76	55	131	21	13	34
3.	Assam	238299	210617	448916	97918	79303	177221
4.	Bihar	934509	431483	1365992	194108	65584	259692
5.	Goa	1685	1518	3203	695	498	1193
6.	Gujarat	344686	273060	617746	128343	77972	206315
7.	Haryana	243053	212953	456006	82981	53644	136625
8.	Himachal Pradesh	101330	85540	186870	44260	30080	74340
9.	Jammu & Kashmir	44319	31978	76297	19338	13368	32706
10.	Karnataka	628798	514716	1143514	190306	126423	316729
11.	Kerala	160061	148962	309023	107421	101501	208922
12.	Madhya Pradesh	839654	560606	1400260	296313	120532	416845
13.	Maharashtra	928345	836835	1765180	357412	255013	612425
14.	Manipur	3073	2867	5940	1030	920	1950
15.	Meghalaya	2965	2944	5909	825	721	1546

Table 23.31: (*Contd.*)

1	2	3	4	5	6	7
16. Mizoram	0	0	0	0	0	0
17. Nagaland	0	0	0	0	0	0
18. Orissa	450000	287000	737000	118000	73000	191000
19. Punjab	429912	378761	808673	153359	113255	266614
20. Rajasthan	662000	245000	907000	245000	62000	307000
21. Sikkim	2490	2280	4770	610	518	1128
22. Tamil Nadu	893540	738824	1632364	362825	262528	625353
23. Tripura	42055	34160	76215	9895	9804	19699
24. Uttar Pradesh	1815479	765518	2580997	615132	161778	776910
25. West Bengal	1176675	1012271	2188946	382175	352211	734386
26. A & N Islands	0	0	0	0	0	0
27. Chandigarh	7208	6412	13620	3280	2656	5936
28. D & N Haveli	224	174	398	99	93	192
29. Daman & Diu	294	308	602	168	137	305
30. Delhi	113125	95154	208279	53840	42841	96681
31. Lakshadweep	0	0	0	0	0	0
32. Pondicherry	10173	10211	20384	6926	6969	13895
India10935830		7601593	18537423	3700922	2152901	5853823

* As on September 30, 1995.

Table 23.31: (*Contd.*)

State/UTs	Sec./Hr. Sec.			Hr. Education		
	Boys	Girls	Total	Boys	Girls	Total
1	8	9	10	11	12	13
1. Andhra Pradesh	356351	149671	506022	25963	12211	38174
2. Arunachal Pradesh	9	6	15	38	11	49
3. Assam	60770	46087	106857	10643	5377	16020
4. Bihar	77974	18964	96938	17049	1847	18896
5. Goa	343	231	574	38	33	71
6. Gujarat	82770	44450	127220	22301	11478	33779
7. Haryana	32403	14030	46433	5849	1296	7145
8. Himachal Pradesh	23739	12078	35817	3846	1602	5448
9. Jammu & Kashmir	8988	3895	12883	961	414	1375
10. Karnataka	132439	60086	192525	29245	9165	38410
11. Kerala	66397	75192	141589	6326	9147	15473
12. Madhya Pradesh	188663	57833	246496	18043	3354	21397
13. Maharashtra	261483	146075	407558	75138	32884	108022
14. Manipur	1241	1428	2669	773	791	1564
15. Meghalaya	755	478	1233	223	120	343
16. Mizoram	0	0	0	0	0	0

Table 23.31: *(Contd.)*

1	8	9	10	11	12	13
17. Nagaland	0	0	0	0	0	0
18. Orissa	78852	30051	108903	7622	1662	9284
19. Punjab	80072	52364	132436	8732	7053	15785
20. Rajasthan	124000	17000	141000	13416	1158	14574
21. Sikkim	323	273	596	21	28	49
22. Tamil Nadu	192985	104232	297217	28337	16599	44936
23. Tripura	7421	4505	11926	1374	523	1897
24. Uttar Pradesh	408381	70630	479011	64261	4917	69178
25. West Bengal	125116	53875	178991	17364	7753	25117
26. A & N Islands	0	0	0	0	0	0
27. Chandigarh	1333	1233	2566	154	154	308
28. D & N Haveli	111	65	176	0	0	0
29. Daman & Diu	159	119	278	27	8	35
30. Delhi	35212	27354	62566	5286	3012	8298
31. Lakshadweep	0	0	0	0	0	0
32. Pondicherry	3393	3021	6414	753	492	1245
India	2351683	995226	3346909	363783	133089	496872

Table 23.32: Sexwise, Stagewise and Statewise Enrolment of Scheduled Tribes, 1995-96*

	States/UTs	Primary			Middle		
		Boys	Girls	Total	Boys	Girls	Total
	1	2	3	4	5	6	7
1.	Andhra Pradesh	352012	235022	587034	65763	26489	92252
2.	Arunachal Pradesh	57670	46968	104638	14149	10324	24473
3.	Assam	381832	316382	698214	125716	95388	221104
4.	Bihar	475862	302363	778225	103395	55685	159080
5.	Goa	91	70	161	74	55	129
6.	Gujarat	552429	393530	945959	147028	86198	233226
7.	Haryana	0	0	0	0	0	0
8.	Himachal Pradesh	17280	13250	30530	7790	4240	12030
9.	Jammu & Kashmir	0	0	0	0	0	0
10.	Karnataka	209812	165192	375004	57928	37923	95851
11.	Kerala	19050	17588	36638	9471	9013	18484
12.	Madhya Pradesh	991112	577163	1568275	244467	115983	360450
13.	Maharashtra	613715	505528	1119243	171239	108184	279423
14.	Manipur	52740	44930	97670	16820	13740	30560
15.	Meghalaya	116412	116248	232660	31503	28370	59873
16.	Mizoram	60919	54975	115894	21181	20245	41426

Table 23.32: (*Contd.*)

	1	2	3	4	5	6	7
17.	Nagaland	115201	105871	221072	29235	27051	56286
18.	Orissa	549000	268000	817000	118000	50000	168000
19.	Punjab	0	0	0	0	0	0
20.	Rajasthan	465000	174000	639000	178000	41000	219000
21.	Sikkim	9050	8310	17360	2190	2070	4260
22.	Tamil Nadu	43437	32550	75987	14881	9792	24673
23.	Tripura	81148	60215	141363	16318	12698	29016
24.	Uttar Pradesh	20121	11573	31694	6491	2331	8822
25.	West Bengal	286712	271767	558479	112115	92730	204845
26.	A & N Islands	1852	1638	3490	789	777	1566
27.	Chandigarh	0	0	0	0	0	0
28.	D & N Haveli	10671	7080	17751	2505	1318	3823
29.	Daman & Diu	1076	924	2000	442	345	787
30.	Delhi	371	315	686	262	160	422
31.	Lakshadweep	4665	3912	8577	2064	1472	3536
32.	Pondicherry	0	0	0	0	0	0
	India	5489240	3735364	9224604	1499816	853581	2353397

* As on September 30, 1995

Table 23.32: (*Contd.*)

	States/UTs	Sec./Hr. Sec.			Hr. Education		
		Boys	Girls	Total	Boys	Girls	Total
	1	8	9	10	11	12	13
1.	Andhra Pradesh	62927	20755	83682	5564	1512	7076
2.	Arunachal Pradesh	9516	4733	14249	2211	627	2838
3.	Assam	84598	57693	142291	15105	7919	23024
4.	Bihar	43156	21980	65136	7954	3395	11349
5.	Goa	42	19	61	2	0	2
6.	Gujarat	84450	50960	135410	20336	12946	33282
7.	Haryana	0	0	0	0	0	0
8.	Himachal Pradesh	5050	2474	7524	1334	644	1978
9.	Jammu & Kashmir	0	0	0	0	0	0
10.	Karnataka	29348	13939	43287	8042	2351	10393
11.	Kerala	4122	4467	8589	121	233	354
12.	Madhya Pradesh	183454	53890	237344	11918	2357	14275
13.	Maharashtra	99591	54092	153683	15467	5736	21203
14.	Manipur	9445	7227	16672	1855	1158	3013
15.	Meghalaya	17253	15288	32541	4196	3372	7568
16.	Mizoram	13601	12820	26421	3335	2340	5675

Table 23.32: *(Contd.)*

	1	8	9	10	11	12	13
17.	Nagaland	15953	13004	28957	3082	1973	5055
18.	Orissa	52526	34075	86601	5359	1306	6665
19.	Punjab	0	0	0	8	2	10
20.	Rajasthan	89000	9000	98000	9250	427	9677
21.	Sikkim	1684	1177	2861	149	126	275
22.	Tamil Nadu	7990	4696	12686	1242	513	1755
23.	Tripura	10309	4907	15216	632	228	860
24.	Uttar Pradesh	3719	1419	5138	1341	541	1882
25.	West Bengal	22284	12163	34447	775	284	1059
26.	A & N Islands	460	453	913	34	30	64
27.	Chandigarh	0	0	0	73	40	113
28.	D & N Haveli	1042	614	1656	0	0	0
29.	Daman & Diu	191	122	313	105	16	121
30.	Delhi	272	158	430	421	252	673
31.	Lakshadweep	1006	687	1693	0	0	0
32.	Pondicherry	0	0	0	0	0	0
	India	852989	402812	1255801	119911	50328	170239

Table 23.33: Enrolment Ratio of Students Belonging to Scheduled Tribes, 1995-96

S. No.	States/UTs	Class I-V (6-11 Age Group)			Class VI-VIII (11-14 Age group)		
		Boys	Girls	Total	Boys	Girls	Total
1	2	3	4	5	6	7	8
1.	Andhra Pradesh	144.09	100.82	122.96	48.35	20.30	34.60
2.	Arunachal Pradesh	121.15	98.62	116.26	56.60	41.30	48.90
3.	Assam	196.62	171.11	184.18	116.30	92.61	104.70
4.	Bihar	90.73	62.82	77.40	35.53	20.81	28.34
5.	Goa	13.00	11.66	12.38	18.50	13.75	16.10
6.	Gujarat	122.04	112.37	140.91	67.60	42.25	55.30
7.	Haryana	—	—	—	—	—	—
8.	Himachal Pradesh	105.36	96.01	101.09	84.67	47.64	66.40
9.	Jammu & Kashmir	—	—	—	—	—	—
10.	Karnataka	162.39	135.85	149.52	76.42	53.04	65.00
11.	Kerala	124.51	118.04	121.32	101.84	99.04	100.40
12.	Madhya Pradesh	93.95	59.07	77.18	41.01	21.04	31.40
13.	Maharashtra	137.79	121.08	129.71	67.05	45.30	56.50
14.	Manipur	123.51	127.64	125.38	72.81	62.74	67.90
15.	Meghalaya	102.47	123.14	111.86	49.46	45.03	47.20
16.	Mizoram	118.98	132.47	125.02	71.56	72.05	71.00

Table 23.33: *(Contd.)*

1	2	3	4	5	6	7	8
17.	Nagaland	143.64	161.39	151.62	62.60	60.93	61.70
18.	Orissa	121.86	58.15	89.64	46.96	19.32	32.90
19.	Punjab	—	—	—	—	—	—
20.	Rajasthan	121.66	49.21	86.84	80.87	20.21	51.70
21.	Sikkim	96.28	105.19	100.35	43.80	43.13	43.40
22.	Tamil Nadu	147.24	73.15	132.15	78.32	54.10	66.00
23.	Tripura	151.11	135.31	143.95	55.69	46.00	50.90
24.	Uttar Pradesh	99.12	63.94	82.54	56.94	23.08	41.00
25.	West Bengal	123.53	122.64	123.09	82.50	71.06	76.80
26.	A & N Islands	51.44	45.50	48.47	41.53	43.17	42.30
27.	Chandigarh	—	—	—	—	—	—
28.	D & N Haveli	127.04	102.61	116.02	55.67	32.95	44.90
29.	Daman & Diu	—	—	—	—	—	—
30.	Delhi	—	—	—	—	—	—
31.	Lakshadweep	137.21	134.90	136.14	121.41	86.59	104.00
32.	Pondicherry	—	—	—	—	—	—
	India	129.96	94.87	113.03	61.59	37.63	50.04

Table 23.34: Growth of Enrolment in Universities, 1976-77 to 1995-96

Year	Total Enrolment	Increase over the Preceding Year	%age increase
1976-77	24,31,563	5,454	0.2
1977-78	25,64,972	1,33,409	5.5
1978-79	26,18,228	53,256	2.1
1979-80	26,48,579	30,351	1.2
1980-81	27,52,437	1,03,858	3.9
1981-82	29,52,066	1,99,629	7.3
1982-83	31,33,093	1,81,027	6.1
1983-84	33,07,649	1,74,556	5.6
1984-85	34,04,096	96,447	2.9
1985-86	36,05,029	2,00,933	5.9
1986-87	37,57,158	1,52,419	4.1
1987-88	40,20,159	2,63,001	7.0
1988-89	42,85,489	2,65,330	6.6
1989-90	46,02,680	3,17,191	7.4
1990-91	49,24,868	3,22,188	7.0
1991-92	52,65,886	3,41,018	6.9
1992-93	55,34,966	2,69,080	5.1
1993-94	58,17,249	2,82,283	5.1
1994-95 +	61,13,929	2,96,680	5.1
1995-96 +	64,25,624	3,11,695	5.1

+ Estimates

Source: Annual Report 1995-96, University Grants Commission, New Delhi.

Table 23.35: Statewise Enrolment in Universities (Excluding PUC/Inter/Pre-professional), 1995-96

S. No.	State/UT	Enrolment	Increase over the Preceding year	%age incr--ease	Average Annual Compound Rate of Growth during the period 1991-92 to 1995-96
1	2	3	4	5	6
1.	Andhra Pradesh	451173	23521	5.5	5.9
2.	Arunachal Pradesh	3431	191	5.9	6.6
3.	Assam	154541	6371	4.3	4.2
4.	Bihar	499467	24237	5.1	4.8
5.	Delhi	143365	6827	5.0	5.0
6.	Goa	17979	1002	5.9	6.9
7.	Gujarat	435615	19157	4.6	4.9
8.	Haryana	148582	6262	4.4	4.3
9.	Himachal Pradesh	37440	2086	5.9	6.9
10.	Jammu and Kashmir	46811	2059	4.6	4.9
11.	Karnataka	514865	27303	6.0	6.0
12.	Kerala	187615	7562	4.2	3.3
13.	Madhya Pradesh	393226	18010	4.8	4.8
14.	Maharashtra	995640	44694	4.7	5.1
15.	Manipur	29695	1441	5.1	5.5
16.	Meghalaya/ Nagaland/Mizoram	20544	1089	5.6	5.7
17.	Orissa	216181	11076	5.4	5.5
18.	Punjab	197444	10647	5.7	5.1
19.	Rajasthan	217528	12313	6.0	6.1
20.	Tamil Nadu	442070	25416	6.1	6.9
21.	Uttar Pradesh	892168	44905	5.3	4.5
22.	West Bengal/ Sikkim/Tripura	369710	14902	4.2	3.9
23.	Pondicherry	10534	624	6.3	5.8
	Total	6425624	311695	5.1	5.1

Table 23.36: Faculty-wise Enrolment in the Universities, 1991-92 to 1995-96

Faculty	1991-92		1992-93		1993-94		1994-95		1995-96	
	Enrolment	% of Total	Enrolment	% of Total	Enrolment	% of Total	Enrolment	% of Total	Enrolment	% of Total
1. Arts (including oriental learning)	21,29,418	40.4	22,38,626	40.4	23,52,970	40.4	24,73,027	40.4	25,92,925	40.4
2. Science	10,33,614	19.6	10,86,353	19.6	11,41,680	19.6	11,99,830	19.6	12,60,200	19.6
3. Commerce	11,54,804	21.9	12,13,688	21.9	12,75,478	21.9	13,40,560	21.9	14,10,119	21.9
4. Education	1,21,115	2.3	1,27,304	2.3	1,33,797	2.3	1,40,620	2.3	1,47,720	2.3
5. Engineering/Technology	2,58,028	4.9	2,71,213	4.9	2,85,045	4.9	2,99,583	4.9	3,15,720	4.9
6. Medicine	1,79,040	3.4	1,88,989	3.4	1,97,786	3.4	2,07,874	3.4	2,19,918	3.4
7. Agriculture	55,292	1.1	58,120	1.1	61,091	1.1	64,200	1.1	67,990	1.1
8. Veterinary Science	13,356	0.3	13,840	0.3	14,550	0.3	15,285	0.3	16,201	0.3
9. Law	2,79,092	5.3	2,93,353	5.3	3,08,314	5.3	3,24,038	5.3	3,42,440	5.3
10. Others	42,127	0.8	44,280	0.8	46,538	0.8	48,912	0.8	52,401	0.8
Total	52,65,886	100.0	55,34,966	100.0	58,17,249	100.0	61,13,929	100.0	64,25,624	100.0

Source: Annual Report 1995-96, University Grants Commission, New Delhi.

Table 23.37: Stage-wise Enrolment in Universities and Affiliated Colleges, 1995-96

Stage	University Departments/ Colleges	Affiliated Colleges	Total	% in affiliated Colleges		
				1995-96	1994-95	1993-94
Graduate	6,93,423	49,73,977	56,67,400 (88.2%)	87.8	87.8	87.8
Post-graduate	2,62,744	3,41,265	6,04,009 (9.4%)	56.5	56.5	56.5
Research	60,080	10,602	70,682 (1.1%)	15.0	15.0	15.0
Diploma/ Certificate	47,280	36,253	83,533 (1.3%)	43.4	43.4	43.4
	10,63,527	53,62,097	64,25,624	83.4	83.4	83.4

Note: Figures in brackets indicate the percentage of enrolment at each stage to total enrolment.

Source: *Annual Report 1995-96*, University Grants Commission, New Delhi.

Table 23.38: Sexwise, Stagewise and Statewise Enrolment in Indian Universities.

B.A./B.A.(Hons)

States/UTs				Scheduled Castes			Scheduled Tribes		
	Boys	Girls	Total	Boys	Girls	Total	Boys	Girls	Total
1	2	3	4	5	6	7	8	9	10
1. Andhra Pradesh	55233	34853	90086	9705	4305	14010	1722	461	2183
2. Arunachal Pradesh	1967	686	2653	14	7	21	1623	525	2148
3. Assam	71785	48020	119805	7018	4144	11162	11270	6370	17640
4. Bihar	139535	39705	179240	10899	1104	12003	4675	2495	7170
5. Goa	1222	2728	3950	2	4	6	1	0	1
6. Gujarat	91150	92900	184050	13400	8150	21550	14500	10500	25000
7. Haryana	33948	27159	61107	3355	808	4163	0	0	0
8. Himachal Pradesh	20173	13394	33567	2330	1092	3422	831	471	1302
9. Jammu & Kashmir	6767	7293	14060	247	201	448	0	0	0
10. Karnataka	118969	63100	182069	17962	5484	23446	5371	1387	6758
11. Kerala	20914	37539	58453	2490	3519	6009	51	100	151
12. Madhya Pradesh	56851	38998	95849	8539	1760	10299	6430	1458	7888
13. Maharashtra	252240	159462	411702	42468	19494	61962	8985	3257	12242
14. Manipur	5908	6011	11919	427	524	951	1317	844	2161
15. Meghalaya	3739	4192	7931	149	67	216	2804	2544	5348
16. Mizoram	2794	2083	4877	0	0	0	2784	2073	4857
17. Nagaland	2659	1924	4583	0	0	0	2430	1780	4210

Table 23.38: *(Contd.)*

1	2	3	4	5	6	7	8	9	10
18. Orissa	56976	22916	79892	5068	1004	6072	3156	839	3995
19. Punjab	50700	57773	108473	6595	5730	12325	0	0	0
20. Rajasthan	43952	23992	67944	8773	717	9490	6503	286	6789
21. Sikkim	562	441	1003	13	21	34	120	105	225
22. Tamil Nadu	47465	45867	93332	9761	5743	15504	412	171	583
23. Tripura	4156	3750	7906	653	370	1023	357	178	535
24. Uttar Pradesh	231576	149286	380862	41344	3186	44530	574	305	879
25. West Bengal	60033	92204	152237	6002	4161	10163	332	212	544
26. A & N Islands	690	581	1271	0	0	0	34	29	63
27. Chandigarh	1431	4371	5802	57	54	111	19	13	32
28. D & N Haveli	0	0	0	0	0	0	0	0	0
29. Daman & Diu	157	100	257	12	4	16	81	8	89
30. Delhi	33490	34973	68463	2210	2063	4273	153	142	295
31. Lakshadweep	0	0	0	0	0	0	0	0	0
32. Pondicherry	1158	1483	2641	211	148	359	0	0	0
India	1418200	1017784	2435984	199704	73864	273568	76535	36553	113088

Source: *Selected Educational Statistics 1995-96*, Planning, Monitoring and Statistics Division, Department of Education, Ministry of Human Resource Development, Government of India, New Delhi.

Table 23.39: Statewise Percentage of Women Enrolment to Total Enrolment in Universities, 1995-96.

S No.	State/UTs	Total Enrolment	Women Enrolment	Percentage of Women
1	2	3	4	5
1.	Andhra Pradesh	451173	142068	31.5
2.	Arunachal Pradesh	3431	782	22.8
3.	Assam	154541	50641	32.8
4.	Bihar	499467	93028	18.6
5.	Delhi	143365	64003	44.6
6.	Goa	17979	9181	51.1
7.	Gujarat	435615	171789	39.4
8.	Haryana	148582	57375	38.6
9.	Himachal Pradesh	37440	14328	38.3
10.	Jammu and Kashmir	46811	18657	39.9
11.	Karnataka	514865	176954	34.4
12.	Kerala	187615	98260	52.4
13.	Madhya Pradesh	393226	117916	30.0
14.	Maharashtra	995640	362240	36.4
15.	Manipur	29695	12706	42.8
16.	Meghalaya/ Nagaland/Mizoram	20544	8151	39.7
17.	Orissa	216181	69883	32.3
18.	Punjab	197444	100804	51.1
19.	Rajasthan	217528	71275	32.8
20.	Tamil Nadu	442070	176467	39.9
21.	Uttar Pradesh	892168	238471	26.7
22.	West Bengal/ Sikkim/Tripura	369710	131400	35.5
23.	Pondicherry	10534	4759	45.2
	Total	64,25,624	21,91,138	34.1

Source: Annual Report 1995-96, University Grants Commission, New Delhi.

Table 23.40: Sexwise, Stagewise and Statewise Enrolment in Universities.

B.Com./B.Com.(Hons)

State/UTs			Scheduled Castes			Scheduled Tribes			
	Boys	Girls	Total	Boys	Girls	Total	Boys	Girls	Total
1	2	3	4	5	6	7	8	9	10
1. Andhra Pradesh	59746	32884	92630	4069	2427	6496	867	217	1084
2. Arunachal Pradesh	172	22	194	6	1	7	111	13	124
3. Assam	11760	1960	13720	1155	344	1499	1225	488	1713
4. Bihar	197952	43424	241376	1391	64	1455	1561	205	1766
5. Goa	3473	3308	6781	5	12	17	0	0	0
6. Gujarat	71450	47000	118450	4150	1500	5650	2900	1000	3900
7. Haryana	9134	5926	15060	352	69	421	0	0	0
8. Himachal Pradesh	4407	1345	5752	465	148	613	131	37	168
9. Jammu & Kashmir	2927	1003	3930	69	14	83	0	0	0
10. Karnataka	42132	32608	74740	3418	1506	4924	860	364	1224
11. Kerala	8095	8770	16865	804	966	1770	10	23	33
12. Madhya Pradesh	44288	4264	48552	2978	204	3182	1560	78	1638
13. Maharashtra	124344	93041	217385	10201	4928	15129	2319	997	3316
14. Manipur	407	125	532	26	13	39	40	35	75
15. Meghalaya	578	120	698	20	13	33	404	96	500
16. Mizoram	201	59	260	0	0	0	201	59	260
17. Nagaland	299	55	354	0	0	0	234	20	254

Table 23.40: *(Contd.)*

1	2	3	4	5	6	7	8	9	10
18. Orissa	13246	1806	15052	611	126	737	555	122	677
19. Punjab	9394	6433	15827	384	184	568	0	0	0
20. Rajasthan	13777	3493	17270	436	56	492	115	21	136
21. Sikkim	124	24	148	5	3	8	9	4	13
22. Tamil Nadu	31467	22156	53623	3421	2113	5534	141	60	201
23. Tripura	1732	67	1799	247	10	257	90	1	91
24. Uttar Pradesh	49964	3208	53172	2984	28	3012	77	3	80
25. West Bengal	62915	6712	69627	5892	138	6030	218	12	230
26. A & N Islands	127	71	198	0	0	0	0	0	0
27. Chandigarh	851	713	1564	5	25	30	0	0	0
28. D & N Haveli	0	0	0	0	0	0	0	0	0
29. Daman & Diu	162	86	248	10	3	13	13	1	14
30. Delhi	26901	8611	35512	1670	307	1977	58	19	77
31. Lakshadweep	0	0	0	0	0	0	0	0	0
32. Pondicherry	431	723	1154	59	49	108	0	0	0
India	792456	330017	1122473	44833	15251	60084	13699	3875	17574

Source: *Selected Educational Statistics 1995-96*, Planning, Monitoring and Statistics Division, Department of Education, Ministry of Human Resource Development, Government of India, New Delhi.

Table 23.41: Sexwise, Stagewise and Statewise Enrolment in Universities.

B.Sc./B.Sc.(Hons)

State/Union Territory				Scheduled Castes			Scheduled Tribes		
	Boys	Girls	Total	Boys	Girls	Total	Boys	Girls	Total
1	2	3	4	5	6	7	8	9	10
1. Andhra Pradesh	69155	39118	108273	5627	3094	8721	936	357	1293
2. Arunachal Pradesh	171	40	211	6	2	8	132	30	162
3. Assam	21560	4410	25970	1372	441	1813	1372	490	1862
4. Bihar	55089	7837	62926	2605	286	2891	901	263	1164
5. Goa	1172	1644	2816	5	4	9	1	0	1
6. Gujarat	26500	15000	41500	1000	400	1400	500	200	700
7. Haryana	7481	5825	13306	306	52	358	0	0	0
8. Himachal Pradesh	6178	2832	9010	496	194	690	149	72	221
9. Jammu & Kashmir	14272	5532	19804	441	128	569	0	0	0
10. Karnataka	40061	24501	64562	3291	1124	4415	705	343	1048
11. Kerala	21580	37115	58695	1785	3045	4830	15	45	60
12. Madhya Pradesh	40038	14335	54373	1840	435	2275	932	230	1162
13. Maharashtra	69575	45390	114965	6542	2677	9219	1028	400	1428
14. Manipur	4892	2708	7600	301	249	550	264	187	451
15. Meghalaya	980	600	1580	39	33	72	637	360	997
16. Mizoram	240	188	428	0	0	0	240	181	421

Table 23.41: (*Contd.*)

	1	2	3	4	5	6	7	8	9	10
17.	Nagaland	342	114	456	0	0	0	330	109	439
18.	Orissa	16257	4585	20842	892	223	1115	834	125	959
19.	Punjab	6517	7959	14476	404	279	683	0	0	0
20.	Rajasthan	16500	6188	22688	1379	126	1505	729	32	761
21.	Sikkim	186	108	294	3	4	7	20	17	37
22.	Tamil Nadu	70962	59687	130649	9104	5892	14996	486	217	703
23.	Tripura	1368	526	1894	196	70	266	37	26	63
24.	Uttar Pradesh	82189	28336	110525	5783	310	6093	149	43	192
25.	West Bengal	48203	23206	71409	3895	3172	7067	111	41	152
26.	A & N Islands	239	175	414	0	0	0	0	0	0
27.	Chandigarh	165	1144	1309	8	26	34	0	0	0
28.	D & N Haveli	0	0	0	0	0	0	0	0	0
29.	Daman & Diu	62	37	99	1	0	1	0	0	0
30.	Delhi	7977	6535	14512	335	115	450	13	15	28
31.	Lakshadweep	0	0	0	0	0	0	0	0	0
32.	Pondicherry	919	1008	1927	138	110	248	0	0	0
	India	630830	346683	977513	47794	22491	70285	10521	3783	14304

Source: *Selected Educational Statistics 1995-96*, Planning, Monitoring and Statistics Division, Department of Education, Ministry of Human Resource Development, Government of India, New Delhi.

Table 23.42: Sexwise, Stagewise and Statewise Enrolment in Universities.

B.Ed./B.T.

State/Union Territory				Scheduled Castes			Scheduled Tribes		
	Boys	Girls	Total	Boys	Girls	Total	Boys	Girls	Total
1	2	3	4	5	6	7	8	9	10
1. Andhra Pradesh	4390	3351	7741	567	453	1020	181	45	226
2. Arunachal Pradesh	29	6	35	0	0	0	21	4	25
3. Assam	1584	968	2552	204	87	291	193	145	338
4. Bihar	1348	902	2250	142	47	189	102	180	282
5. Goa	45	166	211	0	0	0	0	0	0
6. Gujarat	3050	1800	4850	380	150	530	350	200	550
7. Haryana	1556	1830	3386	253	111	364	0	0	0
8. Himachal Pradesh	245	80	325	55	11	66	10	4	14
9. Jammu & Kashmir	502	494	996	26	10	36	0	0	0
10. Karnataka	3652	2581	6233	399	110	509	141	33	174
11. Kerala	830	2858	3688	172	295	467	4	15	19
12. Madhya Pradesh	3187	2547	5734	410	89	499	107	52	159
13. Maharashtra	27643	10518	38161	2739	932	3671	871	315	1186
14. Manipur	140	121	261	2	1	3	40	5	45
15. Meghalaya	155	303	458	1	1	2	64	135	199

Table 23.42: (*Contd.*)

1	2	3	4	5	6	7	8	9	10
16. Mizoram	121	28	149	0	0	0	110	27	137
17. Nagaland	47	30	77	0	0	0	29	24	53
18. Orissa	1232	698	1930	173	77	250	146	46	192
19. Punjab	834	2960	3794	181	346	527	0	0	0
20. Rajasthan	4381	2842	7223	986	175	1161	558	41	599
21. Sikkim	0	0	0	0	0	0	0	0	0
22. Tamil Nadu	1133	2078	3211	242	281	523	8	2	10
23. Tripura	254	65	319	126	17	143	39	11	50
24. Uttar Pradesh	9990	7583	17573	1320	275	1595	27	17	44
25. West Bengal	5020	4213	9233	470	42	512	31	9	40
26. A & N Islands	15	39	54	0	0	0	0	1	1
27. Chandigarh	74	408	482	24	26	50	5	5	10
28. D & N Haveli	0	0	0	0	0	0	0	0	0
29. Daman & Diu	31	36	67	4	1	5	11	7	18
30. Delhi	279	541	820	21	54	75	10	2	12
31. Lakshadweep	0	0	0	0	0	0	0	0	0
32. Pondicherry	66	206	272	5	42	47	0	0	0
India	71833	50252	122085	8902	3633	12535	3058	1325	4383

Source: *Selected Educational Statistics 1995-96*, Planning, Monitoring and Statistics Division, Department of Education, Ministry of Human Resource Development, Government of India, New Delhi.

Table 23.43: Sexwise, Stagewise and Statewise Enrolment in Universities.

M.A.

State/Union Territory				Scheduled Castes			Scheduled Tribes		
	Boys	Girls	Total	Boys	Girls	Total	Boys	Girls	Total
1	2	3	4	5	6	7	8	9	10
1. Andhra Pradesh	6222	2160	8382	1210	343	1553	251	82	333
2. Arunachal Pradesh	242	75	317	0	0	0	180	41	221
3. Assam	2974	2455	5429	221	142	363	298	183	481
4. Bihar	7935	2798	10733	548	93	641	195	67	262
5. Goa	132	265	397	1	1	2	0	0	0
6. Gujarat	9500	8500	18000	1750	900	2650	1250	850	2100
7. Haryana	4871	3313	8184	729	130	859	0	0	0
8. Himachal Pradesh	1737	1143	2880	285	110	395	128	47	175
9. Jammu & Kashmir	789	836	1625	45	17	62	0	0	0
10. Karnataka	4369	2140	6509	917	300	1217	121	44	165
11. Kerala	2297	4004	6301	334	462	796	5	8	13
12. Madhya Pradesh	10300	7864	18164	1330	400	1730	946	227	1173
13. Maharashtra	30403	17257	47660	6349	2517	8866	1106	355	1461
14. Manipur	319	325	644	3	2	5	18	11	29
15. Meghalaya	392	329	721	12	5	17	231	197	428
16. Mizoram	0	0	0	0	0	0	0	0	0

Table [illegible]. (*Contd.*)

	1	2	3	4	5	6	7	8	9	10
17.	Nagaland	47	36	83	0	0	0	45	35	80
18.	Orissa	4169	2308	6477	316	99	415	143	41	184
19.	Punjab	1779	4485	6264	276	251	527	0	0	0
20.	Rajasthan	5700	2283	7983	1566	58	1624	1191	39	1230
21.	Sikkim	0	0	0	0	0	0	0	0	0
22.	Tamil Nadu	4425	4116	8541	853	394	1247	25	11	36
23.	Tripura	214	244	458	47	33	80	3	8	11
24.	Uttar Pradesh	56733	27206	83939	11202	945	12147	345	159	504
25.	West Bengal	5125	5642	10767	302	175	477	13	2	15
26.	A & N Islands	25	22	47	0	0	0	0	0	0
27.	Chandigarh	771	1039	1810	50	20	70	48	22	70
28.	D & N Haveli	0	0	0	0	0	0	0	0	0
29.	Daman & Diu	0	0	0	0	0	0	0	0	0
30.	Delhi	3108	3370	6478	289	193	482	86	38	124
31.	Lakshadweep	0	0	0	0	0	0	0	0	0
32.	Pondicherry	306	224	530	60	17	77	0	0	0
	India	164884	104439	269323	28695	7607	36302	6628	2467	9095

Source: *Selected Educational Statistics 1995-96*, Planning, Monitoring and Statistics Division, Department of Education, Ministry of Human Resource Development, Government of India, New Delhi.

Table 23.44: Sexwise, Stagewise and Statewise Enrolment in Universities.

M.Com.

State/Union Territory				Scheduled Castes			Scheduled Tribes		
	Boys	Girls	Total	Boys	Girls	Total	Boys	Girls	Total
1	2	3	4	5	6	7	8	9	10
1. Andhra Pradesh	2434	409	2843	449	157	606	193	86	279
2. Arunachal Pradesh	25	6	31	0	0	0	20	5	25
3. Assam	686	56	742	58	18	76	51	9	60
4. Bihar	10826	3372	14198	41	15	56	20	7	27
5. Goa	78	79	157	2	2	4	0	0	0
6. Gujarat	4500	3500	8000	550	200	750	320	100	420
7. Haryana	278	352	630	86	4	90	0	0	0
8. Himachal Pradesh	157	63	220	21	5	26	7	2	9
9. Jammu & Kashmir	168	90	258	6	2	8	0	0	0
10. Karnataka	1054	787	1841	151	59	210	49	27	76
11. Kerala	540	681	1221	78	72	150	0	6	6
12. Madhya Pradesh	8770	1638	10408	575	52	627	310	50	360
13. Maharashtra	9924	3954	13878	1532	484	2016	291	66	357
14. Manipur	45	31	76	1	1	2	1	3	4
15. Meghalaya	21	9	30	0	0	0	0	0	0

Table 23.44; *(Contd.)*

1	2	3	4	5	6	7	8	9	10
16. Mizoram	0	0	0	0	0	0	0	0	0
17. Nagaland	12	1	13	0	0	0	9	1	10
18. Orissa	1265	87	1352	18	3	21	12	8	20
19. Punjab	41	223	264	1	12	13	0	0	0
20. Rajasthan	1153	387	1540	91	4	95	80	0	80
21. Sikkim	0	0	0	0	0	0	0	0	0
22. Tamil Nadu	2304	1112	3416	326	73	399	8	3	11
23. Tripura	123	4	127	9	0	9	3	0	3
24. Uttar Pradesh	13112	458	13570	637	46	683	35	2	37
25. West Bengal	2145	205	2350	22	3	25	1	0	1
26. A & N Islands	0	0	0	0	0	0	0	0	0
27. Chandigarh	32	19	51	8	2	10	0	0	0
28. D & N Haveli	0	0	0	0	0	0	0	0	0
29. Daman & Diu	0	0	0	0	0	0	0	0	0
30. Delhi	820	805	1625	79	13	92	11	3	14
31. Lakshadweep	0	0	0	0	0	0	0	0	0
32. Pondicherry	122	49	171	19	0	19	0	0	0
India	60635	18377	79012	4760	1227	5987	1421	378	1799

Source: *Selected Educational Statistics 1995-96*, Planning, Monitoring and Statistics Division, Department of Education, Ministry of Human Resource Development, Government of India, New Delhi.

Table 23.45: Sexwise, Stagewise and Statewise Enrolment in Universities.

M.Sc.

State/Union Territory				Scheduled Castes			Scheduled Tribes		
	Boys	Girls	Total	Boys	Girls	Total	Boys	Girls	Total
1	2	3	4	5	6	7	8	9	10
1. Andhra Pradesh	3923	1957	5880	472	230	702	73	51	124
2. Arunachal Pradesh	0	0	0	0	0	0	0	0	0
3. Assam	2180	1003	3183	160	75	235	167	74	241
4. Bihar	2261	572	2833	63	21	84	40	21	61
5. Goa	100	146	246	1	1	2	0	0	0
6. Gujarat	2800	1700	4500	200	50	250	100	50	150
7. Haryana	1126	971	2097	95	19	114	0	0	0
8. Himachal Pradesh	281	167	448	43	14	57	8	4	12
9. Jammu & Kashmir	567	627	1194	32	4	36	0	0	0
10. Karnataka	2086	1720	3806	293	90	383	94	17	111
11. Kerala	1152	2586	3738	205	327	532	6	6	12
12. Madhya Pradesh	6024	2956	8980	876	204	1080	107	48	155
13. Maharashtra	7948	5139	13087	868	246	1114	100	60	160
14. Manipur	290	163	453	1	1	2	9	8	17
15. Meghalaya	114	85	199	2	1	3	56	40	96
16. Mizoram	0	0	0	0	0	0	0	0	0

Table 23.45: *(Contd.)*

1	2	3	4	5	6	7	8	9	10
17. Nagaland	5	5	10	0	0	0	5	4	9
18. Orissa	1802	784	2586	106	33	139	46	9	55
19. Punjab	444	1059	1503	18	27	45	0	0	0
20. Rajasthan	1362	715	2077	185	22	207	74	8	82
21. Sikkim	0	0	0	0	0	0	0	0	0
22. Tamil Nadu	6427	5213	11640	614	341	955	9	4	13
23. Tripura	98	64	162	8	4	12	1	0	1
24. Uttar Pradesh	18168	5311	23479	746	102	848	30	11	41
25. West Bengal	2612	1302	3914	148	15	163	7	2	9
26. A & N Islands	17	13	30	0	0	0	0	0	0
27. Chandigarh	149	348	497	0	0	0	0	0	0
28. D & N Haveli	0	0	0	0	0	0	0	0	0
29. Daman & Diu	0	0	0	0	0	0	0	0	0
30. Delhi	990	965	1955	32	10	42	5	3	8
31. Lakshadweep	0	0	0	0	0	0	0	0	0
32. Pondicherry	309	218	527	44	17	61	0	0	0
India	63235	35789	99024	5212	1854	7066	937	420	1357

Source: *Selected Educational Statistics 1995-96*, Planning, Monitoring and Statistics Division, Department of Education, Ministry of Human Resource Development, Government of India, New Delhi.

Table 23.46: Sexwise, Stagewise and Statewise Enrolment in Universities.

B.E./B.Sc.(Engg)/B.Arch.

State/Union Territory				Scheduled Castes			Scheduled Tribes		
	Boys	Girls	Total	Boys	Girls	Total	Boys	Girls	Total
1	2	3	4	5	6	7	8	9	10
1. Andhra Pradesh	24507	5969	30476	3262	718	3980	1052	70	1122
2. Arunachal Pradesh	235	27	262	12	1	13	124	9	133
3. Assam	2946	300	3246	336	81	417	290	71	361
4. Bihar	5942	330	6272	275	12	287	135	10	145
5. Goa	589	233	822	10	1	11	0	0	0
6. Gujarat	13043	2790	15833	825	107	932	405	41	446
7. Haryana	2834	305	3139	503	23	526	0	0	0
8. Himachal Pradesh	570	59	629	81	8	89	36	1	37
9. Jammu & Kashmir	712	38	750	39	2	41	0	0	0
10. Karnataka	64372	9651	74023	2814	492	3306	679	129	808
11. Kerala	9990	3120	13110	319	332	651	10	8	18
12. Madhya Pradesh	9904	1416	11320	1090	84	1174	1273	111	1384
13. Maharashtra	69983	10397	80380	2958	420	3378	335	50	385
14. Manipur	0	0	0	0	0	0	0	0	0
15. Meghalaya	0	0	0	0	0	0	0	0	0
16. Mizoram	0	0	0	0	0	0	0	0	0

Table 23.46: *(Contd.)*

1	2	3	4	5	6	7	8	9	10
17. Nagaland	0	0	0	0	0	0	0	0	0
18. Orissa	2503	122	2625	228	13	241	287	19	306
19. Punjab	2778	383	3161	539	32	571	6	0	6
20. Rajasthan	4425	126	4551	0	0	0	0	0	0
21. Sikkim	0	0	0	0	0	0	0	0	0
22. Tamil Nadu	30805	8212	39017	3163	1145	4308	153	45	198
23. Tripura	402	77	479	88	19	107	102	4	106
24. Uttar Pradesh	13714	515	14229	86	3	89	64	0	64
25. West Bengal	7292	395	7687	320	12	332	50	3	53
26. A & N Islands	0	0	0	0	0	0	0	0	0
27. Chandigarh	21	18	39	2	1	3	1	0	1
28. D & N Haveli	0	0	0	0	0	0	0	0	0
29. Daman & Diu	0	0	0	0	0	0	0	0	0
30. Delhi	3532	415	3947	405	33	438	73	4	77
31. Lakshadweep	0	0	0	0	0	0	0	0	0
32. Pondicherry	855	282	1137	137	53	190	0	0	0
India	271954	45180	317134	17492	3592	21084	5075	575	5650

Source: *Selected Educational Statistics 1995-96*, Planning, Monitoring and Statistics Division, Department of Education, Ministry of Human Resource Development, Government of India, New Delhi.

Table 23.47: Sexwise, Stagewise and Statewise Enrolment in Universities.

M.B.B.S./Ayurved

State/Union Territory				Scheduled Castes			Scheduled Tribes		
	Boys	Girls	Total	Boys	Girls	Total	Boys	Girls	Total
1	2	3	4	5	6	7	8	9	10
1. Andhra Pradesh	4319	3514	7833	602	484	1086	289	143	432
2. Arunachal Pradesh	0	0	0	0	0	0	0	0	0
3. Assam	1667	631	2298	119	45	164	239	89	328
4. Bihar	12565	1547	14112	1085	205	1290	325	147	472
5. Goa	328	326	654	12	8	20	0	0	0
6. Gujarat	1172	667	1839	46	21	67	11	5	16
7. Haryana	1223	986	2209	170	80	250	0	0	0
8. Himachal Pradesh	422	227	649	70	20	90	34	6	40
9. Jammu & Kashmir	836	634	1470	56	36	92	0	0	0
10. Karnataka	5324	1964	7288	0	0	0	22	7	29
11. Kerala	2108	1259	3367	139	129	268	20	22	42
12. Madhya Pradesh	3290	1450	4740	405	126	531	253	103	356
13. Maharashtra	14677	11738	26415	1481	1186	2667	432	236	668
14. Manipur	308	100	408	12	0	12	166	65	231
15. Meghalaya	0	0	0	0	0	0	0	0	0
16. Mizoram	0	0	0	0	0	0	0	0	0

Table 23.47: *(Contd.)*

1	2	3	4	5	6	7	8	9	10
17. Nagaland	0	0	0	0	0	0	0	0	0
18. Orissa	2289	517	2806	210	84	294	180	97	277
19. Punjab	1654	1710	3364	334	192	526	2	2	4
20. Rajasthan	2607	1410	4017	0	0	0	0	0	0
21. Sikkim	0	0	0	0	0	0	0	0	0
22. Tamil Nadu	6563	4753	11316	853	617	1470	0	0	0
23. Tripura	0	0	0	0	0	0	0	0	0
24. Uttar Pradesh	5318	1592	6910	159	22	181	40	1	41
25. West Bengal	2812	958	3770	313	35	348	12	3	15
26. A & N Islands	0	0	0	0	0	0	0	0	0
27. Chandigarh	0	0	0	0	0	0	0	0	0
28. D & N Haveli	0	0	0	0	0	0	0	0	0
29. Daman & Diu	0	0	0	0	0	0	0	0	0
30. Delhi	2245	1853	4098	245	224	469	12	26	38
31. Lakshadweep	0	0	0	0	0	0	0	0	0
32. Pondicherry	612	275	887	80	56	136	0	0	0
India	72339	38111	110450	6391	3570	9961	2037	952	2989

Source: *Selected Educational Statistics 1995-96*, Planning, Monitoring and Statistics Division, Department of Education, Ministry of Human Resource Development, Government of India, New Delhi.

Table 23.48: Sexwise, Stagewise and Statewise Enrolment in Universities.

Ph.D./D.Sc./D.Phil.

State/Union Territory				Scheduled Castes			Scheduled Tribes		
	Boys	Girls	Total	Boys	Girls	Total	Boys	Girls	Total
1	2	3	4	5	6	7	8	9	10
1. Andhra Pradesh	1330	366	1696	55	17	72	0	6	6
2. Arunachal Pradesh	7	0	7	0	0	0	4	0	4
3. Assam	180	114	294	6	3	9	12	7	19
4. Bihar	602	151	753	34	25	59	62	24	86
5. Goa	112	57	169	0	0	0	0	0	0
6. Gujarat	600	400	1000	30	20	50	20	20	40
7. Haryana	605	277	882	25	1	26	0	0	0
8. Himachal Pradesh	504	265	769	22	8	30	14	2	16
9. Jammu & Kashmir	155	115	270	0	0	0	0	0	0
10. Karnataka	1585	650	2235	174	45	219	33	6	39
11. Kerala	848	678	1526	31	19	50	0	0	0
12. Madhya Pradesh	7635	1000	8635	25	15	40	11	2	13
13. Maharashtra	3238	1787	5025	149	68	217	9	9	18
14. Manipur	58	20	78	0	0	0	4	3	7
15. Meghalaya	140	118	258	6	1	7	60	40	100
16. Mizoram	0	0	0	0	0	0	0	0	0

Table 23.48: *(Contd.)*

1	2	3	4	5	6	7	8	9	10
17. Nagaland	0	0	0	0	0	0	0	0	0
18. Orissa	276	79	355	19	7	26	19	5	24
19. Punjab	84	90	174	11	6	17	0	0	0
20. Rajasthan	50	61	111	3	1	4	2	0	2
21. Sikkim	0	0	0	0	0	0	0	0	0
22. Tamil Nadu	1295	674	1969	87	29	116	4	3	7
23. Tripura	0	0	0	0	0	0	0	0	0
24. Uttar Pradesh	6210	2193	8403	300	40	340	10	2	12
25. West Bengal	872	411	1283	36	19	55	3	0	3
26. A & N Islands	0	0	0	0	0	0	0	0	0
27. Chandigarh	69	63	132	0	0	0	0	0	0
28. D & N Haveli	0	0	0	0	0	0	0	0	0
29. Daman & Diu	0	0	0	0	0	0	0	0	0
30. Delhi	3120	1797	4917	98	31	129	30	19	49
31. Lakshadweep	0	0	0	0	0	0	0	0	0
32. Pondicherry	301	100	401	47	1	48	0	0	0
India	29876	11466	41342	1158	356	1514	297	148	445

Source: *Selected Educational Statistics 1995-96*, Planning, Monitoring and Statistics Division, Department of Education, Ministry of Human Resource Development, Government of India, New Delhi.

Table 23.49 : Sexwise and Statewise Drop-out Rates in Classes I-V, 1995-96$

	States/UTs	Boys	Girls	Total
1.	Andhra Pradesh	56.27	54.36	55.44
2.	Arunachal Pradesh	55.49	52.46	54.19
3.	Assam	39.83	41.75	40.69
4.	Bihar	61.46	64.03	62.37
5.	Goa	1.56	9.45	5.39
6.	Gujarat	35.49	41.15	38.02
7.	Haryana	5.78	7.32	6.48
8.	Himachal Pradesh	20.18	27.00	23.43
9.	Jammu and Kashmir	53.13	41.48	48.36
10.	Karnataka	34.88	35.72	35.28
11.	Kerala	-4.93	-1.99	-3.49
12.	Madhya Pradesh	28.06	33.23	30.25
13.	Maharashtra	21.79	27.36	24.40
14.	Manipur*	35.04	36.30	35.64
15.	Meghalaya**	59.61	62.53	61.07
16.	Mizoram	57.71	72.28	57.20
17.	Nagaland	39.93	31.40	35.98
18.	Orissa	52.88	53.79	53.24
19.	Punjab	22.86	22.52	22.70
20.	Rajasthan	50.57	56.00	52.38
21.	Sikkim	61.97	53.74	58.17
22.	Tamil Nadu	14.88	16.97	15.85
23.	Tripura	53.49	57.27	55.24
24.	Uttar Pradesh	22.31	22.94	22.53
25.	West Bengal	49.93	66.84	58.72
26.	A and N Islands	7.84	13.43	10.56
27.	Chandigarh	30.68	30.98	30.82
28.	D and N Haveli	31.21	50.80	39.57
29.	Daman and Diu	-10.24	-11.76	-10.96
30.	Delhi	18.15	30.53	24.37
31.	Lakshadweep	-0.42	7.37	3.16
32.	Pondicherry	-4.07	-7.06	-5.49
	India	37.92	41.31	39.37

$ Provisional

* Decrease is due to exclusion of enrolment of Class I-A from Class I and considered against pre-primary in 1991-92.

** Increase is due to students in classes A and B (aged 6 and above) promoted in Class-I as per new Education Structure w.e.f. 1991-92

Table 23.50 : Sexwise and Statewise Drop-out Rates in Classes I-VIII, 1995-96*

	States/UTs	Boys	Girls	Total
	1	2	3	4
1.	Andhra Pradesh	71.11	74.86	72.73
2.	Arunachal Pradesh	70.16	69.83	70.02
3.	Assam	68.58	73.21	70.66
4.	Bihar	75.96	81.76	77.95
5.	Goa	10.44	19.21	14.73
6.	Gujarat	53.76	62.76	57.78
7.	Haryana	26.44	36.55	30.99
8.	Himachal Pradesh	9.63	27.00	17.84
9.	Jammu and Kashmir	50.13	72.40	59.24
10.	Karnataka	54.02	66.69	60.15
11.	Kerala	0.32	0.52	0.42
12.	Madhya Pradesh	45.96	64.82	54.04
13.	Maharashtra	42.30	52.77	47.24
14.	Manipur	70.66	70.89	70.77
15.	Meghalaya	48.76	48.13	48.46
16.	Mizoram	69.71	67.45	68.65
17.	Nagaland	42.99	45.20	44.08
18.	Orissa	60.90	72.84	65.67
19.	Punjab	39.07	42.78	40.78
20.	Rajasthan	76.20	82.15	78.10
21.	Sikkim	69.28	64.98	67.33
22.	Tamil Nadu	28.60	37.11	32.54
23.	Tripura	73.39	74.46	73.88
24.	Uttar Pradesh	32.28	48.86	38.11
25.	West Bengal	67.47	74.19	69.08
26.	A and N Islands	23.42	24.90	24.13
27.	Chandigarh	18.46	17.18	17.86
28.	D and N Haveli	59.33	66.55	62.29
29.	Daman and Diu	10.49	15.70	12.88
30.	Delhi	30.35	15.26	23.03
31.	Lakshadweep	26.85	33.18	29.88
32.	Pondicherry	5.25	-0.29	2.69
	India	54.99	61.70	57.77

* Provisional

Table 23.51: Growth of Recognised Educational Institutions, 1950-51 to 1995-96.

Year	Primary	Upper Primary	High/Hr. Sec. School/Inter/ Pre-Degree Jr. Colleges	College for General Education	College for Professional Education	Universities
1950-51	209671	13596	7416	370	208	27
1955-56	278135	21730	10838	466	218	31
1960-61	330399	49663	17329	967	852	45
1965-66	391064	75798	27614	1536	770	64
1970-71	408378	90621	37051	2285	992	82
1975-76	454270	106571	43054	3667	**3276	101
1980-81	494503	118555	51573	3421	**3542	110
1985-86	528872	134846	65837	4067	**1533	126
1990-91	560935	151456	79796	4862	866	@184
1991-92	565786	152077	81747	5058	950	@196
1992-93	571248	158498	84608	5334	989	@207
1993-94*	572923	155707	88411	5639	1125	@213
1994-95*	581305	163605	92252	6089	1230	@219
1995-96*	590421	171216	98134	6569	1354	@226

* Provisional

** Includes Institutions for Post-matric Courses

@ Includes Deemed To Be University and Institutions of National Importance.

Source: Selected Educational Statistics 1995-96, Planning, Monitoring and Statistics Division, Department of Education, Ministry of Human Resource Development, Government of India, New Delhi.

Table 23.52: Statewise Number of Recognised Educational Institutions, 1995-96.

S. No.	States/UTs	Primary	Middle	High/Hr. Sec. School/Inter/ Pre-Degree Jr. Colleges	College for General Education	College for Professional Education @	Universities*
1	2	3	4	5	6	7	8
1.	Andhra Pradesh	49125	7298	9801	750	109	18
2.	Arunachal Pradesh	1210	301	154	4	1	1
3.	Assam	30140	7237	4047	245	31	6
4.	Bihar	53220	13558	4133	742	73	18
5.	Goa	1027	108	432	20	7	1
6.	Gujarat	14457	19169	5690	302	78	11
7.	Haryana	5385	1606	3016	128	26	5
8.	Himachal Pradesh	7732	1000	1116	55	5	3
9.	Jammu & Kashmir	9784	2668	1278	33	9	3
10.	Karnataka	23457	18916	7746	712	133	13
11.	Kerala	6725	2998	3294	173	39	8
12.	Madhya Pradesh	75060	17790	6126	448	40	16
13.	Maharashtra	41198	21509	13779	841	427	24
14.	Manipur	2547	547	554	29	3	2
15.	Meghalaya	4225	849	428	26	1	1
16.	Mizoram	1232	691	316	20	1	0
17.	Nagaland	1422	427	249	19	1	1

Table 23.52: *(Contd.)*

1	2	3	4	5	6	7	8
18.	Orissa	42104	12096	6411	476	31	5
19.	Punjab	12585	1687	3136	177	33	4
20.	Rajasthan	34504	11585	4596	191	50	10
21.	Sikkim	536	119	91	2	0	1
22.	Tamil Nadu	30431	5542	5910	280	119	19
23.	Tripura	2026	437	518	14	2	1
24.	Uttar Pradesh	86436	19148	6988	495	54	28
25.	West Bengal	51021	3156	6728	303	62	13
26.	A & N Islands	181	44	78	2	1	0
27.	Chandigarh	27	11	66	12	4	2
28.	D & N Haveli	142	43	15	0	0	0
29.	Daman & Diu	52	20	25	1	1	0
30.	Delhi	2072	531	1263	62	9	11
31.	Lakshadweep	19	4	11	0	0	0
32.	Pondicherry	339	121	139	7	4	1
	India	590421	171216	98134	6569	1354	226

* Includes Deemed To Be Universities and Institutions of National Importance.

@ Includes only College of Engineering/Tech., Medical, Research and Training Colleges.

Source: *Selected Educational Statistics 1995-96*, Planning, Monitoring and Statistics Division, Department of Education, Ministry of Human Resource Development, Government of India, New Delhi.

Table 23.53: Statewise Increase in Number of Colleges, 1991-92 to 1995-96.

S. No.	States/UTs	1991-92		1992-93		1993-94		1994-95		1995-96#		Increase during the period 91-92 to 95-96
		No. of Colleges(UC +AC)	Increase Over the Preceding year	No. of Colleges(UC +AC)	Increase Over the Preceding year	No. of Colleges (UC +AC)	Increase over the Preceding year	No. of Colleges (UC +AC)	Increase over the Preceding year	No. of colleges (UC +AC)	Increase over the Preceding year	
1	2	3	4	5	6	7	8	9	10	11	12	13
1.	Andhra Pradesh	686	94	717	31	790	73	879	89	945	66	259
2.	Arunachal Pradesh	4	0	4	0	4	0	4	0	4	0	0
3.	Assam	210	25	218	8	225	7	225	0	230	5	20
4.	Bihar	664	0	715	51	716	1	720	4	738	18	74
5.	Goa	30	3	30	0	34	4	34	0	36	2	6
6.	Gujarat	370	14	385	15	388	3	435	47	448	13	78
7.	Haryana	155	1	155	0	166	11	171	5	177	6	22
8.	Himachal Pradesh	53	11	54	1	54	0	61	7	63	2	10
9.	Jammu and Kashmir	46	2	46	0	48	2	53	5	56	3	10
10.	Karnataka	790	75	846	56	984	138	1001	17	1057	56	267
11.	Kerala	225	32	225	0	226	1	228	2	230	2	5
12.	Madhya Pradesh	631	0	631	0	636	5	638	2	640	2	9
13.	Maharashtra	1191	90	1216	25	1385	169	1474	89	1550	76	359
14.	Manipur	44	19	50	6	50	0	51	1	51	0	7
15.	Meghalaya	20	0	20	0	20	0	20	0	20	0	0
16.	Mizoram	10	0	10	0	10	0	10	0	10	0	0

Table 23.53: (*Contd.*)

1	2	3	4	5	6	7	8	9	10	11	12	13
17.	Nagaland	13	0	13	0	13	0	13	0	13	0	0
18.	Orissa	289	12	303	14	312	9	543	231	555	12	266
19.	Punjab	217	4	221	4	229	8	230	1	234	4	17
20.	Rajasthan	256	1	268	12	269	1	270	1	274	4	18
21.	Sikkim	2	0	2	0	2	0	2	0	2	0	0
22.	Tamil Nadu	380	23	384	4	385	1	431	46	439	8	59
23.	Tripura	19	2	19	0	19	0	19	0	19	0	0
24.	Uttar Pradesh	949	5	953	4	954	1	954	0	957	3	8
25.	West Bengal	390	1	391	1	392	1	399	7	402	3	12
26.	A and N Islands	3	0	3	0	3	0	3	0	3	0	0
27.	Chandigarh	20	0	20	0	20	0	20	0	20	0	0
28.	D and N Haveli	0	0	0	0	0	0	0	0	0	0	0
29.	Daman and Diu	1	0	1	0	1	0	1	0	1	0	0
30.	Delhi	80	1	80	0	82	2	85	3	87	2	7
31.	Lakshadweep	0	0	0	0	0	0	0	0	0	0	0
32.	Pondicherry	13	0	13	0	13	0	17	4	17	0	4
	Total	7,761	415	7,993	232	8,430	437	8,991	561	9,278	287	1,517

UC – University Colleges; AC – Affiliated Colleges; # – Provisional

Source: Annual Report 1995-96, University Grants Commission, New Delhi.

Table 23.54 : Sexwise and Stagewise Distribution of Teachers at School Level, 1950-51 to 1995-96.

(In Thousands)

Year	Primary			Upper Primary			High/Hr. Secondary		
	Male	Female	Total	Male	Female	Total	Male	Female	Total
1950-51	456	82	538	73	13	86	107	20	127
1955-56	574	117	691	132	19	151	155	35	190
1960-61	615	127	742	262	83	345	234	62	296
1965-66	764	180	944	389	139	528	368	111	479
1970-71	835	225	1060	463	175	638	474	155	629
1975-76	965	283	1248	554	224	778	559	200	759
1980-81	1021	342	1363	598	253	851	669	257	926
1985-86	1094	402	1496	663	305	968	793	339	1132
1990-91	1143	473	1616	717	356	1073	917	417	1334
1991-92	1144	492	1636	714	365	1079	931	450	1381
1992-93	1137	514	1651	709	376	1085	941	454	1395
1993-94*	1196	507	1703	710	370	1080	938	467	1405
1994-95*	1181	533	1714	732	390	1122	956	490	1446
1995-96*	1187	553	1740	756	409	1165	982	511	1493

* Provisional

Table 23.55 : Facultywise Number and Distribution of Teaching Staff in University Departments and University Colleges, 1991-92 to 1995-96.

Year	Professors	Readers	Lecturers*	Tutors/ Demonstrators	Total
1991-92	8,216 (12.8)	16,816 (26.2)	36,586 (57.0)	2,567 (4.0)	64,185 (100.0)
1992-93	8,428 (12.8)	17,250 (26.2)	37,530 (57.0)	2,534 (4.0)	65,842 (100.0)
1993-94**	8,645 (12.8)	17,695 (26.2)	38,498 (57.0)	2,702 (4.0)	67,540 (100.0)
1994-95**	8,868 (12.8)	18,152 (26.2)	39,492 (57.0)	2,771 (4.0)	69,283 (100.0)
1995-96**	9,099 (12.8)	18,624 (26.2)	40,518 (57.0)	2,843 (4.0)	71,084 (100.0)

Note: Figures in parentheses indicate the percentage of the cadres to the total staff in the corresponding year.

* Including Assistant Professors and Assistant Lecturers.

**Estimated

Source: *Annual Report 1995-96,* University Grants Commission, New Delhi.

Table 23.56: Facultywise Number and Distribution of Teaching Staff in Affiliated Colleges, 1991-92 to 1995-96.

Year	Senior Teachers*	Lecturers**	Tutors/ Demons-trators	Total
1991-92	28,979	1,70,327	9,173	2,08,479
	(13.9)	(81.7)	(4.4)	(100.0)
1992-93	30,017	1,76,431	9,502	2,15,950
	(13.9)	(81.7)	(4.4)	(100.0)
1993-94+	31,068	1,82,606	9,834	2,23,508
	(13.9)	(81.7)	(4.4)	(100.0)
1994-95+	32,180	1,89,144	10,186	2,31,510
	(13.9)	(81.7)	(4.4)	(100.0)
1995-96+	33,289	1,95,662	10,537	2,39,488
	(13.9)	(81.7)	(4.4)	(100.0)

Note: Figures in parentheses indicate the percentage of the cadres to the total staff in the corresponding year.

* Comprising Principals, Professors, Readers and Senior Lecturers.

** Including Assistant Professors and Assistant Lecturers.

\+ Estimated

Source: Annual Report 1995-96, University Grants Commission, New Delhi.

Table 23.57: Number of Teachers, 1995-96

S. No.	States/UTs	Primary			Middle			Sec./Hr. Secondary		
		Male	Female	Total	Male	Female	Total	Male	Female	Total
1	2	3	4	5	6	7	8	9	10	11
1.	Andhra Pradesh	74341	35124	109465	28882	18786	47668	77163	45802	122965
2.	Arunachal Pradesh	2019	802	2821	1609	468	2077	2204	579	2783
3.	Assam	59862	19285	79147	38456	8498	46954	43088	13813	56901
4.	Bihar	95769	22416	118185	79657	21294	100951	41995	7380	49375
5.	Goa	984	1873	2857	293	519	812	3356	4367	7723
6.	Gujarat	20945	17053	37998	79573	65591	145164	50150	14990	65140
7.	Haryana	10052	9091	19143	7702	4798	12500	31508	21940	53448
8.	Himachal Pradesh	13920	9253	23173	4790	1530	6320	11060	5463	16523
9.	Jammu and Kashmir	12103	6384	18487	11948	6457	18405	15225	6800	22025
10.	Karnataka	32484	23015	55499	64477	49285	113762	54394	15987	70381
11.	Kerala	14760	32369	47129	17367	33263	50630	34528	64533	99061
12.	Madhya Pradesh	139110	51544	190654	65850	24652	90502	52360	18250	70610
13.	Maharashtra	78929	71902	150831	102937	70604	173541	157617	71607	229224
14.	Manipur	3650	2794	9144	3436	1704	5140	6057	3353	9410
15.	Meghalaya	5380	4042	9422	2472	1685	4157	2740	2330	5070
16.	Mizoram	2314	2012	4326	3312	931	4243	1953	504	2457
17.	Nagaland	4573	2176	6749	3293	1175	4468	2828	1807	4635
18.	Orissa	83332	27208	110540	34631	5862	40493	44038	12061	56099

Table 23.57: *(Contd.)*

1	2	3	4	5	6	7	8	9	10	11
19.	Punjab	18629	26943	45572	4724	4598	9322	28733	29415	58148
20.	Rajasthan	68909	25725	94634	36253	23358	87611	55509	19714	75223
21.	Sikkim	1861	1425	3286	1107	521	1628	1304	953	2257
22.	Tamil Nadu	67733	47483	115216	33006	31386	64392	70701	53524	124225
23.	Tripura	6851	4686	11537	4120	1189	5309	9444	4160	13604
24.	Uttar Pradesh	220641	49818	270459	77939	19392	97331	82439	17318	99757
25.	West Bengal	133124	40511	173635	16091	5137	21228	78547	41766	120313
26.	A and N Islands	450	370	820	324	336	660	1322	1117	2439
27.	Chandigarh	13	231	244	17	167	184	567	2198	2765
28.	D and N Haveli	150	82	232	179	247	426	145	92	237
29.	Daman and Diu	146	210	356	113	68	181	185	107	292
30.	Delhi	10505	16028	26533	2342	4436	6778	18976	27019	45995
31.	Lakshadweep	151	67	218	79	46	125	283	71	354
32.	Pondicherry	880	1244	2124	780	992	1772	2025	1787	3812
	India	1187270	553166	1740436	755759	408975	1164734	982444	510807	1493251

Table 23.58 : Sexwise and Statewise Drop-out Rates in Classes I-X, 1995-96*

	States/UTs	Boys	Girls	Total
	1	2	3	4
1.	Andhra Pradesh	75.67	80.43	77.77
2.	Arunachal Pradesh	75.96	78.74	77.11
3.	Assam	75.71	76.50	76.08
4.	Bihar	83.07	88.97	85.07
5.	Goa	40.54	41.46	40.98
6.	Gujarat	68.72	72.62	70.48
7.	Haryana	57.53	67.07	61.70
8.	Himachal Pradesh	43.96	60.10	51.45
9.	Jammu and Kashmir	66.47	77.95	71.15
10.	Karnataka	64.75	75.16	69.72
11.	Kerala	32.55	20.67	26.73
12.	Madhya Pradesh	62.17	76.90	68.19
13.	Maharashtra	57.01	68.01	62.18
14.	Manipur	74.77	75.16	74.95
15.	Meghalaya	63.62	64.82	64.19
16.	Mizoram	75.08	71.21	73.27
17.	Nagaland	65.31	71.89	68.58
18.	Orissa	72.39	81.20	75.95
19.	Punjab	48.11	53.79	50.74
20.	Rajasthan	79.22	88.89	82.21
21.	Sikkim	87.17	84.38	85.95
22.	Tamil Nadu	60.14	68.20	63.88
23.	Tripura	79.31	83.59	81.26
24.	Uttar Pradesh	50.07	73.63	58.39
25.	West Bengal	74.66	85.89	79.62
26.	A and N Islands	47.70	51.69	49.59
27.	Chandigarh	49.01	39.31	44.56
28.	D and N Haveli	69.90	74.37	71.85
29.	Daman and Diu	**	**	**
30.	Delhi	-13.92	-37.44	-25.25
31.	Lakshadweep	63.90	60.57	62.28
32.	Pondicherry	38.41	32.27	35.57
	India	66.36	74.07	69.58

* Provisional

** Including Goa

PART - FOUR

APPENDICES

SIGNIFICANT DOCUMENTS NOT INCLUDED IN THIRD AND FOURTH SURVEYS

APPENDIX - I

CABE Committee on NPE (1992)*

Introduction

The Government of India, Ministry of Human Resource Development, Department of Education, appointed a National Policy on Education Review Committee (NPERC) in May 1990 to review NPE, 1986, under the Chairmanship of Acharya Ramamurti. The Committee submitted its report on December 26, 1990. With a view to examining the report of the Ramamurti Report Committee, the Central Advisory Board of Education (CABE) appointed a committee with Janardhana Reddy, Chief Minister and Minister of Education, Andhra Pradesh, as its chairman. The Committee gave its report in 1992.

EXTRACTS FROM THE REPORT

Overview (Chapter 2)

After a careful consideration of the recommendations of the NPERC as well as development since, NPE, we have come to the conclusion that while very little of policy required reformulation, the POA needs to be revised considerably.(2.3)

Education of the SCs/STs and other Educationally Backward Sections (Chapter 4)

A standing (CABE) Committee on education of SCs, STs and

---

* Ministry of Human Resource Development, Department of Education, New Delhi, 1993

other educationally backward sections should be constituted; educationists from these groups should have representation in that Committee.(4.4)

Common School System (Chapter 6)

Effective measures need to be taken to implement the provision of NPE, 1986 in regard to Common School System. To this end, disparities between schools should be ended as early as possible by upgrading the quality of ordinary schools and providing amenities for achieving minimum levels of learning. Both the Centre and the States should take determined action in this regard. The privileged schools should accept social accountability by sharing their facilities and resources with other institutions, taking up community activities, and facilitating access to children of the disadvantaged groups. (6.6)

Navodaya Vidyalayas (Chapter 7)

The scheme should continue and a NV should be set up in each district as originally envisaged. Further, the following measures are suggested:

(i) constant review to keep the scheme as cost effective as possible,
(ii) ensuring the continued validity and reliability of the admission tests by periodic evaluation and appropriate modification of admission procedure, and
(iii) more particular attention to the pace-setting role of these institutions. (7.5)

Early Childhood Care and Education (Chapter 8)

The scope of Article 45 of the Constitution need not be enlarged. (8.8).

ICDS and other CSS relating to ECCE should continue as Centrally Sponsored Schemes during the Eighth Five Year Plan. The *Anganwadi* workers should play an expanded role and should be the focal point for a number of activities and support services for women and children, such as child care, family welfare, nutrition and health. The recruitment and training of *Anganwadi* workers should be so organised as to ensure that they have the necessary skills and motivation to discharge the expanded role. (8.8)

Universalisation of Elementary Education (Chapter 9)

What is needed is not so much a Constitutional amendment as suggested by the NPERC as the manifestations of a national will to achieve UEE. The Central and State Governments should bestow overriding priority to adult literacy and UEE and provide programmes in these two areas total support—financial, administrative and political—a support which is commensurate with the priority. (9.2)

Operation Blackboard, being one of the priority strategies for UEE, should continue during the Eighth Plan, in an expanded and extended form. (9.15)

Para 5.12 of NPE, which laid the targets for UPE and UEE, needs to be revised. Every effort should be made to ensure that the Constitutional obligation of providing free and compulsory education upto the age of 14 years becomes a reality before we enter the twenty-first century. (2.6 and 9.17)

The following points deserve priority during the Eighth Five Year Plan in the area of UEE:

(i) Universal enrolment of all children, including girls and persons belonging to SC/ST.
(ii) Provision of primary school for all children within one kilometre of walking distance and of facility of non-formal education for school drop-outs, working children and girls who cannot attend schools.
(iii) Improvement of ratio of primary school to upper primary schools from the existing 1:4 to 1:2, this being a pre-condition for larger opportunity for widening girls' participation at upper primary stage;

(iv) Reduction of drop-out rates between Classes I to V and I to VIII from the existing 45 per cent and 60 per cent to 20 per cent and 40 per cent respectively.

(v) Improvements of school facilities by revamped Operation Blackboard, to be extended to upper primary level also;

(vi) Achievement of minimum levels of learning by approximately all children at the primary level, and introduction of this concept at the upper primary stage on a large scale;

(vii) Local level committee, with the representation to women and teachers, to assist in the working of primary education and to oversee its functioning;

(viii) Improvement of the monitoring system for universalisation of elementary education to see to the achievement of above mentioned goals.

NPE and POA may be revised accordingly. (9.18)

Adult and Continuing Education (Chapter 10)

The "dual-track approach" of promoting simultaneously UEE and adult literacy should continue in educational planning; the special needs of women and of disadvantaged group like SCs and STs should be specially attended to. (10.1)

Programmes of post-literacy and continuing education should be planned for neo-literates and youth passing out of primary education system (through the school system or non-formal education programme) and these programmes should be planned simultaneously with literacy campaigns and be made effective as soon as large numbers of persons complete literacy courses. (10.9)

Secondary Education (Chapter 11)

It would be necessary to bring about a planned expansion of secondary education facilities all over the country in order to cope with new demands for secondary education. (11.3)

Efforts should be made to bring about uniformity in the management structure for secondary education in all States. (11.4)

It is necessary to recognise the Boards of Secondary Education and vest them with autonomy so that their ability to provide academic inputs to secondary education is enhanced. (11.5)

Time-bound measures should be taken by the Central and State Governments to implement the directions contained in para 10.7 of NPE and to empower the Headmasters with administrative, academic and financial powers. Training of the heads of institutions requires particular attention. (11.6 and 17.15)

Open learning should be given utmost encouragement and that the National Open School should play the same lead role within the open school system as IGNOU with open universities. (11.11)

Vocationalisation of Education (Chapter 12)

The existing vocational stream at the +2 level may be suitably strengthened and, wherever possible, the vocational courses may be started from class IX also. (12.12)

The idea of a core vocational course, mooted by the NPERC, is attractive. Generic vocational courses may be introduced on a selective basis; to begin with generic vocational courses may be tried out in about ten per cent of the schools. (2.5 and 12.12)

The Work Experience programme may be systematically implemented by allocating 12.5 per cent to 20 per cent of the school time for these activities; the activities should have a practical orientation in relation to various subjects under this programme. The vocational 'core' would find place at the secondary and higher secondary stages; Work Experience/SUPW would relate to elementary education. (12.12)

Higher Education (Chapter 13)

It is not advisable to set up a national level statutory mechanism to regulate the opening of non-standard and sub-standard universities and colleges. The proliferation of colleges without adequate facilities can be curbed to a large extent if the universities exercise rigorous control and insist on creation of necessary infrastructure and educational facilities before granting affiliation and if the State Governments respect the decision of the universities in these matters. The establishments and operationalisation of State Councils of Higher Education will go a long way in the planned development of higher education. (13.3)

A Central Council of Rural institutes is necessary to provide the much needed fillip to rural education on Gandhian lines; it should be set up immediately. (13.6)

Management of Education (Chapter 18)

The idea of educational complex may be tried on an experimental basis in selected areas. (18.2)

The District Boards of Education should be set up and operationalised expeditiously. (18.3)

It would be necessary to hasten the process of consultation with States and to give concrete shape to the idea of IES with due regard to the views and concerns of the States. (18.4)

On Centrally Schemes the decisions of the 43rd meeting of the NDC held on 23-24 December, 1991, are reiterated. Launching of new CSSs in some priority areas not so far covered, such as advancement of educationally backward minorities, are also suggested, after due process of consultations with the States. (18.7)

Constitution of specialised State Education Tribunals is desirable. The details of setting up of these tribunals may be worked out in consultation with the State Governments. (18.8)

"Making the System Work" has to be treated as non-negotiable. Formulation and implementation of an Action Plan to put into practice the strategy outlined in para 7.3 of the NPE is strongly recommended. (18.10)

Resources for Education (Chapter 19)

The practice of treating education as a residual sector in the matter of allocation of resources should be reversed; para 11.4 of NPE should be implemented forthwith. Need-based financing requires to be provided for priority areas like Universalisation of Elementary Education, Adult Literacy and Vocationalisation. (19.4)

Higher budgetary allocation for education should be complemented by other measures such as:

(i) Prioritisation within the Education Sector in the matter of allocation of governmental resources.
(ii) Progressively making higher education and technical and management education largely self-financed by revising the fee structure with appropriate support to the needy students by way of student loans.
(iii) Institutional finances for development of educational infrastructure.
(iv) Incentive to academic institutions to augment income by way of consultancy and other studies.
(v) Encouraging community and the cooperative sectors to financially support education, The time and effect given by thousands of unpaid volunteers in the Total Literacy Campaigns is a concrete demonstration of the possibility of raising social capital without any opportunity cost.
(vi) Efficiency and effectiveness of expenditure which would imply that programmes should be judged not only with reference to the financial expenditure or coverage in terms of geographical area or number of beneficiaries but also in terms of outcomes. (19.5)

APPENDIX - II

Education For All : Delhi Summit Declaration*

Introduction

Heads of State and Government of Nine High Population Countries, all of which are developing countries accounting for more than half of the World's population, held a Summit in Delhi on December 13-16, 1993 to discuss the Goal of Education For All. (Only two heads, however, attended the Summit — President Sukarno of Indonesia and Prime Minister P. V. Narasimha Rao of India. The rest of the countries were represented by Ministers of their governments). Given below is the Text of the DECLARATION adopted on the concluding day of the Summit December 16, 1993.

— Editor

Declaration

We, the leaders of nine high population developing nations of the world, hereby reaffirm our commitment to pursue with utmost zeal and determination the goals set in 1990 by the World Conference on Education For All and the World Summit on Children, to meet the basic learning needs of all our people by making primary education universal and expanding learning opportunities for children, youth and adults. We do so in full awareness that our countries contain more than half of the world's people and that the success of our efforts is crucial to the achievement of the global goal of Education For All.

---

* *Progressive Educational Herald,* 8(2), January, 1994.

We recognise that:

The aspirations and development goals of our countries can be fulfilled only by assuring education to all our people, a right promised both in Universal Declaration of Human Rights and in the Constitution and law of each of our countries.

Education is the pre-eminent means for promoting universal human values, the quality of human resources, and respect for cultural diversity.

The education systems in our countries have made great strides in offering education to substantial numbers, and yet have not fully succeeded in providing quality education to all our people, indicating the need for developing creative approaches, both within and outside the formal systems.

The content and methods of education must be developed to serve the basic learning needs of individuals and societies, to empower them to address their most pressing problem — combating poverty, raising productivity, improving living conditions, and protecting the environment — and to enable them to play their rightful role in building democratic societies and enriching cultural heritage.

Successful education programmes require complementary and convergent actions on adequate nutrition, effective health care and appropriate care and development of the young child, in the context of the role of the family and the community.

The education and empowerment of girls and women are important goals in themselves and are key factors in contributing to social development, well-being and education of present and future generations, and the expansion of the choices available to women for the development of the full potential.

The pressure of population growth has seriously strained the capacity of education systems and impeded needed reforms and improvements. Moreover, given the age structure of the population in our countries, it will continue to do so throughout the coming decade.

Education is and must be, a societal responsibility, encompassing governments, families, communities and non-governmental organisation alike, it requires the commitment and participation of all in a grand alliance that transcends diverse opinions and political positions.

Conscious of the vital role that education must play in the development of our societies, we hereby pledge that, by the year 2000 or at the earliest possible moment, we will ensure a place for every child in a school or appropriate education programme according to his or her capabilities, in order that no child be deprived of education for lack of a teacher, learning material or adequate space. We pledge this in fulfilment of our commitment under the Convention of the Rights of the Child which we have ratified.

We will consolidate efforts towards the basic education of youth and adults from public and private sources, improving and expanding our literacy and adult education programmes within the context of an integrated strategy of basic education for all our people.

We will eliminate disparities of access to basic education arising from gender, age, income, family, cultural, ethnic and linguistic differences and geographical remoteness. We will improve the quality and relevance of basic education programmes by intensifying efforts to improve the status, training and conditions of teachers, to improve learning contents and material and to carry out other necessary reforms of our education systems.

We will, in our actions, accord to human development the highest priority at national and other levels, ensuring that a growing share of national and community resources is dedicated to basic education and improving the management of existing resources for education.

We will rally all sectors of our society towards 'Education For All' as we hereby endorse the framework of action accompanying this declaration and undertake to review our progress at the national level and to share our experiences among ourselves and with the global community.

We hereby call upon:

International collaborators to raise substantially their support for our efforts to expand our national capacities for expanding and improving basic education services.

International financial institutions, in the context of structural adjustments to recognise education as a critical investment without imposing predetermined ceiling on such investments to promote an international environment to enable countries to sustain their socio-economic development.

The 1993 Kuala Lumpur Declaration on Education For All*

SIXTH REGIONAL CONFERENCE OF MINISTERS OF EDUCATION AND THOSE RESPONSIBLE FOR ECONOMIC PLANNING IN ASIA AND THE PACIFIC, KAULA LUMPUR, 21-24 JUNE, 1993

The Sixth Conference of Ministers of Education and those responsible for Economic Planning in Asia and the Pacific, meeting in Kuala Lumpur from 21 to 24 June, 1993, examined a broad range of educational challenges facing the countries of the region today. The size and complexity of this region, which accounts for nearly two-thirds of the world's people and is predicted soon to become the largest force in the global economy, would suggest that a consensus on educational priorities would be difficult to achieve.

The Conference agreed, however, that two overarching concerns stood apart from all others. The first was the importance of values, ethics and culture in education; the second, the need to improve the situation of women and girls within the education systems of the region. These two imperatives are integral parts of education as the foundation of socio-economic development.

The Conference expressed the profound conviction that the only path to the restoration of a balance in its value system in a world increasingly shaped by materialism was to assign a significant place for the teaching of ethics, values and culture in the school curriculum. On the subject of women and children, consistent with

---

* *Progressive Education Herald* 8(1) October, 1993.

the Universal Declaration of Human Rights and in particular with the spirit and letter of paragraph 26 relating to the right to education, equity, that is the quality of fairness or justice, must lie at the centre of national and regional educational plans.

Since women and girls constitute half the population of the region and, in many parts of the region, are deprived of equity in education and employment, they must receive special emphasis in the preparation of national educational plans.

Bearing the foregoing in mind, the Conference called upon the countries of the region, on UNESCO and on international community to:

— review their existing education systems with a view to formulating appropriate values education within the curriculum at all levels of the education system;
— promote the use of effective pedagogical strategies and curriculum to inculcate ethical, cultural and moral values;
— ensure their education systems play a positive interventionist role in the promotion of women's status by developing targeted action plans, removing both women's illiteracy and barriers inhibiting their access to, and retention in, education;
— emphasize women's participation in scientific, vocational, technical and professional education;
— foster development of new values through gender appropriate curricula, learning measures, and the enhanced awareness of gender issues amongst teachers, planners, and administrators;
— continuously monitor the progress of education for women and girls.

The Conference further called upon international agencies and non-governmental organizations to give top priority in their developmental programmes to the education of women and girls; and upon the United Nations to place on the agenda of the forthcoming World Conference on Women, the issue of women and girls' education, with emphasis on access and equity.

ASIA AND THE PACIFIC: A RENEWED COMMITMENT TO EDUCATION FOR ALL

Countries of the Asia-Pacific region renewed their commitment to Education For All and the increased access of women and girls to education at all levels at the conclusion of the Sixth Regional Conference of Ministers of Education and those Responsible for Economic Planning in Asia and the Pacific (MINEDAP VI) organised by UNESCO in Kuala Lampur, Malaysia, from 21 to 24 June.

Thirty-one Member States pledged to work out more effective programme monitoring and assessment in order to improve learning achievement, strengthen staff support for greater decentralization of Education For All activities (EFA), improve the data-bases on which EFA-related decisions are made, reinforce parental and community support for basic education through a closer partnership with the media and non-governmental organizations and step up the involvement of women as experts and resource persons.

Addressing delegates at the closing of the Conference, UNESCO's Assistant Director General for Education, Colin Power, expressed satisfaction with the work that had been accomplished. "I like to think", he said, "that there is a near-complete identity of views between professional educators and policy-makers."

The Conference adopted most of the recommendations proposed by the Advisory Committee on Regional Co-operation, which met earlier in Kuala Lumpur from 14 to 17 June.

To UNESCO, the Conference recommended the strengthening of the Asia-Pacific Programme of Education For All (APPEAL), greater decentralization of funds to field offices, redoubled efforts to obtain extra-budgetary support, the reinforcement of education of women, minorities, refugees, the disabled and other disadvantaged groups, and a broader, more intensive media role.

Member States pledged to forge stronger links between general education and technical and vocational education, and between technical and vocational education and industry, agriculture and other fields.

The Asia-Pacific Programme of Educational Innovation for Development (APEID) was urged to give special attention to problems of the environment, population, health and nutrition, AIDS and drugs.

The Conference recommended that UNESCO help in upgrading teacher education, developing learning materials and providing opportunities for teacher educators to study abroad in order to enhance their knowledge, skills and understanding.

In their Declaration adopted at the end of the Conference, the ministers called upon the countries of the region, on UNESCO and on the international community to give top priority to the education of women and girls. The United Nations, they suggested, should place this issue on the agenda of the 1995 World Conference on Women, with emphasis on access and equity.

Finally, the Conference urged UNESCO to give special and urgent attention to populous countries with high illiteracy rates, to small island States and to the landlocked, newly independent Central Asian Republics. It recommended that the allocation in the 1994-95 Draft Programme and Budget for the Pacific Member States be increased and that UNESCO assess and analyse needs and policies in the context of national reform and reconstruction in response to requests from member States.

Three round tables on matters crucial to the future shape of education were organised during MINEDAP VI. They dealt with funding, education and the world of work and values in education.

The question of resources is an acute one in nearly all countries. Donor agencies who spoke at the round tables stated that they acted only in an advisory capacity and had no prescriptive role to play. As such, priorities had to be set by the countries themselves, and the demand for assistance in education could, at times, be preceded by demands for nutrition or clean drinking water.

Delegates agreed that the importance of technical and vocational education could not be over-emphasized, given that education was meant to equip the learner with skills and training for life. They recommended that UNESCO encourage its Member

States to promote the mutual recognition of qualifications in co-operation with industry. The Organisation, they said, should support the co-operative development of curricula which link science, humanities and cultural and traditional values to the world of work in each country.

Values education emerged as a pervasive theme in MINEDAP VI. If poverty eradication and human resources development were pre-conditions of peace, then the inculcation of values was a necessary part of education, for it was through values that the individual and society find their worth.

RECOMMENDATIONS

I. Education For All

A. The Conference *recommends* that Member States renew their commitment to EFA goals and further strengthen EFA programmes and continue to make use of the Asia-Pacific Programme of Education For All (APPEAL), with an emphasis on:

1. More effective programme monitoring and assessment as a means of improving learning achievement with a view to reporting in 1995 on the progress towards EFA 2000 goals.
2. Strengthening staff support and professional development for decentralized planning and management of EFA programmes.
3. Improving the data base on which EFA-related decisions are made and its reliability.
4. Reinforced community and parental support for basic education by means of strengthened partnership with the media, NGOs, and other relevant Ministries.
5. Greater involvement of women as experts and resource persons in EFA programmes.

B. The Conference *recommends* to UNESCO that:

6. APPEAL be strengthened in order to better fulfil the objectives of the programmes, giving due consideration to the specific needs and expectations of the Member States and field offices of the region.
7. Further, decentralization of EFA funds to PROAP, APIA, and other field offices be foreseen in 27C/5 with particular references to target countries in the region (large countries, small island states and least developed countries).
8. Efforts to obtain multilateral and bilateral financial support for EFA programmes be strengthened for the forthcoming biennium and through the remainder of the decade.
9. Partnership with UNESCO National Commissions as well as national mechanisms and institutions of relevance to EFA's goals be promoted.
10 Programmes to support the involvement of the media and other social service sectors in parental and community support for basic education be foreseen in the approved work plan of the Organization for 1994-95.
11. Continued vigorous support be given to re-inforce national efforts on behalf of girls and women as well as to minorities, refugees, the disabled, children of the border areas where there is a mingling of cultures, languages and traditions, the urban poor and other disadvantaged groups.
12. APPEAL's efforts for the improvement of curriculum, learning materials and training of personnel of EFA including literacy and continuing education be strengthened.
13. Support be given to the priority efforts of the government of Bangladesh in the eradication of illiteracy and in their establishment of a Centre for Non-formal Education, which would promote exchange of experiences among countries of the region.

II. Education for Women and Girls

The Conference *recommends* that Member States commit themselves to the:

14. Development of targeted action plans to increase access of girls and women to education at all levels.
15. Development of educational contents, materials, and methods in both formal and non-formal systems, that take into account the unique needs and problems of women and girl learners and introduce changes which will contribute to their equal participation in all aspects of learning.
16. Priority placement of education programmes for girls and women, as well as training on gender issues for those in education, within the framework of national development plans which reflect an adequate analysis of the social and educational situation of girls and women.
17. Establishment of monitoring systems to prepare a progress report on women's education to the International Forum of Education for All and the United Nations World Conference on Women in 1995.

III. Quality and Relevance of Education

A. *Educational Research and Innovation for Development*

The Conference *recommends* that, in order to strengthen its recognised mandate, the programmes and activities of the Asia and Pacific Programme of Education Innovation for Development (APEID):

18. Continue to focus on multi-disciplinary and educational innovation and research in curriculum, educational management, delivery systems, evaluation, teaching material curriculum, educational management, delivery

systems, evaluation, teaching materials and methodologies, with emphasis on development materials for the teaching of thinking skills, educational technology, distance education and teacher education;

19. Focus on the problem of developing normative and culture-specific life quality indicators with special attention being paid to the environment, population health/nutrition, AIDS and drugs education.
20. Support programmes for the development of entrepreneurial and leadership skills in children with due regard for the need for a balance with promoting attitudes which reflect a concern for the environment, the community and international understanding.

Further *recommends* that UNESCO encouraged member States:

21. To support the 1974 Recommendation on International Understanding and Peace and Associated Schools project, in order to foster humanistic, ethical/moral and cultural values and international education for peace.
22. To make more systematic reviews and evaluations of the APEID-related programmes of National Development Groups (NDGs) and Associated Centres (ACs).
23. To increase technical support and voluntary financial contributions to APEID to enable it to respond to Member-States requests for assistance in educational innovation and research for development.

B. *Education for the World of Work*

The Conference *recommends* that UNESCO encourage Member-States to:

24. Promote stronger links between general education and technical vocational education, and between

technical vocational education and industry, agriculture and other fields, both within each country and across the Region in application of the Revised Recommendation concerning Technical and Vocational Education and the Convention on Technical and Vocational Education.

25. Promote the mutual recognition of qualifications in co-operation with industry.
26. Support the co-operative development of curricula and learning materials in technical and vocational education subjects.
27. Support the cooperative development of curricula which link science, humanities, and cultural and traditional values to the world of work in each Member-State.
28. Develop appropriate credit transfer, twining arrangements, articulation and recognition, procedures within and outside the Region.
29. Exploit open learning approaches to deliver TVE programme to areas for which access is currently difficult.

Further recommends that Major Programme Area I continue to accord a high priority and appropriate resources to education for the world of work and technical and vocational education in general, and to UNEVOC in particular, with a view to:

30. Effectively mobilising APEID, its associated centres, and the technical and vocational unit at PROAP for programme coordination to assist institutions, organizations and statutory bodies involved in technical and vocational education.
31. Supporting co-operative regional projects to develop technical and vocational educational programmes that integrate school and work experience in the curriculum.

32. Developing co-operative regional projects to promote learning for the work place, and in conjuction with the Associated Centres network, support the UNEVOC project within in the region.

C. *Teacher Education*

The Conference *recommends* to the Director General that UNESCO provide technical advice and other forms of assistance to member countries to:

33. Strengthen and upgrade their systems of teacher education at both the pre-service and in-service levels.
34. Assist with the development of teaching and learning materials and appropriate delivery systems to improve the professional developments of teacher educators.
35. Provide opportunities for key teacher educators in member countries to study abroad in order that they can develop improved knowledge, skills and understandings to upgrade their own countries' systems of teacher education.

D. *Higher Education*

The Conference *recommends* that the Director-General:

36. Transmit to the forthcoming session of the General Conference the proposal to establish a Centre for Higher Education for Asia-Pacific, paying special attention to the principle of programme concentration and administrative decentralization, together with the feasibility study undertaken by UNESCO.
37. Support regional and national programmes for monitoring the quality of education in private universities.

38. Increase the level of resources required to render the UNITWIN and UNESCO chair programmes more effective in the region and to suggest other forms of university network.
39. Support regional and national programmes for providing the recognition of learning acquired via different pathways in university and distance education and technical training and to ensure that there is a linkage between higher education and the world of work, especially in those nations in a state of economic transition.

IV. International and Regional Co-operation in Education

A. *APEID and APPEAL*

The Conference *recommends* that the Directors-General:

40. Give further clarification and an operational definition of the APEID and APPEAL mandates,
41. Establish a Regional Committee on Education with a broad-based participation and including representatives of funding agencies and NGOs in order to plan, monitor and assess all the PROAP's activities in the area of education, it being understood that this Committee would replace the Advisory Committee and the separate Regional Conference.
42. The full name of the APEID Secretariat be expanded to the "Asia and Pacific Centre of Educational Innovation for Development", while retaining the abbreviated form ACEID, since the acronym is widely known.

B. *Policy and Management*

The Conference *recommends* that through the Director-General:

43. Assistance be given to Member-States to establish or strengthen education management information systems.
44. Needs assessments, policy analysis and sector reviews be carried out in the context of national reform and reconstruction initiatives in response to Member States requests and in partnership with National Commissions as well as other United Nations Agencies.
45. The educational authorities of each Member State of the region be urged to designate one internal department as the liaison organ for exchange of educational legislative and policy information, this organ providing information upon request about educational legislation and innovation of its own country to other Member-States.
46. Special attention be paid to the needs of countries with major educational needs such as those with large populations, those with high illiteracy rates, small islands states, least developed countries, or those with a rapidly evolving socio-economic environment.
47. Assistance by given to Member-States to develop physical environments suitable for life-long learning by making use of existing schools, religious centres and parks and stimulating community participation in construction, maintenance and ecological landscaping.
48. In welcoming the proposed new UNDP-UNESCO initiative, UNESCO-PROAP be asked to work out the details necessary to launch and coordinate this plan, particularly the regional project on Basic Education in close consultation with UNDP, bearing in mind the guidelines presented by Members attending the Seventh Session of the Advisory Committee.
49. UNESCO convey to the Asian Development Bank the appreciation of the six regional Member States concerned for its assistance in formulating national EFA plans of action which are worthy of emulation;

50. UNESCO take initiative to mobilize all partners of the Jomtien Conference and other donor agencies to provide additional resources, mostly in grant form, so as not to overburden those who are already suffering from debt burdens.
51. Agencies such as UNESCO, UNDP, UNICEF and the World Bank concentrate their efforts on Basic Education for All, working together so that in least developed countries and countries with high population and high illiteracy rates, EFA goals are achieved according to their national policies.
52. Support be given for developing a system of effective indicators for monitoring the performance and quality of education which reflects the specificity of the countries of the region.
53. Considering that UNESCO field offices in the Asia Pacific region have grown under the conflicting stresses of needs and demands, with some offices working as integrated units and others as single discipline units, and keeping in view the large distances and vast area of the region, UNESCO be urged to undertake a complete review of all the field offices to make them more efficient and functional.
54. To provide PROAP with the requisite facilities including reinforced staff, budget and decentralized authorities to enable it to efficiently implement major regional programmes such as APEID and APPEAL, working in co-operation with sub-regional education advisers.
55. Adequate emphasis be placed on training and research activities in rural education within the UNESCO Programme and Budget for 1994-95.
56. Support given to the priority efforts of China for the establishment of an International Centre for Research and Training in Rural Education in China considering that the majority of the population in

developing countries live in these areas and that the international Symposium on Rural Education reaffirmed the need to reform, strengthen, and integrate rural education programmes.

57. The allocation in the 1994-95 Draft Programme and Budget for the Pacific Member-States be increased to atleast the current levels, in view of the Basic Education and Life Skills (BELS) programme and other emerging education activities in the region, and that this recommendation be presented to the General Conference through MINEDAP VI.

58. Realising that illiteracy is a most outstanding problem of the region, UNESCO be urged to consider the most populous countries with high illiteracy rates as a separate priority target groups, with specific focus, resources, and priority attention in the design and implementation of UNESCO's education programme and budget, and to present such to the General Conference through MINEDAP VI.

59. Recognizing the specific nature and difficulties of the land-locked newly independent Central Asian Republics, UNESCO be likewise urged to consider the countries in these categories as a separate priority target group, to be given specific focus, resources, and priority attention in the design and implementationUNESCO's education programme and budget, and to present such to the General Conference through MINEDAP VI.

APPENDIX - IV

Expert Group on Status-cum-Impact Evaluation of Literacy Campaigns in India (1993)*

Introduction

An Expert Group was constituted in April 1993 under the Chairmanship of Professor Arun Ghosh to undertake the Status-cum-Impact Evaluation of Literacy Campaigns launched in different parts of the country since 1991. The objectives proposed were as under:

(a) (i) To measure the outcome of literacy campaigns among learners/participants with respect to prescribed levels of literacy as per National Literacy Mission Norms.

(ii) To analyse the estimated number of persons made literate by gender, age group and social groups (SC/ST and others).

(b) The process and effectiveness of environment building/mass mobilisation through mass literacy campaigns.

(c) Involvement and partnership between Government bodies and voluntary groups in literacy campaigns.

(d) Duration of implementation of the campaign with special emphasis on the duration of teaching/learning.

(e) Resources available and mobilised for mass literacy campaigns including the cost effectiveness of the campaign.

(f) To study and assess the fall-out impact of the literacy campaign on related socio-economic development programmes,

---

* Ministry of Human Resource Development, Department of Education, New Delhi, 1994

such as primary education, health, nutrition, family welfare, gender sensitivity, women and child development programmes, national integration, etc.

The Expert Group held 19 meetings, interacted with a number of social science institutions and evaluation agencies, held extensive discussions with field functionaries, programme implementors, policy-makers, educationists, academicians and social activists, visited several States like Maharashtra, Goa, Gujarat, Rajasthan, Madhya Pradesh, Karnataka, West Bengal, Orissa, Bihar and Uttar Pradesh for on-the-spot study and submitted its findings on the evaluation of the Literacy Mission.

RECOMMENDATIONS

(a) Literacy Campaigns

1. Adoption of an appropriate approach for mass support from various quarters including a strong political commitment, constitution of a strong core group committed to Literacy.
2. Integration of TLC with NFE, improvements in the teaching learning materials, training and the monitoring and evaluation system.
3. Carrying out accurate initial survey of the non-literates.
4. Adequate facilities and provisions in the learning centres.
5. Constitution of a core group at State and district level to guide and support the programme.
6. Emphasis on voluntary character of this programme which was deemed essential for its success.
7. Concentration on Hindi belt where there are about half of the non-literates in India.

(b) Post-literacy Measures

1. Bringing internal evaluation procedure close to the external evaluation procedure and continuing interaction

between internal and external evaluation agencies.

2. Adoption of adequate representative sample for reliable evaluation of TLCs, assessing at least 10 per cent of the learning centres.
3. Adoption of appropriate design for external evaluation based on stratified random sampling design including blocks, panchayats and villages.
4. Validity of target population and absenteeism.
5. Assessing at least 80 per cent of the learners.
6. Assessing the impact of the TLC and adopting proper procedure for storage of TLC data.
7. Conducting impact evaluation studies.

APPENDIX - V

UNICEF: Promoting Basic Education: 40 Lessons from China and India*

Education-Development Interaction

1. The relationship between basic education and aspects of national development is better explained and understood as a non-linear and interactive process rather than as a direct cause-and-effect relationship.
2. The crucial question is not whether and how much basic education is necessary, but how to maximise its beneficial consequences.
3. The inner workings of basic education – its content and Quality, as well as overall development parameters – policies, objectives and priorities in development, which also affect educational programmes have to be looked at simultaneously.
4. The synergy between basic education and national development falls into place naturally when human development becomes central to national development.
5. The programmes for poverty alleviation need to combine economic measures with basic education components.
6. Basic education facilities shift of the surplus workforce from farming to non-farm employment
7. Primary education and literacy help make mass communications educationally more potent.
8. A large measure of decentralized local decision-making in development activities is an essential step for enhancing benefits of basic education.

---

* *Progressive Educational Herald,* 8(4), July 1994.

Learning Goals: Skill for Further Learning and for Life

9. Learning skills, life skills and post-primary and post-literacy transitional learning mainly in preparation for the world of work, are the most important contributions of basic education to development.
10. Where illiteracy is still a significant problem, "primary education-plus" and "literacy-plus" should be the core of basic of education.
11. Primary education needs to be freed from its "hidden" subservience to secondary school preparation.
12. A common school system based on comprehensive local planning and diversified approaches to serve all children in a locality is a precondition for universalization of basic education.
13. A common school system needs to be supported by appropriate legislation.

Qualitative Criteria: Universality and Equity Supported by Assessment of Learning

14. Universality and equality of access and opportunity must be included in the definition of quality in basic education.
15. Assessment of learning achievement using sampling techniques should become an integral part of a functioning educational management information system (EMIS).

New Model of Pedagogy and Teachers' Performance

16. Teachers' performance is a critical area of action to improving cost-effectiveness of basic education.
17. Current practices in teachers' training and the model for teachers' performance almost totally neglect the central goals of basic education – learning skills and life skills.
18. An "internship" approach rather than institutional training will help teachers acquire essential qualities and competencies.

19. Rewards and incentives for teachers in basic education have to be recognised in order to attract and retain competent people in the profession.
20. Primary education teachers' role and functions have to be differentiated to introduce possibilities of professional growth and a career ladder, changing the present situation of a "dead-end" occupation.

Decentralization and Participation

21. Major decentralization with greatly enhanced local responsibility and popular involvement is crucial for creating a conducive environment for solving key problems of basic education.
22. A political choice has to be made to adopt decentralization and devolution of authority as a key strategy for giving national development efforts a human development focus.
23. Legislative measures will help establish structures of effective decentralization and participation, such as village education committees with statutory functions.
24. A multi-level system of technical support is needed for capacity-building at local and subnational levels.
25. A competent cadre of basic education planners and managers at the local and regional/subnational levels has to be built up; the total neglect of this critical need has to be remedied urgently.
26. Voluntary organizations, social activists and the higher levels of the government have to serve as countervailing forces to entrenched local structures of domination and exploitation.
27. A norm of partnership between local government, voluntary organisations and the private sector has to be developed to meet the diverse basic learning needs of the entire community.

Overcoming Chronic Under-financing: A Political Choice

28. A radical rethinking is needed to solve the problem of chronic

and serious under-resourcing of basic education – recognizing the total inadequacy of the conventional approach.

29. New criteria which ensure adequate finances for social priorities should guide the allocation of national resources for basic education.
30. In absolute terms, expenditures for basic education in China and India need to increase in the next ten years by four to six times, which would mean atleast a doubling of the GNP share for basic education.
31. A major increase in finances for basic education with a measure of equity will require that different levels of government, non-education sectors, communities and the direct beneficiaries share the burden.
32. Access to and participation in basic education on an equitable basis has to be recognized as an entitlement of all citizens, especially of children.
33. Greater efficiency in the use of resources is essential for generating and sustaining increased support for basic education.

Continuity and Consistency of Policies

34. A sense of direction and effectiveness of programme implementation have been the casualties of frequent politically inspired shifts in policies.
35. If provinces/states were to emerge as major centres of new policy and programme initiatives in both China and India, there would be 25 or 30 centres of innovation and creativity, which could further stimulate local initiative - instead of essentially one at present at the centre level.
36. How school leavers are employed and remunerated has a major effect on the choice of content and goals of basic education even if it is not directly linked to employment.

Building a Consensus

37. Basic education policies and priorities need to be protected

from the vagaries of the frequent shifts in political winds by building a broad national consensus based on wide-spread popular involvement in deciding key priorities and strategies.

38. Policy statements need to be backed up by realistic strategies and mechanisms for implementation.

39. Testing new policies and actions on a "pilot" basis before wide replication can help make policies realistic and enhance their implementability.

40. Rationale and strategies for resource raising and cost sharing should be on the agenda of policy-making bodies and public forums for ensuring continuity and support for basic education policies and priorities.

Source: Ahmed, Manzoor, Cheng Kai Ming, A.K. Jalaluddin and K. Ramachandran, *Basic Education and National Development: Lessons from China and India*, UNICEF, New York, 1991.

APPENDIX - VI

Vice-Chancellors' Conference on Decentralisation of Higher Education (1991)*

A National Seminar on 'Decentralisation of Higher Education System' was organised on October 8, 1991 at University of Kerala, Thiruvananthapuram. As many as 100 Vice-Chancellors/Directors of other University level institutions of higher learning participated in seminar. The following were the sub-themes:

1. Decentralisation in the University Grants Commission—Regional Officer and State Councils of Higher Education.
2. Decentralisation within the University System—Academic, Administrative and Financial.
3. Decentralisation in the Relationship of the Universities with the Colleges and that of Colleges with the Government.
4. Decentralisation: Financial Authority and Accountability.

Consensus and Recommendations (Chapter 1 of the Report)

Recognising that a decentralised system of higher education will be more conducive for enriching human resources by promoting scientific temper and inculcating the values of universalism, humanism, egalitarianism, tolerance and democracy in a cross-section of the society;

---

* *Decentralisation of Higher Education System: A Report on the Proceedings of the Vice-Chancellors' Conference held on October 8, 1991, at University of Kerala, Thiruvananthapuram*, Association of Indian Universities, New Delhi, 1992

Hoping that vertical delegation of well-defined powers in respect of administrative, and financial matters will generate a better sense of responsibility and accountability among various constituents and functionaries of the system.

Anticipating that a decentralised system of higher education will be able to better address the specific requirements of different geographic regions for promoting balanced regional development.

Noting that in view of multi-cultural characteristics, and vastness of the country, a decentralised system is imperative for raising efficiency by way of introducing socially useful economically relevant programmes.

1. Decentralisation of the University System at National Level

1.1 Administrative Decentralisation

1.1.1 The University Grants Commission (UGC) should establish at least four regional offices—one each in the North, South, East and West, and possibly a separate fifth one for the north-eastern region, with a view to ensuring effective implementation and monitoring of its programmes throughout the country. The regional offices should be vested with well-defined powers to take decisions, issue sanctions and pass orders at their levels and should not become mere processing units of the UGC in which final decisions continue to be taken at the central level.

1.1.2 The National Policy on Education (1986) stipulated the establishment of State Councils of Higher Education (SCHE) and consequently various Committees have further upheld this recommendation by laying down the specificities for its constitution. Necessary steps should, therefore, be taken to expeditiously establish the proposed Councils in each State.

1.2 *Academic Decentralisation*

1.2.1 The mis-match between the supply of. and demand for university graduates has got aggrieved due to the increasing pressure of enrolment on the system of higher education. In order to ameliorate such conditions, substantial number of students are required to be diverted, preferably at the stage of Class X and Class XII towards vocational streams; and only those who have the real motivation and relevant aptitude to benefit from higher education should be admitted to the universities. To this end, effective manpower planning should be initiated keeping in view the requirements of the agricultural, industrial and service sectors at the regional and national level.

Besides, the concentration of enrolment in universities and colleges in certain regions is found to have been highly disproportionate in terms of total working population or the ratio of students in higher education in the relevant age-group. Appropriate policy measures, therefore, need to be initiated at the national level for ensuring more even distribution of enrolment across different regions so that the benefits of higher education could be extended to all parts of the country in a balanced manner.

1.2.2 The degree and nature of relationship between the extent of decentralisation and academic and administrative performance at various levels should be studied and evaluated so as to obtain necessary feedback from the experience of the existing institutions/departments for policy formulation. To this end, a high level committee may be constituted.

1.3 *Financial Decentralisation*

1.3.1 The Central and State Universities should receive uniform treatment from the funding agencies as far as the creation of facilities and provision of finances are concerned.

1.3.2 (a) The prevailing system of block-grant, which is fixed for a period of 3 to 5 years, is preferable for providing maintenance grants to the universities;

(b) Suitable norms and formula need to be evolved for determining the financial requirements of these institutions; and

(c) the grant should be released in time.

1.3.3 Universities should have full autonomy to decide upon the manner in which block-grants are to be utilized for realising their specific objectives.

1.3.4 The UGC should do away with the 'matching grant' system and provide 100 per cent development grants to the universities.

1.3.5 With a view to reducing excessive dependence upon governmental grants and to finance the new programmes, the universities should be encouraged and empowered to mobilise revenues from such sources as fees, donations and contract research. Such increase in revenue should be treated as expenditure for development and the grant should not be reduced rupee for rupee. The grant released should be as per criteria.

1.3.6 Financial autonomy of universities is to be jealously safeguarded. The funding agencies must exercise restraints in interfering in the functioning of the universities. By the same token, it is incumbent on the universities to ensure accountability with regard to their financial performance and cost-effectiveness of the educational programmes.

2. Decentralisation within the University System

2.1 *Administrative Decentralisation*

2.1.1 In order to relieve the Vice-Chancellor from work of routine, it is necessary to make arrangements for proper devolution of powers within the university system. The Vice-Chancellors should be able to devote more time for reviewing and monitoring of ongoing, as well as for planning of developmental programmes of their respective institutions. Their focus should be on academic development and not on institutional administration.

2.1.2 With a view to overcoming the problems of overlapping responsibilities and concentration of powers in the hands of the apex authorities/officers, it is necessary to make arrangements for clearcut divisions and separations of powers *vis-a-vis* responsibilities among the authorities and officers of the university.

2.1.3 For efficient supervision of undergraduate education and closer liaison with the colleges, Administrative Sub-Centres (ASC) should be set up for a unit of 20 to 25 Arts, Science, Commerce and multi-disciplinary affiliated colleges, in the case of large universities. An ASC, to be headed by an officer of the rank of a Pro-Vice-Chancellor, should be given sufficient administrative and financial autonomy for all the works connected with evaluation, inspection, conduct of examinations as well as co-ordination of various developmental programmes available for colleges.

2.1.4 Every affiliating or federating university should have a Collegiate Wing to be governed by a Collegiate Council, for maintenance of standards of education in colleges, including curriculum development and selection of teachers for colleges. The Council should be presided over by the Vice-Chancellor, and should include such members as Pro-Vice-Chancellors of different campus/ASCs and a few members from each sub-campus, some Professors from the university teaching departments whose subjects are taught in the colleges, besides experts from industry, research institutions, etc.

2.2 *Academic Decentralisation*

2.2.1 Each Faculty should have a Faculty Council, which should have the representation of all the concerned departments, as well as other functionaries so as to ensure participation of faculty members. The Faculty Council should play a co-ordinating and supervisory role by fixing guidelines for teaching, research and extension programmes of the department. The Faculty Council should also act as a channel of communication between the departments and the highest authority of the university system.

2.2.2 Every academic department should have a Departmental Council and its composition should offer adequate opportunities to all the members of the department. Within the broad policy guidelines laid down by the Academic Council and the Faculty Council, the Departmental Council should have the freedom to frame their syllabi, courses of study, examination schemes, and research and extension programmes.

2.2.3 The individual Schools/Departments should be made both administratively and financially self-contained, so that academic programmes and other related activities could be freed from undue bureaucratic controls. Therefore, once the budgets of the individual Schools/Departments are sanctioned by the appropriate authorities, the Directors/ Heads of the Departments should be entrusted with the powers to manage funds and co-ordinate academic programmes. In turn, they should be responsible for releasing their set objectives of teaching and research.

2.2.4 Each Centre of Advanced Studies should be autonomous and responsible for all administrative, financial and academic matters of the Centre.

2.2.5 The moves towards granting academic autonomy to colleges should be further declared and the objectives of making all colleges autonomous should be realised within a definite time-frame.

2.3 *Financial Decentralisation*

2.3.1 The Finance Committee of each university should be made more effective in allocation and management of funds and also for proper procedural review of its utilisation.

2.3.2 Financial powers of the university (Syndicate) should be delegated to the Vice-Chancellor and other officers like the Registrar, Registrar (Evaluation), the Deputy Registrars, Assistant Registrars, Finance Officers, Deputy Finance Officer, the Librarian, the Deputy Librarian, the Dean of Students' Welfare, Director of Publications, Director of Printing Press, Director of Correspondence Courses, Principals of Colleges managed by the University, Director of College Development Council, and the like.

2.3.3 The structure and composition of the Finance Committee should be suitably changed to allow for major participation of academics in it.

2.3.4 Distinctive provisions should be made to delegate financial powers of the university to the Heads of Departments, and from them down to those incharges of the sub-units of the Departments engaged in different specialisations. They should be accountable for utilizing funds on approved projects and in the manner laid down by the appropriate authority.

2.3.5 The university and its fraternity of academics should try to display better financial accountability to make the system of decentralisation in financial administration a success.

APPENDIX - VII

Committee for Mobilisation of Resources for Technical Education (1994)*

Introduction

A high-power committee for mobilisation of additional resources for technical education was set up by the Human Resource Development Minister in 1992 in his capacity as the Chairman of the All India Council for Technical Education (AICTE) to look into these matters.

The 18-member Committee was headed by Dr. D. Swaminathan. The member of the Committee included Vice-Chancellors of Benaras Hindu University, Anna University, Madras, Aligarh Muslim University and Punjab Agricultural University; Directors of IIT, Madras, Birla Institute of Technology and Science, Pilani and Director General of Confederation of Indian Industries.

RECOMMENDATIONS

A national loan scheme may be set up under Educational Development Bank of India (EDBI) and details of the scheme worked out for soft loans for needy students.

All Government of India grants to institutions presently given for the payment of PG Scholarships shall be given as a grant to institutions for teaching/research assistantship.

The plan allocation for technical educational sector, both Central and State, should be based and related to the plan outlays in the industrial and service sectors.

---

* Ministry of Human Resource Development, 1994.

Revenues generated through enhanced fee structure, consultancy and other activities should not be offset against Government grants.

The AICTE should establish liaison with the Ministry of Finance regarding tax benefits to the donors and setting up of EDBI as recommended.

The Government-funded and aided institutions may be given specific approval to increase intake by up to 20 per cent in undergraduate courses and 20 per cent in management and PG courses.

The industries may consider adoption of one or more existing institutions.

Linkages may be established with technical institutions in various academic and R&D activities and research activities may be sponsored.

Institutes should promote consultancy activities involving all staff by sharing profits.

Academic and non-academic supporting may be reduced to optimal levels, and contract service may be used wherever possible.

The national level institutions should establish industrial foundations.

Attempts should be made to quantify various types of subsidies which should gradually be reduced and finally eliminated.

The Committee has emphasised the need for rationalisation of fee structure in the technical institutions and pointed out that at present the tuition fee contributes only about 1 to 5 per cent of the recurring expenditure per student per year in government-funded and aided institutions. It says that there is need to rationalise the fee structure with freeships and soft loans to protect the interests of economically weaker students.

APPENDIX - VIII

Role and Impact of Teaching Curricula in Meeting National Needs: Case Study of IITs (1991-94)

Department of Science and Technology, Government of India sanctioned the research study to the Department of Electrical Engineering, Indian Institute of Technology, Kanpur in September, 1991. The Research Study Advisory Committee included faculty members of IIT (Kanpur), experts from industry, Government of India as well as other academicians. The principal investigator was Naresh C. Mathur and the duration was upto November 30, 1994.

CONCLUSIONS AND RECOMMENDATIONS

CHAPTER 6

This study of the IITs regarding the role and impact of teaching curricula and other related factors in meeting national needs has brought many interesting issues to light. The collection of views from the alumni, industry and the IIT faculty shows a large agreement regarding areas of strength, concerns, and ideas on where we have failed and what should be done. The picture that emerges shows we have much to be proud of and we are going in the right direction. Only certain areas need to be looked into and some steps need to be taken to modify priorities in the future. In this chapter we include the broad conclusions that can be drawn.

6.1 Institution Building

Since Independence in 1947, the country has purposefully embarked on building certain institutions of national importance in chosen areas of professional education. These institutions include the five IITs, the four Indian Institutes of Management (IIMs), and the All India Institute of Medical Sciences (AIIMS). They were created with a great vision originating in the thinking of Jawaharlal Nehru. Their success is indicated by the status and reputation they enjoy both in the country and abroad. Much of this success is owed to the vision and personality of the individuals who were the first heads of these institutions. In the case of IIT Kanpur, for example, it is difficult to find a single individual who does not attribute the institution's strength to the vision and foresight of its founding Director, the late Professor P.K. Kelkar. In fact, each of these institutions carries the stamp of its founding Director. This is an important lesson in institution building and is also well known and accepted. However, even for institutions which have been created and established very meticulously, the head of the institution plays a very significant leadership role in the future growth of the institution. An institution, painstakingly built by men of high stature, can quickly degenerate and disintegrate in the absence of the right man at the top. Leadership in an academic institution, particularly is one of the institutes of national importance such as the IITs, is a much more difficult task than in any other organization. The presence of fiercely independent faculty having the highest credentials who vociferously express their views and opinion, and who refuse to be led, makes the task of providing leadership extremely difficult and challenging. Many in the IITs and outside feel that the government have sometimes failed in their duty to appoint, and appoint in time (see below), such leader to lead the IITs.

The delay in the appointment of a successor head is a peculiar problem of the Indian system. A great misfortune of institutions in India is to remain headless for extended periods of time due to government indecision. Headless institutions tend to be incendiary and the head, when he eventually comes, has little else to do but to do fire-fighting. He has little time left to provide academic leadership. It is pathetic to see the large number of institutions in India which are allowed to remain headless and drift almost aimlessly for extended periods of time, thereby destroying a stature that has been built after years of effort. Such institutions include institutions of national importance, universities, public sector enterprises, etc. This kind of misfortune has befallen the IITs time and again and many place the blame for some of the ills of the IITs on this factor. The role of leadership has been stressed by a large number of persons. We have, therefore, decided to include this section here.

6.2 The Role of Curricula

There is an overwhelming agreement about the role of the curricula in the overall education of the students. The curricula of the IITs has been recognized as of world class. The teaching has also been recognized to be of the highest quality. (Amongst the 1023 responses of the alumni there were only 2 or 3 which had criticized the teaching). The ability of the IITs to set up and maintain high quality facilities and the high calibre faculty deserves all credit. The organization and conduct of an all India competitive examination for admissions which has run successfully and without blemish for over 30 years is a big achievement. In the Indian context, the running of an educational programme with clockwork precision in terms of admission, classes, examinations, declaration of results and holding of convocations every year is also a great achievement. In fact many parents and students choose an IIT education for these characteristics only (even if engineering is not their main concern). The creation and operation of a new (to India) system of internal evaluation, course-wise promotion and offering of elective courses is also a contribution to the Indian educational scene.

There are two aspects which have caused concern. One is the inadequate attention paid to summer training, industrial tours and B.Tech. projects. The other aspect is the lack of exposure of the students to the Indian scene through the contents of the lectures and through organization of lectures by persons from the industry. In this context the role of the Academic Senates leaves something to be desired. Even when the curriculum review committees have recommended an increased emphasis on this aspect and have suggested ways and means of achieving this, there has been no positive action taken. Many feel that in the Senate meetings, decision making is dominated by the vociferous few resulting in what has been described as the 'tyranny of the minority'. The inability of the Chairmen in such cases to have the curriculum review committee recommendations implemented somehow creates a feeling of lack of leadership. This is unfortunate because few institutions have gone about the task of curriculum review so methodologically as the IITs have done through their review committees. That these reviews are not effectively utilized is a matter of concern.

Another matter in which IITs have failed to create a proper example is the creation and adoption of a system of student evaluation of the programme and of the teachers. Such evaluation is even more important in the IITs than in the conventional university system because of the enormous responsibility placed on the teacher and the power given to him. A proper procedure evolved in this regard will go a long way in setting a new tradition in the country.

6.3 The Science and Technology Scene

With regard to the impact on the science and technology scene of the country there are undoubtedly areas where the IITs have contributed greatly through their students and their faculty. These include major thrust areas like space, defence, electronics, computers, atomic energy, etc. The industry also has benefited greatly from the quality and temper of the manpower generated by the IITs. IITs have also contributed towards the growth of entrepreneurship although they have not met people's expectations in this regard. It is generally felt that the contribution of the IITs is far more than what is generally known due to the poor public relations posture adopted by them.

Nevertheless, the overall interaction with industry is not as much as expected (or as is prevalent in western countries). The consequent lack of exposure of students to our industrial scene has many consequences. Many alumni also feel that even when the faculty members are deeply involved in research, their research activity is not highlighted in the teaching. The students remain unaware of the work being done by their teachers. All this has contributed to the alienation of the students from the Indian scene. In the process the country has missed a great deal of what might have been contributed by the faculty and the students.

The new economic policy and the consequent liberalisation and globalisation have added a new dimension to the thinking of our industries. It is felt that this will remove some of the barriers which prevented institution industry interaction. Some effects are already becoming visible. In that sense it will not only lead to greater exposure of the students and the faculty to the industrial scene but will also create a new challenge for the graduates which they presently lack.

6.4 National Pride and Role Model

Every country has certain landmarks of success and achievement which create a sense of pride amongst its people. They help boost the national ego and are a great source of strength to its people. They are quoted by other countries as evidence of the strength of its character and ability. In the modern environment, they serve as a measure of the country's ability to achieve results and thus generate confidence about itself in other countries and organizations. This confidence is of great value which is not measurable in terms of costs. The return of such investments are often hidden and not directly visible.

In this context, the country's decision to set up institutes of national importance and its success in setting up of the IITs has become a matter of national pride. These institutions are recognized the world over as institutions of excellence because of the calibre of the students and of the faculty. Their facilities are appreciated even in the well developed western countries and are superior to the best found in the developing countries. Nationally they have set standard of honest and unbiased admission on merit, teaching regularity and quality, and an environment of freedom which has few parallels in the country. Their contributions to the national pride is itself an achievement which is noteworthy. One needs examples to emulate and IITs provide such an example to the technical education institutions.

The role of a pace-setter and a model imposes high responsibility on the system. In this context the negative impact of the IITs has been mentioned in Section 5.2. This needs careful consideration.

6.5 Alumni as a Resource

One of the strengths of the education system in the west is the participation of the alumni in the development and growth of the institutions. While IITs are often seen as having copies the western system, their relationship with the alumni is far from what is practised in USA, for example. In the present context of reorientation of our economy and funding of higher education, the alumni can play a very significant role and a strong interaction with them is necessary. The responses of the alumni show that, apart from possible monetary contributions, their participation can have meaningful impact on the teaching programme as well as efforts at more meaningful research and industrial interaction. This needs to be taken up as a matter of priority.

6.6 Recommendations

The overall findings of this project lead to identification of certain areas which the IITs need to strengthen to enhance their utility and impact. These are listed below:

1. A new course of action needs to be adopted to enhance the exposure of the B.Tech students to the industrial scenario of the country. Various steps in this direction have been suggested by the curriculum review committees of the IITs.

These include a well planned and supervised summer training programme and industrial tour for the students. The quality of the B.Tech project needs improvement with greater relationship to the actual needs of the industry. This can only be achieved if the faculty have greater involvement with the industry and the institute as a whole invites more participation from industry personnel through lectures in courses, extra-mural lectures and adjunct professorships. All these are feasible and need only the will to achieve them.

2. The involvement of the faculty in the industrial scene requires a multi-pronged approach. The following are amongst the possible steps:

   (a) Incentives to faculty who participate in industrial interaction in one way or the other;
   (b) Changing the rules regarding sabbatical leave so that greater leave can be utilized for industrial participation;
   (c) A tilt towards favouring industrial experience as a desirable qualifications when considering candidates for faculty recruitment;
   (d) Encouraging consultancy by reducing the amounts that go to the institute as overheads from consultancy income;
   (e) Changing rules so that faculty can draw part of their salary from project funds in return for reduced teaching load; and
   (f) Encouraging faculty to start their own industry and providing suitable facilities and benefits (as has already been started in IIT, Kharagpur).

3. The IITs must start a concerted effort at getting top class textbooks written for use in India which emphasize the Indian work environment and developments in India. Some IITs have already started this scheme. However, a much greater

effort needs to be made with proper incentives and remunerations. This should be considered equivalent a teaching load and a definite time frame should be set.

4. IITs must develop a system of student evaluation of both the teaching programme and the teachers. Such systems are widely used in the USA and provide an input for faculty assessments as well as course improvement. When used for faculty assessment, they provide both an incentive and a check to maintain standards.

5. The contact with the alumni needs to be increased to encourage financial contributions and increase their participation in the growth and development of the institutes.

APPENDIX - IX

AIACHE Committee on College Libraries, (1994)

The Committee was appointed in August 1994 consisting of the following members:

1. Prof. K.A. Isaac, Retired University Librarian and Professor of Library and Information Science, University of Kerala, Trivandrum (Chairman)
2. Mrs. Anne Dayanandan, Associate Librarian, Madras Christian College, Tambaram, Madras
3. Mr. G.P. Reuben, Librarian American College, Madurai.
4. Mrs. Nisha Cairae, Librarian, AIACHE, New Delhi.

Terms of Reference

1. To study the present state of the libraries of the member colleges of All India Association for Christian Higher Education (AIACHE);
2. To suggest ways and means of improving their functioning and how AIACHE can help in the process; and
3. To examine the question of computerisation and electronic networking of libraries.

A status report on college libraries was prepared on the basis of the details collected through the questionnaire and the observations made by the chairman. The present position regarding each of the factors that are pertinent to the satisfactory working of libraries is given in the status report. The Committee held its second and last meeting on 6th and 7th July, 1995 in the Department of

Library and Information Science University Library, Trivandrum and examined each of these factors in the background of the existing situation. Its findings, views and recommendations are given below:-

Recommendations

1. *For Universities and State Governments*

(i) The rates of library fees collected from students should be enhanced wherever they are low now to ensure the availability of a responsible amount for library expenditure especially in the context of the steadily increasing price of books and journals. The case of colleges of education and other professional colleges where the enrolment of students is low deserves special attention in this connection. The fees per student per annum should be not less than the rates suggested below:

Pre Degree	–	Rs. 25
Degree	–	Rs. 50
P. G.	–	Rs. 100
M. Phil	–	Rs. 150
Ph.D.	–	Rs. 250

(ii) The quantum and quantity of library staff should be strengthened. Every college library from its inception, should be headed by a qualified librarian. Librarians should be given academic status and should have membership of academic bodies like the Staff Council. UGC pay scales should be implemented for them exactly in the same manner as for teachers. The library and librarians should form an integral part of the academic system.

(iii) The education system especially the methods of teaching and examination should be so redesigned as to make library use by students compulsory.

(iv) Library personnel should be given all facilities to undergo continuing education programmes and courses for the improvement of their qualifications on a par with faculty improvement programmes.

(v) College libraries should be kept open for atleast 10 hours daily on 300 days in a year. The additional staff required for the purpose should be sanctioned.

2. *For University Grants Commission (UGC)*

(i) The UGC grant available for books and journals during a Plan period should be made known as early as possible and should be released annually instead of in one or two instalments as at present, to facilitate a planned collection development. The grant should be earmarked for the development of a centralised library collection that would meet the requirements of the different departments.

(ii) UGC should provide financial assistance for the computerisation of libraries and also for the provision of reprographic and audio visual services.

(iii) Continuing Education Programmes for college librarians like refresher courses conducted by the UGC at present should be continued on a recurring basis.

(iv) UGC should provide building grant to each college library to ensure the availability of a functional and aesthetic building and comfortable furniture. Wherever there are rare materials, an air conditioned room should be made available for their preservation. There should be special UGC grant for equipments and their maintenance.

(v) UGC should initiate steps for the formulation of College Library Standards.

3. *For College Managements*

(i) Efforts should be made to enhance the financial resources available for college library development. Apart from the conventional sources of finance, financial assistance, if sought from individuals especially alumni, societies, firms, etc. may be forthcoming.

The possibility of creating a Library Endowment Fund with the help of AIACHE and organisations like Parent Teacher Associations, the interest from which can be utilised for collection development, should be explored.

(ii) The librarian should have independent charge of the college library and should be assigned a crucial role in the selection and purchase of books.

(iii) User education programmes suitable for different levels of college education should be organised to facilitate the effective exploitation of library resources by students.

(iv) There should be guided tours arranged for students to enhance library use.

(v) Documentation services should be organised especially for the benefit of the P.G. Students, research scholars and teachers.

(vi) All colleges especially those offering PG courses and research programmes should subscribe for advanced journals in the subjects concerned.

(vii) The inevitable loss of books that occurs in libraries especially those that follow open access should be written off as suggested by the UGC and the Central Government.

(viii) A rational policy should be evolved for the periodic weeding out of obsolete and superseded books from libraries.

(ix) The register system of issuing books on loan which is laborious and time consuming should be replaced by the ticket or card system or the computerised issue system.

(x) Every college should have an integrated and centralised library system with provision for the long term loan of a specified number of frequently required books, to the departments. Departmental libraries, wherever they exist now, should be merged with the central library.

(xi) The librarian should be associated with the planning and designing of library buildings as he is the person who knows best the functional requirements of the library.

(xii) There should be a Library Committee with the Principal as Chaiman and the Librarian as Member Secretary and representatives of teachers and students. It should function in an advisory capacity advising the college authorities on all matters relating to the library.

4. *For All India Association for Christian Higher Education (AIACHE)*

(i) AIACHE should conduct not only refresher courses for qualified college librarians, but should also conduct short term training programmes for the untrained staff.

(ii) AIACHE should sponsor the establishment of an electronic network of the libraries of member colleges.

(iii) The conduct of special programmes like workshops in information technology especially computerisation and networking of libraries should be undertaken by AIACHE in the context of the need for modernising library organisations, operations and services. The coverage of as wide a section of the library personnel as possible within a short time frame should be attempted by these programmes.

(iv) AIACHE should develop facilities to function as a clearing house of information regarding library matters among member colleges. It would be great help to the colleges if AIACHE keeps them informed of UGC's policies and programmes relating to college libraries.

(v) AIACHE, with its contacts with UGC and other organisations interested in higher education, should function as an agency for creating awareness of libraries and lobbying support for them.

(vi) AIACHE should take the initiative of getting a model college library manual prepared.

(vii) AIACHE should sponsor the compilation of a checklist of books and periodicals for college libraries and its periodic updating.

We trust that this report will be made available to the Principals and librarians of colleges as well as the decision-makers and administrators in various agencies that are related to the college libraries. We express our gratitude to all those who cooperated with us in the execution of this study and Dr. Mani Jacob, General Secretary of AIACHE, who consistently guided and supported the ommittee in its work.

INDEX